Hotspots

Hotspots

The Legacy of Hiroshima and Nagasaki

Sue Rabbitt Roff

CASSELL

Cassell
Wellington House
125 Strand
London WC2R 0BB

215 Park Avenue South
New York, NY 10003

First Published 1995

British Library Cataloguing-in-Publication Data
A catalogue record for this book is available from the British Library

Library of Congress Cataloging-in-Publication Data
Rabbitt Roff, Sue
    Hotspots: the legacy of Hiroshima and Nagasaki/Sue Rabbitt Roff.
      p. cm.
    Includes bibliographical references and index.
    ISBN 0–304–33437–5 (ppc). — ISBN 0–304–33438–3 (pb)
    1. Nuclear warfare—Health aspects—Research—Evaluation.
2. Hiroshima-shi (Japan)—History—Bombardment. 1945. 3. Nagasaki-shi
(Japan)—History—Bombardment, 1945. 4. Atomic bomb victims—Japan.
5. Radiations injuries—Research—Evaluation. 6. Leukemia, Radiation-
induced—Research—Evaluation. I. Title.
RA648.3.R33 1995
363.17'99—dc20
                                95–15514
                                    CIP

ISBN 0–304–33437–5 (hardback)
       0–304–33438–3 (paperback)

Front cover picture © Greenpeace.

Typesetting and Design Ben Cracknell
Printed and bound in Great Britain by Biddles Ltd, Guildford & King's Lynn

Contents

Preface

This study has been supported over the past three years by many individuals and institutions. Travel grants for research have been received from several American sources: the History of Science Society, North East Asia Committee of the Association for Asian Studies, Rockefeller Archives Center, the Ferry Foundation, the Samuel Rubin Foundation and the *Knowledges* conference of the University of Minnesota. Lorna Arnold and Roger S. Clark were indefatigable in writing in support of my applications for funding.

As well as financing the archival and library research in the United States, these grants enabled me to present progress reports to the History of Science Congress, Washington DC in December 1992; the Women in Technology and Science Conference in Melbourne and the Peace Research Centre, Australian National University in Canberra during 1993 and the *Knowledges* Conference, University of Minnesota in April 1994. I have also given papers from the study to the History of Medicine Group, University of Edinburgh in May 1994 and the 34th International Congress of History of Medicine in Glasgow in September 1994. Each audience helped me to clarify my ideas and I was gratified by the support expressed for the study.

Librarians and archivists also have been very supportive during my research trips, facilitating access to materials and often making illuminating suggestions about where best to look for material. I am particularly indebted to the staff of the Medical Library, University of Dundee. Thomas E. Rosenbaum and Darwin H. Stapleton of the Rockefeller Archives Center, Patricia M. Redman of the Alfred Taubman Medical Library of the University of Michigan and her colleagues in the Bentley Historical Library, Robert L. Worden of the Library of Congress, Daniel Barbiero of the National Academy of Sciences, the staff at Sterling Memorial Library of Yale University, the Columbia University Libraries, the Eisenhower Library of The Johns Hopkins University, the Wellcome History of Medicine Unit, Oxford and the Science Library, Oxford

University were very responsive to my requests.

Dr Alleyn Seymour, Sir Mark Oliphant and Professor James V. Neel were generous with their time in granting me interviews. Lynn R. Anspaugh of the Lawrence Livermore National Laboratory, Henry Kohn of the Rongelap Reassessment Project and Marcus Duke of the Fisheries Research Institute of the University of Washington were good enough to send me materials I requested.

Good friends gave me fine accommodation and good advice during these travels. I particularly remember the good conversation along with the fine wines with Dave Aronson, Pearl Bowman, Jane Irwin, Belinda and Anthony Lamb, and Donna and Larry Rabbitt. Dave Aronson and Pearl Bowman served as my first critical readers, criticized and lived to tell the tale.

Deborah Murtagh, Joy Crosby, Jan Shephard and Tahmina Ismail helped me beyond the call of duty with literature retrieval, bibliographical typing and wordprocessing. Pearl Bowman, Peter Carey, John Parkinson, Will Peakin and Trevor Royle advised me on the publication possibilities. Carol Bernstein Ferry, Eleanor Seagraves and Cora Weiss continued to support my not-always-comfortable work as they have for the past decade. Colleagues at the Centre for Medical Education at the University of Dundee, and in particular Professor Ronald M. Harden, encouraged me to do it my way. Jane Greenwood and her staff at Cassell have committed their talents and resources to publishing the book.

I was supported in my decision to write a study in the history of science with never a mention of Foucault by my two closest advisers, William R. Roff and Sarah Roff – each of whom would probably have done it differently, and certainly better. But my husband in particular made this book possible, as before, by making space for it in our lives. Ultimately, of course, for all its faults, this book was written for the seven-year-olds, particularly Emily Ann Roff who has always paid me the compliment of thinking it natural that mothers write books about atomic bombs.

Glossary

Though I could not avoid knowing something about the outcome of events, I could nevertheless approach the everyday stuff of administration and action with a relatively open mind, since I had no special knowledge of the nuclear weapons testing program.

Relying instead on my background in American history, the history of science and technology, and military history, I resolved to read the documents in as nearly chronological order as I could manage, and write the book the same way. Perhaps I could thus more easily avoid the hindsight that too often mars the history of controversial events. I could not be oblivious to the future, of course, but I could focus on contemporary perspectives. And so I did. That secondary accounts did not yet exist made the choice easier, but as they began to appear I set them aside until I had drafted my own version. Always my first goal was getting the story straight, I have consistently sought to keep my analysis and criticism restricted to what a knowledgeable observer might have attained at the time. Only in lengthy epilogues to each book have I allowed myself to comment on the past from a present-day viewpoint.

Barton C. Hacker 'Radiation safety, the AEC, and nuclear weapons testing: writing the history of a controversial program',
***The Public Historian*, 1992:14:1:31–53.**

† Death certificate studies

The accuracy of cause of death data from death certificates also depends on a number of factors, such as whether an autopsy has been performed, the age of the deceased, whether the physician filling in the death certificate knows the deceased, the recording physician's attention to detail, avoidance of reporting a cause of death if "stigma" is attached, incorrect coding of disease, and variations in the quality of medical care in regions or over time.... Thus, among a cohort of exposed or potentially exposed individuals, the effect of underascertainment of disease is most likely to bias the magnitude of the association under investigation toward the null.'

* Gray

A unit of radiation dose equal to 100 rads.

* Induced radioactivity

Radioactivity produced in certain materials as a result of nuclear reactions, especially by the absorption of neutrons.

Ingested radioisotopes

'Hazards from ingested radioisotopes may arise from two principal ways: (1) the ingested material may be absorbed and deposited in some "critical organ" where it will continue to irradiate surrounding tissue for a period of time determined by the radioactive half-life and the biological turnover time for the particular element in the particular organ; and[2] the unabsorbed radioisotope will irradiate the gastrointestinal tract during its passage through the tract.... Inhalation is beyond doubt the most significant industrial hazard encountered in the handling of radioactive materials and the least well understood in so far as biological mechanisms are concerned. An intensive program of research on biological mechanisms and toxic consequences is in progress at Hanford....'
R. C. Thompson, W. J. Blair, S. Marks and M. F. Sullivan, 'Evaluation of internal exposure hazard for several radioisotopes encountered in reactor operation', *Proceedings of the Second United Nations International Conference on the Peaceful uses of Atomic Energy*, Geneva, September 1958: 23:283–9.

Inhaled radioisotopes

'Inhalation has long been considered the most important route of entry into the body of hazardous materials in industry. Ingestion is the next most likely route. Frequently the inhalation route, because of deposition in the gastrointestinal [GI] tract of material cleared from the lung, becomes primarily an ingestion type of exposure. While the basic principles remain the same in considering either radioactive or nonradioactive aerosols, certain factors assume relatively greater importance when radioactive materials are concerned. For example, (a) the total weight of material is usually very much smaller; (b) an external radiation hazard may exist even though the material does not enter the body; (c) material in the GI tract may damage the radiosensitive cells of the lining epithelium whether or not the element is absorbed; and (d) radiation damage, including the induction of cancer, may occur from relatively small deposits in th lung, pulmonary lymph nodes, or other portions of the reticulo-endothelial system.'

J. N. Stannard (University of Rochester School of Medicine and Dentistry) 'An evaluation of inhalation hazards in the nuclear energy industry', *Proceedings of the Second United Nations International Conference on The Peaceful Uses of Atomic Energy*, Geneva, September 1958: 23:306–12.

* Internal radiation dose
Radiation dose to internal organs due to radioactivity inside the body; may consist of any combination of alpha, beta and gamma radioactivity.

Maximum permissible dose
'The rapid changes in the values and ideas in relation to the maximum permissible external doses ... are only an indication of the enormous amount of work that remains to be done in the field of radiological safety. The long-term effects, both somatic and genetic, which result from humans being subjected to steady regular doses of radiation for very long periods of time, have not been experimentally studied for obvious reasons. An ideal spot to make such studies would be an area that is reasonably well populated and that has a radiation field significantly higher than background. Such an ideal area exists in the southernmost region of the west coast of India. Here in a strip of land adjoining the sea, which is 150 miles long and about 0.25 miles wide, extensive monazite sand areas occur. This sand contains thorium and to a smaller degree uranium and daughter products. The population of about 100,000 residing in this area is being and has been subjected to low-level chronic irradiation for generations.'

D. S. Bharatwal and G. H. Vaze, 'Radiation dose measurements in the Monazite areas of Kerala State in India', *Proceedings of the Second United Nations International Conference on the Peaceful Uses of Atomic Energy*, Geneva, Sepember 1958:23:156–8.

* Neutron

An elementary particle that is electrically neutral. Neutrons together with protons form the nucleus of an element (except the normal hydrogen nucleus, which consists of a single proton). Neutrons are stable in the nucleus, but unstable in free air, disintegrating into a proton and an electron.

† Null Hypothesis

'Formally, in planning an investigation, an epidemiologist poses a hypothesis to the effect that the exposures and health outcomes under study are not associated. Under this hypothesis, the value of the measure of association used is theoretically expected to be approximately 1. This is termed the *null hypothesis* or the hypothesis of no association. The measure of association derived from the investigation is then tested statistically. To "reject the null hypothesis", or to conclude that exposures and events are not independent, is to conclude that there is evidence of an association.'

† Proportionate mortality studies

'In analytical epidemiology, proportionate mortality studies are generally considered most valuable in the initial stages of an evaluation. They provide an inexpensive and rapid way of taking an early look at a set of data. Results of proportionate mortality studies must be interpreted carefully, since a proportionate excess can reflect either an excess in the absolute rate for the disease in question or a deficit in the absolute rates for some of the other causes. Large proportionate excesses, however, are unlikely to be produced in that way. Although a proportionate mortality study is usually considered a type of retrospective cohort study, it is convenient to consider the proportionate mortality study as equivalent to a case-control study in which the cases have died from the cause of interest and the controls are selected from deaths from all other causes.'

† Publication bias

'It has been well documented in biomedical research that studies with a statistically significant finding are more likely to be published than studies with nonsignificant results. Thus, evaluations of disease–exposure associations based solely on published literature could be biased in favor of showing a positive association.'

* Rad

A unit of dose equal to the deposition of 100 ergs of energy per gram of material being irradiated.

* Radioactivity

The spontaneous release of energy from the nucleus of an atom, in the form of gamma, beta, and/or alpha radiation. Releases of beta and alpha radiation result in the transformation of the atom into a different element (known as transmutation).

Radioisotope

'Radioisotopes are formed at the time of the detonation of an atomic bomb and are formed in two ways, one by fission or splitting of the nucleus of a uranium or plutonium atom, the other by the capture, by a stable isotope, of a neutron. The former are known as fission products, the latter as induced radioisotopes or non-fission products. The fission products are radioisotopes of elements that are about one-half the atomic weight of uranium or plutonium. The induced radioisotopes are isotopes of any elements that are present in the area of the neutron flux that occurs at the time of the detonation of the bomb and that have the ability to capture a neutron.'

Allyn N. Seymour, Division of Biology and Medicine, US Atomic Energy Commission 1959.

* Radionuclide

The radioactive isotope of an element.

* Rem

A unit of dose that takes into account the relative biological damage due to various kinds of radiation energy absorbed by tissue. In general, the larger the amount of energy deposited per unit length of tissue, the greater the radiation damage per unit of absorbed radiation energy; that is, the greater the ratio of rems to rads.

* Roentgen

A unit measuring gamma radiation dose. A roentgen is equal to 0.94 rads.

* Sieveret

A unit of effective dose equal to 100 rems.

* TNT equivalent

The unit most commonly used to measure the energy released in nuclear explosions. One ton of TNT is assumed to be equivalent to one billion calories of energy. The energy released by nuclear explosions is generally measured in kilotons and megatons of TNT equivalent.

Whole body monitoring

Whole body monitoring by high pressure ionization chambers or scintillation counters has developed into a very valuable health physics tool.... Originally whole body monitors were constructed in connection with investigations of the natural radioactivity of human beings. More recently they have been used for checking personnel involved in nuclear weapons trials, before and after their participation, for ingested or inhaled fission products. Whole body monitors have also been found useful for investigating articles contaminated by the escape of activity as a result of reactor accidents or by fall-out from nuclear weapons trials.'

Denis Taylor, 'Some special problems in health physics instrumentation', *Proceedings of the Second Annual United Nations International Conference on the Peaceful Uses of Atomic Energy*, Geneva, September 1958:23:404–7.

* Yield

The energy released by a nuclear explosion.

Definitions marked * are taken from *Radioactive Heaven and Earth*. A report of the International Physicians for the Prevention of Nuclear War (IPPNW) International Commission to Investigate the Health and Environmental Effects of Nuclear Weapons Production and the Institute for Energy and Environmental Research. (IPPNW, 1991).

Definitions marked † are taken from *Veterans and Agent Orange: Health Effects of Herbicides Used in Vietman*. (Washington, National Academy of Sciences, Institute of Medicine, 1994).

Note British spellings are used in the running text. Cited extracts and names of organizations retain their original spelling.

Abbreviations of organizations

AAAS	American Association for the Advancement of Science
ABCC	Atomic Bomb Casualty Commission (US)
AEA	Atomic Energy Authority (UK)
AFEB	Armed Forces Epidemiological Board (US)
AOWG	Agent Orange Working Group (US)
BEIR	Biological Effects of Ionizing Radiation (UN)
BNFL	British Nuclear Fuels Limited
CAC	Committee on Atomic Casualties (US)
CDC	Centre for Disease Control (US)
EPA	Environmental Protection Agency. Formerly FRC (US)
FRC	Federation Research Council. Became EPA (US)
HASL	Health and Safety Laboratory (US)
HSE	Health and Safety Executive (UK)
ICRP	International Commission on Radiation Protection (UN)
LSS	Life Span Study (US)
JNIH	Japanese National Institute of Health
NAE	National Academy of Engineering (US)
NAS	National Academy of Sciences (US)
NCRP	National Council on Radiation Protection (US)
NIH	National Institute of Health (US)
NRC	National Research Council (US)
NRS	National Research Services (US)
OSRD	Office of Scientific Research and Development (US)
OTA	Office of Technology Assessment (US)
RERF	Radiation Effects Research Foundation (Japan)
UNSCEAR	United Nations Scientific Committee on the Effects of Atomic Radiation
USAEC	United States Atomic Energy Commission

Introduction

'I just want to know how it happened. Was it my fault?' Two mothers sitting on a small pier built by Robert Louis Stevenson's father in a fishing village on the east coast of Scotland, on a glorious summer's day in 1994. Our daughters were rehearsing a play about Robert Louis' childhood and adolescence, before he fled the tubercular climate of Edinburgh for the South Seas.

Her child had been conceived two days after the Chernobyl reactor exploded, in late April 1986. 'It was a Saturday. My husband played golf with our priest. Father came home to dinner. They were both soaked to the skin. News of Chernobyl was all over the television. Father had been worried about the lighting bills at the church. They joked that they were so radioactive they would glow in church the next day and there would be no need for electricity. She was conceived that night.'

My child had been conceived in December 1986, in the next fishing village. I had spent the early part of December in the South Seas, monitoring the fourth plebiscite on the question of whether the Republic of Palau should retain its nuclear-free constitution which was preventing the United States building a nuclear submarine port in the island territory.[1] I had flown home to New York for a week, then to Paris for a conference with my husband. We went to our house in Scotland for Christmas and there I became pregnant.

Our daughters were now seven and six years old. They go to the same primary school. Her daughter had spent five years battling leukaemia. Her parents and sisters had fought it with her. She was winning. But her mother seemed to be carrying this burden of guilt. 'Why her? Why my family? Was it Chernobyl? Did we do something wrong? Why did it take the doctors so long to diagnose it? I told them something was wrong and she is my third child. I knew. They should have known. When you go to the Sick Children's Hospital in Edinburgh you see a ward full of children with leukaemia. We have known so many who died. Most of them are coming from one primary school.'

She was dabbling her feet in the water at the base of the pier, but I wasn't. I knew that we were fifty miles downstream from Rosyth Naval Dockyard where Britain's (and America's) nuclear submarines berthed on the Firth of Forth at Edinburgh. Past the lighthouses that Robert Louis' father had built, I could see the Dunbar nuclear power station. Even the limited information that appeared in our local press about the radionuclide count in this very harbour were enough to make me reluctant to paddle.

Six months earlier, the golf course where her husband had played that Saturday afternoon had been covered in snow. We went sledging there, enjoying one of the first snowfalls my daughter had experienced in six years of life in New York and Scotland. Almost exactly forty years earlier, snow had fallen in the South Seas, in the Marshall Islands, on Rongelap and Utirik and other atolls downwind of Bikini, where the United States was firing its *Bravo* weapons test. Shortly after the test the people living on Rongelap saw what they thought were snowflakes falling from the cloud passing over their atolls. It was so heavy the children frolicked in it and smeared it all over their bodies. Even though they eventually bathed in the salt sea, within hours they were vomiting and suffering intense diarrhoea. Burns began to appear on their skin within days. Like the Japanese fishermen caught in the *Lucky Dragon* vessel by the same fallout – and perhaps like the children in the leukemia ward in Edinburgh – they had become victims of fallout.

Whose fault was it? I had been pondering this question for more than a decade, since I first began to work with the women of Palau to defend their right to a nuclear free constitution and a territory free of nuclear substances. Very early on in New York I had read Neal O. Hines' history[2] of the Washington University Fisheries Laboratory, which carried out the studies into the impact on the food chain of the American tests at Bikini in the 1940s. Neal Hines was an administrator and science journalist at the Laboratory. The deputy director, Alleyn Seymour, has since told me that Hines' book was considered the official history of the Laboratory and the radiobiological studies they had carried out.[3]

The 239 people of Rongelap, Utirik and Ailingnae atolls together with 28 US servicemen on Rongirik atoll were evacuated after three days by the United States Navy. They have since been monitored for forty years for the effects of whole body doses of irradiation from the *Bravo* tests. I met several of the Marshallese in New York throughout the 1980s, en route to the Brookhaven National Laboratory in Long Island where they were sent for testing and treatment for thyroid problems in particular. As well as the scar of thyroidectomies, they had one other common aspect to their medical history. They had very complicated reproductive histories. The men were worried about their 'conceptual outcomes', and the lack of them. The women each had a long history of miscarriages and sometimes deformed births. In the worst cases, they spoke of 'jelly babies', conceptual products which clearly had some elements of being human but were far too deformed to live for more than a few hours, or were born dead.

Yet Hines had remarked that although the construction firm of Holmes and Narver had been contracted to build barracks for both men and women in the Pacific Proving Ground in preparation for the tests on Bikini, no woman – scientist, clerk or member of the US Armed Forces – had ever been assigned to the test site. Dr Seymour confirmed this when I interviewed him in Seattle in 1993. Later, I read in Jonathan Weisgall's account[4] of the Operations Crossroads tests, the first series at Bikini held less than a year after the bombing of Hiroshima and Nagasaki, that no woman journalist had been permitted to observe the tests although 40,000 men had been present at them in one capacity or another. Weisgall also quotes a 'theme song' composed by some of the journalists en route to the Marshall Islands which had the refrain,

> *'We're all signed up and ready to go,*
> *To offer up our testicles for UNO'.*

When I asked Sir Mark Oliphant in Canberra in 1993[5] why no woman scientist or service person had ever been sent to the Pacific Proving Grounds he suggested that it was because of a traditional chivalry. 'You don't put women in the frontline', he said. But the Marshallese women had been in the front line of the United States tests. There had even been suggestions that in 1954 the populations of Rongelap, Ailingnae and Utirik – 239 Marshallese – had been deliberately not evacuated from the predictable path of the fallout cloud of the *Bravo* tests until at least 48 hours after the 'snow' had fallen.[6]

Even as I was flying to Australia to interview Sir Mark, I fell into conversation with the passenger next to me on the leg out to Hawaii. He was a 52-year-old Mexican welder who had just been to his father's funeral in Nevada. He made the best money working in nuclear power plants. I asked him how the dose monitoring system worked. 'Oh, we throw those away. You can't make overtime if you wear those so no-one does.' 'Don't you worry about radiation exposure?' I asked him. 'Well,' he replied, 'they always choose older men for the dangerous jobs, those who have completed their families.' He told me that his sister-in-law and his wife both had thyroid problems. They grew up in Nevada and Idaho, downwind from the United States' continental nuclear test site. He was childless.

Hines had acknowledged in his 1962 history of the radiobiological studies in the Pacific Proving Ground that the tests series from Operations Crossroads to Hardtack were concerned with investigations into medical and biological aspects of the weapons as well as their military capacities. 'If these investigations sometimes fell short of total and comprehensive attacks on basic problems, they were, at least, acknowledgements of responsibility beyond the purely technical and administrative, and were as disciplined, imaginative and productive as the resources and the state of knowledge would allow.'But were they? Is it sufficient to accept the reassurances of the official historians of the weapons development establishments and biomedical laboratories?

Had the scientists and biomedical researchers been motivated by what J. Robert Oppenheimer had called 'technical sweetness'? He recalled to the Personnel Security Board of the United States Atomic Energy Commission a few weeks after the *Bravo* tests in 1954 how the momentum for building the first atomic weapons had caught up the scientists in Los Alamos and Alamagordo back in 1945. Now he was expressing reservations about the immense power he had been so pivotal in creating. His loyalty to the United States was in question. He acknowledged that he had no reservations until the bombings of Hiroshima and Nagasaki. 'However, it is my judgement in these things that when you see something that is technically sweet, you go ahead and do it and you argue about what to do about it only after you have had your technical success.'

Echoes of Oppenheimer's early position, the legitimacy of technical sweetness, were expressed by Dr Harold Agnew nearly forty years later in December 1992. Dr Agnew, now in his seventies, had been one of the team of three scientists who had flown on the mission to drop the atomic bomb on Hiroshima in August 1945 which killed more than 150,000 people. At a ceremony at London's Science Museum to open an exhibit of the replica of the first controlled self-sustaining nuclear reactor that had been built at Stagg football field at the University of Chicago fifty years earlier, Dr Agnew said he found it hard to understand the public reaction to the bomb. 'It's technically so sweet ... just a beautiful reaction. From a single molecule of uranium you can liberate 70 million times the amount of energy that you can from a molecule of carbon. The media doesn't appreciate this and tends to emphasize the bogeyman aspects ... they like to scare people.'[7]

In 1990 I read a Greenpeace publication, John May's *Nuclear Age: The hidden history of the human cost*[8]. On his opening page, May remarked, 'Because the effects of radiation take decades to reveal themselves, almost all the stories in this book are current, even though some of them begin in the mid-1940s. In this context, information develops its own half-life – the amount of time it takes for official truth to leak out of the canisters in which it is contained.'

I took this as a challenge. Always inclined to work from primary sources rather than secondary commentaries, I wondered if I – a social scientist rather than a scientist or biomedical researcher – could go back to the beginnings, to read the literature on human radiation injury since the 1940s and understand it. Could I gain access to the archives containing the minutes, the correspondence, the memos, the research designs of the researchers? Could I trace out the growth of knowledge about human radiation injury from fallout in order to assess Hines' defence of the researchers – that they had been as 'disciplined, imaginative and productive as the resources and the state of knowledge would allow'? As a sociologist of knowledge, I felt I had the basic research competence to embark on this project. In 1991 I found myself working in a British medical school, with access to a full medical library. Over the next three years I secured enough funding to travel several times to the United States and Australia to interview surviving researchers and to study the deposited papers of those who had died.

It was a three-year journey for me to come to a decision about where the responsibility lies. I would like to take the reader through this journey so that you can make up your own mind. Nineteen ninety-five is the fiftieth anniversary of the bombing of Hiroshima and Nagasaki. The bipolarity of the Cold War has given way to a potential proliferation of minor nuclear states. The bombs that devastated Hiroshima and Nagasaki were commonly referred to as 'baby bombs' less than a year later. We face the possibility that they will be treated as mere 'tactical weapons'. Are we informed enough about their consequences – to both victor and vanquished – to include them in the arsenal of a just war?

It is important to note that all contemporary scientific and biomedical discussions about the types and extent of injury caused to humans by ionizing radiation are grounded in the biomedical studies of the survivors of the August 1945 bombings of Hiroshima and Nagasaki. So many of the current results from studies of, for instance, leukaemia clusters around nuclear power stations, are assessed against the data and results generated by the studies conducted in Japan.

In discussing the genetic consequences of exposure to ionizing radiation, for instance, Professor P. M. B. Walker CBE FRSE[9] notes that our current understanding of the epidemiology of cancer resulting from low level environmental or occupational radiation is grounded in the baselines that are assumed to have been established by the Life Span Study of survivors in Hiroshima and Nagasaki. 'This study has shown that children born to mothers exposed to high doses of radiation (around 2 Sv) at Hiroshima and Nagasaki, but not irradiated in *utero*, do not have a higher incidence of childhood leukaemia compared to unirradiated controls. Neither does the incidence of a number of other markers, including the occurrence of abnormal proteins, increase. For these and similar reasons, irradiation at near background levels has not been thought to be a significant factor for the children of workers who may have been exposed to the normal permitted levels in, particularly, the nuclear industry.' In Britain this means that the interpretation of what are thought to be 'leukaemia clusters' in the vicinity of nuclear power stations such as Sellafield and Dounreay are very controversial because 'the dosage received by the fathers is about twenty times less than that received by the parents in the Hiroshima and Nagasaki studies.' A lot depends, then, on the assumption that the studies in Hiroshima and Nagasaki were well conducted.

Professor Walker points out that even after fifty years we do not actually understand much about the mechanism of injury from ionizing radiation, or about the amount or dose required to cause injury. The studies of the survivors of Hiroshima and Nagasaki are always considered to be studies of people who received a massive instantaneous dose of radiation. But radiation and radon are present in low doses throughout our environment. Controlled doses of radiation can be used to marvellous therapeutic effect in medicine. As Professor Walker explains, 'The major problem with very low radiation doses is whether their biological effects remain proportional to the absorbed dose or whether there is a threshold below which radiation has no effect.' The argument for the threshold revolves around the ability of the cell to repair damage. It is known that therapeutic doses of X-rays have fewer side effects if they are divided or fractionated.

We have not yet established even in sub-human species such as mice the precise relationship between radiation and dose. Even with the mouse, millions would be required. According to Professor Walker, 'The regulatory authorities therefore assume that these effects are essentially stochastic, that is that they follow statistically at random with a given probability after irradiation. There is therefore no threshold and biological limits for radiation have been set accordingly.' As we shall see, this is not necessarily the view that informed forty years of research on the survivors of Hiroshima and Nagasaki, yet it is now the consensus view of the newer generation of biomedical and health physics researchers.

American physicians writing for the organization Physicians for Social Responsibility[10] agree that 'Most, but not all, scientists believe that such stochastic or probabilistic effects of radiation are also directly related to the radiation dose, and that they can occur at any dose, no matter how small. This is called the *linear, no-threshold hypothesis*; it means that all exposure to radiation presents some risk to human health.'

But this hypothesis is still controversial. 'Until recently, most radiation scientists felt that, because cells repaired themselves, no association with cancer would be found at radiation doses below a certain threshold. This was the majority view of the National Academy of Sciences committee that, in 1980, produced its third report on the biological effects of ionizing radiation (BEIR III). But BEIR IV, published in 1990, unanimously accepts the linear, no-threshold hypothesis – a significant change in scientific opinion.'

Some scientists believe there is evidence that low doses produce more cancer per unit of radiation than high doses – the *supralinear hypothesis*. Others suggest that because radiation occurs naturally, it is essential to human life and in fact can be beneficial – this is the notion of *hormesis*.

Clearly, one hundred years after Roentgen detected the X-ray, the only certainty is uncertainty. Please bear this in mind as you read on into my reconstruction of the history of the biomedical legacy of Hiroshima and Nagasaki. I do think some of the researchers forgot it. The best they can urge on us non-scientists is a sort of stochastic stoicism. Just hope that the laws of chance will mean that you and yours are spared from the injurious effects of man-made radiation fallout. But surely this is the greatest argument for cessation of nuclear testing. Are we going to go on polluting our atmosphere and that of our children? Are we going to continue to proliferate manufactured radionuclides beyond the capacity of the planet to tolerate them? Or are we going to reassess the work of the first generation of nuclear and biomedical researchers and claim back the Earth and its atmosphere for our children and their children?

Notes

1. See my *Overreaching in Paradise: US Policy in Palau since 1945* (Juneau Alaska, The Denali Press, 1991); and Amy Boss, Roger Clark, Else Hammerich, Sue Roff and David Wright, *Report of the International Observer mission to the December 1986 Plebiscite in Palau* (International League for Human Rights and Minority Rights Group, New York (United Nations Document T/Com.10/L.374) (13 May 1987).

2. Neal O. Hines, *Proving Ground: An Account Of The Radiobiological Studies in the Pacific 1946–61*, (University of Washington Press, 1962).

3. Interview with Alleyn Seymour Seattle, 20 June 1993.

4. Jonathan M. Weisgall, *Operations Crossroads: The Atomic Tests at Bikini Atoll*, (Maryland, Naval Institute Press, 1994).

5. Interview with Sir Mark Oliphant, Canberra, Australia, November 1992.

6. See *inter alia* Robert A. Conard, *Fallout: The Experiences of a Medical Team in the Care of a Marshallese Population Accidentally Exposed to Fallout Radiation*, (New York, Brookhaven National Laboratory, Informal Report BNL 46444, September 1992).

7. Susan Watts, 'Scientist recalls nuclear dawning', *The Independent*, 2 December 1992.

8. John May, *The Greenpeace Book of the Nuclear Age: The Hidden History of the Human Cost.* (London, Victor Gollancz Ltd, 1990).

9. Professor P. M. B. Walker CBE FRSE, *Nuclear Energy and Radiation Dictionary* (Edinburgh, Chambers, 1992).

10. Kenneth L. Lichtenstein and Ira Helfand, 'Radiation and health: nuclear weapons and nuclear power' in Eric Chivian *et al.* (eds.) *Critical Condition: Human Health and the Environment, a report by the Physicians for Social Responsibility* (Cambridge Mass. and London, The MIT Press, 1993).

Testing for technical sweetness

... it is my judgement in these things that when you see something that is technically sweet, you go ahead and do it and you argue about what to do about it only after you have had your technical success.

J. Robert Oppenheimer, Hearings before Personnel Security Board, United States Atomic Energy Commission, 1954

... it is proper to remember that there are no known fallout casualties among the 220,000 Japanese hurt and killed in Hiroshima and Nagasaki.

Robert L. Corsbie of the Atomic Energy Commission to the Military Operations Subcommittee of the Committee on Government Operations of the House of Representatives of the United States, 1961

One

On Friday, 10 August 1945 the 78-year-old Secretary of War of the United States, Henry L. Stimson, wrote in his diary, 'Today was momentous. We had ... packed up and the car was ready to take us to the airport ... for our vacation when word came that the Japanese had made an offer to surrender.... That busted our holiday.'[1]

Exactly fifty years after Roentgen had first detected the X-ray, the Japanese city of Hiroshima had been bombed with a uranium atomic weapon on 6 August 1945; Nagasaki was bombed with a plutonium weapon on 9 August 1945. The deployment of two atomic weapons in less than a week was designed to achieve the unconditional surrender of Japan's military forces, yet the next day the US Secretary of War, the person who acknowledged [2] that his was the primary responsibility for advising President Roosevelt and then President Truman on the use of atomic energy as a weapon of war, was preparing to leave Washington for his retreat in New York. What had he – and the President and the scientists who developed and the military personnel who deployed the weapons – expected from their use?

In February 1947 Stimson published his account of the decision to use the atomic bomb in *Harper's Magazine*. The former Secretary of War recorded that he had first heard about atomic energy in late 1941. President Roosevelt appointed a committee consisting of Vice-President Wallace, General Marshall, Dr Vannevar Bush, Dr James B. Conant and Stimson which was involved in all major decisions of policy on the development and use of atomic energy. Stimson was directly responsible to the President for the administration of the undertaking from May 1943 until his resignation on 21 September 1945. His chief advisers were Marshall, Bush, Conant and Major General Leslie R. Groves, the military officer in charge of what came to be known as the Manhattan District Project.

Stimson says that the policy adopted by the President and this group of advisers was to spare no effort in securing the earliest possible development of an atomic weapon because of the conviction that the German scientists, who had achieved atomic fission in 1938, must be working to the same end, 'and it was vital that they should not be the first to bring atomic weapons into the field of battle'. Stimson insists, 'At no time, from 1941 to 1945, did I ever hear it suggested by the President, or by any other responsible member of the government, that atomic energy should not be used in the war. All of us of course understood the terrible responsibility involved in our attempt to unlock the doors to such a devastating weapon; President Roosevelt particularly spoke to me many times of his own awareness of the catastrophic potentialities of our work. But we were at war, and the work must be done. I therefore emphasize that it was our common objective, throughout the war, to be the first to produce an atomic weapon and use it.'

To Stimson and his scientific advisers, 'The possible atomic weapon was considered to be a new and tremendously powerful explosive, as legitimate as any other of the deadly explosive weapons of modern war. The entire purpose was the production of a military weapon; on no other ground could the wartime expenditure of so much time and money have been justified.'

A weapon based on atomic energy, then, was seen as primarily an explosive device by the Secretary of War – and his scientific advisers. The exact circumstances of its use as a tactical weapon were not known until 1945, but it was built to be used. 'As time went on it became clear that the weapon would not be available in time for use in the European Theater', but 'in the spring of 1945 it became evident that the climax of our prolonged atomic effort was at hand.'

But it was not all clear sailing for the pro-use scientists advising the Secretary of War. Stimson talked with President Roosevelt on 15 March 1945 for what turned out to be the last time before the President's death in April. In his memo of this meeting, which he reproduced in part in his *Harper's* statement in 1947, Stimson remarks that the President and he discussed the suggestion that an independent committee of scientists be called together to evaluate the Manhattan Project 'because rumors are going around that Vannevar Bush and Jim Conant have sold the President a lemon on the subject and ought to be checked up on.' Stimson countered by pointing out to President Roosevelt that the Manhattan Project included four Nobel Prize winners and practically every physicist of national standing.

He then outlined to the President 'the two schools of thought that exist in respect to the future control after the war of this project, in case it is successful, one of them being the secret close-in attempted control of the project by those who control it now, and the other being the international control based upon freedom both of science and of access.' The Secretary of War warned the President that 'those things must be settled before the first projectile is used.' to which the President agreed.

The next time the Secretary of War discussed atomic energy with the President of the United States was on 25 April 1945 after Roosevelt's death. Stimson noted of President Truman that he 'accepted this responsibility with the same fine spirit that Senator Truman had shown before in accepting our refusal to inform him.' An Interim Committee was formed to advise the new President on 'the various questions raised by our apparently imminent success in developing an atomic weapon.' This Interim Committee, far from constituting a review panel of the advisory group who had surrounded the Secretary of War and President of the United States since the inception of the atomic weapons development project, consisted of James F. Byrnes as personal representative of the President, Ralph A. Bard, Under-Secretary of the Navy, William L. Clayton, Assistant Secretary of State, Dr Vannevar Bush, Director, Office of Scientific Research and Development and President of the Carnegie Institution of Washington, Karl T. Compton, Chief of the Office of Field Service in the Office of Scientific Research and Development, and President of the Massachusetts Institute of Technology, and James B. Conant, Chairman of the National Defense Research Committee and President of Harvard University. This Interim Committee was assisted by a Scientific Panel consisting of Dr A H Compton, Dr Enrico Fermi, Dr E O Lawrence and Dr J. R. Oppenheimer who, as Stimson acknowledged, all held positions of great importance in the atomic project from its inception.

On 1 June 1945 after discussions with the Scientific Panel, the Interim Committee recommended to President Truman that the bomb should be used without prior warning against Japan as soon as possible on a dual target – 'that is, a military installation or war plant surrounded by or adjacent to houses and other buildings most susceptible to damage.'

The first atomic weapon was exploded in the Alamogordo desert on 6 July 1945. Kenneth T. Bainbridge, Director of this Trinity test, probably expressed the views of most of the other scientists who developed the atomic bomb in the early 1940s when he reflected:

> My residence in England during the influx of refugees in 1933-34, and a taste of war for two months in 1941, sped the soul-searching undergone before agreeing to work on nuclear weapons. An inherent abhorrence of totalitarianism was increased when I was told by a famous theoretical physicist of the death of his parents and how they had been murdered. The pronouncement by Hitler that Nazi Germany would rule the world for

the next thousand years strongly affected my resolution as it did so many others.[3]

Bainbridge had heard first-hand accounts of incidents in the evacuation of Crete, Guadacanal, the Battle of Britain. 'From these stories it was obvious that in the space of a few years the war was getting dirtier, and Hitler's threats and deeds gave me a somewhat bloodthirsty viewpoint on the war, and I would be glad to do what I could to help get there first with atomic weapons. I know that this background finally made me want to go to Los Alamos, and later, in another way, contributed to my lack of euphoria after the explosion at the Trinity test.'

Another Los Alamos scientist, Frederic de Hoffman, agreed: 'Basically, there was a sense of common mission which pretty well transcended all that might divide us.'[4] Joseph O. Hirschfelder [5] said 'At Los Alamos during World War II there was no moral issue with respect to working on the atom bomb. Everyone was agreed on the necessity of stopping Hitler and the Japanese from destroying the free world. It was not an academic question – our friends and relatives were being killed and we, ourselves, were desperately afraid.'

But there were dissidents among the scientists working on the bombs. Donald L. Collins recalled [6] that 'prior to the use and public announcement of the bomb, it was estimated by the Security Department that some 200 persons were officially knowledgeable of the end product of the project. A social consciousness developed which was difficult to explore within the security limits. Nevertheless, we did manage a few meetings and organized the Association of Atomic Scientists. One of the persistent organizers in 1945 was Dr Eugene Rabinowitch. His *Bulletin of the Atomic Scientists* is still an outlet for dissenters and anti-establishment propaganda, which often serves the useful purpose of causing us to rethink our positions.' The heart of the dissident movement was in the Metallurgical Laboratory in Chicago, where the director appointed a Committee of Social and Political Implications composed of three physicists, James Franck, D. Hughes and Leo Szilard; three chemists, T. Hogness, E. Rabinowitch and G. Seaborg; and a biologist, C. J. Nickson. Szilard and his colleagues tried to reach President Roosevelt through the good offices of Albert Einstein to inform him about the implications of the use of atomic energy as a weapon, but the President died before they were able to see him. In June 1945 the Chicago Committee sent what is known as the Franck Report to Secretary of War Stimson.[7]

The Franck Report argued for the demonstration of the weapon on a barren island or in the desert, in the presence of United Nations observers, rather than its use against one or more Japanese cities. These scientists argued that first use by the United States of this unprecedented weapon would only hasten the arms race that was sure to take place anyway and prejudice the possibility of reaching an international agreement on the future control of such weapons. They were of course correct in both predictions. But where the dissident scientists failed was in depicting eloquently enough the horror that the use of the weapons would cause. 'All of us familiar with the present state of nucleonics,' they wrote to the Secretary of War, 'live with the vision before our eyes of sudden destruction visited on our own country, of a Pearl Harbor disaster repeated in thousand-fold magnification in every one of our major cities' if this new invention was deployed as a tactical weapon.

The seven physicists, chemists and biologist made the point to the Secretary of War that the United States had stockpiles of poison gas but that recent polls had shown that public opinion would disapprove of their use even to accelerate the winning of the war against Japan. 'It is true that some irrational element in mass psychology makes gas poisoning more revolting than blasting by explosives, even though gas warfare is in no way more "inhuman" than the war of bombs and bullets. Nevertheless, it is not at all certain that American public opinion, if it could be enlightened as to the effect of atomic explosives, would approve of our country being the first to introduce such an indiscriminate method of wholesale destruction of civilian life.'

On 16 June 1945 the Scientific Panel considered a memorandum similar to the Franck Report but concluded 'we can propose no technical demonstration likely to bring an end to the war; we can see no acceptable alternative to direct military use.'

Stimson maintained in 1947 in his explanation to the American public that he and the President had sought the best advice they could, while acknowledging their personal responsibility for the final decision. Based on the scientists' views, in which the dissenting voices were barely heard, Stimson and Truman decided to deploy two atomic weapons to destroy completely the influence of the Japanese militarists while protecting the position of the Emperor who was thought to be essential to post-war stability.

On 2 July 1945 Secretary of War Stimson advocated that a warning should be given to Japan which 'was designed to promise destruction if Japan resisted, and hope, if she surrendered.' The warning was issued in the form of the Potsdam ultimatum of 26 July. The first successful detonation of an atomic fission weapon had been achieved at Alamogordo, New Mexico on 16 July 1945 while President Truman was in Potsdam. 'We had developed a weapon of such revolutionary character that its use against the enemy might well be expected to produce exactly the kind of shock on the Japanese ruling oligarchy which we desired, strengthening the position of those who wished peace, and weakening that of the military party.' But on 28 July Japan's Premier Suzuki rejected the Postdam ultimatum as 'unworthy of public notice'.

The scientists and politicians were now free to test the 'technical sweetness' of the atomic bomb in two different compositions (the bomb detonated at Hiroshima was a uranium device whereas that at Nagasaki was based on plutonium) on two different cities, on 6 August and 9 August. Stimson argued in his *Harper's Magazine* article that the use of the atomic weapon helped the Emperor's faction to prevail over the die-hard Japanese militarists.

A weapon developed in fear of Germany's capability to develop and deploy it first had been used to end the war with Japan. The Secretary of War and the President of the United States had made a utilitarian calculation – Japan still commanded five million armed forces; there had already been 300,000 Allied battle casualties in the war against Japan and Japan's own territory had not yet been penetrated. In March 1945 the first incendiary raids had been launched on Tokyo, with more than 100,000 deaths – much the same death rate as had occurred in the fire bombings of Dresden. As Secretary of War Stimson recalled in 1947, 'On August 6 one B-29 dropped a single atomic bomb on Hiroshima. Three days later a second bomb was dropped on Nagasaki and the war was over.' He quoted Dr Karl Compton, 'it was not one atomic bomb, or two, which brought surrender; it was the experience of what an atomic bomb will actually do to a community, *plus the dread of many more*, that was effective.' The destruction of Hiroshima and Nagasaki and the immediate death of more than 100,000 of their citizens put an end to the Japanese war. 'It stopped the fire raids, and the strangling blockade; it ended the ghastly specter of a clash of great land armies.' Or as J. Robert Oppenheimer told the Personnel Security Board of the United States Atomic Energy Commission in 1954, 'it is my judgement in these things that when you see something that is technically sweet, you go ahead and do it and you argue about what to do about it only after you have had your technical success.'[8] For both the scientists and politicians – and indeed for the American public – the deployment of the first tactical atomic weapons at Hiroshima and Nagasaki was a technical success which was sweet. The US Strategic Bombing Survey Summary of the Pacific War, however, was oddly equivocal about the bombing of the two cities with atomic devices. On the one hand, it estimated[9] that the damage and casualties caused at Hiroshima by one atomic bomb dropped from a single plane would have required 220 B-29s carrying 1200 tons of incendiary bombs, 400 tons of high explosive bombs, and 500 tons of antipersonnel fragmentation bombs, if conventional weapons rather than an atomic bomb had been used. One hundred and twenty five B-29s carrying 1200 tons of bombs would have been required to approximate the damage and casualties at Nagasaki. But the US Strategic Bombing Survey also concluded 'based on a detailed investigation of all the facts, and supported by the testimony of the surviving Japanese leaders involved, it is the Survey's opinion that certainly prior to 31 December 1945, and in all probability prior to 1 November 1945, Japan would have surrendered even if the atomic bombs had not been dropped, even if Russia had not entered the war, and even if no invasion had been planned or contemplated.'

Notes

1. Henry L. Stimson quoted by Barton J. Bernstein, 'The perils and politics of surrender: ending the war with Japan and avoiding the third atomic bomb', *Pacific Historical Review*, from Henry L. Stimson, Diary, 10 August 1945, Stimson Papers, Yale University.

2. Henry L. Stimson, 'The decision to use the Atomic Bomb', *Harper's Magazine*, 194:1161:February 1947:97–107.

3. Kenneth T. Bainbridge, 'Prelude to Trinity', *Bulletin of the Atomic Scientists*, April 1975 p.430.

4. Frederic de Hoffman, 'Pure science in the service of wartime technology', *Bulletin of the Atomic Scientists*, January 1975, p.41.

5. Joseph O. Hirschfelder, 'The scientific and technological miracle at Los Alamos' in Lawrence Badash *et al.* (eds.) *Reminiscences of Los Alamos, 1943–1945*, (London, D. Reideil Publishing Company, 1976).

6. Donald L. Collins, 'Pictures from the past: Journeys into health physics in the Manhattan District and other diverse places', in Kathren and Ziemer (eds.) *Health Physics; A Backward Glance*, (Oxford, Pergamon Press, 1980) pp.37–45.

7. The Franck Report is published in Edward Fogelman (ed.) *Hiroshima: The Decision to use the A Bomb* (Scribner Research Anthologies, 1964).

8. 'In the matter of J. Robert Oppenheimer, Transcript of hearing before Personnel Security Board and texts of principal documents and letters', United States Atomic Energy Committee, Washington DC, 12 April 1954 through 6 May 1954, (Cambridge Mass. and London, The MIT Press 1970 and 1971).

9. 'US Strategic Bombing Survey summary of the Pacific War', published in *Japanese War Mobilization and the Pacific Campaign, 1941–1945*, edited by W. Victor Madej (Allentown PA, Game Publishing Company, 1985) pp.71–2.

Two

On Saturday morning, 28 July 1945 Lieut Col William F. Smith Jr, deputy commander of the 457th Bomber Group, was trying to find La Guardia Field in a heavy mist. Deciding to head for Newark Airport instead, he turned his twin-engined B-25 back over New York City. At 9.49 a.m. workers in the Catholic War Relief Services offices on the 78th floor of the Empire State Building looked up from their work preparing for a trip to Europe to see a plane swerving into their windows at an angle of 15 degrees. The recently decorated bomber pilot slammed into the tallest office building in the world, killing himself and a dozen office workers, about a thousand feet above Thirty-Fourth Street and Fifth Avenue. Flames shot out as high as the observatory on the 86th floor; cascading torrents of flaming petrol poured through the floors where the plane's fuselage had entered the building and parts of the landing gear crashed into a lift shaft and fell to the sub-cellar a quarter of a mile below. It was, said *The New York Times*, the worst local tragedy of the war.

Little more than a week later the B-29 *Enola Gay* detonated a bomb over Hiroshima, a major military target of 318,000 civilians and soldiers who were busy travelling from their homes to the military installations and armaments plants for the day's work. Early reports from Hiroshima were unclear, said the War Department, because 'an impenetrable cloud of dust and smoke' still masked the city from the reconnaissance planes. Two days later, a different type of atomic bomb was detonated over Nagasaki. Both devices – the uranium bomb for Hiroshima and the plutonium bomb for Nagasaki – were detonated at much the same height as the Empire State Building. Yet they are until this day referred to as air bursts rather than ground bursts. For this reason, it is still said, they did not leave any significant amount of residual radioactivity. A senior official of the Atomic Energy Commission (AEC) was to tell a Congressional Committee in 1961 that 'it is proper to remember that there are no known fallout casualties among the 220,000 Japanese hurt and killed in Hiroshima and Nagasaki.'

According to General Groves[1], overall commander of the Manhattan District Project, it did not occur to the builders of the first atomic bomb – detonated in the New Mexico desert at Alamogordo in early July, 1945 – to worry about radioactive fallout until early 1945. Joseph O. Hirschfelder[2], a young researcher in Hans Bethe's Theoretical Physics Division at Los Alamos, was given the problem of predicting what radioactive fallout would do after an atomic explosion. Hirschfelder and his colleagues studied the formation of the ball of fire, which involved aerodynamics including the radiative transport of energy.

They used an astrophysics textbook on the dynamics of nebulae and chemical engineering books on heat transport. The second problem was the rise of the fire ball and the generation of winds along the ground and around the fire ball itself. Sir Geoffrey Taylor, world authority on turbulent and convective aerodynamics, helped with this part of the work. They had to figure out the fate of the radioactive materials inside the fire ball. What size distribution of the particles could be expected? There were two possibilities, according to Hirschfelder, depending on whether the fire ball was sufficiently high above the ground that debris from below wasn't picked up and mixed with the bomb's own ingredients. If the fire ball were high enough above the ground, Hirschfelder and his group argued theoretically that the small particles of the radioactive materials would condense on the interface between the fire ball and the surrounding cold air currents. They modelled their understanding of this entirely new phenomenon – the release of radioactive fallout – on the commercial manufacturing process of carbon black for use in rubber tyres since one of the group – John Magee – had worked at the Goodrich Rubber Company laboratory at the beginning of the war. They also used Volmer's book, *Homogeneous Nucleation*. 'On the basis of the Volmer theory and the carbon black, we convinced ourselves that homogeneous nucleation could only produce very small radioactive particles. However, to clinch the matter, John and I made experiments in which we vaporized metals and chilled the vapor by mixing with cold air. Sure enough, we got a blue smoke of metal particles less than a micron in diameter, in agreement with our theory.'

They realized that if the bomb were detonated within half a mile of the ground – or within *twice* the height of the Empire State Building – the air currents sweeping along the ground would pick up dirt, rocks and assorted debris, some of which would pass through the fire ball and get plated with radioactive materials. They looked at Department of Agriculture Soil Conservation reports and Bagnard's study of the Sahara Desert, *The Physics of Blown Sand* and concluded 'The thing that is amazing is that the size of the distribution of these particles depends very, very little on the kind of terrain that this crud has been picked up from'.

They then needed to establish how the fallout particles would spread and fall with the passage of time. They studied air pollution from industrial smoke and particulates emitted from smokestacks, the spreading of airplane trails and chemical warfare reports on how poison gases distribute themselves with respect to hills and valleys. They concluded 'Most of the radioactive fallout occurs in the valleys, leaving the hills relatively uncontaminated. At the Alamogordo bomb tests this was important because most of the people in the area lived on hilltops, so they were not in danger. However, their cattle spent most of their time grazing in the valleys and quite a few cows suffered from skin tumors. Since cows don't bathe and can't wash off this radioactive dust, people have an additional advantage.'

Hirschfelder and his group consulted with the military meterologists about air circulation in the upper atmosphere for distances of thousands of miles. 'Our biggest concern was the washing out of radioactive particles by rain, since that was not predictable.'

In the first week of July 1945, as Oppenheimer and his group were about to conduct the first atomic test, codenamed Trinity, at Alamogordo, 'very few people believed us when we predicted radiation fallout from the atom bomb', Hirschfelder recalled thirty years later. But they could not ignore the possibility and Dr Stafford Warren – medical director of the Manhattan District Project and soon to be elected the founding dean of UCLA Medical School – was put in charge of monitoring fallout. He had a very small team including Hirschfelder and Magee and a few old vehicles. Warren remained with the high command at six miles from ground zero and sent a number of agents out to monitor the situation downwind. 'Unfortunately, he misinterpreted the wind direction and the radiation monitors were deployed *upwind*. This became apparent in talking to him through my unreliable walkie-talkie. By the time this got straightened out, it was too late to move the monitors to places where they would be useful. At this point I took a catnap in the automobile while the cold rain continued to fall.'

Immediately after the Trinity Test Hirschfelder and Magee set out in their car to follow the radioactive clouds and to monitor the fallout from them – and if necessary to evacuate the area if the radioactivity readings were too high. About 25 miles from ground zero they came upon a mule who must have looked directly at the explosion; 'his jaws were wide open, and his tongue hanging down, and he was completely paralyzed. When we passed the same spot in the afternoon, the mule was gone so he must have recovered.'

Later in the day they visited an army searchlight post where the soldiers had bought huge T bone steaks. 'When we arrived they were just roasting the meat and it smelled delicious. However, at the same time, the fallout arrived – small flaky dust particles gently settling on the ground. The radiation level was quite high. So we sent the searchlight crew back to their base camp and told them to bury their steaks.'

When Hirschfelder and Magee got back to base camp their vehicle was so radioactive that the Geiger counters read 4 roentgen per hour in the driver's seat. It was still sufficiently radioactive four days later to throw Geiger counters in nearby laboratories off the scale. General Groves wouldn't let the two men ride with him to Albuquerque in his car.

After telling these stories in a public lecture series at the Santa Barbara campus of the University of California in 1975, Hirschfelder was asked how he felt about the atomic bombing of Hiroshima and Nagasaki. He replied that while there had been scientists working from Chicago who opposed the use of the bombs in 1945, 'At Los Alamos we never questioned that it should be used in a military engagement'. The atomic bomb was more efficient than the fire raids on Tokyo, Dresden or Hamburg because 'if the atom bomb is exploded high above the ground (as it was at Hiroshima and Nagasaki) very few of the casualties are produced by radiation – most of the casualties are produced by falling rubble, blast and fire as in conventional air attacks.' One bomb delivered the equivalent of 20,000 tons of TNT. His questioner pursued him about whether his calculations about residual radioactivity from such a weapon were accurate in 1945. 'Actually', Hirschfelder replied, 'in Hiroshima and Nagasaki there was no residual radioactivity left on the ground. The height of the detonation was so high that the fire ball did not come in contact with the ground. The result was that the radiation exposure of people was mainly gamma rays. If people were in a region where they got a dose of neutrons, they were killed by the blast and by fires and by all sorts of other things as well as by radiation. At Hiroshima and Nagasaki, I do not believe' said the man responsible for the fallout predictions thirty years later, 'that there were more than one or two thousand people who were left with radiation burns (but not killed). It is a surprisingly small number.'

General Groves also remembered thirty years later that at the time of the Trinity Test his main concerns were pollution by plutonium release and fallout. While he feared spillage of the plutonium,

the hazard that I feared the most was that of radioactive fallout on the area over which the radioactive cloud would pass. This had not been considered for too many months as it was only at the turn of the year that Joseph Hirschfelder had brought up the possibility that this might be a serious

problem. I learned later that the possibility of this danger had been indicat-
ed in the British Maud report, but I had been unaware of the existence of
this report. It was this fallout hazard that caused us to be fearful of explod-
ing the bomb when rain was likely, since we thought rain would be certain
to bring down excessive fallout over nearby areas. We could also not ignore
the old tales that heavy battle cannonading had sometimes brought on rain,
although we knew of no scientific basis for any such phenomenon.

The scientist in charge of the Trinity Test was Kenneth T. Bainbridge. He recalled[3] the anxiety over the weather because the politicians wanted a demonstration of the weapon to strengthen President Truman's hand at Potsdam. There had been two delays due to the weather. 'We would have preferred no inversion layer at 17,000 feet but not at the expense of waiting over half a day.' In the event, 'the bomb was detonated at T=O=5.29:45 a.m. I felt the heat on the back of my neck, disturbingly warm. Much more light was emitted by the bomb than predicted, the only important prediction which was off by a good factor.' When the light diminished 'I looked directly at the ball of fire through the goggles. Finally I could remove the goggles and watch the ball of fire rise rapidly. It was surrounded by a huge cloud of transparent purplish air produced in part by the radiations from the bomb and its fission products. No one who saw it could forget, a foul and awesome display.'

Three weeks later the tail gunner of the *Enola Gay*, the plane that bombed Hiroshima, described[4] what he saw as he looked back on the detonation. 'The mushroom itself was a spectacular sight, a bubbling mass of purple-gray smoke and you could see it had a red core in it and everything was burning inside. As we got further away, we could see the base of the mushroom and below we could see what looked like a few-hundred-foot layer of debris and smoke and what have you.'

But Norman Ramsey, Chief Scientist at Tinian Airbase when the *Enola Gay* took off with its atomic payload, has gone on record[5] as saying that 'The people who made the decision to drop the bomb made it on the assumption that all casualties would be standard explosion casualties.' They thought that 'The region over which there would have been radi-ation injury was to be a much smaller one that the region of so-called 100 per cent blast kill.' As Ramsay put it, it was expected that 'Any per-son with radiation damage would have been killed with a brick first.' Despite all the evidence that was to come from Hiroshima and Nagasaki over the next fifty years, the belief that there was no significant residual radiation left at Hiroshima and Nagasaki because the bombs were 'air bursts' has become an article of faith in the radiobiological studies of the long-term effects of the first atomic detonations on human communities.

One of the earliest American investigators into Hiroshima and Nagasaki after the bombings was a Manhattan District health physicist, Donald L. Collins[6], whose job it was to measure radioactivity.

I reported to General Nichols and received orders to take my emergency instruments and join the Atomic Bomb Investigation Committee under Col Stafford Warren, head of the Medical Division of the [Manhattan] District. We flew to Tinian where we saw the Enola Gay, *which had delivered the first bomb. While en route, we received word that the war was over. We were addressed by General Farrell who told us more specifically that our mission was to prove that there was no radioactivity from the bomb. In my typical attitude (I didn't particularly consider myself military), I didn't mind talking back to him. I said, 'Excuse me, General. I thought we were going to measure the radioactivity.' Well, that's what we did. While we were sitting, waiting to get into Japan — we were scheduled to have been there, but we weren't quite there — we read in the Stars and Strips [sic] the results of our findings!*

From Okinawa they flew to Nagasaki arriving on 19 September. It was overcast with breaks in the clouds, as it was reported to have been on the day of the bombing. Collins' principal assignment was to measure the residual radioactivity and to draw contour lines of equal radiation intensity on the local maps. From this he tried to extrapolate to time-zero and to calculate exposures. Collins traced fallout from the bomb some 32 miles out to sea in one direction. The background radiation readings were about three times the normal six weeks after the explosions.

Dr Shields Warren arrived at Sasebo on 24 September 1945. A major naval base 88 kilometres from Nagasaki, Sasebo had sustained extensive damage from conventional bombing but was now a base for US military personnel as well as the main base for Japanese being repatriated. When Warren arrived, a rumour was 'rampant' that the 2nd US Marine Division was being withdrawn from Nagasaki due to the intense radiation effects. But Warren claimed[7] that his standard monitoring instruments showed that Nagasaki's streets and hospitals were now, six weeks after the explosions, back to background levels of radiation.

On 5 October 1945 Shields Warren also began to track the fallout from the bomb. He found that the radioactive cloud had crossed the mountains in a northeasterly direction towards the town of Isahaya. He noted that there had been a team of Japanese researchers from Kyoto University who only stayed in Hiroshima for a week at a time 'because of commonplace rumors about the uninhabitability' of the city. But eleven members of this team had been killed by a typhoon on 17 September.

Warren discussed the detonations with Kenzo Sassa, a vulcanologist and director of the Siesmology Institute and Observatory. Sassa told him that 90 per cent of the bomb explosion had remained in the air and only 10 per cent had been absorbed by the earth. In a volcanic explosion, Sassa maintained, the proportions are the reverse – most of the energy in a volcanic eruption is absorbed by the earth rather than going into the atmosphere. Warren concluded from this discussion that the fission products of the bombs had been dispersed and that there was little residual radioactivity at ground level in the two cities.

Colonel Crawford Sams MC was Chief of the Public Health and Welfare Division, Military Government Section, US Army in the Pacific. On the creation of MacArthur's Supreme Allied Command on 2 October 1945 he was transferred to Tokyo. As soon as he arrived in Tokyo Sams[8] 'was flooded with A-bomb investigators from the United States, General Farrell, Stafford Warren, Scotty Oughterson, and the Strategic Bomb Survey Team. Their major anxiety concerned the question of safety from deadly radiation injury at Hiroshima, since many Japanese and Americans were predicting that any person setting foot in that city in the next 75 to 100 years was certain to die.' But in the opinion of the battle-hardened Chief of Public Health and Welfare, 'It was just a case of a town burned down.'

A Joint Commission for the Investigation of the Effects of the Atomic Bomb in Japan entered Hiroshima and Nagasaki in September and October 1945. The team of US Army, Navy and Manhattan District medical investigators had been hastily brought together to investigate the increasing reports of radiation sickness among the survivors of Hiroshima and Nagasaki who had not been killed by the heat, blast and aftermath of the bombs. In May 1946 the leader of the Joint Commission, Colonel Ashley Oughterson wrote to the Surgeon General of the US Army urging him to recommend that the National Research Council (NRC) initiate a long-term study of the survivors.

Two radiobiologists, Austin Brues and Paul Henshaw, were commissioned to go to Japan in the winter of 1946 to investigate the feasibility of such a long-term study. Brues subsequently became Director of Biomedical Research at the Atomic Energy Commission's Argonne National Laboratory at the University of Chicago. In a talk[9] to the Chicago Literary Club fifteen years later he said he had anticipated that there might be some radioactivity worth measuring and had smuggled out some instruments for that purpose. He was accompanied by Dr Paul Henshaw, 'one of the pioneers in radiation biology'.

Brues told his Chicago audience in 1961, 'Happily enough, nobody higher up had got interested enough in our business to dignify it with some title such as "Operation Meathead". Somewhere along the line, while standing on a windy corner waiting for transportation, Paul got the idea that we should have a name and suggested the "Atomic Bomb Casualty Commission" because it would be called ABCC.'

Japan immediately after the cessation of hostilities was not an easy place to work in and gradually 'it began to dawn on my consciousness that we might almost actually be feather merchants. These were people who, through some tenuous connection with the occupation, got to Japan and then stayed on, leading a hebephrenic life until found out, living on a combination of wits and dollars in varying proportions. As nearly as I was able to sense the definition of the term, the feather merchant differed from the carpetbagger of an earlier time by virtue of the pointless nature of his activity.'

The Brues mission was facilitated by Dr Masao Tsuzuki, a Rear Admiral of the Japanese Navy who had studied radiobiology at the University of Pennsylvania in 1925 and 1926. Immediately after the bombings of Hiroshima and Nagasaki, the National Research Council of Japan had established a comprehensive investigation organized in ten sections. Dr Tsuzuki chaired the Medical Section which had 30 committee members, 150 researchers and about 1000 assistants. It presented its first findings of the medical effects of irradiation from Hiroshima and Nagasaki to a meeting on 20 November 1945. Tsuzuki's first field reports were available in March 1946 and the investigators described disturbances in sexual function among males, residual radioactivity and menstrual changes. On meeting the American investigators at General MacArthur's headquarters in Tokyo, Dr Tsuzuki said, 'I did the experiments years ago, but only on a few rats. But you Americans, you are wonderful. You have made the human experiment!'

Brues, too, was cavalier about the significance of residual radiation. Fifteen years later he said,

> I wanted some relief from courtesy calls on minor politicians and clinic administrators, and Tsuzuki must have also, for when I suggested a visit to the area of radioactive fallout around the Nishiyama Reservoir, he offered quickly to come along. It was a day of relaxation, visiting farmer Nakao who supplied soil, vegetables, and parts of a couple of rabbits and chickens, and collecting soil and water from the reservoir. We got a bit of almost everything that would characterize the fallout field except silt from the bottom of the reservoir. The project turned out of less value than it might have, because in a few years some better fallout fields were made; but it was a pleasant experience to see the hills in the tropical midwinter, and farmer Nakao, grateful for the honor of a visit to his humble place, gave me a pair of handmade straw slippers.

Brues showed some Japanese journalists that Nagasaki was less radioactive than his watch. He told his Chicago audience the story of Professor Nagai, Chief of Radiology at Nagasaki Hospital who had long suffered from chronic leukaemia and had already received massive X-ray treatment. At the time of the detonation in Nagasaki he was standing at the window of his office a few hundred yards from ground zero. 'Nagai, escaping death from flying and falling objects, was so well irradiated that for several years he seemed to have been fully cured. He was quite well at the time I saw him, and lived another six years.'

The Brues-Henshaw Report to the Secretary of War and the National Academy of Sciences said it would be absolutely inexcusable if a comprehensive study were not carried out, and already a year and a half had passed in which the unsupported Japanese had worked vigorously on their own and hardly made an impression. According to Brues in Chicago in 1961, 'the report was accepted and the ABCC passed from the hands of some feather merchants, many of whom continue to advise and to work for it, to a duly constituted, permanent arm of the National Academy of Sciences'.

The Brues-Henshaw Report recommended the initiation of studies of the long-term effects of the A-bomb to complement the studies of the short-term effects being conducted by Oughterson and his colleagues currently in Japan as the Joint Commission. Almost immediately upon the return of Brues and Henshaw to the United States, the Committee on Atomic Casualties (CAC) was convened by the National Research Council and met for the first time on 15 March 1947.

Notes

1. Lt General Leslie R. Groves, 'Some recollections of July 16, 1945' *Bulletin of the Atomic Scientists*, June 1975: 21–7.

2. Joseph O. Hirschfelder, 'The Scientific-Technological miracle at Los Alamos' in Lawrence Badash *et al.* (ed.) *Reminiscences of Los Alamos, 1943–1945* (London, D. Reidel Publishing Company, 1976).

3. Kenneth T. Bainbridge, 'A foul and awesome display', *Bulletin of the Atomic Scientists*, May 1975:40–46.

4. Quoted by Richard Rhodes, *The Making of the Atomic Bomb* (New York, Simon and Schuster, 1986) p.648.

5. Quoted by James V. Neel, *Physician to the Gene Pool* (New York, John Wiley and Sons, 1994, p.79) from P. Wyden, *Day One: Before Hiroshima and After* (New York, Simon and Schuster, 1984) p.16.

6. Donald L. Collins, 'Pictures from the Past: Journeys into health physics in the Manhattan District and other diverse places', in Kathren and Ziemer (eds.), *Health Physics: A Backward Glance* (Oxford, Pergamon Press, 1980) pp.37–45.

7. Shields Warren's diary as quoted by John Z. Bowers in 'Draft typescript history of the Atomic Bomb Casualty Commission', dated 15 February 1984, found in Papers of John Z. Bowers, ACC:89–73:1.

John Z. Bowers served as Deputy Director of the Atomic Energy Commission from 1947 to 1950 and President of the Macy Foundation 1965 to 1980; he was also associated with the Rockefeller Foundation. His papers are deposited at the Rockefeller Archive Center, Tarrytown, New York.

8. Colonel Sams' memoirs, on file at the Hoover Institute for War and Peace, Stanford University, are quoted by John Z. Bowers in his 'Draft typescript history of the ABCC' dated 15 February 1984.

9. Austin Moore Brues, 'The chrysanthemum and the feather merchant', read before the Chicago Literary Club, 13 February 1961, found at Bowers, ACC:83–79:1.

Three

Hines wrote that 'If these investigations sometimes fell short of total and comprehensive attacks on basic problems, they were, at least, acknowledgements of responsibility beyond the merely technical and administrative, and were as disciplined, imaginative and productive as the resources and state of knowledge would allow.'

What was the state of knowledge about atomic radiation when Hiroshima and Nagasaki were bombed fifty years ago? Hiroshima was bombed with a uranium device, whereas Nagasaki was obliterated with a plutonium weapon. While uranium is abundant throughout the world as an ore, plutonium only occurs in minute quantities in nature. It was the discovery of how to manufacture plutonium and its vast proliferation beyond the equilibrium established by nature that marks the past fifty years. The harnessing of the awesome energy of the fission process of these elements for war as well as domestic energy has surely been a landmark moment in the history of the planet.

There had been fifty years of laboratory knowledge of radiation prior to the atomic bombings. It was realized that uranium in particular was a hazardous substance, though the potency of plutonium came to be understood only by tragic trial and error.

Dr Robert S. Stone was the director of the Health Division of the Manhattan District Project and its Plutonium Project. His Medical Section performed all the usual functions of a good industrial medical department – physicals, X-rays, routine blood and urine tests. It closely monitored the hands of the employees, because they were most vulnerable to radiation burns.

As Dr Stone explained in 1946,[1] at the beginning of the Plutonium Project in the early 1940s, the blood count was considered by most radiologists and the National Advisory Board on X-ray and radium protection to be the best indicator of over-exposure of the whole body to radiation. But a review of the literature revealed that very few accurate studies of normal people had in fact been undertaken and also that normal variations in the blood counts of any individual were so great that minor fluctuations could not actually be relied on. The blood of the workers on the Manhattan District Project was continually monitored, and Dr Stone maintained that 'It has been the good fortune of the Project to keep radiation exposures within the range of that considered tolerable, and the blood counts have revealed no significant changes.' But, 'since the basic mechanism of the action of radiation is not known, empirical approaches had to be used' to try to develop a clinical indicator of changes from low level radiation exposures.

The literature had shown that uranium was an extremely toxic substance once it entered the body, but Dr Stone took comfort from the reports that workers at the Port Hope factory in Canada, where radium had been extracted for years from uranium ore, had not shown any signs of injury. 'This encouragement was still further borne out when mice placed in one of the project laboratories where uranium oxide dust was extremely thick were found to develop into more healthy mice than controls in the animal farm.' A great deal of work had been done on uranium toxicity and 'It has been found that if uranium succeeds in getting in the blood it is a toxic substance, but that many of the compounds are difficult to get through the lung or intestines, and that on the whole the hazard can be satisfactorily controlled.' Dr Stone felt confident in 1946 that 'unless there is an acute reaction from overexposure, there is not likely to be any serious chronic damage' from exposure to uranium externally, or by ingestion, inhalation or absorption through the skin.

The Director of the Health Division of the Manhattan District Project did acknowledge that 'owing to a lack of knowledge of how to measure radiations, as well as to a lack of understanding of their action on the human body, many hundreds of physicists, physicians, manufacturers, and laborers were damaged by X-rays and radium gamma rays in the first few years of their use.' The Health Physics section was responsible for radiation protection – and therefore for radiation detection and measurement in a situation where nuclear chain reactor piles and chemical separation plants were being built. Health physics was therefore very interested in the shielding properties of different materials and with the disposal of waste radioactive products. It was also interested in the weather conditions necessary for adequate dispersal of radioactive products to levels that would not be injurious to humans or our habitat.

Dr Stone remarked that when the Health Division of the Plutonium Project was set up there were established dose levels, or maximum permissible exposures, for X-rays and gamma rays but 'these rested on rather poor experimental evidence. There was little knowledge of the tolerance for fast neutrons, and none for slow and thermal neutrons, or for alpha or beta rays.' It was realized that strontium, barium, tellurium, cesium and iodine can all enter the body through absorption from the gastro-intestinal tract and that many of these fission products 'seek' the bones. It was known that iodine was taken up into the thyroid. 'The lungs retain some of the inhaled radioactive elements for considerable periods of time and thus are exposed to the radiations even if they are only weak beta radiations. The human lung retains a considerably larger per cent of inhaled small particles than do the lungs of rats and other small animals.'

The researchers in the late 1940s expected on the basis of its alpha activity and long half-life that plutonium would be about one-fiftieth as dangerous as radium. But this was shown to be wrong for acute effects, and it was determined that one microgram of plutonium was about as dangerous as one microgram of radium. The Medical Division and Biological Research Section were trying to find out how to hasten the elimination and excretion of radioactive substances from the body.

Two years after the bombings of the two Japanese cities, Dr Stone listed in an editorial in the professional journal *Radiology*[2] what radiologists and health physicists still did not know after fifty years of laboratory work, several major accidents, and the bombing of Hiroshima and Nagasaki. Chief among them was the determination of the maximum dose of radiation that humans – and animals – could be exposed to without injury.

> *The scientific data on which it was based were found to be very sketchy. What are the first changes produced by exposures just above the tolerance level? Is the peripheral blood picture as reliable an indicator of over-exposure as radiologists have considered it to be? Are there any other changes produced that can be detected by known or newly developed clinical tests? Can a person ever recover completely and entirely from any dose of radiation big enough to produce detectable effects? How much radiation is necessary to kill a man?*

In April 1947 Dr Stafford Warren, Professor of Radiology at the University of Rochester who had served as director of the Medical Division of both the Manhattan Project and later the Operations Crossroads Tests in July 1946, addressed the Yale Institute of Occupational Health and Safety[3] He said that when the Manhattan District Project was organized in 1943, two groups at Chicago and Berkeley were already working under Dr Stone on the special hazards.

> *The program had to start from scratch with a great many things. Take one dust problem. Those of you who are in industrial hygiene know that there have been no real criteria, no good animal experiments to set the maxi-*

mum allowable concentrations of lead fumes in the air. The data are based on empiricism. They are just guesses by a group of people who have had a little experience, and who may have measured a concentration in one plant or another, and then found that it was at a certain level and since nobody died or got lead poisoning in those particular plants, therefore, that was considered to be the safe level. There was no level established for dust and fumes which could be used as a baseline for our problems.

'But', said the Medical Director of the Manhattan District Project, the Japanese survivor studies and the first Pacific tests, 'we had to come up with answers, some kind of a practical answer within the first year, about the amount of, say, uranium oxide that could be permitted, that would be safe in a manufacturing area, because the engineers had to put ventilating facilities down on blueprints, and they had to cast the walls and the buildings in concrete. Some of these walls were phenomenally thick for protective reasons, and they couldn't wait. So various committees and individuals did some empirical calculating from quick, short animal experiments and gave engineers these figures. Fortunately, we have come pretty close to being correct for a short time exposure of, say, two years.'

Dr Warren reminded this audience of fellow professionals in 1947 that a tenth of a roentgen per day had been the conventional maximum dose set for hospital workers and industrial workers. 'It has been set for many, many years. But in looking back, you will find that a "committee" got together and agreed upon a tenth of a roentgen, with no data to support it. When you talk to the old timers who sat on that committee, you will find that they thought that this level would be too hard to achieve, that it was probably the practical limit of safety that could be built into radiology departments, in lead and other protective devices.'

Dr Stone and his group had also started out with the standard 0.1 roentgen (r) per day but 'As it turned out, at the end of two and a half years of experience, 0.1 r is not really safe. At the end of two years of daily exposure, with Sundays off, changes occur in the number of sperm, and aspermia appears; and, of course, with the aspermia, sterility. Probably the reason why this has not been a problem before this is because radiologists and their personnel in hospitals don't receive 0.1 r per day every working day. In our laboratories and plants no-one did either so that we have really had this level tested out in practice. This is fortunate in view of the experimental results.'

Blood counts proved equally unreliable, as Dr Stone had indicated. Although they had been performed in their millions and analysed statistically, 'when it comes down to the individual, we are in a position to say now that we don't really know from his blood picture when a person has had a small amount of exposure to radiation. It is only when he has had a moderately large dose, or has had such a chronic damage to the bone marrow that you have a steadily developing anemia or leukemia, that it is of any value.' In 1947, one of the pivotal scientists in the study of radiation injury told his professional colleagues, 'We believe from the animal experiments, that any radiation exposure at all is bad and it should be avoided if it can be.'

He was not convinced of the capacity of the damaged cells to regenerate. 'The irradiated cell is never quite the same again. The evidence of damage is apparently cumulative. It shows up in the genes. It is easier to demonstrate genetically than it is organically. In other words, you find it in the second and third generations more readily than you can find it in the original cell. A lot of experimental and genetic data are now accumulating which show also that a tenth of a roentgen per day is too much exposure if it is given every day for more than two or three years.' This conclusion was based on work on a quarter of a million mice and 150,000 Drosophila fruit flies.

Dr Warren – who had just become the founding dean of the UCLA Medical School – had been one of the first American researchers into Hiroshima and Nagasaki in late 1945. The Manhattan District Project physicists and medical researchers understood that uranium and plutonium fallout was hazardous to humans, but they under-estimated the extent and dangers of both fallout and residual radiation. The first medical officers who entered the Japanese cities were more concerned with, and perhaps overwhelmed by, the effects of heat and blast on the survivors. Captain Shields Warren, Professor of Pathology at Harvard Medical School, was a member of the US Navy's Medical Corps and he was in the cities within a month of the bombings. He reported his first findings in his Presidential Address to the American Association for Cancer Research in March, 1946.[4]

> As we studied our patients it became apparent that there was no segregation of injury among them, but that an individual might well be suffering from blast effect, thermal injury and radiation injury simultaneously. Of the 80,000 people who died at Hiroshima and 45,000 that died at Nagasaki, it is very difficult to say what proportion was killed by one or another type of energy. Our primary interest is in those who died as a result of short-wave or neutron irradiation. Since the biologic response to these different types of ionizing radiation are essentially similar, they will be considered en masse.'

Captain Warren told his audience, 'The disorganization of the Japanese was so great that no adequate material exists to determine the exact nature of immediate effects. We may assume, however, that they parallel experimentally induced changes in animals and represent the syndrome of radiation sickness carried to an extreme degree.'

As well as these two assumptions – that all types of ionizing radiation are essentially similar in the injury they cause humans, and that the radiation sickness caused by the bombs was essentially the same as that seen in laboratory experiments on animals and fruit flies, Shields Warren was convinced that there was no residual radiation of any biological significance in either of the two cities. He formed this opinion in his first days in the devastated cities and held it unmodified throughout his involvement in the research studies conducted on the survivors. A decade after this statement, when another member of the advisory committee of the Atomic Bomb Casualty Commission on which he had served since its inception, asked about the significance of the 'black rain' which had been reported in Nagasaki shortly after the bombing, Shields Warren said it had no relation to radiation.

> It was simply the cloud of dust that had been picked up in the stem of the cloud, and had been precipitated when it had come in contact with the moisture down wind. The measurements of the areas in which these rains had fallen were not at a radiation level of biological significance. It was important not to expect mysterious happenings in response to radiation levels that were no greater than those which existed in a large number of places in this country.[5]

The early researchers into the long-term effects of the bombs were aware that radiation injury could be caused by inhalation and ingestion of residual radiation. John E. Wirth, Director of the Tumor Clinic at the United States Marine Hospital in Baltimore, had told a Symposium on Atomic Energy in Industry in October 1946[6] that 'there are maximum allowable concentrations or tolerance of exposure to external radiations and to isotopes which may be taken into the body by inhalation or ingestion'.

Shields Warren's narrow understanding of fallout and residual radiation was apparent in his address to the annual convention of the Association of Military Surgeons in November 1947;

> Since the explosions at Hiroshima and Nagasaki were air bursts, relatively little of the fission products remained at the site, but instead were widely disseminated through the stratosphere. Consequently, every bit of bombed area is safe for habitation and for cultivation. Owing to the abundant wood ashes which have fertilized the soil, it is not unusual to hear those with gardens in the two sites report that their crops are more abundant than is usually the case.[7]

Another military medic, Colonel Elbert De Coursey, a member of the US Army Medical Corps, reflected this article of faith in mid-1948:

The detonation of an atomic bomb is said to result in rays that cover the entire length of the spectrum. The intensity of the thermal radiation was so great in Nagasaki that there were flash burns on such things as wood, oranges, tile and people [sic]. *Such thin things as leaves, blades of grass, or clothing acted as filters and offered protection to their shadows. Ionizing radiation, the agent which makes the atomic bomb unique among all other weapons, not only contributed to the morbidity and mortality but also by hindsight contributed in Japan a biological experiment of unprecedented scope.*[8]

The researchers who went into Hiroshima and Nagasaki within a few weeks of the explosions and who continued to work there over the next forty years assumed – on the basis of very rudimentary initial measurements – that induced radiation, fallout and residual radiation were negligible in the two cities. The earliest research teams early formed the impression that approximately a third of the populations of each city had been killed outright by the bombs, another third had died of injuries before the end of 1945, and the last third would survive despite the inadequate medical care that was available for the first year or two after the devastation.[9]

But these assumptions were made even as another researcher, R. R. Newell, was telling the 35th annual meeting of the Radiological Society of North America in December 1949[10] that a group of more than fifty scientists working in radiation therapy and experimental radiobiology who had met a year earlier had been unable to agree on the human tolerance, or maximum permissible dose, for whole body irradiation. Dr Newell subsequently circulated a questionnaire which invited specialists to indicate where in the range from 25 to 1000 r they thought the maximum permissible dose might lie. 'The important results,' he told his professional colleagues in 1949, 'is not these evaluations or averages of opinion with regard to human tolerance for radiation but rather the very wide range exhibited in the answers received from supposed experts in the field. Take for instance the question concerning dose to render 50 per cent of those exposed ineffective – one thought 50 r, three thought 1000 r but every one of the intermediate values received at least one vote and none more than four votes. Three questions actually received answers over the entire range from 25 r to 1000 r.'

Despite this clear lack of consensus among the radiologists, the biomedical researchers in Hiroshima and Nagasaki continued to assume that the residual radiation, induced radiation and fallout were biologically negligible and could be excluded from their research designs into the long term effects of the two bombs. J. N. Crawford, for instance, wrote in 1950:

> *When the bomb explodes, many fission products are carried upward in the 'atomic cloud' by the heat that is produced and are dispersed by the wind. They gradually settle over large areas and emit radioactivity. These products are hazardous only if they are concentrated in a contaminated area. Secondary radioactivity must also be considered, but such radioactivity from ground and normal structural materials will have decreased to below the dangerous level within two minutes of the instant of explosion[11].*

Brigadier General De Coursey, now Director of the Armed Forces Institute of Pathology in Washington DC, told a 1951 conference of clinical radiologists[12] that:

> *The nuclear radiations of greatest biologic importance are the gamma rays which originate chiefly from the fission products in the fireball. These fission products have half-lives varying from microseconds to thousands of years; therefore as seconds and minutes pass, the dosage of radiation falls tremendously. Meanwhile, the fireball rises at an average speed of 10,000 feet per minute, thus lengthening the distance from source to ground, with consequent reduction of ground dosage (by inverse square law and absorption in air). The radiation continues for about ninety seconds, approximately, 15 per cent being delivered in the first 0.1 second after detonation, 50 per cent by the end of one second, and 80 per cent in ten seconds. Beyond the limits of a two-mile radius of such a bomb burst, dosage is less than 1 r; at a distance of 4,000 feet, 400 to 500 r are delivered, and at ground zero (about 2,000 feet) more than 10,000 r.*

The chief pathologist of the United States Armed Forces reassured his colleagues in 1951 that 'induced residual radiation seems to be of only academic importance. Alpha and beta particles have such short range that they do not reach the earth immediately. They may be present in the "fallout" of fission products from the cloud. As sources of injury within a few miles of the explosion, these particles are of no importance.'

The assumption that air bursts produce little residual radiation was shared by the British military. An Air Ministry handbook in 1957[13] advised confidently:

> *With a true air burst (ie where the fireball does not touch the ground), the up-draught caused by the rapidly rising mushroom cloud may be sufficient to draw upwards a stream of dust and debris from the ground. This stream rises upward towards the centre of the toroid or smoke ring of the main*

cloud and appears to join the main cloud and so form the stem of the mushroom. In fact, the stream of dust particles and debris pass through the centre of the toroid and curl round down the outside but do not mix with the main cloud. Any radioactivity originally induced in the dust and debris of this stream is not significantly increased nor do the particles act as centres on which the unfissioned or vaporized weapons materials of the fission products condense. When this dust and debris falls out there is relatively little residual radiation from it. The original weapons material and fission products in the toroid which have already condensed into much smaller particles will rise much higher, take longer to fall, be so much more widely spread and decay before reaching the ground, so that they too cause little residual radioactivity.

British Air Force instructors were told that 'If evidence points to a burst of this type there should be no need for the whole radiological defence organisation to go into action.' There was one exception, however. The manual advised that 'residual radiation is of no military significance from a high or medium air burst except in the case of low yield weapons (less than 10 kilotons) burst in rain, when rainout may be a hazard.' Although what were described as 'black mists' were reported by Aboriginal Australians after the 1953 *Totem* series of British tests at Maralinga in South Australia[14] and the Japanese researchers had from the beginning pointed out that 'black rain' had fallen in Nagasaki in particular immediately after the bombing, the hazards of rainout were dismissed and ignored throughout the first two decades of research into the long-term effects on the survivors in Japan.

Notes

1. Robert S. Stone, 'Health protection activities of the Plutonium Project', *Proceedings of the American Philosophical Society*, January 1946:90:1:11–19

2. Editorial, 'The Plutonium Project', *Radiology*, September 1947:49:3.

3. Stafford Warren, 'Radioactivity, health and safety', mimeo of address delivered to Yale Institute of Occupational Health and Safety, 1 April 1947, at Darling:770:111:68:74.

4. Captain Shields Warren (MC) US Navy, 'The pathologic effects of an instantaneous dose of radiation', Presidential Address delivered to the 37th meeting of the American Association for Cancer Research, 11 March 1946, and published in *Cancer Research*, September, 1946:9:449–53.

5. Minutes of the 23rd meeting of the Advisory Committee of the Atomic Bomb Casualty Commission, 5 January 1957, at Bugher 2:1:2:9:106.

6. John E. Wirth, 'Essential safeguards in production and use of atomic energy', presented at a Symposium on Atomic Energy in Industry and Medicine at the 7th Annual Congress on Industrial Health, 2 October 1946, published in Robert S. Stone (ed.), *Industrial Medicine and the Plutonium Project* (New York, McGraw Hill, 1951).

7. Shields Warren, MD, 'The Nagasaki survivors as seen in 1947', presented to the 54th Annual Convention of the Association of Military Surgeons, 13–15 November 1947 and published in *The Military Surgeon*, February 1948:98–100.

8. Colonel Elbert De Coursey MC US Army, 'Human pathologic anatomy of ionizing radiation effects of the atomic explosions', *The Military Surgeon*, June 1948:427–32.

9. Leon O. Jacobsen, R. S. Stone and J. Garrott Allen, 'Physicians in an atomic war' *Journal of the American Medical Association*, January 1949:139:138–40.

10. R. R. Newell MD, 'Human tolerance for large amounts of radiation', presented at 35th annual meeting of the Radiological Society of North America, 4–9 December 1949, published in *Radiology*, April 1950.

The doyen of American health and safety monitors, Merril Eisenbud, tells the story of the 'taxicab standard' for beryllium exposure in his *An Environmental Odyssey* (University of Washington Press, 1990:55–6):

> In the absence of an epidemiological basis for establishing a standard, it was decided to assume that, atom for atom, beryllium was as toxic as the most toxic metals, such as mercury, lead and arsenic. However, these are heavy metals, whereas beryllium is very light. If allowance is made for differences in the atomic weight of the metals, the beryllium standard would be much lower than the standard for the heavy metals. We had been discussing this matter for some weeks when the time came for a decision because a new laboratory which would use beryllium was in the final stages of design at Long Island.... One morning I was riding to the new laboratory by taxi with Dr Willard Machle. He was a medical consultant to the company that was building the laboratory, and had been involved with beryllium disease almost from the beginning. We knew that when we arrived we would be expected to provide the laboratory designers with design criteria and decided that a tentative MPC [Maximum permissible concentration] should be two micrograms per cubic meter. In view of the circumstances, this standard has been dubbed the 'taxicab standard' in recognition of the seemingly flimsy basis on which it was established.

11. J. N. B. Crawford, 'Medical Aspects of the Effects of Atomic Explosions', *Canadian Medical Association Journal*, June 1950:62: 529–34.

12. Brigadier General Elbert De Coursey MC USA, 'Injury from atomic bombs', presented at the 18th Annual Meeting of Teachers of Clinical Radiology, 10 February 1951, published in *Radiology*, May 1951:645–52

13. United Kingdom Air Ministry, *The Nuclear Handbook for Instructors and Staff Offices*, 1957: 142, quoted in *Radioactive Heaven and Earth: A Report of the IPPNW International Commission to Investigate the Health and Environmental Effects of Nuclear Weapons Production and the Institute for Energy and Environmental Research* (New York, The Apex Press and London, Zed Books, 1991) p.127.

14. See for instance the discussion of black mists in Lorna Arnold, *A Very Special Relationship: British Atomic Weapons Trials in Australia* (London, HMSO, 1987).

Four

Although many scientists felt that more data on atomic energy and its applications – and consequences – could now be obtained from laboratory experiments, two more weapons were detonated barely a year after the first Trinity Test and eleven months after the devastation of Hiroshima and Nagasaki.

Several observers[1] have seen the tests conducted on Bikini Atoll in the Marshall Islands in July 1946 as the US Navy's determination to demonstrate a role for a nuclear navy at a time when the Army and Air Force was claiming the Japanese detonations as a triumph for air power and armed forces cooperation. The primary purpose of the Operation Crossroads series was to test the effects of air blast, intense heat, high waves, underwater shock and pressure on ships. A secondary purpose, according to Vice-Admiral W. H. P. Blandy USN, Commander of the Joint Army-Navy Task Force One in a briefing to journalists on 26 April 1946[2] was to 'learn more of the various effects of the atomic bomb against living beings, in order to provide much-needed information upon protection, early diagnosis – which we didn't get at Hiroshima and Nagasaki – and treatment of personnel who may hereafter be exposed to atomic explosions, either in war or peace.'

By bombing battleships, cruisers and carriers lined up in various formations from both above (air bursts) and below (underwater bursts) the Navy would be able to improve both its ship designs and battle plans to survive nuclear attacks. Forty thousand servicemen and scientists were gathered in the Marshall Islands to observe and monitor these tests, which were estimated to cost half a billion US dollars. Seventy-five foot towers housing cameras, television and other devices were built around the atoll to gauge the radiation contamination as well as physical impacts of the detonations. The fauna and algae of the atoll had been surveyed and the whole atoll sprayed with DDT to rid it of flies, over the objections of the biologists who feared contamination of their specimens.

Vice-Admiral Blandy told the press 'we don't make any bones about it – this is not presumed to be a test for the benefit of science. We hope it is being properly scientifically carried out and that there will be some benefit to science. It is primarily a technical military test for military purposes to gain what knowledge we can.' Dismissing the press from the briefing, Vice-Admiral Blandy barked, 'My last remark is that the Senate Naval Affairs Committee's harsh criticism in peacetime has been that we were busily engaged in the last war, instead of the next one. Here's a case where we're trying to prepare for the next one, if there should be one and it should unfortunately be an atomic war.'

Observers including military attachés from Washington embassies, civilian scientists and parliamentarians were shipped out to Bikini Atoll to form the first international panel to see the atomic weapons. Their reaction, like that of journalists such as William L. Laurence, was mixed. On the one hand, they found the actual explosions anticlimactic; on the other, they began to understand the lethality of residual radiation.

The observers were berthed on the USS Panamint and the Passengers Wardroom produced several issues of a daily newspaper[3] which contained verbatim many of the comments made after the explosions. Dr Parker D. Trask, Professor of Geology at the University of Wisconsin said two things had impressed him about the first bomb, Test Able. The first was that some of the participants were allowed into the lagoon within six hours from the time the bomb exploded which 'meant that the water did not have enough radioactivity at that time to be considered dangerous for ships such as the one we were on'. The second 'is the fact that the waves caused by this bomb do not seem to have been tremendous.' There had been no chain reaction burning up the atmosphere. There was no big hole in the lagoon; the water did not visibly boil; there was no tidal wave. On first impressions, one bomb certainly did not seem to be capable of destroying a fleet, if it was in a wide formation.

Two British observers, Flight Lieutenant F. Beswick and Commander A. Noble, reported after this first Test Able that 'Our opinion, for what it is worth from observation only and without access to official data and records, is that an atomic bomb dropped at such a height over a fleet is lethal to small or old cruisers, destroyers and transports, within a radius of 440 yards and causes serious damage within a radius of about 880 yards. Outside of a circle of that radius structural damage falls off very rapidly and only scorching of paintwork is seen.' They did think it was important not to 'belittle' the importance of the bombs given that only five old vessels were sunk because it may be that the effect on humans had not yet been appreciated and they could see that the structural damage within a populated area in cities such as Hiroshima and Nagasaki would be very significant. But 'The atmosphere among the United Nations observers aboard the *USS Panamint* since the dropping of the bomb is one of anti-climax. Something more spectacular seems to have been anticipated…. In particular the Egyptian and Russian observers express themselves as being satisfied that the danger from atomic bombs has been greatly exaggerated [*sic*].'

Test Baker, the second test, was more spectacular because it was an underwater detonation resulting in a great plume of water and spray. But Commander S. H. K. Spurgeon, the Royal Australian Naval Attaché in Washington DC, remarked that there had been a major change of attitude in the observers in the two weeks between the first and second tests. 'Before Test Able watertight doors and deadlights in the ship seemed to me to be much more generally closed than before Test Baker. The ship was at only half the distance, and broadside to, instead of bows on to the direction of the explosion. I think this is very important, as it indicates the general feeling that prevailed amongst all of us. We were not so fearful about what to expect, in this the second test.'[4] The new weaponry had already become almost routinized.

Some of the observers were reporting to President Truman as his Evaluation Commission, and some to the Joint Chiefs of Staff. After the first test, the President was advised, 'We are of the unanimous opinion that the first test amply justified the expenditure required to conduct it and that the second test is equally desirable and necessary. You made a wise decision when you approved the plans for these tests and they have been carried out with extraordinary skill, diligence and ingenuity. The test just completed has again proven that the atomic bomb is a weapon of terrific power when used on land or sea.'[5]

The Joint Chiefs were informed that 'Effective precautions appear to have been taken to safeguard personnel against radioactivity and associated dangers.' The Evaluation Board thought 'The radioactive residue dissipated in the manner expected.' They also felt that 'Once more the importance of large-scale research has been dramatically demonstrated.' It was clear to this Board that 'only by further large-scale research and development can the United States retain its present position of scientific leadership. This must be done in the interests of national safety.'[6]

Two weeks later, however, the President's Evaluation Commission were decidedly less complacent about radiation contamination generated by the second test. 'All but a few of the target ships', they reported to President Truman, 'were drenched with radioactive sea water, and all within the zone of evident damage are still unsafe to board. It is estimated that the radioactivity dispersed in the water was equivalent to that from many hundred tons of radium.' What the observers now referred to as 'the deadly effects of persistent radioactivity' would, they realized, have been even more severe in the second blast, which was an under-water detonation, than in the first, air blast detonation. They urged changes in ships' size, design and structure both above and below the water-line. 'Such changes can afford increased immunity to flash and blast effect, but protection from catastrophe by deadly gamma and neu-tron radiations lies rather in the spacing of task forces and decentraliza-tion of navy yards, repair and loading facilities, of ships within ports and amongst all available harbors. We are convinced [as Captain Mahan had been before them] distance is the best defence.'[7]

The Joint Chief of Staff's Evaluation Board was clearly shocked by the implications of the second test. They reported that the explosion *looked* exactly as the scientists had predicted.

> At the moment of explosion, a dome, which showed the light of incandes-cent material within, rose upon the surface of the lagoon. The blast was followed by an opaque cloud which rapidly enveloped about half of the tar-get area. The cloud vanished in about two seconds to reveal, as predicted, a column of ascending water. From some of the photographs it appears that this column lifted the 26,000-ton battleship Arkansas for a brief interval before the vessel plunged to the bottom of the lagoon.

They thought the diameter of the column of water was about 2200 feet and its height about 5500 feet but spray rose to a much greater height. There were one-hundred-foot waves. The column must have contained roughly ten million tons of water – all of it, the observers realized, radioactive. 'Great quantities of radioactive water descended upon the ships from the column or were thrown over them by waves. This highly lethal radioactive water constituted such a hazard that after four days it was still unsafe for inspection parties, operating within a well-established safety margin, to spend any useful amount of time' in the target area. The well-established safety margin had of course been established by the Trinity Test and the first Crossroads test on assumptions about the dis-persal of fission products in the atmosphere which had been modelled on non-atomic particles. The Joint Chiefs of Staff panel, which included K. T. Compton and other longstanding advisers to the President of the United States, now realized that 'the radiological effects have no parallel in conventional weapons'. However, the same panel still maintained that in the air-burst bombs (such as Trinity, Hiroshima, Nagasaki and Able), 'Those surviving immediate effects would not have been menaced by radioactivity persisting after the burst'.[8]

But the Operations Crossroads tests did begin to make the civil defence planners at least consider the problems of residual radiation. Dr Stafford

Warren, who had been Medical Director for Operations Crossroads as he had been for the Trinity Test, told the Yale Institute of Occupational Medicine and Hygiene in April 1947[9] a little over six months after the second test at Bikini, that the warships were still contaminated.

> *They are too dangerous to live on. Some of them have areas where you can't stand for more than a few hours because of the gamma radiation that is still being given off. Six months from now these spots will be half as active. You can stand there twice as long. A year from then it would be a quarter as strong as it is now, and so on.*

Dr Warren went on,

> *Now there are two ways of using these bombs, and I am sure both will be used. One is to smash the city from above, like we did with Japan, and destroy the transportation and all of the resources and kill about three-quarters of the population that is within a radius of three miles. If bigger bombs are used higher, they will destroy and kill over a greater area. Half of the bombs have been dropped over the cities, and all of the major cities that any country has require only a small number as bombs go when you consider one or two, or at the most, five bombs per city. And you have poisoned the substratosphere with fission products equivalent to hundreds of thousands of tons of radium equivalent.*

The second way, Dr Warren suggested, is to drop the bomb in the water in front of the city at the same time or shortly after the air detonation.

> *These bombs are best detonated in the afternoon or the evening when you have a good onshore wind (and you don't have to break a window in the city), but let that mist drift down over the city and radioactive material can be deposited on a city quite readily, I am sure, in amounts that will be equivalent to lethal doses in one hour more or less. So you have the prospect of evacuating your already destroyed city within less than an hour or hiding them all in deep basements or caverns for an unpredictable time. Your ventilation problem is tremendous, because there is no mask, no filter, no type of precipitator — nothing that will stop all of these small particles for very long.*

Stafford Warren now considered that only after a week or so, when the gamma radiation intensity begins to fall, could people cautiously come into the outskirts of the city with Geiger counters:

> *After three to four weeks, you can probably actually go into the city for an hour or so, if you are very careful where you go and watch where you go. After four or five months, you can probably work in the city from eight to*

ten hours. If you consider only the gamma radiation from the contamina-
tion of your environment, such is the case. But don't forget that every-
where in the city, on the window sills, on the roofs, in the gutters, on your
grass, on your farms, on the street, everywhere, are small or large amounts
of fission materials with long half-lives. Those are the ones that you get
into your body by inhalation. They are going to be in next year's crop,
and they get in the protein of your crop; that is, in the seeds. Those are the
things you eat and I eat. They are the things our animals eat. Our ani-
mals get contaminated. The milk and water are contaminated. It is in the
successive year's crops for a long and unpredictable time. You will have to
carefully measure everything you eat to be certain of it.

The Dean of the UCLA Medical School warned occupational health
workers,

If you bring a family of three children, your wife and yourself, back into
such a city area, you can pretty well expect that one out of your family of
five, over a period of years, will accumulate enough of these fission materi-
als, bone seekers, alpha emitters or beta emitters, probably a hundred
micrograms or less is enough, to cause this progressive aplastic anemia.

The food chain, too, would be contaminated. 'How and when will you
know that contaminated rain has fallen on your farm, and to what
extent?' Dr Stafford Warren drew a rather different moral from vulcanology than Shields Warren had drawn from his conversation with a
Japanese vulcanologist the previous year.

Look up in the Encyclopedia Britannica or any other source you might
have, the description of the Krakatoa volcanic eruption in 1883. Fine
dust was tossed about seventeen miles in the air. The first three bomb
explosions tossed their radioactive materials about two-thirds as high.
That is about twice as high as the first Bikini test.... The underwater
one, of course, didn't throw water up high enough to get into the sub-
stratosphere.

In the case of Krakatoa, within six weeks after the explosion of the vol-
cano, ten degrees on either side of the equator was contaminated with
dust around the globe. Within several months, the dust contamination
could be noticed in Norway and the Cape of Good Hope. 'That was
only one volcanic eruption, and that was innocuous dust.'

Dr Warren considered the implications of this new awareness of residual radiation for the biomedical effects of atomic bombs. The Japanese
data that the Joint Commission and other researchers were collecting was
indicating in April 1947 that at least in some men the aspermia had

disappeared after a year and a quarter. 'Some of the ovarium dysfunctions have likewise cleared up. Menstrual cycles have returned, and in several cases children were born to the women who were previously amenor-rhetic. But that amenorrhea does not prove anything, because that was not an uncommon thing in Japan, nor is the aspermia, when you consid-er the fact that they were on such a low dietary intake for such a long time.'

The reproductive rate, or at least the child-bearing rate, had increased all over Japan, and the increase was approximately the same in Hiroshima and Nagasaki, in so far as the researchers had been able to determine. Laboratory studies of induced aspermia in dogs had been going on for the past two and a half years. There had been a very slow increase in the number of sperm in a few of the animals but some of the dogs had not shown any return of sperm, even after about six months without expo-sure. Further studies were done on goats and other large animals at Bikini during Operation Crossroad[10] But Dr Warren warned in 1947 that 'We are now faced with the prospect that most of the acute experimental work has been done, and we will have to start all over again with the long-term experiments. And those are going to be time-consuming and rather unspectacular.'

While the bombing of Hiroshima and Nagasaki was surely one of the most dramatic events in the history of the earth, the investigation of the biomedical effects on humans was going to be very tedious and boring. This sort of research, Dr Warren warned, involves 'a lot of scut [tedious] work, much like that required in obtaining this information about the tenth of a roentgen per day. But when you realize that we had about 50,000 people potentially exposed to radiation, we had to really know and be able to confront a jury, or certainly a lawyer, with evidence that it was safe or wasn't safe.' Dr Warren also saw a time when 'Particularly if we have a depression, we will have a lot of people who will want to coast along on the government charities, and who will come up with the story that they worked for the Manhattan District somewhere, or they passed down the street to windward of a plant, and therefore they deserve com-pensation. It is going to be a very serious problem.'

But eighteen months of observation in Japan by the admittedly disor-ganized research teams enabled Dr Warren to feel confident enough in early 1947 to 'lay one ghost. At least in the mice and Drosophila fly experiments, there are no unusual abnormalities. You only increase the number of normally occurring abnormalities. In other words, the things you have already seen occur with greater frequency after exposure to radiation. We don't know what the frequency is yet.' But even in this rush to judgement, Dr Warren acknowledged that any genetic mutations were more likely to occur in second and subsequent generations – 'Large-scale experiments by Spencer and Stern with Drosophila, Charles with mice, and Donaldson with fish, have shown this to be the case'. It would therefore be reasonable to assume that what was true of mice, fruit flies and fish would be true of human beings.

Whatever conclusions Stafford Warren drew from his observations at Bikini, he did not seem to apply them retrospectively to what he had observed at Hiroshima and Nagasaki shortly after the bombings in 1945. He was not alone in this. George C. Darling had attended the Crossroads series as a civilian observer in his capacity as Professor of Human Ecology at Yale University. The mimeo copy of Warren's 1951 Yale speech was found among Dr Darling's papers from his years as Director of the Atomic Bomb Casualty Commission in Japan.

Claude R. Schwob of the US Naval Radiological Defence Laboratory was not so dismissive of residual radiation in 1951[11]:

An atomic bomb, in one sense, may be considered to be a device for efficiently and rapidly producing untold amounts of radiation and radioactive substances. If the radioactive material so produced is spread over an area, that area is said to be contaminated. Once deposited, the material continues to give off harmful rays for a long time, and nothing known to science can stop this process. This so-called residual radiation is as deadly as the instantaneous radiation: it has been calculated that at the time of deposition on some of the Bikini-Baker target ships, the resulting radioactivity was of the order of 50,000 r per hour. Not only are surfaces of objects contaminated, but so is dust. The latter is often disturbed during and immediately after a blast and can find its way inside the body. Thus, we have both an external and internal hazard.

But even Dr Schwob continued to reaffirm the article of faith that air-bursts were 'clean'. He still maintained after the Operations Crossroads tests that 'in an air burst, which incidentally is considered the most efficient for destruction, the danger of contamination is so small that it may be neglected. However, underwater, underground and surface bursts will cause widespread contamination. In such instances, the fission products are trapped by the water or the soil and, instead of being dissipated in the stratosphere, are returned to the surroundings by the force of gravity.' He told his professional colleagues in 1951, 'There is no neutralization of radioactivity: nothing that we poor mortals can do will influence the radioactive process in any way.' Nevertheless he recommended using soap and water to wash down contaminated surfaces or bodies and then 'Flush it down the drain. If it is from a bomb detonation, there will undoubtedly be very rapid decay. By the time it gets to its ultimate destination, it will be fairly harmless.' As for the future of atomic waste disposal, 'I have heard such suggestions as putting the stuff in rockets and shooting it up high enough to follow a permanent orbit around the earth, or to shoot it up to the moon.'

Notes

1. Including Lloyd L. Graybar, 'Bikini revisited', *Military Affairs*, October 1980, 117–23. Graybar commented: 'The Bikini tests did make a few observers and participants more aware than they had been of the profound dangers of radiological contamination. However, this was just the start of an educational experience whose basic lesson took nearly two decades for the nuclear powers to absorb.'

2. Transcript of 'Off the record conference with the press' held by Vice-Admiral W. H. P. Blandy USN, Commander, Joint Army–Navy Task Force One, Washington 26 April 1946, mimeo found at Darling 770:V:91:1065.

3. Mimeo issues of *USS Panamint* Passengers Wardroom Newspaper found at Darling 770:V: 9l:1066. George C. Darling was one of the observers.Letter from Flight Lieutenant F. Beswick and Commander A. Noble to Mr Hector McNeil dated 5 July 1946 reprinted in Roger Bullen *et al.* (eds.) *Documents on British Policy Overseas*, Series I, Volume IV, HMSO, London, 1987, with microfiche copy of documents.

4. 'Bikini on Baker Day: first impressions of a bomb test' (Baker Day 25 July 1946) as told by various observers on board *USS Panamint*, mimeo found at Darling 770:V:9l:1066. The journalist William L. Laurence published his observations on 'The Bikini tests and public opinion', *Bulletin of the Atomic Scientists*, 1946:2:7 2 and 17.

5. 'Report of the first Bikini atom bomb test' made to the US President by President's Evaluation Commission, 11 July 1946, found at Darling 770:V:91:1066.

6. Report of the Joint Chiefs of Staff Evaluation Board for the Atomic Bomb Tests, 11 July 1946, found at Darling 770:V:9:1066.

7. 'Report of the second Bikini Atom bomb test' made to the US President by President's Evaluation Commission, dated 2 August 1946, found at Darling 770:V:9l:1067.

8. 'Preliminary report following the second atomic bomb test', report by the Joint Chiefs of Staff Evaluation Board for the Atomic Bomb Tests, 30 July 1946, mimeo found at Darling 770:V:91:1067.

9. Dr Stafford Warren, 'Radioactivity, health and safety' address to Yale Institute of Occupational Medicine and Hygiene, 1 April 1947, found at Darling: 770:111:68:74.

10. See *inter alia*:

John L. Tullis (MC) USN and Shields Warren MC(S) USNR., 'Gross autopsy observations in the animals exposed at Bikini', *Journal of the American Medical Association* 134:14:1155–1158; and Eugene P. Cronkite, 'Clinical manifestations of acute radiation illness produced in goats by exposure to an atomic bomb, Test Able, Bikini, 1946, with comments on therapy', Naval Medical Research Institute, National Naval Medical Center, Bethesda Md Project NM 007, 039 Report No. 10, 1948.

11. Claude R. Schwob Ph.D, 'Radioactive decontamination', presented to the 18th Conference of Teachers of Clinical Radiology, 10 February 1951, published in *Radiology*, May 1951:670–4.

Five

The view of atomic bombs as primarily explosive devices which would kill more people by heat and blast as in conventional weapons than by radiation – immediate or residual – carried over into early civil defence planning in the United States.

Typical of the public information was a pamphlet issued by the National Security Resources Board of the US Civil Defense Office in 1950[1] It reassured the public, 'To begin with, you must realize that atom-splitting is just another way of causing an explosion. While an atom bomb holds more death and destruction than man has ever before wrapped in a single package, its total power is definitely limited. Not even hydrogen bombs could blow the earth apart or kill us all by mysterious radiation.'

Because the power of all bombs is limited, the average American's chances of surviving an atomic attack are much better than he or she may have thought.

> In the city of Hiroshima, slightly over half the people who were a mile from the atomic explosion are still alive. At Nagasaki, almost 70 per cent of the people a mile from the bomb lived to tell their experiences. Today thousands of survivors of these two atomic attacks live in new houses built right where their old ones once stood. The war may have changed their way of life, but they are not riddled with cancer. Their children are normal. Those who were temporarily unable to have children because of the radiation now are having children again.

According to this pamphlet, one 20,000 ton bomb would not create nearly as much damage as 10,000 two-ton bombs dropped a little distance apart. 'This is because the larger bombs "waste" too much power near the center of the explosion.' It was held that a 'modern atomic bomb' can do heavy damage to houses and buildings roughly two miles away, but doubling its power would extend the range of damage to only about two and a half miles. A bomb one hundred times as powerful, on this principle, would reach out only little more than four and a half, not a hundred, times as far.

Blast and burns from an A-bomb were at least as dangerous as radiation according to this 1950 government statement. Radioactivity is the only way, apart from size, in which the effects of A- or H-bombs differ from ordinary bombs. 'But, with the exception of underwater or ground explosions, the radioactivity from atomic bursts is much less to be feared than blast or heat.' Radioactivity has always been with us; it occurs naturally – 'we actually know much more about radioactivity and what it does to people than we know about infantile paralysis, colds or some other common diseases.' The trouble comes from being exposed to too much radioactivity, just like sunburn. 'In the same way, the harm that can come to you from radioactivity will depend on the power of the rays and particles that strike you, upon the length of time you are exposed to them, and on how much of your body is exposed.' The pamphlet does not mention ingestion, inhalation or latency as aspects of radioactivity.

The injury range for an atomic bomb was said to be about one mile, *If* the bomb exploded about 2000 feet in the air. If it was detonated much higher, some of the radiation would reach the ground so the danger would be less. If it exploded much lower than 2000 feet, the radiation 'also may not reach out as far, because it would be blocked by the ground or by buildings.' Some objects may become radioactive as a result of the blast, but they would still be usable. 'Lingering radioactivity may become a danger when atomic bombs are exploded on the ground, underground or in the water. Air bursts leave no dangerous lingering radioactivity.' This lingering radioactivity will take the form of particles which will be very difficult to remove from surfaces. But:

> In spite of the huge quantities of lingering radioactivity loosed by atomic explosions, people fortunately are not very likely to be exposed to dangerous amounts of it in most atomic raids. Since high-level bursts do the greatest damage, that is the kind we can expect most often. When atomic weapons are exploded in mid-air, the violent, upward surge of super-hot gases and air quickly sweeps practically all of the radioactive ashes and unexploded bits of bomb fuel high into the sky. Most of them are carried harmlessly off in the drifting bomb clouds. High-level explosions definitely will not create 'areas of doom', where no man dares enter and no plant can grow. In fact, they will leave very little radioactivity on the ground, even near the point of explosion. Firefighters and rescue teams can move promptly toward the center of destruction with little danger of facing harmful radiation.

The US government reassured its public in 1950 that:

regardless of all you may have heard or read concerning the dangers of radioactive clouds, after the first minute and a half there is actually little or nothing to fear from those produced by high-level bursts. While most of the radioactive materials swept up into the sky eventually fall back to earth, they are so widely and so thinly spread that they are very unlikely to offer any real danger to humans. Thousands of bombs would have to be set off in the air before serious ground contamination would be found over really large areas. There was no ground-level pollution of any importance following either of the two Japanese atomic bombings.

While 15 per cent of the Japanese A-bomb deaths or injuries were caused by radioactivity, 'not one of them was caused by the lingering kind. Explosive radioactivity caused them all.' However, any rain immediately after an atomic explosion was considered dangerous. But an airburst would leave no lingering radioactivity of importance, so after a few minutes it would be safe to go out to fight fires or help people who may need it.

While lingering radioactivity that occasionally follows some types of atomic bursts may be dangerous, still it is no more to be feared than typhoid fever or other diseases that sometimes follow major disasters. The only difference is that we can't now ward it off with a shot in the arm; you must simply take the known steps to avoid it.

The understanding of immediate and residual radiation among those scientists and biomedical researchers responsible for generating civil defence plans in the United States does not seem to have been much more sophisticated than the information they were giving the public five years after the detonations at Hiroshima and Nagasaki.

Cities such as New Haven, the 59th largest city in the United States, located on the rail link between Boston and New York, and home to both Yale University and a longstanding armaments industry, commissioned studies on how they were to prepare for civil defence. Two Yale doctors produced *A Civil Defense plan for New Haven, Connecticut with Special Reference to Medical Problems.*[2] It was realized that cities such as this were for the first time in history threatened with the possibility of 'sudden, direct and brutal attack'. A single atomic bomb cost less than the intercontinental plane by which it would be delivered – or it could be smuggled into a harbour by submarine.

The civil defence planners looked at the Japanese experience five years earlier.

At Hiroshima, 70–80,000 people were killed outright and an equal number were severely injured by the one bomb. Before the explosion there were 33 modern fire stations, afterwards the six remaining units could not begin to cope with the fires which sprang up everywhere. Of nearly three hundred doctors, only thirty were able to work and they were almost completely without medical supplies or trained assistants. Four square miles of the city's center were flattened to the ground, the only exception being a few of the reinforced concrete building which were partially collapsed and internally gutted. Most of the people in this area were crushed or pinned down by the falling buildings or flying debris. For a considerable distance beyond that zone, brick buildings and frame houses were flattened. Windows, doors and partitions were hurled at high velocity through those buildings which did not collapse.

These medical civil defence planners knew that in addition to the tens of thousands of casualties due to crushing injuries and fire burns, there were many thousands of people who suffered from damage characteristic of radioactive explosions. Flash burns were common for more than one mile from the centre of detonation, and gamma radiation sickness occurred as a delayed effect in most of those who were within two and a half miles of the target centre.

Fire control was impossible. 'The civil defense organization, even though disciplined by years of war, was overwhelmed by the completeness of destruction. It was more than three days after the bombing before any semblance of organized medical care could be brought to the wounded and dying.'

The authors, Dr Bloomer and Dr Livingston, predicted that

If a 'baby' bomb of the kind used over Japan were to be exploded in the air over New Haven, it would demolish nearly the whole of the city. Even though the bomb were delivered within only one half mile of the target center, the whole of the business and harbor section of the city would be almost completely flattened. Immediately under the point of explosion it would be difficult to decide where the principal streets had been. The sky scrapers would all be structurally damaged and many of them would lose their facing, not to mention their partitions and floors. Other buildings in this area would be pulverized. The major police, fire and medical installations would be knocked out of commission. There would be fifty thousand people dead in the first few minutes and probably seventy to eighty thousand additional persons seriously wounded.

Whereas the area of destruction of a 'baby' bomb such as those used at Hiroshima and Nagasaki is approximately four square miles, that of a hydrogen bomb developed in the late 1940s would be approximately eighty square miles, with flash burns up to twenty miles away.

The New Haven consultants advocated sending a dozen men away for training by the Army or Navy auspices so they could return to train special fire, police and rescue personnel. Their training ought to include a grounding in the physics of radioactivity, in the health hazards of the radioactive contamination of food, clothing and equipment, and the immediate and delayed effects on the body of external and internal irradiation. They should also understand the special problems of radioactive contamination of open wounds. Their training must emphasize the basic principles of health physics so that they could advise quickly on the extent of body radiation permissible in a given duration of time. Radiation monitors should be consulted in regard to the establishment of civil defence posts so that workers would not be gathered in radioactively 'hot' or contaminated areas.

All civil defence personnel should be equipped with dosimeters. The Yale doctors considered that these workers could tolerate 50 roentgen per day for three days of total body irradiation but warned that 'Minute amounts of radioactive materials which may become deposited in body structure can supply a small dose of irradiation over an extended period of time, a period depending on the duration of radiation of the ingested particle, and therefore the hazards of inhalation, ingestion or absorption from contaminated skin abrasions or wounds is indeed very grave.'

By this time, 1950, the investigation into the long-term effects of the survivors of atomic bombings had been underway for a year or more. When Austin Brues and Paul Henshaw returned to the United States in 1947 they had recommended the initiation of studies of the long-term effects of the A-bomb to complement the studies of the short-term effects being conducted by Oughterson and his colleagues currently in Japan as the Joint Commission.

Almost immediately upon the return of Brues and Henshaw to the United States, the Committee on Atomic Casualties (CAC) was convened by the National Research Council (NRC). The membership consisted of Thomas M. Rivers, Director of the Rockefeller Institute's hospital; George H. Whipple, Head of Pathology and Dean at the University of Rochester; George W. Beadle, a geneticist; Raymond E. Zirkle, Director of the Institute of Radiobiology and Biophysics at the University of Chicago; Stafford Warren who had just been demobilized and selected as founding dean of the new medical school at UCLA; George M. Lyon, Chief of Radioisotopes at the Veterans Administration; Detlev Bronk; Shields Warren, the Harvard Medical School pathologist;

Austin Brues; and C. P. Rhoads. They met as the CAC for the first time on 15 March 1947.

Shields Warren was planning to go to Japan in April 1947 and he was designated CAC's first representative there. Upon arriving in Nagasaki twenty months after the bombing, Warren heard that many of the survivors of the bomb were returning to the city. Since he assumed that radiation had extended at most three or four miles from the hypocentre, and that residual radiation was insignificant, Warren argued that there would be now be a sufficient population of survivors for the ABCC studies without going to another city such as Sasebo to find a control group of unexposed people – 'such a study could be conducted on an intrinsic basis in Nagasaki itself'[3] This early decision by one of the most senior biomedical researchers in the United States was to shape the studies for the next fifty years – and shape their results.

In a discussion with twelve Japanese doctors, Warren learned that 60 per cent of the burns suffered by the survivors were accompanied by keloids; those on the face and hands were especially susceptible to infection. But the proposed ABCC studies would have to be undertaken with no existing bacteriological facilities. It would be difficult to obtain autopsies and there was a shortage of medical personnel. 'In the light of these problems', he concluded, 'Let the keloid problem ride.'[4]

Like Brues six months earlier, Shields Warren was still dismissive of the significance of residual radiation in Nagasaki in mid 1947. This was despite the fact that he met with Dr Sato on his studies of the effects of neutrons on camphor trees' germinating seeds. Sato reported that at a distance of one to one and a half kilometres trees were showing rapid germination and increased growth rates. He also met with Professor Hirai, who studied soil and micro-organisms and found that vegetables had developed deformed leaves and colour variations after the bomb. Some sweet potato bushes near the hypocentre were alive but unproductive.

The Japanese investigators were particularly concerned about the fallout that had landed in the Nishiyama Reservoir area. In his 1947 trip, Shields Warren visited Nishiyama several times, once to study the effects of the detonation on female breasts. He also undertook a series of haematologic studies on an exposed goat and on the day before his departure from Nagasaki he killed the goat to perform an autopsy. He found three kids in the womb, due in about five weeks. He determined that all organs and tissues of the mother were normal, then carved several chunks of meat for his assistants to enjoy as food. The animal's bones were preserved for studies on radiochemistry. Warren and his associate James V. Neel performed sternal marrow biopsies on 57 patients in May 1947. During one of these biopsies, a needle broke and had to be extracted with pliers. The patient refused a second try, leading Warren to write in his diary, 'Stoicism of the Japanese not too marked'. He also noted of the survivors he dealt with that 'all have some haziness of memory about events just after the bomb.'[5]

Shields Warren had been centrally involved in designing the animal experiments in the Operations Crossroads tests at Bikini nine months earlier. In his report he had indicated that he had not been shaken from his assumptions about the nature of residual radiation and fallout in what were considered to be air bursts (which is to say in the case of Hiroshima and Nagasaki, detonations that took place at the height of the Empire State Building). Two years after the detonations at Hiroshima and Nagasaki, Warren and his co-worker at Bikini, John L. Tullis (a Commander in the Medical Corps of the US Navy) wrote, 'an underwater atomic bomb explosion is more lethal than an air explosion, since the spray which showers down on the ships in the vicinity carries with it fission products which contaminate their surfaces, cannot be removed easily and remain dangerously radioactive for long periods of time.'[6]

Two years later Shields Warren became the part-time director of the Division of Biology and Medicine of the newly-formed Atomic Energy Commission (AEC). Merril Eisenbud, one of the earliest employees of the New York Operations Office (NYOO) of the AEC who became one of the United States' most distinguished radiation safety monitors, recalled[7] that Warren did not see the need for the NYOO Medical Division. 'Warren's opposition to our laboratory was largely the result of his lack of familiarity with the practical requirements of industrial hygiene. His orientation was towards medical science, not the applications of the physical sciences to the solution of medical problems in industry.'

Shields Warren's blinkered view of the nature of fallout and residual radioactivity also shaped the work that Eisenbud and his colleagues were able to do in tracking the fallout from the early Nevada tests. Eisenbud notes that when fallout from Nevada was registered by the Eastman Kodak company at their film plant in Rochester, New York in 1951

> there was little appreciation of the fact that some of the nuclides present in the bomb debris were capable of being absorbed by plants and animals and could eventually find their way into food and the human body. Such information was available from studies that had been conducted at Hanford and other nuclear centers, but the information was still secret in 1951, and at HASL [Health and Safety Laboratory which Eisenbud now directed] we didn't know it existed. What is disappointing in retrospect is that the Division of Biology and Medicine at AEC headquarters had paid so little

attention to the matter that there were no advance preparations for fallout measurement.'

Even though Merril Eisenbud became the doyen of health physics and radiation monitoring in the United States, throughout his working career he too held the article of faith that there had been no significant fallout at Hiroshima and Nagasaki. Writing perhaps in sight of the Empire State Building in 1990 after he had retired as Professor Emeritus at New York University, he explained:

Dangerous fallout of radioactive particles occurs when a nuclear bomb is exploded so close to the ground that particles of soil and other materials are sucked into the cooling fireball as it rises. When bombs are exploded at greater altitudes, the debris takes the form of fine particles that settle to the ground, usually with rain or snow, at great distances from the explosion, after which most of the short-lived radionuclides have decayed. The two bombs dropped on the Japanese cities were exploded high in the air, which tended to minimize fallout, but rain showers shortly after the explosions did result in slight, but measurable levels of fallout at both Hiroshima and Nagasaki.'

Shields Warren and Merril Eisenbud were not the only senior members of the Atomic Energy Commission to hold this article of faith. Robert L. Corsbie was an architect who went to Washington in 1951 to head up the AEC office concerned with the 'development and dissemination of facts on the effects of nuclear explosions on man and his environment'[8] His primary concern was with the shielding effect of construction materials against radiation. A decade later, in 1961, on the sixteenth anniversary of the Hiroshima and Nagasaki bombings and after extensive series of physics and biomedical studies in association with the weapons test series in the Pacific and Nevada Proving Grounds, Mr Corsbie testified to the Military Operations Subcommittee on Government Operations of the House of Representatives. He explained to the Congressional overseers of the Atomic Energy Commission:

a nuclear weapon, when detonated so that the fireball comes into contact with the surface, draws up a vast amount of earth. The earth is melted and mixed with the fission products in the process; and when the temperature drops, radioactive substances condense with the particles of earth. In a matter of minutes the particles will commence to fall toward the surface and be deposited in a rough circle around the point of detonation under the mushroom cloud and then downwind.

Corsbie then distinguished between early and delayed fallout. 'Early fallout is defined as that which reaches the ground during the first 24 hours following a nuclear explosion. It is the early fallout from surface, subsurface and low air bursts that is capable of producing radioactive contamination over large areas with an intensity great enough to present an immediate biological hazard.' Delayed fallout, on the other hand, 'that arriving after the first 24 hours, consists of very fine, invisible particles that settle in low concentrations over a considerable portion of the earth's surface. The radiation from delayed fallout is greatly reduced in intensity as a result of radioactive decay during the relatively long time that the particles remain suspended in the atmosphere. Delayed fallout radiation generally poses no immediate danger to health, although there may be a long-term hazard.'

But, the AEC expert reassured the Congressmen, 'it is proper to remember that there are no known fallout casualties among the 220,000 Japanese hurt and killed in Hiroshima and Nagasaki.'

Notes

1. Executive Office of the President, National Security Resources Board, Civil Defense Office, *You Can Survive*, United States Government Printing Office, 1950, found at Darling 770:111:68:74.

2. By William E. Bloomer MD and Robert B. Livingston, MD, found at Yale: Darling: 770:111:61:616.

3. John Z. Bower, 'Draft typescript history of the ABCC', Chapter 3, dated 28 February 1984.

4. Diary of Shields Warren, 26 April 1947, quoted in John Z. Bower, Draft Typescript of history of ABCC, Chapter 3, dated 28 February 1984

5. Diary of Shields Warren, quoted by John Z. Bower, 'Draft typescript history of the ABCC', Chapter 3, dated 28 February 1984.

6. John L. Tullis and Shields Warren, 'Gross autopsy observations in the animals exposed at Bikini', *Journal of the American Medical Association*, 2 August 1947:1155–8.

7. Merril Eisenbud, *An Environmental Odyssey* (University of Washington Press, 1990) p.47.

8. Statement by R. L. Corsbie on 'The effects of nuclear explosions' before the Military Operations Subcommittee of the Committee on Government Operations of the House of Representatives of the United States, 4 August 1961, found at Bugher 1:2:14:195.

Designing 'Do-able' Science

I did the experiments years ago, but only on a few rats. But you Americans — you are wonderful. You have made the human experiment!

**Professor Masao Tsuzuki,
General Macarthur's Headquarters, Tokyo 1945**

Whatever the diagnostic shortcomings of the experience to date may be, it is felt these shortcomings are almost equally distributed between the 'irradiated' and the control material...

**James V. Neel, 'Evaluation of the accuracy of
abnormality reporting during 1948 and early 1949',
Committee on Atomic Casualties, 17 October 1949.**

Six

On 26 November 1946 the Atomic Bomb Casualty Commission (ABCC) was created by a Presidential Directive 'to undertake a long-range, continuing study of the biological and medical effects of the atomic bomb on man.' The ABCC was organized by the Atomic Energy Commission but operated by the National Academy of Science and the National Research Council. A Committee on Atomic Casualties was established to advise the ABCC on scientific matters and it was envisaged that the Japanese National Institute of Health would participate in the ABCC in some collaborative way.

The ABCC was a direct outcome of the Brues-Henshaw Report which had argued the urgency of setting up a research programme on the Japanese survivors now that nearly eighteen months had passed since the bombings. The joint armed forces medical teams were producing early reports on the sequelae of the burns and blast injuries suffered by the survivors, but were unable systematically to study the phenomenon of radiation sickness, much less the as yet unrecognized long-term effects of whole body ionizing radiation.

Eighteen months after the ending of the Second World War, many men in the armed forces – including those in the medical corps – were being demobilized and taking up new careers in the universities and burgeoning private sector. Very few were willing to remain in the services to work in occupied Japan, in the two bombed cities.

As Stafford Warren, himself just appointed the founding dean for the medical school at UCLA, told his Yale audience in April 1947, 'Since we came home from Japan after the initial bombing, the Manhattan District, the Army, the Navy and the National Research Council have been trying to get people interested in going back on a long-term basis, but it has been impossible to find people to do that. As you know, most of you people participated in it too, and I plead guilty to the same thing, there is a great urge to get out of the armed forces.' But someone was available, albeit a very junior biomedical researcher. 'At the present time we have a young lieutenant over there who is a trained geneticist. He got his PhD in genetics, and he is an MD. He is in for a year, and he will spend that year in Japan. He went happily, however, because he was interested in the program.'[1]

This was James V. Neel. The Brues–Henshaw Report had contained an appendix prepared by Neel who was attached to the mission. Neel reported that a Japanese group under Ikuzo Matsubayashi had begun to study the genetic effects in the Hiroshima area by checking the progress of pregnancies of the women who registered for additional food and clothing allowances available for mothers. Neel identified[2] two major shortcomings in this Japanese study – there were no control series and the vital statistics did not include a complete record of abortions and miscarriages. Many survivors had left the cities, reducing the amount of clinical material for study and increasing the urgency of the need for a large enough survey that would permit the very small magnitude of genetic changes expected in the first generation to be detected. But even Neel acknowledged that his proposed research plan – which would also rely on the ration registration system but would include a control sample at Kure and a closer follow-up of abnormal termination of pregnancy and congenital malformations – 'at best, will detect only a fraction of the dominant mutations'.

The Brues-Henshaw mission put a considerable effort into negotiating collaboration on these studies with Japanese counterparts such as the Japanese National Institute of Health, facilitated by Dr Tsuzuki. James Neel, who had just begun his active service after finishing medical school and genetic studies at the University of Rochester, was to remain in Japan to continue these negotiations. Brues and Henshaw left Japan in January 1947 while Neel, Block and Ullrich continued to develop the groundwork for the proposed research enterprise.

Warren reviewed Neel's proposals for the study of pregnancies and their outcomes. On 28 April 1947 he radiogrammed to the CAC in Washington urging them to accept Neel's research protocol 'to prevent further loss of data'. The Committee on Atomic Casualties voted unanimous approval. Although Neel worked hard to try to negotiate a joint study with the appropriate Japanese institutions, particularly the National Institute for Health, he was unable to get the Japanese to commit to a programme led by American investigators. Neel was in Nishiyama examining fallout effects on seven patients and a goat when he received Warren's letter of authorization to undertake 'a continuing study of the biological and medical effects of the atomic bomb on man' under the auspices of the NRC.

Thirty years old, Neel had completed his graduate work at the University of Rochester (where Warren had been Professor of Radiology) in 1939 and then gone on to an MD because of his growing interest in human genetics. During the war period, the Drosophila geneticist Curt Stern and the mouse geneticist Donald Charles were both working on Manhattan District-related research on the biological effects of ionizing radiation at the University of Rochester.[3]

After several weeks in Japan with the Brues-Henshaw mission, talking among others with the early Japanese researchers into the genetic effects on the survivors, Neel developed a preliminary research protocol which was appended to the Brues-Henshaw Report. Within a month of the formation of the Atomic Bomb Casualty Commission and its Committee on Atomic Casualties, Neel was called to Washington to defend his proposals before a very high-level panel of geneticists.

Neel had discussed his proposals with department heads at Nagasaki Medical School and he had warned them that any effect on the first generation born to the survivors would be very small and very difficult to detect. The detection programme would be very dependent on an accurate register of births and indeed on the outcomes of every conception in both cities and in the control areas. Even so, from the outset Neel conceded that abortions before the fourth month would not be recorded (because registration for extra rations began in the fifth month of pregnancy) and would be very difficult to spot. Professor Yasuchi Mitani of the Department of Obstetrics and Gynaecology said that he considered the proposed programme feasible and that registration should begin as quickly as possible. He added that since 1938 there had been fewer stillbirths at Nagasaki than at Hiroshima and Kure; he estimated the difference to be about half.[4]

During this feasibility study period, Shields Warren met Hiroshima's Mayor, Shinso Hanai, who told him that the city's population had been 400,000 at the beginning of the war, but following a series of evacuations, had dropped to 150,000. Just after the bombing it fell further to an estimated 130,000, although the Mayor thought this was too high a figure since some people registered twice for food. On the basis of data from the rationing programme he estimated the population in May 1947 had grown to 210,000. The Mayor pointed out that there were problems in relying on pregnancy registrations as Hiroshima was now so poor that pregnant women moved out to the country to their family homes to await the birth. There was no maternity hospital in the city in the aftermath of the bombing.

The June 1947 review conference for the genetics studies proposed by Neel, barely out of graduate school, included Hermann J. Muller who had just won the Nobel Prize for 1946 for his work on fruit fly genetics. It also included Donald R. Charles from Rochester, Charles H. Danforth, Professor of Anatomy at Stanford and member of the National Academy of Sciences, and Laurence H. Snyder who had just moved from the Ohio State University to become Dean of the Graduate School at Oklahoma University.

Neel's research proposal rested on the hypothesis that genetic effects detected in mice and fruit flies from ionizing radiation doses administered under laboratory conditions would be paralleled in the human survivors of the two atomic detonations at Hiroshima and Nagasaki. He proposed an observational, epidemiological study of a sufficiently large sample of the survivors to establish whether there were statistically significant differences between observable genetic damage in the radiated group and the control group, who were assumed to have not received any radiation in the explosions.

John Beatty has explained that Neel was proposing to test a null hypothesis.

> The usual form of a null hypothesis is that exposure to some treatment (in this case radiation from the bombs) does not have a particular effect (in this case a genetic effect). To test the null hypothesis, one checks to see whether the frequency of the hypothesized effect in the exposed group is sufficiently greater than in the control group – that is, sufficiently great to refute the null hypothesis and thus establish a connection between the treatment and the effect. The point of having a sufficiently large ('statistically significant') difference is to rule out the possibility that the difference is simply a matter of chance.

In the case of the survivors at Hiroshima and Nagasaki, for instance, Neel had to guard against the possibility that 'one would expect some mutations among the radiation-exposed group as well as among the control group, since mutations occur "naturally"' (i.e. for reasons other than radiation exposure). Even if the bombs had no effect, the exposed group might, just by chance, have more mutations. The question, then, is whether the exposed group has a sufficiently greater number of mutations to rule out a chance discrepancy and thus refute the null hypothesis that the explosions had no genetic effects.[5]

William J. Schull, Neel's associate in the genetics studies over the next forty years, considered that the point of the studies was:

> to help determine the extent of mutational damage to offspring of people who were exposed to the ionizing radiation released with the detonation of the bombs. We knew, from the studies of Hermann Muller and others,

that such damage occurred in experimental animals, and we presumed it would occur also among human beings. We did not know, however, whether the mutability of human genes would be the same as or different from that of animal species that had been studied, nor what form the damage might take. We did know that most newly arising mutations are deleterious, and we assumed that they might be manifested as an increased frequency of birth defects, fetal and infantile mortality, and retarded mental and motor development.[6]

The trouble was that Hermann Muller in particular questioned every one of the assumptions of the research methodology designed to test the extent of damage to humans from the tests. When the chairman, Dr Beadle, polled the geneticists who met in June 1947 to consider the research protocol on their attitude towards the proposed project after extensive discussion, Dr Muller felt that on the basis of Charles' work on mice (and Charles was a member of the conference) it should be possible to demonstrate a genetic effect, but stressed that there would be a large amount of genetic damage not apparent in the first generation offspring. It might be better to work with 'an appropriate mammal'. Dr Danforth and Dr Charles expressed a similar view. But Dr Snyder felt that under the circumstances the Committee on Atomic Casualties could not pass up the opportunity to carry out the studies. According to the summary report of the conference 'There was some discussion as to the extent to which our thinking was being influenced by "non-scientific" considerations.' It was suggested that experimental work on primates might be more productive than the proposed study of the survivors of Hiroshima and Nagasaki, nearly two years after the bombings. There was also discussion of the central concept in Neel's methodology, of surveying the survivors epidemiologically rather than a case by case clinical study of a representative sample – might it not be more informative to study different samples of radiated and non-radiated couples to see the outcomes of their pregnancies? Would it not be better to conduct laboratory studies since 'this material is too much influenced by extraneous variables and too little adapted to disclosing genetic effects'?[7]

There was one overriding consideration for pursuing the study as outlined by Neel on the survivors of Hiroshima and Nagasaki – to reassure the survivors and the general public that there would not be massive genetic damage as a result of the bombings. In presenting the report of the Conference on Genetics to the Committee on Atomic Casualties two days later[8] Dr George M. Beadle said there was a real concern among the geneticists about the 'misunderstandings and misinterpretations that might arise in connection with the study', but they also felt it was a unique opportunity which could not be missed, even if the study was unlikely to reveal statistically significant results. It would be an expensive undertaking that might yield little information. But Dr Beadle also 'referred to the need for publicity to counteract the false impressions that are prevalent regarding the genetic effects of the bomb, with special reference to the occurrence of monsters.' However, it 'was the belief of the conference that from a purely scientific standpoint more can be learned from experiments on chimpanzees and monkeys than can be learned from the study of the Japanese survivors.' Dr Neel stressed that it would be at least a decade before the data would yield results of statistical significance. Even so, only a very small fraction of the total range of genetic effects would be evident in the first post-bomb generation.

Despite these reservations, the Committee on Atomic Casualties decided unanimously to authorize the project as proposed by Neel. Dr Lewis H. Weed of the sponsoring National Research Council said that he fully agreed with Dr Beadle but that even though a negative answer might be revealed by the study, 'this fact in itself would be of tremendous value from the standpoint of morale'. Dr Detlev Bronk said the Committee would assume a heavy responsibility if it decided not to undertake the study, since this was an 'opportunity to explore the results of a unique experiment' and it would be a serious matter not to attempt the study even though the obstacles seemed insurmountable. The projected cost of $100,000 for the first year would be justified by the unique scientific information that would be obtained as well as the morale factor involved. Dr Beadle said it was his personal belief that the study should go forward although he also remarked that 'the geneticists who had considered the program were not convinced that the study could be justified on purely scientific grounds, although there was general agreement that the program would result in the accumulation of valuable data on inheritance.' Dr Beadle also reminded the Committee that Dr Muller was not convinced that the study would show much as to genetic damage resulting from the bomb, although Dr Muller was sure that such damage had occurred. Dr Raymond E. Zirkle brought the discussion back to the morale factor. 'He felt that the study would remove much uneasiness if the results of the study were negative and that it would be comforting to the public to know that the possible genetic effects of the bomb were to be investigated by competent scientists.' Dr Shields Warren moved the motion, and Dr Zirkle seconded it, and the Committee agreed unanimously to approve the recommendations made by the conference on genetics. These recommendations had read in part:

Although there is every reason to infer that genetic effects can be produced and have been produced in man by atomic radiation, nevertheless the conference wishes to make it clear that it cannot guarantee significant results from this or any other study of the Japanese material. In contrast to laboratory data, this material is too much influenced by extraneous variables and too little adapted to disclosing genetic effects. In spite of these facts, the conference feels that this unique possibility for demonstrating genetic effects caused by atomic radiation should not be lost.[9]

The conference of geneticists insisted that a caveat be published in *Science* expressing their reservations. This warned that 'inasmuch as the majority of mutations occurring in animals are recessive, only the relatively small proportions of mutations which are dominant may be expected to show effects in the first post-bomb generation. The potential range in their effects is very wide. Dominant mutations with large, clear cut manifestations can be expected to be much more rare than those with smaller, but possibly quite significant, effects on bodily dimensions, life span, etc. But the detection of the latter is a matter of great difficulty with present techniques.' For practical reasons the investigation would have to concentrate on such gross mutations as would lead to stillbirths, to live births with gross external abnormality or to internal defects causing death or serious illness in infancy.[10]

As well as the sieve being necessarily wide-holed, it would need to be a statistical rather than a pathological investigation since 'It is unlikely that any individual and specific pathology in a post-irradiation generation can ever be attributed with certainty to the effects of the bomb'. If a sufficiently large, controlled sample of survivors showed a definite increase in the frequency of abortions, miscarriages, stillbirths and abnormal products of conception, this might be surmised to be a genetic effect of the bombing. But it would be a very large-scale undertaking to produce a very soft result – it would be looking for a needle in a haystack and ignoring anything that did not look like a needle as known heretofore. It would be totally observational in methodology, relying on the quality of training of the investigators and the gathering of their data. It was a crude approach to a new phenomenon in human experience, and it was in danger, as Muller pointed out in the 1950s, of falling into the 'fallacy that what cannot be seen or felt need not be bothered with'.[11] At the least, appropriate control studies in other Japanese cities were essential to the design of the research, which should extend over at least a decade and preferably over two or more generations.

Despite Dr Muller's reservations, the Committee on Atomic Casualties authorized the study and placed on record[12] a statement of appreciation of Neel's 'unusual abilities in the conduct of studies on Japanese survivors [and his] mastery of the methods and techniques necessary to the investigation of the complicated medical and biological problems resulting from atomic radiation.' A few weeks later Neel was given the title of Acting Director of the ABCC in Japan and the permanent title of Research Associate in Charge of Genetic Studies under the ABCC in Japan'.[13]

Notes

1. Stafford Warren, 'Radioactivity, health and safety', mimeo of address to Yale Institute of Occupational Medicine and Hygiene, 1 April 1947, found at Darling 770:111:68:74. Warren's talk to the Yale group was hardly likely to have encouraged family men in particular to volunteer to work in Hiroshima and Nagasaki to do scut work in a difficult and perhaps dangerous environment!

2. According to John Z. Bowers' Draft typescript of history of ABCC, Chapter 3, dated 28 February 1984, found at Bowers:ACC:89–73: Brues–Henshaw Report, 1947 p.59, quoted in Bower's 'Draft typescript history of the ABCC', Chapter 3, dated 28 February 1984. Dr Tsuzuki's remark was quoted by Philip Morrison, 'The laboratory demobilizes...', address at the Atomic Energy Session of *New York Herald-Tribune Forum*, 29 October 1945, reprinted in *Bulletin of the Atomic Scientists*, 1946:2:5:5–6.

3. See John Beatty, 'Genetics in the atomic age: The Atomic Bomb Casualty Commission 1947–56', in Keith R. Benson *et al.* (eds.) *The Expansion of American Biology*, (Rutgers University Press, 1991:284–324) and also James V. Neel, *Physician to the Gene Pool* (John Wiley and Sons, 1994).

4. Diary of Shields Warren, 7 May 1947 quoted John Z. Bower, 'Draft typescript history of the ABCC' dated 25 February 1984.

5. John Beatty, 'Genetics in the atomic age: The Atomic Bomb Casualty Commission, 1947–56' in Keith R. Benson *et al.* (eds.) *The Expansion of American Biology*, (Rutgers University Press, 1991) p.299.

6. William J. Schull, *Songs of Praise* (Harvard University Press, 1990) p.4.

7. Conference on Genetics, Summary of Proceedings, 24 June 1947, National Research Council, NAS.

8. Minutes of the CAC, dated 26 June 1947, NAS.

9. 'Recommendations of the Conference on Genetics to the Committee on Atomic Casualties', Appendix A to Minutes of the CAC, dated 26 June 1947, NAS.

10. 'Genetic effects of the atomic bombs in Hiroshima and Nagasaki', Genetics Conference, Committee on Atomic Casualties, National Research Council, *Science*, 10 October 1947: 331–3.

11. H. J. Muller, 'How radiation changes the genetic constitution', prepared for the United Nations Conference on the Peacetime Uses of Atomic Energy, 1955.

12. Minutes of the CAC, dated 26 June 1947.

13. Minutes of the CAC, dated 10 September 1947.

Seven

Although the Committee on Atomic Casualties had authorized the epidemiological studies of pregnancies and their outcomes in the two bombed cities with Kure as a control city, funding – the lifeblood of scientific and biomedical research in the post-war era – for the Atomic Bomb Casualty Commission was problematic from the start. Organized under the auspices of the National Research Council and the National Academy of Sciences, the ABCC was nevertheless dependent for its funding on the newly formed Atomic Energy Commission. It had to compete with developmental weapons tests and laboratory studies for funding at the height of the early Cold War.

The Minutes of the meetings of the Committee on Atomic Casualties give a blow-by-blow account of the discussions of the appointed experts as they grappled with the spiralling costs of a research agenda in inflationary Japan. They permit an insight into the accommodations that scientists and biomedical researchers are required – and willing – to make in order to be able to pursue their research interests – and careers – within the constraints determined by the managers of science and biomedical research. If science is the art of the do-able, it may follow that the science which is done is constrained by practicalities. And those practical constraints may be dictated by non-scientific considerations. How does science respond? Does good science necessarily result?

Less than a year after the Committee on Atomic Casualties had authorized the genetics studies with an initial budget of $100,000 for the first year, the costs had risen to over a million dollars. The Committee at its April 1948 meeting was urgently looking at ways to cut costs. Even though a Conference on Haematology had been told by its Chairman, Dr John S. Lawrence, in September 1947[1] that the Japanese had reported a persistent leukocytosis in the Nishiyama Reservoir region of Nagasaki, which had received marked fallout because of prevailing winds at the time of the explosion, it was still thought that the population of Nagasaki divided clearly into those who had been exposed to radiation in the instant of the bomb, and those who had not. Dr Lawrence presented a detailed analysis of all the observations, both Japanese and American, which had been made but argued that the inconsistencies in the data were of such a magnitude as to raise serious questions concerning the significance of the findings. He also spoke of the poor character of the bone marrow smears which he had seen, but said that the Japanese had told him that their best preparations had been appropriated by American researchers.

Faced with a million dollar discrepancy between the best estimates the Committee's staff could prepare and the amount of money the AEC felt it could make available, Dr Shields Warren reaffirmed[2] his belief that internal controls would be possible in Nagasaki. Despite the evidence from Nishiyama, he still maintained that the bombs were exploded sufficiently high above the cities that the fission products were carried upward. He told his colleagues on the Committee on Atomic Casualties in April 1948 that in Nagasaki there was practically no induced radioactivity and the bombed area was below tolerance levels after 23 September 1945. There probably was no significant radiation twelve hours after the bombing. The fission products of the Nagasaki bomb did fall out to some extent in the Nishiyama valley, but white blood cell counts of the valley residents performed by American investigators revealed no significant effects, and Japanese reports of leukocytosis were not confirmed. Accordingly, he was of the opinion that internal controls could be arranged in Nagasaki and that there probably was no significant objection, from the genetic standpoint, to doing this.

Dr Warren was assuming on the basis of very primitive measurements made in very difficult conditions in late 1945 that radiation was so localized and instantaneous that only those people within two kilometres of the hypocentre had been irradiated. Everyone else who was in Nagasaki at the time could be regarded as 'non-exposed' and serve as control subjects for those who had been 'exposed' and survived. It was thought that the similarities between the environment, diets and socio-economic status of 'non-exposed' survivors and 'exposed' would be controlled by having this 'intrinsic' control sample instead of comparing the pregnancies of the population of Nagasaki as a whole against the reproductive outcomes of a comparable Japanese city such as Sasebo.

Could the same argument be made for Hiroshima? One Committee member, Dr Owen, thought that there were many people now living in Hiroshima who had not been there in August 1945; Dr Neel pointed out that many of these newcomers were returned soldiers, and therefore would be mostly men. Dr Rivers, the Committee's Chairman, asked about the possible cost savings to the project if it were restricted to

Hiroshima and Nagasaki. But Dr Wigodsky pointed out that a major saving would not be achieved since the same number of people would have to be examined. Dr Winternitz suggested it would be possible to use one control to four exposed persons. Dr Rivers asked again if a control city was really required. Dr Neel replied that he believed a control city was desirable, especially since Dr Snell believed that the individuals who had moved into the cities since the bombings were not entirely adequate controls because of the different environments, food intakes and so on between them and those who had endured the devastation after the bombings.

The Chairman then asked for expressions of opinion from the Committee members on the question of the control sample. Dr Weed pointed out that although the dose of radiation was said to be below tolerance levels, this might not be true from the standpoint of the genetic effects, and although no detectable physical evidence could be seen now, the possibility existed that genetic effects might be uncovered eventually. Dr Shields Warren countered this argument by saying that when the level of radiation descends to the background level, it could be assumed that the affected area is safe. But if the returned Nagasaki population was predominantly male, it would be advantageous to have one control city. Dr Zirkle pointed out that 25 years on, adequate controls would be critical for the entire programme and had to be provided now, even if one *exposed* city had to be dropped from the programme. It was proposed that the programme of study should include the three cities of Hiroshima, Nagasaki and Kure. But discussion on the motion returned again to the possibility of studying only two cities, to save costs. Dr Evans felt that the Committee should bend over backwards on the matter of controls. It was his opinion that if the programme did not contain very adequate controls, the entire project should be dropped. Shields Warren said that because the numbers were so small, it would be desirable to use both Hiroshima and Nagasaki. Dr Neel thought Nagasaki might have more adequate internal controls than Hiroshima. Shields Warren agreed 'since so much of the city was untouched by the bombing'.

But the projected budget for the two years 1947 to 1949 was $1,850,000 and the question was still before the Committee, 'Will we say do it right or not do it at all?' as Dr Rivers put it from the Chair. Dr Lyon noted that negative information would be valuable in offsetting any misinformation published by the Japanese. Dr William Gruelich's report[3] on the physical growth and development of children in Hiroshima, Kure, Nagasaki and Sasebo was accepted but priority was placed on the genetics studies, in the three cities.

Staffing at the ABCC was expanded and in 29 June 1948 Hiroshi Maki MD became the first Japanese Associate Director of ABCC. In July 1949 William J. Schull from the University of Michigan (where Neel had taken up a professorship after the end of his military service) arrived to supervise the genetics studies. After earning a Bachelor and Master of Science at Marquette University in Milwaukee in 1946 and 1947, Schull had moved to Ohio State, where received his doctorate in 1949. He had then joined the Heredity Clinic at the University of Michigan and was subsequently recruited by Neel to manage the programme in Japan on an initial two year contract.[4]

Colonel Tessmer, a radiologist, was appointed Field Director of the ABCC and in September 1949 Harvey Grant Taylor became Tessmer's Deputy Field Director for Research. Taylor had most recently been Associate Dean and Associate Professor of Pediatrics and Bacteriology at Duke University School of Medicine. His premedical studies and a masters degree in bacteriology had been completed at Stanford.[5]

Negotiations for collaboration with the ABCC having failed, the Japanese Welfare Ministry was organizing a study of the long-range genetic effects to be conducted in Hiroshima and Nagasaki with Kure and Omura as the control cities. Although the formation of the ABCC and the initiation of the genetic studies had taken almost two years since the bombings of the cities, it was to be another two years before data collection was really under way in any systematic fashion. The American investigators, however, were too dismissive of the quality of the early Japanese investigations to attempt to use the only available data on the immediate post-bomb effects. In April 1948 the ABCC itself noted that the Japanese investigators had not yet been allowed to publish their findings on the medical effects of the atomic bombs, in spite of the fact that a review of their data disclosed little if anything which would affect the security of the United States. Furthermore, the Japanese investigators were beginning to read in US medical journals published papers similar to their own that had been suppressed; and recently a news report of one of these had appeared in a Tokyo Japanese language paper. 'It is expecting too much of a competent Japanese investigator to ask him to work with a US group under circumstances in which the latter can publish and he cannot.'

In October 1949 Dr Neel reported to the Washington meeting of the Committee on Atomic Casualties.[6] He was worried that the thirty young Japanese physicians doing the genetics observations were identifying only 80 per cent of the pregnancies in the three cities. The 20 per cent lost 'may very well be weighted with abnormalities'. The ABCC was now registering roughly 20,000 pregnancies per year, but only two fifths to one half of these were to parents who were in the cities at the time of the bombing. Dr Neel thought about 10 per cent of the total group would have had significant amounts of radiation; it would take ten years to have 10,000 babies born to this group. As Dr Neel told his advisory committee in late 1949, 'A great deal depends upon the level of significance which is chosen.'

Dr Wearn asked if the next ten years were critical, and Dr Neel said they were. The first year after the bombings had been the most important, but no data had been collected (by the American researchers) then. Dr Wearn suggested increasing the size of the sample but Dr Neel said that it was almost at its peak for the two bombed cities and could only be increased by expanding the study to other cities to which survivors had migrated since the war.

Dr Lyon inquired as to the distortion of the sample caused by some exposed and injured persons emigrating from the bombed cities. Dr Neel acknowledged that there was a possibility of distortion since among those who emigrated might be those who had been closest to the hypocentre and had lost everything. Some thought had been given to attempting to track down such individuals but it was believed this would be scarcely worth the effort.

Dr Rivers inquired whether the parents of the babies being examined by the genetics programme were being examined and Dr Neel (who was now based in Michigan and directing the studies through Dr Schull) said he thought so. So far in the pregnancy termination studies, it had been possible to examine the children only once – shortly after birth. Dr Neel noted that the Prefectural Eugenics Committee reported several hundred 'spontaneous' terminations each month which were not being seen by ABCC. These were required for a complete study. A pilot study was being conducted on this question. When several hundred such cases had been examined, it would be possible to determine if they involved a high number of radiated parents.

By the later 1940s, the post-war reconstruction of Japan meant that the food situation was improving and therefore use of the pregnancy rations as an incentive for registering for the ABCC studies was becoming visibly less effective in attracting the survivors to the study. The Committee agreed to allocate up to $20,000 a year for financial incentives or goods to attract subjects.

Dr Dowdy asked about the validity of a patient's history regarding petechiae and epilation. Were the patients reporting their symptoms accurately or were they exaggerating them in order to qualify for ABCC attention? Dr Neel thought that the results obtained so far seemed to agree with those obtained by the Joint Commission, but that perhaps this was due to both studies being subject to the same errors.

Dr Bowers of the Division of Biology and Medicine of the AEC had been to Japan to assess the work of ABCC in August 1949 and he reported to the CAC Executive Session in October, 1949[7] He was worried that while the programme was established originally primarily to determine the effects of the two bomb explosions on the Japanese, 'there is a grave question whether adequate coverage is being given to the exposed persons by virtue of the effort being made to gather control data. There is a question as to whether or not too much emphasis is being placed on research projects at the expense of screening.' He was concerned as to whether or not the administrative and construction aspects of the work were getting too far ahead of the scientific portion of the programme and considered the possibility that the ABCC might end up with handsome, well-equipped facilities, but not enough work to justify their existence.

More fundamentally, Dr Bowers raised the question of whether or not the ABCC programme was turning as closely as possible about the problem of radiation effects. Only the Field Director, Colonel Tessmer, had experience with the effects of radiation but he was devoting 90 per cent of his time to administration.

There was concern about whether the massive investment of time and energy in the routine physical examinations of the epidemiological studies were being undertaken without reference to the research goals of the ABCC. It was expected that the physicals would lead to the recognition of new conditions which would lead to research investigations. But, as Dr Rivers pointed out, since the ABCC didn't know what they were looking for in terms of unpredicted sequelae of radiation injury, the whole enterprise was one of research. The trouble was that it was intensely tedious and the research goals were often lost in the predictability of the routine examinations. As Dr Bronk expressed it, would it not be more fruitful to examine fewer cases in a clinical pathological way than to continue a large broadbrush survey of the most obvious predictable and externally observable injury and mutation? It was already apparent that even an epidemiological study required full medical facilities. This raised the question of cost and the Committee was staggered by both the size and the cost of the programme indicated by their deliberations. The staff had already grown to 80 Americans and 400 Japanese. Yet, as the Chairman of the CAC himself pointed out, the scientific direction of the research agenda was still piecemeal. 'As staff members were added, each was encouraged to start on some particular small phase of the program for which he was best suited. When a sufficiently large number had accumulated, these parts were then integrated into the whole.'

In October 1949 the Committee on Atomic Casualties thought it would be best on the one hand to initiate control studies as simultaneously as possible with studies of exposed persons, and on the other hand to examine in Hiroshima and Nagasaki only 'the unique population' – those who had been closer than two kilometres to the hypocentres and who were therefore assumed to have been exposed. Kure was still the site of the control sample and building construction was underway there and in Hiroshima; no major building investment could be planned for Nagasaki because of the cost implications. The Committee, that is, were content to commission what they thought would be a complete examination of a representative (not complete) sample of the exposed population and a simultaneous study of a comparable control population in Kure.

Dr Bronk reminded his colleagues on the Committee that he had questioned the advisability of engaging in the work in Japan when it was first proposed. It appeared to be a long-range gamble.'Everyone concerned with the establishment of the ABCC had experienced periods of misgiving. However, once a decision was made to engage in such work the important thing is to reach a firm decision at this time as to whether everyone is prepared to continue with the program regardless of whether or not it is a gamble.' It was agreed to halt the construction work at Kure in order to contain costs, even though staff members of the ABCC were commuting three hours a day to Hiroshima. A comprehensive census of the bombed population was still not available.

Neel appealed to the October 1949 meeting of the Committee[8] for more personnel, and centralized office space for the genetics studies. 'The bulk of the working time of these physicians is occupied with riding about in jeeps trying to locate the address of newborn babies (the Japanese system of numbering streets is impossible), with nine-tenths of the babies proving upon examination to be completely normal. This is not professionally exciting work.' The Genetics section, though ably led by Schull, was 'woefully undermanned'.

Neel told the Committee[9] that it was not yet feasible to reach an accurate evaluation of the reporting of major malformations; he thought the survey was seeing 80 per cent of the major malformations even though he acknowledged that there was a considerable subjective element in the determination of minor external malformations. Dr Neel thought if anything there was a tendency to overdiagnose among the young physicians, and in some conditions he would put the accuracy at only 10 to 20 per cent. Only if it was possible to accumulate a thousand autopsies in each of the three cities over the next decade, together with the radiation histories of the parents, would first approach to the question of the incidence and significance of internal malformations be feasible.

But at least, reported Dr Neel, 'Whatever the diagnostic shortcomings of the experience to date may be, it is felt these shortcomings are almost equally distributed between the "irradiated" and control material, although one cannot exclude a possible greater tendency of irradiated parents to disclose an abnormality because of the "out" offered by the atomic bomb. The comparison of the results obtained in these two groups appears to have a high degree of validity at the present time, even if the absolute level of diagnostic accuracy improves with the passage of time.'

Neel and his colleagues did feel able to report their preliminary findings on the incidence of consanguinity, or cousin-marriage, in Japan, which they calculated as being six times more frequent that in Europe, based on[10] special surveys in the Katayama district of Kure and the Hijiyama district of Hiroshima which were 'selected as more or less typical of the city as a whole', as well as Midori Machi near Kure, an Eta village whose social isolation was assumed to be likely to result in higher consanguinity; and Daniu fishing community six miles from Kure, which apart from its proximity to a large city, 'may be regarded as more or less typical of the smaller agricultural and fishing villages of Southern Honshu, the main island of Japan'.

Neel and his co-authors emphasized in their first report on consanguinity in Japan 'a fact already recognized by many students of human genetics, namely, that the weaknesses which exist in the present day data concerning the genetics of human populations are no less extensive than the weaknesses in our mathematical tools for dealing with such data if they did exist. Valid studies of gene frequencies by indirect methods are as dependent upon an improvement in the quality of case reports and our knowledge of the breeding structure of human populations as on developments in mathematical theory.' But they still felt confident in hypothesizing that 'Induced recessive mutations may be expected to manifest themselves significantly more rapidly in Japanese than in European populations if this [six fold] difference in the coefficient of inbreeding persists'. That is, the epidemiological survey for dominant mutations in the survivors of the bombings at Hiroshima and Nagasaki should have an enhanced chance of success statistically because of the relatively high rate of close-relation marriage in the sample. In another early report circulated to the Committee on Atomic Casualties in October 1949, a Columbia University researcher reminded the scientific advisers[11] that Neel was only studying pregnancies after the fifth month. 'It is really necessary to know if early pregnancy wastage differs between the radiation and the control groups [in the first twelve weeks of pregnancy].' He proposed a pilot study in Hiroshima to clarify this point, which would rely on individual case studies rather than a population survey.

But the problems of accumulating a sufficiently numerous sample of survivors, and controls, were still being governed by cost considerations at the next meeting of the Committee on Atomic Casualties, in February 1950.[12] Housing shortages still meant long commutes for the 105 American and allied nationals and 600 Japanese now on the staff of the ABCC and was affecting the rate at which subjects could be examined – only ten or twelve a day. A control census had been undertaken in an attempt to evaluate the several areas in which the ABCC were working in order to answer the problem raised by extrinsic as compared to intrinsic controls.

The Chairman, Dr Rivers, recapitulated the problem for the Committee, nearly five years after the bombings.

In the beginning the CAC did not have clearly in mind the best procedure to follow. In succeeding months, ideas were crystallized and it was agreed that a genetics program should be developed but that it would not be adequate in itself. It was decided that the program of investigation required the periodic examination of cross-sections of the exposed and unexposed populations. This would require adequate laboratory facilities. Originally the Committee intended to use the two bombed cities, Hiroshima and Nagaski, and two control cities, Kure and Sasebo. Later it was decided to omit Sasebo but to retain Kure as the extrinsic control city.

Cost constraints had led to termination of the construction of laboratories at Kure.

The Field Director, Colonel Tessmer, told his advisory committee that it was his opinion that using Kure as an extrinsic control had always been a calculated risk because people there 'do not have the incentive of exposure to the atomic bombs in their background' and it might be difficult to get them to return to the laboratories periodically for examinations. There were other reasons also why the use of Kure was open to question. It was in some respects a dying city. Prior to the war, it had been completely dependent upon the naval yard. Now that the yard was reduced to an almost inactive state, the population was diminishing slowly. Kure had been a closed city for many years, the population being controlled by the Navy, and undoubtedly this had resulted in some demographic distortions.

Colonel Tessmer reminded the Committee in early 1950 that the problem of residual radioactivity in Hiroshima and Nagasaki had disturbed members of the staff of the ABCC in regard to the utilization of individuals in those cities for so-called intrinsic controls. It was not difficult to visualize questionable control cases which might arise because of the inhalation or ingestion of radioactive particles. But there certainly was no obvious danger at that time in either of the bombed cities.

Colonel Tessmer – the Field Director of the Atomic Bomb Casualty Commission and its only trained radiologist – told the Committee he would be willing to give up Kure as an adult control if the census currently being conducted on 10 per cent samples in the two cities indicated that there would be sufficient internal controls.

Notes

1. Conference on Hematology, CAC, 8 September 1947, NAS

2. Minutes of the CAC, dated 20 April 1948, NAS.

3. William W. Gruelich, *A Report on the Physical Growth and Development of Children in Hiroshima, Kure, Nagasaki and Sasebo*, 9 March 1948, NAS.

4. William Schull joined the Institute of Human Biology at the University of Michigan and in 1956 was appointed a member of faculty. He stayed at Michigan until 1972.

5. Taylor became Director in early 1951 after Tessmer went to Fort Knox. Soon thereafter Taylor launched a strenuous effort to terminate the programme at Nagasaki. He was supported by John C. Bugher of the AEC who argued that there was not enough money to support both Hiroshima and Nagasaki.

6. Minutes of the CAC, dated 17 October 1949, NAS.

7. Minutes of the CAC Executive Session, dated 17 October 1949.

8. James V. Neel, Report on activities in Japan during the period 8 May 1949 to 13 July 1949 to CAC, Appendix II to Minutes of the CAC, dated 17 October 1949.

9. James V. Neel, Consultant in Genetics, 'Evaluation of the accuracy of abnormality reporting during 1948 and early 1949', Appendix B to Minutes of the CAC, dated 17 October 1949, NAS.

10. 'The Incidence of consanguinity in Japan, with remarks on the utilization of this data in the estimation of comparative gene frequencies and the expected rate of induced recessive mutations', James V. Neel, Masuo Kodani, Richard Brewer, Ray C. Anderson, ABCC Japan, Appendix III to Minutes of the CAC, dated 17 October 1949, NAS

11. Earle T. Engle, Columbia University College of Physicians and Surgeons, Report on Fertility Studies of the ABCC, May 8–July 8, 1949 to National Research Council on Atomic Casualties, dated 18 August 1949, Appendix I to Minutes of the CAC, dated 17 October 1949, NAS

12. Minutes of the CAC, dated 21 February 1950, NAS

Eight

The study of the long term effects of radiation on the survivors of Hiroshima and Nagasaki was now restricted to the two bombed cities on the assumption that those inhabitants who had been further than 2000 or 3000 metres from the hypocentre of the explosions had not received any radiation, or at least not any of significance. We have seen how this assumption evolved from the earliest days of the first biomedical research team into Japan, and the ways in which pivotal individuals on the managing committee of the research agenda in Hiroshima and Nagasaki insisted on its acceptance. From the beginning, then, the biomedical research agenda of the Atomic Bomb Casualty Commission took as received wisdom – assumed – something which it might have been expected to test. Were people more than two or three kilometres from the centre of the explosion in fact not irradiated? Was it legitimate to include them with incomers to the city after the bombings as part of the *control* sample against which the findings in the epidemiological survey would be evaluated?

The men who served on the Committee on Atomic Casualties and those who were invited to its meetings as expert contributors were involved in more committees than the CAC. They were themselves researchers in the scientific and biomedical studies of the effects of nuclear energy. They were a small group of perhaps thirty men who met often and worked together. How did they deal with emerging evidence that the primary assumption of the ABCC research agenda might be fallacious?

The Minutes of the Committee on Atomic Casualties give almost verbatim reports of the interplay between the various members. As such, they provide us with a way of listening in on how scientists and biomedical researchers converse – at least in formal meetings – about the possibilities and problems in their work.

At its February 1950 meeting the CAC heard from Dr Phillip Abelson about the early findings on radiation-induced cataracts in Hiroshima.[1] He recalled that a survey of induced radioactivity in Hiroshima and Nagasaki had been made in October 1945 by taking measurements along two diameters, at right angles, through the hypocentre. These investigators found that at one and one half kilometres from the hypocentre, the readings were equivalent to the background readings for that area. Their data fitted a smooth curve. The Naval Research Laboratory, utilizing this data, had made a number of calculations and had obtained data 'which was better fitted to theory'.

Dr Abelson told his colleagues that neutrons were known to behave in a peculiar manner. When they collide with a nitrogen atom, they bounce off elastically and they go through fifty to one hundred such elastic collisions before being captured. In the instant after the explosion of the atomic bomb, there is almost literally a sea of neutrons. These do not travel in straight lines. The formula for the intensity of neutrons would contain several terms, one being the inverse square law, a second being an exponential decrease with distance, and a third a constant. Such a formula could be established and it was found that the data collected at Hiroshima and Nagasaki and utilized by the Naval Resarch Laboratory agreed with this theory. The equation was normalized and utilizing the published statement that the bomb was equivalent to 20,000 tons of TNT (which was based on Fermi's methods for establishing the yield of the Trinity Test with a piece of paper dropped from four feet high, ten kilometres from the hypocentre) it was possible to obtain estimations of the neutron flux at various distances from the hypocentre.

With only one exception in the cases so far examined, all of the cataracts found in Japan were within 1080 metres of the hypocentre. This was in agreement with the neutron flux predicted on the basis of the theoretical calculations and the estimated amount of radiation required to produce cataracts with the cyclotron. As Dr Abelson remarked to the CAC in February 1950, 'The agreement between the theory and the observation appears to be almost too good to be true. The finding of the cataracts throws light on the problem of which is the most important in an atomic bomb explosion, the neutrons or the gamma rays. Originally it was believed that the gamma rays were the most important but it would appear that the neutrons produce the greater effects.'

Dr Abelson believed one could obtain a relatively good flux versus distance curve if it were possible to take all of the existing data into account. 'The radiation cataracts and other effects represent a tremendous biological experiment which has not yet been completely evaluated.' It took from two to eight years for radiation cataracts to develop. Dr Abelson said that the curve of the neutron flux falls off so rapidly that it would appear to be unlikely that any cataracts would be found beyond one and a half kilometres, almost certainly not beyond two kilometres. While some committee members felt that the survivors beyond two kilometres must be studied, others such as Dr Owen felt that a point of diminishing returns would be reached quite soon beyond two kilometres from the hypocentre. But there was considerable excitement at the possibility that the study of cataracts could serve to develop a 'biologic dosimeter' which would show a neat linear relationship between distance from the bomb, dose of radiation received and damage suffered.

Dr Winternitz wondered what the effects of neutrons on the gonads had been, and what impact that would have on the genetic studies. Dr Wilson pointed out that there was a difference between Hiroshima and Nagasaki because the cities had been bombed with two different bombs. Dr Winternitz said he felt that the radiation cataract problem raised the question of intrinsic controls to a new level. Dr Evans urged the extension of the study out to 3000 metres. Dr Abelson pointed out that each individual who had survived within 1000 metres of the hypocentre represented a unique biological specimen. He recommended that roughly half of the effort of the ABCC be devoted to this group.

Dr Bronk pointed out that going beyond 1.2 kilometres would be a study of distance effects whereas studying individuals within 1.2 kilometres would be a study of neutron effects in general. Dr Evans asked if it was not highly desirable to go beyond 1.2 kilometres. He suggested 3 kilometres because of known errors in the data. Dr Abelson, however, countered that the slope of the neutron flux curve is such that it falls off very rapidly with distance. If he were pressed, he would recommend only going as far as 1.5 kilometres. Colonel Tessmer pointed out that the case for neutrons being the most important agent was not completely proved. The epilation curve which had been worked out by the Joint Commission indicated that there were serious gamma effects extending for a very great distance beyond 1.2 kilometres. Dr Abelson said that there was reason to believe that if epilation occurred beyond 2 kilometres one must look for some reason other than any which had so far come to light. Dr Wilson pointed out that there was 'a very valuable problem' in the fact that two different kind of bombs had been utilized in Japan. There was a real possibility that more neutrons were produced by one than by the other and that gamma ray production might be quite the reverse. Careful measurements were needed in both instances in order to determine the neutron–gamma differences and that one might anticipate that the gamma ray intensity probably was much greater in Nagasaki.

Dr Neel remarked that the non-existence of radiation at various distances from the hypocentre had made the genetics work much more difficult. He asked if there were no radiation beyond 3000 metres. Dr

Abelson replied that there was reason to believe the radiation at 2 kilometres was quite small. Colonel Tessmer pointed out that the epilation data did not agree with Dr Abelson's statements since at 3000 metres there was a very real incidence of epilation. Dr Abelson suggested a possible explanation for the variation between the material he had presented and the epilation data. He had assumed that the bomb explosion was symetrical. However, even if it was asymmetrical, tongues of radiation may have extended out for some distance. A study of the epilation data might reveal such extensions.

Dr Lyon pointed out that Dr Stafford Warren had made calculations which indicated that there were spikes which went out radially in the course of the explosion and that these were not necessarily continuous. Dr Wilson corroborated this. Dr Evans reported some observations made recently in his laboratory which were preliminary in nature but which if proved to be true, would have great bearing on the problem in Japan. His laboratory had been experimenting with the combined effects of burns and radiation and found that a patient receiving 50 r and burns may have suffered effects which might be totally different from an individual who received 100 r but no burns.

The Field Director of the ABCC, Colonel Tessmer, then introduced another complexity. He remarked that there was reason to believe that the cataract patients must have been at least partially shielded or they would have died. Some of the cataract cases had burns about the head indicating that other parts of the body probably were shielded. No accurate shielding data had been obtained, however. Dr Evans remarked that there might be a great discrepancy between the epilation data and the cataract data because of many factors.

Colonel Tessmer asked whether or not, given concise details of the location of the person at the time of the bombing, it would be feasible to reconstruct the dose of radiation received, including the dosage resulting from scattering effects. Dr Abelson said he doubted that this would be possible but Dr Wilson said he thought such an approach would be very worthwhile. It might answer some of the questions which had been raised; it would be difficult without such an analysis to apply the type of data that Dr Abelson had developed. Preferential shielding was extremely important and that in the final analysis it was the quantity of radiation which reached the individual that caused the biological effects.

Dr Winternitz asked whether the data on the cataracts affected Dr Neel's feelings in regard to the genetics programme. Dr Neel replied that it was known that neutron units are three to four times as effective as gamma units in terms of ionization in tissue. In terms of mutations, gamma rays and neutrons might not differ in their effects. From Dr

Abelson's curve, it seemed that the neutron concentration falls off so fast beyond one and one-half kilometres that there is not much likelihood of a genetic neutron effect beyond this distance. At the same time, the genetics programme was not registering a large number of births from survivors within the one and one-half kilometres from the hypocentre. There were a number of variables which must be considered and in addition secondary factors such as the effect of temperature on the gonads might be even more important. Colonel Tessmer asked whether sterility was a factor in the studies. Dr Neel replied that it apparently was not and that it had been assumed that most of the survivors did not receive a sterilizing dose.

Dr Rivers said that 'it seems inappropriate to question the consequence' of the genetics study each year. Instead the effort should be directed towards getting the work accomplished. 'There being no method of obtaining an *a priori* answer, the experiment [*sic*] must be done.'

However, this discussion of these potentially confounding factors did not influence the discussion on the acceptability of dropping not only Sasebo but also Kure as external controls on the sample being studied by the ABCC. When Dr Zirkle raised the question of intrinsic controls again at this February 1950 meeting he was primarily concerned to keep Nagasaki – one of the bombed cities – in the study. 'If the program is going to be continued, it is essential that all possible data be obtained. Since Nagasaki represents one-fourth to one-third of the radiation data, studies must be continued there.'

Dr Rivers asked if the Committee could afford to sacrifice Kure in the genetics studies. Dr Neel indicated that he felt that this was a crucial decision and that the Committee should state its position clearly on the record disregarding the factor of cost. If after careful consideration it was found that the programme outlined by the Committee was too costly, then the decision as to what must be eliminated should be made by the AEC. Dr Neel acknowledged that he was disturbed by the cost in terms of what could be done in basic genetic research in the United States for a similar amount.

Dr Rivers said the Nagasaki subjects should not be dropped because their numbers were already so small; Dr Evans agreed that the mathematics of the problem were such that dropping Nagasaki might make the entire study worthless; it was already apparent that questionable results might be obtained even with Nagasaki included. Dr Winternitz asked Dr Neel what his opinion was about keeping Kure in the study. Dr Neel replied that there appeared to be a relatively large group of individuals in Hiroshima and Nagasaki who could be utilized as instrinsic controls. If something had to be dropped from the programme he would recommend that Kure be dropped before Nagasaki. However, eliminating either of these two cities would be undesirable. Dr Winternitz said he felt that intrinsic controls and other factors made Nagasaki more important than Kure and he would rate in importance, from greatest to least, Hiroshima, Nagasaki and Kure.

Dr Neel – the contracted consultant – reminded the Committee on Atomic Casualties that if the original considerations which formed the basis for the present programme were sound, then all three cities were required. However, if the AEC could not support studies in all three cities, then the Committee must be forced to drop Kure.

The Committee then moved into Executive Session. Dr Winternitz said that questions regarding the possible returns from the study had been raised from the beginning and there had never been a clear picture as to whether the cost and the work involved would be returned in kind with data on the fundamental problem of the medical and biological effects of the atomic bombings. Throughout there had been a great deal of concern about the financial implications. The second control city, Sasebo, was dropped over two years before. 'No one can be blamed for the changed financial situation, for the changed point of view of the project, or for the energy which has been expended in developing them.' But after three years, it had become evident that the Advisory Committee in Biology and Medicine of the AEC and the Committee on Atomic Casualties were not seeing entirely eye to eye and it was felt desirable for an *ad hoc* group composed of members of these two Committees to meet, and they had done so on 4 February. This meeting had requested the ABCC staff to prepare a budget, which was submitted to Dr Shields Warren on 9 February. The projected budget was $2,000,000 a year for Hiroshima plus a one-time cost of $500,000 for housing to cut down the 100,000 working hours lost each year in travelling between the staff accommodation in Kure and the laboratories in Hiroshima. There was only $2,500,000 – the amount required to operate in Hiroshima and one other city – Nagasaki or Kure. The CAC must choose.

Dr Winternitz said that the *ad hoc* meeting had served to clarify his own point of view regarding the project in Japan. He emphasized that the researchers in Japan must be in close contact with the work in America and that results of animal experiments in this country should be made available as rapidly as possible to the workers in Japan to assist them in focusing their efforts.

Dr Warren said that he would have to make every effort possible in order to obtain even $2,500,000 and that he felt certain that the budget group in the AEC would not entertain a request for additional funds at a later date. It was his opinion that, as things developed, items in the Los

Alamos budget, for example, would take precedence over items such as those in Japan. But once the programme was established at a certain level of operations and once results began to come out, it would be possible to maintain the programme at that level. The rocky period was the period of preparation; a similar experience was occurring in relation to the Brookhaven laboratories.

Dr Lyon and Dr Winternitz proposed that the Committee operate a full programme in Hiroshima and a paediatrics programme, including the pregnancy termination studies, in Nagasaki. Dr Rivers said the Committee should discuss whether or not such a programme would be scientifically sound. Dr Bronk enquired whether it would include the cataract studies. Colonel Tessmer said that in the minds of the staff of the ABCC, the cataract problem had been incidental in their consideration of the investigative programme as originally established. The cataract survey was a superficial study of the patient to solve only one small point in the programme. It was an inefficient method of study and it detracted from the other parts of the programme. Properly set up, the same information could become available on a much more satisfactory basis if the patients were studied more thoroughly.

Dr Bronk observed that with limited manpower and money, the Committee must decide whether to examine a few individuals very carefully or examine larger numbers less carefully. Dr Rivers noted that it had been postulated that neutrons were the cause of the radiation cataracts but at the same time there appeared to have been fewer neutrons produced in the Nagasaki explosion than in the Hiroshima explosion. Therefore, if one examined the survivors in Nagasaki within one kilometre of the hypocentre, the results might support to the idea that the causative factor in cataract formation is neutrons. Colonel Tessmer was uncertain with the funds being contemplated for Nagasaki whether personnel and facilities could be diverted from other problems.

Dr Evans said there had not been sufficient emphasis on how bad surveys can be. In his personal experience, after twelve hours he would not be doing survey work properly because of fatigue. He found also that by the second day he was becoming somewhat disgusted. This appeared to be one of the very great dangers of the survey approach.

Dr Rivers asked Dr Neel whether, since the genetics programme was one of the large programmes of the ABCC and the first established, would giving up Kure mean that the genetics programme would become impossible? Dr Neel replied that the programme contemplated in Dr Lyon's motion meant that the ABCC would be operating in Hiroshima and Nagasaki under dissimilar circumstances. Every effort had been made in the past to expand the work in each of the centres in order that both the control and the exposed subjects would receive the same amount of attention and as nearly identical study as possible. Now, however, the question arose of the comparability of data of the two areas. The proposed programme changed the problems facing the Committee. If accepted it might mean that the Committee would find itself attempting to compare the Nagasaki exposed personnel to the Hiroshima exposed personnel, and the Nagasaki controls to the Hiroshima controls. Dr Rivers asked whether Dr Neel was willing to go ahead with the study on this basis. Dr Neel replied that he knew the contemplated changes would weaken the programme and that he was greatly concerned about these changes. Dr Bronk suggested it might be reasonable to go ahead for a year on the basis the Committee proposed and then reevaluate the programme at the end of that time. Dr Bronk asked whether such a programme would be scientifically satisfactory. Dr Neel responded that, viewed from the standpoint of a laboratory experiment, the proposed programme left much to be desired. He did not believe it was his responsibility to suggest to the Committee on Atomic Casualties whether or not such a programme would be satisfactory.

Dr Rivers – chairman of the committee charged with advising on the scientific issues before the ABCC – then asked the two field directors, Dr Tessmer and Dr Taylor, if they believed that the 'program as proposed would be a creditable scientific job'. Colonel Tessmer replied that, if the programme were limited in regard to the number of adult patients, there would be a number of problems which could not be answered. For example, in the leukaemia programme it would be necessary to examine large numbers of individuals in order to establish a control incidence. It must be remembered that if it was contemplated that intrinsic controls would be utilized, they would subtract from the number of irradiated patients who could be examined in the same facility. Such a programme would make impossible certain of the things which one would like to know. In reference to intrinsic controls, Colonel Tessmer – a radiologist by training – also raised the technical question of the possible effects of any ingested fission products. These were not measurable with present instruments. He would like to pose this as a question but, if the question were answered to reasonable satisfaction, he would think that Kure was less necessary than Nagasaki.

Dr Zirkle pointed out that working only in Hiroshima and Nagasaki one would really be dealing with three groups. First, those known to be irradiated; second, those who were in the city at the time of the bombing but who were at some distance from the hypocentre and who, presumably, were not irradiated; and third, those people who had moved into the city since the bombings. Dr Lawrence asked whether there was any reason to assume that individuals who had moved into the city since the explosions might have been exposed to residual radioactivity. Dr Wilson replied that his impression was based on measurements which had been made by friends of his and by the Japanese. He believed one did not have to worry about induced radiation and fission products; however, in order to answer the problem satisfactorily, it would be necessary to make a number of calculations. Dr Lyon expressed the opinion that there was very little reason to believe that there had been any internal radiation hazard at either Hiroshima or Nagasaki. Dr Wilson remarked that the explosions at Bikini were different in that they were essentially ground blasts. He said there might have been a few small areas in Nagasaki and Hiroshima where fallout had occurred.

On the basis of these discussions in February 1950, the Committee on Atomic Casualties agreed unanimously that the ABCC conduct a full programme of investigation in Hiroshima and a paediatrics programme, including the pregnancy termination studies, in Nagasaki. Dr Bronk went on record saying that he felt the actions of the Committee had been a good example as to how a National Research Council Committee should function. The Committee had considered the scientific merits of the case and the questions had been settled on that basis.

Dr Bronk and Dr Rivers expressed appreciation for the splendid spirit of Colonel Tessmer and Dr Taylor, who were working in Japan under such difficult conditions. Colonel Tessmer then almost as an afterthought brought up another complication. He raised the question of the desirability of making an attempt to reconstruct a scale model of the various surroundings of individuals who were exposed to radiation in Hiroshima and who survived. Dr Wilson agreed and said it was not necessary for a physicist to assist in the reconstruction work; an engineer or a radiologist could do an equally creditable job. He raised the question, however, as to the possibility of determining the neutron flux which had occurred. These data would, of course, be basic to any further consideration and to any interpretations which the Committee would make. If one were able to collect all of the measurements which had been made on the Alamogordo, Bikini, Eniwetok, Hiroshima and Nagasaki explosions then one might be in a better position to interpret the data accumulated by the ABCC and in particular to make some estimates of the dosages on the basis of the reconstructions of rooms, buildings, streets and so on. Dr Wilson said that to the best of his knowledge no analysis of the physical data had been made which would be suitable for the Committee's purposes. Dr Zirkle moved and Dr Lyon seconded a motion that the Committee authorize Dr Wilson to proceed with the collection and analysis of the quantity of radiation created in all of the atomic bomb explosions. Dr Wilson asked for funds to hire some graduate students to assist him in making the necessary calculations.

Notes

1. Minutes of CAC, dated
21 February 1950.

Nine

It was a full year before the Committee on Atomic Casualties met again to review the work of the Atomic Bomb Casualty Commission. The ABCC was in crisis. The Atomic Energy Commission's Division of Biology and Medicine was prepared to fund it at only $1,000,000 for the fiscal year 1952, rather than the $2,500,000 that had been sought. The members of the Committee on Atomic Casualties were informed of this prospect just before the February 1951 meeting. None of them, including the Chairman, had been involved in the discussions of the Division of Biology and Medicine. The Chairman, Dr Rivers, said[1] that this was merely a polite way of forcing the ABCC to close. Already under pressure to constrict the research agenda, the ABCC was now fighting for its very existence in a Cold War climate that was more interested in nuclear superiority than research on the biomedical effects on the survivors of Hiroshima and Nagasaki.

Committee members agreed that the personnel of the ABCC were excellent and the experimental (*sic*) design sound. Dr Winternitz reminded them that the costs had gone up sharply for a programme which from the first Dr Neel had insisted that results would be dubious at best, and which must continue for a long time. Dr Rivers agreed that the *ad hoc* committee had agreed at the outset that a ten year minimum period would be required for collection of an adequate amount of data. He said that he had understood that a budget of $2,000,000 would be made available yearly.

The Chairman of the advisory committee indicated that he felt that the order to close had best be accepted. The issue was how to close down the operation with the maximum salvage. He called on Dr Neel for suggestions. Dr Neel naturally argued the priority of his genetics programme. He said he understood there was a feeling that studies yielding positive findings like cataracts and leukaemia should be intensified, while studies which may yield negative results such as the genetics work should be cut off. He insisted that establishment of negative results was as important as establishment of positive results. The genetics programme, being intimately connected with all the other programmes, should continue to run with them. But if the genetics programme were to terminate in June 1951, there would have been accumulated data on 50,000 to 55,000 pregnancy terminations and paediatric data on the follow-up of 10,000 babies. These data could be analysed in Michigan in eighteen months, if properly funded.

The main opposition to continuation of Neel's lion's share of the budget was Dr Machle, who thought that the continuation of the somatic studies should have precedence over the genetic epidemiological survey. Dr Machle argued[2] that 'in view of the costs of the Genetics program in relation to the predicted likelihood of significant return from it, it is our opinion that this program should be abandoned forthwith.' This would enable the ABCC to close down the Nagasaki studies, according to Dr Machle. He was supported on cost grounds by both the new field director, Dr Taylor, and by John C. Bugher who was about to become Director of the Division of Biology and Medicine of the AEC.

There was discussion of the possibility of dissolving the Committee on Atomic Casualties and reconstituting it as a committee of the National Academy of Sciences which would bring together all information about radiation casualties, not just those at Hiroshima and Nagasaki. The Committee then resolved that the Atomic Bomb Casualty Commission be terminated because of lack of financial support.

But the Committee's threat to close down the ABCC if the budget allocated by the AEC was a mere million dollars a year succeeded in calling the AEC's bluff. In September 1951 a newly constituted Committee on Atomic Casualties met under the chairmanship of Dr Detlev Bronk (although in fact there were few new faces around the table). The Peace Treaty with Japan was due to be signed in a few weeks, and the Committee needed to consider the implications of the return to full sovereignty of Japan for its status, having been initiated under the Occupation. Dr Bronk suggested that the Committee be renamed in order to 'avoid some bitterness' on the part of former members.[3]

Dr Bugher rehearsed the history of the ABCC for the benefit of the few new faces around the table.

> There has been much change of plan and orientation during the five years of the Commission's existence. At the beginning, two centers for studies of exposed cases, and two more for control studies were planned. Realization of excessive costs involved, and difficulty of operating the controls led to the abandonment of all effort to create a base at Sasebo. At a later date, after the interim construction at Kure had been attempting to serve as a control

for both the Hiroshima and Nagasaki studies, it was decided in view of the high expenses involved, and the lack of enthusiasm of the natives at Kure for studies on themselves when they had not been exposed to the bomb, to abandon the external control studies altogether, and to rely upon internal controls at Hiroshima and Nagasaki. This was considered valid because of the growing realization that residual radioactivity at the bombed localities had dropped to a non-significant level immediately after the explosions.

Dr Bugher said that 'the gloom prevailing last autumn over the indicated excessive cost of the operation, and the questionable wisdom of continuing it in the face of a bad military situation' had passed. 'As a result of many field trips and discussions, and again of the improvement of the military situation, it became clear that the operation could continue, with modification. The administrative pattern, designed for four centers, was too elaborate and expensive; the amount of American personnel of all classes was too high; the scattering of facilities over the Kure–Hiroshima area was inherently expensive in time and cost. Consolidation was imperative.' The ABCC now had more than a thousand employees of whom 918 were Japanese.

But there were clear constraints before the Committee and Dr Neel now cut his cloth accordingly. Dr Goodpasture asked about the necessity for study of 240,000 cases for the genetics programme. Dr Neel replied that estimates varied but that certainly 150,000 must be studied – or 15,000 new cases for ten years. Dr Warren pointed out that the Hiroshima and Nagasaki bombs were different and may differ in their effect. Dr Winternitz inquired what was known of the latent period. Dr Warren pointed out that one fundamental difference between this material and that of the radiologists was that they were studying the effect of a summation of a large number of small doses.

Dr Goodpasture felt that where the genetics programme had been well considered and arranged, the planning of the leukaemia study was weak – for instance, it relied in part on the study of diagnoses from death certificates, although it was recognized that clinical pathology in Japan was unreliable. There were also no accurate records from which to obtain the basic incidence, and the Commission had, therefore, perforce to use US statistics. This raised some question of the validity of the study. Every attempt should be made to overcome these defects. Physical examination of the 1000 metre group may be sufficient for study of the exposed, but what should be the control? The blood survey did not seem to be practical, so how could an adequate statistical control be obtained? He insisted on the importance of valid methods of case finding, since increased leukaemia incidence, if real, would constitute the first and so far the only somatic pathological sequel to the bomb which had been observed first in Japan.

Dr Neel said that examination at birth revealed at least 80 per cent of everything found at nine months. But the later examination was useful because in cold weather the Japanese homes were so uncomfortable that the infants were sometimes examined without undressing them, or uncovering only one limb at a time. In his written report to this meeting[4] Neel argued 'Only about half of the terminations in Hiroshima and Nagasaki presently involve an exposed parent or parents, so that there is available in these two cities a sufficient amount of control material.' The analysis to date of children born 1948–50 to parents one or both of whom were within 2000 metres of the hypocentre showed a '10–15 per cent increase in the gross malformation rate among the children of parents who received significant amounts of irradiation'. It was Neel himself who now asked 'Does the additional data obtained at the nine-month follow-up contribute sufficiently to the program to justify the effort which goes into the accumulation of this data?'

What had been envisaged as a multi-generation study of the survivors could, the principal researcher was suggesting, be cut off after barely four years with only 150,000 examinations rather than 240,000.

Two months later, at the November 1951 meeting of the Committee on Atomic Casualties, Dr Taylor, who was now Field Director of the ABCC, reported[5] that approximately 62,000 of the (revised) goal of 150,000 genetics samples had been studied. Dr Neel said the genetics studies should continue for eight to ten years but the geneticists felt ready to begin to publish their preliminary findings.

Dr Taylor mentioned that contrary to the assumptions about residual radiation, nine cases of epilation had been found beyond 4000 metres. Members responded to this anomaly by asking what new information was available on residual radiation. Dr Taylor replied that there were only rumours from the Tracerlab chemists of residual radiation, but their report was highly classified. A Japanese report on the subject was being translated.

Dr Lawrence noted that researchers working in Hiroshima and Nagasaki had no knowledge of the probable amount of exposure of patients because of these classification difficulties. Collection of spot examples was inadequate. Mr Eisenbud said that biological, especially human material, would be useful to determine the effect of ingested radioactive substances. Dr Taylor said that at one time these were readily available; scores of Nagasaki bomb victims had been re-inhumed in a common grave but collection of bone samples had not been undertaken by the ABCC. Considerable discussion ensued on the existence and whereabouts of various materials brought back from Japan since 1946 for residual radioactivity studies which were scattered in various research offices and laboratories in Washington. Some soil samples collected at the Nishiyama reservoir spillway were thought to be in Dr Brues' possession, while biological material consisting of wheat, insects and lizards collected near the Mitsubishi steelworks were stored in Washington. Three soil samples were in the CAC office. In addition much material had been collected in 1949 to 1950 by Mr Yamasaki. Dr Bugher observed that this illustrated the unsatisfactory nature of piecemeal assignments. All samples should be recorded and studied. The Committee invited Dr Bugher and Mr Eisenbud to write up their proposals to correct this situation.

But in opening the next meeting of the CAC, in March 1952, the chairman, Dr Lawrence noted[6] what he termed the continued preoccupation with residual radiation. Mr Eisenbud reported that bones from an individual who had entered Hiroshima immediately after the blast and had subsequently died of leukaemia were found to be free from significant amounts of deposited radioactive elements. The 200 or so specimens of soil and ashed vegetation collected in both cities in 1950 were only very slightly radioactive and this was attributed to natural potassium. There was therefore no evidence that residual radiation was a factor complicating the problems of dosage and shielding.

Dr Bugher said that calculations on radiation at Hiroshima were uncertain, since the bomb was of a type not tested previously or since. The energy spectrum was unknown. If enough information on the Hiroshima-type bomb became available to make a study of dosage, shielding and backscatter profitable – and they were all very difficult problems – the study should be made at Los Alamos rather than in Japan. The Committee asked Dr Bugher, Dr Hodges and Dr Lawrence to determine what the ABCC should request of the AEC in the way of shielding studies and related problems – five years after the ABCC was initiated, seven years after the bombings, and on the eve of the completion of the genetics studies.

Dr Brandt commented that while the ABCC programme was excellent it still retained the features of a survey. It was very difficult to maintain enthusiasm for repeated physical examinations while no indications of change were detectable. Extensive discussion followed but no means of avoiding a great amount of tedious work was seen. It was repeated that lack of sequelae, if well established, would be 'the most gratifying of findings'.

Three months later at the June 1952 meeting of the CAC Dr Neel reversed himself. He said[7] that while it had been originally estimated that ten years' accumulation of information would be necessary, extension had been possible in two directions – the inspection of infants and the study of early pregnancy terminations. He now maintained that each passing year afforded progressively less pertinent data on exposed parents, and even if the amount of data were doubled the error would decrease by only approximately 30 per cent. 'The indication is that at the end of the first five years a significant level may have been reached and the investigation of further cases can be discontinued.' He did acknowledge that the level of significance required of this foreshortened data remained unsettled. But he proposed to divert the major effort to analysis at the end of 1952, while maintaining minimal activity in collection of further raw data.

Dr Plough felt it unwise to discontinue data collection as soon as a significant level was reached. Dr Davison pointed out that figures obtained from now on would depend more and more on prepubertal exposure to radiation. Dr Neel said that there were fewer of these cases than of exposed adults, and that irradiation of immature spermatozoa leads to fewer mutations than does irradiation in maturity, while in the female all ova are present at birth. Dr Plough added that with radiation it is generally considered easier to sterilize the female permanently than the male; Dr S. Warren remarked that transient sterilization of the male is easier. Dr Brandt mentioned Brookhaven experiments in which it was shown that the stage of development of Drosophila eggs determines their sensitivity to irradiation. Dr Neel suggested that there was a difference in that ova in the human progress to a certain stage of development and then become quiescent.

At this point, according to the minutes 'Leaving the discussion', the CAC resolved that the assembly and analysis of genetics data obtained through the calendar year 1952 be made; that accumulation of genetics data be continued for an indefinite time; and that further recommendations be based upon study of the completed analysis. These recommendations should be made by a committee appointed to examine the completed analysis of genetics data consisting as far as practicable of the original committee on genetics. Dr Plough recommended the inclusion of individuals not connected with the NRC or the AEC. But the Committee resolved that Dr Bronk and Dr Neel should make the final selection of the members of this review committee of Dr Neel's work.

Dr Davison reported on the growth and development programme. Approximately forty children a day were being examined and there were already several important findings. The high incidence of microcephaly (7 of 11) in children born to women who were in the first three months of pregnancy and were within 1200 metres of the hypocentre when the bomb exploded, contrasted with the absence of microcephaly in all others, raised, according to Dr Davison, the serious question of the advisability of sterilization or abortion of gravid females after exposure to heavy irradiation. Another study had shown 15 per cent of children within the 1200 metre radius had cataracts. Dental surveys showed hypoplasia and delayed eruption of teeth. Numerous differences in growth and development had been found between the exposed and control groups, although destitution had possibly played a role in this. Congenital dislocation of the hip showed an initial incidence of 15 per cent at birth but dropped spontaneously to 3 per cent at nine months. Altogether the growth and development programme had been so productive that any curtailment at present would be most undesirable. There were clear differences in the number of survivors in the under 2000 metres range in the two cities who had experienced epilation. While it was thought that publication of these results without clear statements of the dosages that had caused the microcephaly would be dangerous, it was decided it was better to publish than to be thought to be suppressing the evidence.

Mr Eisenbud reported on residual radiation studies. Of one hundred samples of vegetable ash and soil from Hiroshima and Nagasaki, fifty exhibited slight radioactivity. Identification of the active matter, if possible, would be difficult. Bones from a human skeleton were found negative. The findings of residual radiation, as reported by Dr Stafford Warren in 1945, were summarized. The highest radiation measurement at Hiroshima (6 October 1945) was 0.4 mr/hr, which would represent a total dose of about 4.2 r to an individual who remained at the hypocentre for sixty days following the instant of detonation. At Nagasaki the highest radiation measurement (26 September 1945) was 1.8 mr/hr, representing a cumulative dose of 14.2 r to an individual who remained at the hypocentre. These cumulative values were considered to be insignificant in comparison with the dose these individuals would have received from prompt gamma and neutron radiation. Dr Shields Warren corroborated this last statement. Japanese white counts were worthless because of the poor quality and condition of their pipettes, but the American group, using good equipment, found normal counts.

The Committee on Atomic Casualties progressively foreclosed on the genetics studies throughout 1953. At its February meeting[8] Dr Davison cautioned against too much faith in the statements by the victims of their locations at the moments of explosion and asked if the uncertainties were sufficient to vitiate the significance of the data collected so far. Dr Davison thought the last two years' compilation to be sound; the earlier data were less satisfactory, but the limits of uncertainty could be fairly well established for these early studies and should be included in the final report.

There was increased optimism about using lens changes as a measure of radiation received, of using the incidence and development of cataracts as a biological dosimeter. As the Committee tried to agree on its priorities between the various clinical studies that had been initiated by various investigators and the genetics survey which was still taking up a third or more of the ABCC's budget, Dr Bronk suggested that Dr Wearn might be able to assemble a small group of medical men to scrutinize the objectives and the results – but he felt that this should not be the present Committee, which was too closely connected with the operation. But according to the Minutes, several of the other committee members thought that 'finding another interested group would be difficult, and that inordinate time would be lost in their indoctrination.' Was the ABCC to continue to conduct a programme to find low level negative results, or a frequently reviewed programme where the basic premises were recurrently questioned? Dr Bronk suggested that it was an indefinite programme but not perennial; annual appraisal of the programme and its objectives was necessary; a geneticists group should evaluate the genetics programme, a medical group should consider the medical aspects. It was time to begin publishing results and findings for lay and scientific circulation.

Dr Shields Warren chaired the September 1953 meeting of the Committee on Atomic Casualties which finally terminated the genetics survey. Dr Neel summarized[9] the preliminary analysis of the genetic data. Parents were classified into five categories with respect to radiation exposure – not present at the bombings, present at a distance greater than 2500 metres, present at a distance between 1845 and 2500 metres, present at a distance less than 1845 metres, exposed followed by epilation or petechiae. These classes were through to correspond roughly to the radiation exposures of zero, minimal, 30 to 60 r, 100 to 150 r, and 200 r or more (300 r average). Evaluation of the dosage received by individuals in groups three and four was very difficult, not least because of the difference between the two bombs. Most disagreement centred on the third category; the text 'Effect of Atomic Weapons' indicated that this group received relatively little irradiation, but the biological data tended to suggest otherwise.

The results to date had been negative in most respects but the Nagasaki sex-ratio differences seemed to be significant. The birth weights of the babies born to those assumed to have been exposed were, contrary to prediction from the laboratory genetic data, heavier than those born to parents who were considered controls, but this anomaly was attributed by Dr Neel to parity differences between the groups under study. Analysis of pregnancy terminations by considering male and female exposures separately failed to reveal positive effects.

Dr Neel then considered the chances of improving the confidence level by continuing observations beyond the present. There had been an unexpectedly large drop in the birth rate in Japan as a result of wide acceptance of the birth control programme. Calculations based on the expected number of pregnancy terminations in the exposed group for the next four years, forecast by extrapolating linearly from the birth figures for the past five years, indicated that only a 14 to 22 per cent decrease in the standard error of the observed differences would result, taking sex-ratio as the reference point. It would appear that the excessive effort required to effect relatively small improvement was not justified and that further collection of raw data for the genetics programme should be discontinued.

Dr Bugher asked how much data had been put aside in excluding mothers over 35 years old. Dr Neel replied 10 per cent in Hiroshima and 15 per cent in Nagasaki. Dr Bugher suggested that since the declining birth rate in Japan was an attempt to solve the problems of population pressures, an equilibrium level would presumably be reached. Linear extrapolation might therefore not lead to a correct estimate of the number of additional pregnancies available in the next four years. Dr Neel explained that linear extrapolation was chosen as the simplest approximation.

Dr Stern pointed out that the genetics programme was started after the genetics conference had met in 1947. Their recommendation, working at a 3 per cent confidence level, was that the study was worthwhile, because so little was known of human genetics. At its next meeting in July 1953 the conference, after examining the preliminary analysis of the six-year accumulation of data, recommended that field work terminated by June 1954. The recommendation was based on the very poor prospect of improving the data now gathered. Dr Stern referred to the uncertainty of human sensitivity to radiation. According to Sewall Wright, exposure to 3 r might double the mutation rate; on the other hand, 300 r might be necessary. In mice 50 r was known to double the rate. With such a factor of uncertainty, the small improvement of confidence level to be gained by continuing the collection of raw data would serve little purpose.

Dr Warren said that the Committee had before it for consideration a clear recommendation by a group of competent geneticists that the gathering of field data for the genetics study be terminated. The Field Director of the ABCC, Dr Taylor remarked that well established negative data were as valuable as positive data. In any case, the Commission's activity must be determined by the availability of personnel, and by public relations. Dr Bugher, Director of the Atomic Energy Commission's Division of Biology and Medicine, said that he wished to record satisfaction with the way in which funds had been utilized and progress had been made despite inflation in Japan. Although not disagreeing with the recommendations of the genetics conference, he felt that something might be said for continuation of the genetics programme until the analysis had progressed so far that all concerned were satisfied. Since much effort had been expended in setting up the programme, it might be desirable to consult with Japanese geneticists for an opinion about continuation.

To Dr Lawrence's suggestions that the generally negative results might possibly be due to insufficiently thorough analysis, Dr Stern replied that the statement of the genetics conference was not intended for distribution as final. He and Dr Taylor urged consultation with Japanese geneticists about continuation. Dr Bugher remarked that as four or five years of additional data would effect only a 14 per cent to 25 per cent improvement in the confidence level, continuation for six months could be expected to contribute practically nothing. The decision to terminate became, therefore, an administrative matter, 'beyond the experience of this Committee, which has the duty of making scientific judgements'. The Committee on Atomic Casualties then resolved unanimously that it concurred with the opinion of the conference of geneticists that the genetics programme of ABCC had developed to a point at which emphasis should shift from the collection of field data to the intensive analysis of the accumulated data of the past six years. The Committee therefore recommended the immediate phasing-out of the field studies in such a way as to cause the minimum administrative dislocation, continuing only such of the studies as the director and the genetics consultants deemed to be scientifically desirable, in particular the continued accumuluation of data on sex-ratios. The director and staff should consult closely with Japanese geneticists so that they would be able to continue under their own direction whichever of the terminating studies they might wish to pursue.

As William J. Schull later remarked,[10] 'In an institutional setting, one's freedom as an investigator can be compromised by institutional needs and by advice that might be sound or might be capricious. A review panel can impose directions without accepting any of the responsibility for misguided advice. There is an oracular element to this process that is troubling. Fortunately, at the ABCC the reviewers rarely imposed their judgement; indeed, their comments were generally uncritical. It was difficult to know, however, whether this signalled approbation or merely a poorly prepared group of referees.'

Notes

1. Minutes of the CAC, dated
3 February 1951 NAS

2. Memo to Dr Winternitz from Dr
Machle, NRS Division of Medical
Sciences, dated 2 February 1951; Analysis
of financial and personnel outlook for
ABCC', appendix to Minutes of the CAC,
dated 3 February 1951, NAS.

3. Minutes of the CAC, dated
24 September 1951, NAS.

4. Report to CAC Appendix II of Minutes
of the CAC, dated 24 September 1951,
NAS.

5. Minutes of the CAC, dated
21 November 1951, NAS.

6. Minutes of the CAC, dated
27 March 1952, NAS.

7. Minutes of the CAC, dated
18 June 1952, NAS.

8. Minutes of the CAC, dated
21 February 1953, NAS.

9. Minutes of the CAC, dated
13 September 1953, NAS.

10. William J. Schull, *Songs of Praise*
(Harvard University Press, 1990) p.222.

Ten

The results of the studies on the effects of exposure to the atomic bomb on pregnancy outcomes in Hiroshima and Nagasaki were presented simultaneously by James Neel to the first International Congress on Human Genetics in Copenhagen and by William Schull to a symposium on genetics organized in Japan by the International Union of Biological Sciences in 1954. Schull recalled[1] his experience in presenting the first results to his colleagues. 'Attendance at this symposium read like a contemporary *Who's Who* in genetics.' It included J. B. S. Haldane, the British geneticist who, like Hermann Muller, had actively supported the Communist Party in the 1930s.

Several of the most distinguished participants in the symposium went on to Hiroshima to participate in an informal review of the genetic activities of the Commission. According to Schull, this informal review had two aims: to determine what further genetic studies, if any, could be done in Hiroshima and Nagasaki, and to draw Japanese geneticists into the work of the ABCC. 'Neither of these objectives was especially well served since, save for myself, none of the other participants, all of whom were experimentalists, had a grasp of the research milieu in Japan nor an appreciation of the complexities of epidemiological studies.'

It was the unanimous recommendation of this panel to shut down the epidemiological studies on the pregnancy outcomes. Hermann Muller had visited the ABCC geneticists in 1951 but Neel and Schull had not felt it necessary to modify their research designs to meet the concerns of the laboratory 'experimentalists', although they often referred to their own study as an experiment. They were falling between several stools and would face criticism from several sides on their methodology. But the unique opportunity to study the first impacts on pregnancy of the two atomic bombs had already been lost – the study did not get under way until early 1948, by which time more than two years of data on reproductive outcomes had been lost, and even then it did not capture data before the fifth month of pregnancy. The sample had been progressively conflated until the distinction between radiated and control samples had virtually been lost, and few observers were confident that the post-war migrants into the two cities were a reliable control sample.

There was increasing appreciation of the role that residual radiation might be playing in reproductive outcomes and the possible genetic cost past the first generation. Neel and Schull had ended up relying heavily on those listed as survivors of the detonations in the 1950 census – and then only those who had not moved out of Hiroshima and Nagasaki. Schull later acknowledged[2] that this census 'had certain important limitations. Since it was conducted more than five years after the event, it provided no basis for determining those survivors who succumbed between 1945 and 1950. Nor did it include those Koreans or American Japanese who had been repatriated in the interim, nor the Australian, Dutch and Indonesian prisoners of war exposed in Nagasaki who returned to their homeland with the cessation of hostilities.' Moreover, Japan's crude birth rate had fallen from thirty or so per thousand to about sixteen during this period as a consequence of a birth control programme. 'This had awesome implications for our study: a fall in the birth rate could be precipitous enough to compromise our ability to collect sufficient data to evaluate the radiation hazard or, worse still, could introduce biases that would be difficult to manage, particularly if pregnancies were more likely to be interrupted if one or more parents had been exposed.'[3]

In their preliminary report released in 1953[4] Neel and his colleagues had argued that their early findings of no statistically significant differences between the group they assumed had been irradiated and those they assumed had not been exposed 'if taken at face value, are entirely consistent with what is known of the radiation genetics of a wide variety of plant and animal material, including Drosophila and mice'. This assumption that laboratory findings in plants and animals could be simply extrapolated to a human population exposed to all but lethal doses of ionizing radiation was questioned in some quarters where it was felt that 'since our expectations came mostly from studies on Drosophila, a genetically peculiar animal in some respects, we really did not have realistic expectations in mammals'.[5]

Others questioned the way the concept of statistical significance was being used with the data. One reminded his colleagues that back in 1923 James Mavor of Union College reported that he had X-rays that were producing mutations in Drosophila, 'but the data weren't significant, and he was rather laughed out of the meeting. We are worshipping significance too much. An insignificant result may mean that you haven't worked at it long enough. Muller demonstrated it about 1927. It was an advance in technique. Muller could do it, and prove it, where Mavor could do it but hadn't proved it.'

Schull recalled that in 1954:

> The evidence was now compelling that the frequency of leukemia was higher among the survivors, in rough proportion to dose. However, we still did not have estimates of individual doses and, of necessity, had to use the distance from the hypocenter of the survivors as a rough measure of exposure. Simple distances have their limitations, however, for they do not take into account the shielding that could have lessened the exposure to some degree nor do they allow for the attenuation of the radiation as it passed through the tissues of the body. These short-comings made it difficult to determine whether there was or was not a threshold, that is, a dose below which no effect of radiation occurred. Since it had been argued on theoretical grounds that a threshold was unlikely, proof of this conjecture was a matter of substantial concern in the regulation of exposures that might occur in the workplace or through accidents.[6]

In 1954 Neel and Schull each published a paper in a book on *Statistics and Mathematics in Biology*[7]. Neel described the studies on the potential genetic effects of the atomic bombs in Japan as being research on single-exposure, whole body irradiation of extreme intensity.[8] He stated clearly his assumption that 'The available evidence, derived from a wide variety of plant and animal forms, indicates that the genetic effect of irradiation of brief duration is proportional to the dosage. There is no evidence for a threshold effect. The question at issue in Hiroshima and Nagasaki is not whether there were genetic consequences of the bomb but rather whether these effects were of sufficient magnitude to result in detectable effects upon the children of irradiated parents.' Although in Japan the social stigma surrounding the birth of a deformed child was greater than in the US, he felt confident that there had been a minimal loss of information through concealment and that they had achieved a 95 per cent level of completement of registration of pregnancies after the fifth month. The work was complex, both logistically and statistically. Hence it was not, now that the results were about to come out, 'an undertaking to be judged by the usual standards of laboratory design. Rather, this is an attempt to extract the maximum amount of information possible from a unique situation which we all sincerely hope will never again materialize. Quite aside from its theoretical implications, information of this type would have a very considerable practical value in allaying vicious rumours in the event of a conflict in which the use of atomic weapons was widespread.'

Schull agreed[9] that 'the question is not whether there were genetic consequences but rather whether the genetic effects were of sufficient magnitude to be measurable in the first-generation children of exposed parents.' He acknowledged that no specific time after the bombings was used as a reference point in determining nonexposure and that this was a tacit assumption that residual radiation was negligible but 'no other course of action seems feasible'. He also emphasized that in all cases the classification of an individual with respect to exposure was based on the history obtained from that person. Moreover, the populations of Hiroshima and Nagasaki were found to differ significantly in mean age and in the amount of consanguinity – both factors which would influence pregnancy outcomes. There were, in Schull's words, 'a plethora of variables' in the study even with the elimination of the two control cities. Schull sought to do 'statistical justice' to these data but warned that they were collected 'with the full knowledge that the neatness in design of a laboratory experiment was out of the question'. However, even in 1954, he felt that it was possible to estimate 'fairly reliably', the upper limit of damage.

But even with these caveats the results from the genetics studies conducted by Neel and Schull were used immediately to reassure other populations who were now being exposed to nuclear detonations. John C. Bugher, Director of the Division of Biology and Medicine of the AEC, and the member of the advisory committee of the ABCC who had probably been most influential in constricting the studies for cost reasons, told[10] a press conference on the eve of the Upshot-Knothole tests in the Nevada desert in 1955:

We've been operating in Japan for several years, in fact since the war, the very important study of the long-term effect of the bombs used at Hiroshima and Nagasaki. An enormous effort has been made to detect in children of persons exposed to those bombs any evidence of genetic change. Now there we're talking of people exposed to large amounts of radiation – in many cases just short of a killing amount. They had doses measured in two hundred, three hundred, four hundred roentgens. It appears at the present time, that by none of the genetic criteria which we have in man, can we find clear evidence of a difference between the children exposed to these radiations and the children of a control population in which the parents were not exposed. Now we think the changes must be there, but they are not statistically significant in comparing these two populations. Now when we come to Nevada, instead of talking about roentgens, we talk about milliroentgens – a fraction of a roentgen, a thousandth of a roentgen.

According to the Official Report of ABCC issued in January 1956[11] 75,000 children had been examined over six years. Dr Neel told the March 1956 meeting of the CAC that the genetics report was about ready; the manuscript had been read extensively by both geneticists and statisticians. 'With a problem of this complexity it was too much to hope for unanimity of outlook with regard to statistical analysis, but the authors were quite well satisfied that there were no major errors in the presentation.'

The report was published in 1956 as an official publication of the National Academy of Sciences and National Research Council (NAS–NRC).[12] The researchers concluded that they had found no 'conspicuous' indicators of human sensitivity to genetic mutation induced by ionizing radiation. From this they inferred that it was improbable that human genes are so sensitive that as little as 3 r or even 10 r would double the present mutation rate 'although it must be admitted that a rigorous demonstration of this belief would be difficult'. They considered that the urgency of setting 'permissible' levels of radiation dosage meant that they must be guided by the data available, even as inconclusive as this. They noted 'There *is* doubt concerning the advisability of calculations which have the appearance of mathematical exactitude to persons not thoroughly indoctrinated in genetics and unfamiliar with the shaky basis of the primary assumptions.' It would be 'as unfortunate, on the one hand, to deny the possibility that low doses are dysgenic at all as it is, on the other hand, to assert that a serious threat to the genetic integrity of mankind is involved.' But they were governed by the practical necessity to set tolerance limits for those involved with ionizing radiation.

Thirteen years after the bombing of Hiroshima and Nagasaki, in August 1958, Schull and Neel published a report on their findings on the sex ratio among children of survivors.[13] They stated explicitly that they had assumed that the increase in gene mutations with increasing radiation is linear over the measurable range of exposures. 'The linearity of the response in gene mutations to dose of radiation is one of the cornerstones of radiation genetics, and rests on a literature far too extensive to review here. Suffice it to say that since linearity obtains in all organisms thus far studied, it seems improbable that a different situation would obtain in man.' Again, that which their studies might have been thought to have been investigating under the mandate of the ABCC – the long-term effects of ionizing radiation on humans – was assumed as a linear relationship.

A year later, in December 1959 Schull and Neel published a paper on *Atomic Bomb Exposure and the Pregnancies of Biologically Related Parents*[14] on 5163 pregnancies of consanguineous parents. They acknowledged that the assumption that exposure was related to distance from the hypocentre was 'considerably less precise than could be desired, or than is frequently imagined'. They had sought 'somewhat more elegant procedures for estimating the dose–genetic effect relationships' than one which required a value judgement in the assignment of almost every dose which may mean that the 'the apparent precision in estimating the genetic effect may well be spurious.' This more elegant procedure was to adopt a classificatory scheme which they said evolved to take into account distance, shielding and symptomatology. But essentially this classification was the same as the simple distance-dose estimates that they were claiming to improve upon. Subjects were asked where they were at the time of the explosion, and what symptoms they had experienced. On the basis of these self-reports, they were classified into five groups – who were *assumed* to range from exposed to non-exposed. That is, throughout the late 1940s and early 1950s, in fact the first decade of the investigations, the relationships between distance, dose and injury were assumed before the investigations into genetic damage even began.

Anomalies were observed. Back in 1949[15] Dr Snell had presented the haematological results to the Committee on Atomic Casualties and he had noted that:

> *The irradiated group was divided roughly on the basis of the amount of epilation sustained, 0 to 1/3 epilation, 1/3 to 2/3 epilation, and 2/3 to complete epilation. This breakdown has no statistical validity but on this basis there appears to be greater depression of the red blood cell count in those with the greater degrees of epilation. One unusual finding was the tendency toward higher red blood counts in those who had been most severely injured (by other than radiation). There is reason to believe that epilation is a valid criterion for estimating the amount of radiation received, but there is no certainty that the answers given on the questionnaires were true. For instance, the questionnaires indicated a 21 per cent incidence of epilation outside the two kilometer ring whereas the Joint Commission found only 8 per cent. The white blood cells are affected by so many factors that it is difficult to interpret the findings. In general, it can be stated that there was deficiency in the absolute number of white blood cells in the circulating blood of both the exposed and control groups.*

Dr Luykx said then that in studies attempting to describe the effects of an agent on a population, some of whom die and some of whom survive, care must be taken in formulating the description on the basis of the conditions found in the survivors, since these conditions may be related to survival and unique in the survivors. Dr Rivers agreed with this but said the ABCC's work was centred on the survivors, and, admittedly, no attempt should be made to interpret the data as an accurate cross-section of the total exposed population. The possibility existed that the researchers might be dealing with a true cross-section of the control on the one hand and a selected cross-section of the population exposed to the bombs – the survivors, and not even all of them – on the other.

Now, a decade later, Schull and Neel noted that the most striking aspect of their study of the outcomes of the consanguineous marriages was the apparent heterogeneity between the two cities. Not only was there a fairly marked difference in the perinatal death rates in the two cities, but the increase in mortality with parental exposure which seemed to occur in Hiroshima was countered by a *decreasing* mortality with increasing exposure in Hiroshima. Within the exposure groups classified according to distance, moreover, there was no apparent significant difference in Nagasaki but there was in Hiroshima. However, 'when the model previously described is fitted to the Hiroshima data, one finds that though the regression removes a significant amount of variation the variation not removed by the regression is also significantly large. In short, the linear model would appear inadequate to account for more than a small fraction of the observed variation. Interesting too, is the finding that on the linear model the regression coefficients associated with mother's exposure and father's exposure differ in sign.' However, the researchers note, 'In most circles, the latter would not be considered consistent with our present knowledge of genetic damage following parental radiation. It must be borne in mind that these seemingly anomalous findings may be due to confounded concomitant variation.' Nevertheless, they felt confident enough to assert that their findings were that 'there is no demonstrable, consistent effect of parental exposure on the frequency of malformed infants or perinatal deaths among the children born to related parents.'

Schull and Neel did not assert that no genetic damage had accrued from the exposure of the populations of Hiroshima and Nagasaki to ionizing radiations in this 1959 paper. They admitted that the data they had managed to accumulate did not 'afford an adequate test of the genetic hypothesis' or the basic premise that inbred children because of their increased homozygosity are a more sensitive indicator of radiation induced genetic damage than other children. But neither did they accept that the data they were presenting had no utility. They argued that 'in point of fact, each "negative" study serves to further isolate the "critical range", that is, that area wherein we must search for genetic differences.' And each negative result, they thought, should further refine future experimental designs.

'Unhappily, however, we are called upon even now to make decisions regarding "permissible doses". These decisions can affect not only the practice of medicine in this country but our national safety as well.' While they advocated keeping to a minimum the exposures to which humans are subjected, Schull and Neel felt they had contributed to an understanding of permissible, tolerable doses of radiation from their study of the survivors of Hiroshima and Nagasaki classified at the outset into assumed doses of radiation on the grounds of reported distance and injury.

The studies commissioned by the Atomic Bomb Casualty Commission were of course not the only work going on into the effects of ionizing radiation on human subjects – but certainly the Hiroshima and Nagasaki survivors were the largest sample available. Stanley H. Macht and Philip S. Lawrence reported[16] their study of the effects of relatively small but frequent doses of ionizing radiation in 2717 US radiologists and 1918 controls in 1955. The results 'indicate that small prolonged doses of radiation produce abnormalities in humans. The differences between exposed and unexposed groups show a consistent trend of higher rates of abnormality in the exposed group within the several parity orders, ages of mother, and decades of birth of offspring. The differences are not of large magnitude and in themselves would not be viewed with alarm. These abnormalities occur, however, in the *first generation* of offspring and visible first genetic effects represent only a small fraction of the total damage that may have been inflicted.' These researchers pointed out that 'Study of the effects of radiation should not be based only upon effects so gross that they are lethal or make it improbable that the affected person would ever reproduce.... Gross defects, while they are an immediate burden in any generation, are not nearly so costly as minor defects transmitted over a very long span of time.'

This of course was Hermann Muller's position, too. He had warned the United Nations Conference on the Peacetime Uses of Atomic Energy that:

> All these questions need to be not only discussed but actually investigated far more realistically than they have been in the past. Otherwise, we may at last find ourselves, genetically, facing a parallel to already accomplished deforestation and erosion, on an even grander scale. This problem is not only one that is concerned with the possible aftermaths of atomic war. It must be faced equally by the proponents of peace if we are to have an atomic age, with its risks of prolonged 'permissible' exposure arising from industrial uses and radioactive products.

But Dr Neel put a different construction on the results, and lack of results, that his research design was producing by the end of 1956. He told the Advisory Committee of the Atomic Bomb Casualty Commission in January 1957[17]:

To sum up the entire genetics study: the results revealed no clear effect of exposure to the bomb on the F1 children. There was no doubt that there had been a genetic effect, as established in theory derived from laboratory experimentation, but it could be said that such effects had not been demonstrable in Japan under the conditions of the study. From this study one can set limits on radiation induced effects. It could be said that the effect had been not greater than a specified magnitude.

Dr Neel then proposed a new study, on the outcomes of pregnancies of the more than 7000 consanguineous matings that had been recorded during the general study. He argued that this study would produce information concerning the accumulation factor – 'what was the store of bad genes which each of us carry?' To this store, compounded in consanguineous matings, radiation-induced mutants were presumably added. The high degree of consanguinity detected in the general study - 7 per cent in contrast to 0.1 per cent in the US – represented an outstanding opportunity to get data on the accumulation factor which entered into every attempt to put radiation genetic risks into quantitative estimates, although he proposed to eliminate the children of the heavily exposed group as they were not large enough to analyse statistically. Both Dr Warren and Dr Bugher spoke in favour of the study because it 'could help narrow the gap between knowledge derived from animal experimentation and its application to human genetics.' No one spoke against it and it was duly funded.

Notes

1. William J. Schull, *Songs of Praise*, (Harvard University Press, 1990) p.156

2. *ibid*: p.77.

3. *ibid*: p.68.

4. J. V. Neel *et al.*, *The Effect of Exposure to the Atomic Bombs on Pregnancy Termination in Hiroshima and Nagasaki: A Preliminary Report*, 6 November 1953.

5. Thomas H. Roderick, 'Summary of general discussion in the symposium on the effects of radiation on the hereditary fitness of mammalian populations', held at Jackson Laboratory, Bar Harbor, Maine, 29 June to 1 July 1964, *Genetics*, 30:1213–1217 November 1964.

6. Schull, *op cit*. p.1220

7. Oscar Kempthorne *et al.* (eds.) *Statistics and Mathematics in Biology* (The Iowa State University Press, 1954).

8. James V. Neel, 'A description of studies on the potential genetic effects of the atomic bombs in Japan, I organizational aspects', in Kempthorne *ibid*,

9. William J. Schull, 'A description of studies on the potential genetic effects of atomic bombs in Japan, II analytical problems', in Kempthorne *ibid*,

10. Transcript of remarks made by John C. Bugher, Director of Atomic Energy Commission's Division of Biology and Medicine, Las Vegas, 13 February 1955. Document 32291, DoE Coordination and Information Center, quoted at footnote 108 in Beatty, 'Genetics in the atomic age: The Atomic Bomb Casualty Commission, 1947–1956 in Keith R. Benson *et al.* (eds.) *The Expansion of American Biology*, Rutgers University Press, 305.

11. Bugher 1:2:9:103

12. J. V. Neel and W. J. Schull *et al.*, *The Effect of Exposure to the Atomic Bombs on Pregnancy Termination in Hiroshima and Nagasaki*, Publication No. 46l, NAS–NRC, 1956.

13. William J. Schull and James V. Neel, 'Radiation and the sex ratio in man', *Science*, 15 August 1958: 343–8

14. William J. Schull and James V. Neel, 'Atomic bomb exposure and the pregnancies of biologically related parents', *American Journal of Public Health*, 1959:49.

15. Minutes of the CAC, dated 18 March 1949.

16. Stanley H. Macht and Philip S. Lawrence, 'National survey of congenital malformations resulting from exposure to roentgen radiation', *American Journal of Roentgenology*, 73: March 1955: 442–66

17. Minutes of the Advisory Committee to the ABCC, dated 5 January 1957 at Bugher 2:1:2:9:10.

SAMPLING
THE DATA

A preliminary, but reasonably inclusive, study of 9000 deaths in Hiroshima over the years 1950–54 shows about a three-fold increase in death rate among the heavily exposed survivors. There also appears to be a definite exposure–distance relationship. This finding is presented with utmost caution and for careful additional analysis. It is potentially a very explosive observation, at least in Japan.

What does this finding mean to the ABCC program? If it be true that there is actually a higher death rate among the heavily exposed, the causes are not known and, under our present investigative effort, it is highly unlikely that they ever will be known.

Robert S. Holmes, Director, Atomic Bomb Casualty Commission to Dr R. Keith Cannan, National Research Council, 10 February 1955.

The Japanese doctors who work at the Atomic Bomb Casualty Commission have an opportunity to observe American methods of medicine and to learn by the example set for them. They may add to their knowledge of experimental design.

Official report of the Atomic Bomb Casualty Commission, 1956.

Eleven

In 1950 William J. Schull and two Japanese employees of the Atomic Bomb Casualty Commission, Dr J. N. Yamazaki, a paediatrician, and Dr S. J. Kimura, an ophthalmologist, had met with sixteen Japanese researchers associated with the Nagasaki Medical College who gave their clinical impressions of the immediate effects of the bombing of Nagasaki. Professor Shirabe, the Professsor of Surgery and one of the few surviving faculty of Nagasaki Medical College (which was 400 metres from the hypocentre) presided.[1]

The Japanese doctors reminded the ABCC investigators that it had rained after the detonations. Dr Yamazaki asked if the rain had been black and Dr Odachi said he thought it was. Dr Sugihara remembered, 'It was as though looking through a veil. One could gaze and clearly define the outline of the sun without feeling the glare.'

The Japanese said that it was the impression of the survivors that in Hiroshima more people were killed by the ceilings falling on them than by the radiation, while in Nagasaki more people died from burns and radiation effects than from external injuries. The wooden houses 'just crumbled and burnt. They afforded no protection at all.' Dr Kimura of the ABCC said that 'In Hiroshima some of the children were having a diving contest and a boy who happened to be underwater when the atomic bomb fell was saved while five others who were out of the water were killed.' Dr Shirabe agreed. 'That sort of things [sic] happened here too. Those who were swimming and happened to be in the water were saved.'

The Japanese also said 'that some deaths occurred to persons who returned to Nagasaki about a week after the atomic bomb explosion. Did radiation have anything to do with those cases?' Dr Odachi recalled that 'Soon after the explosion I was in Urakami for about a week but I did not become ill at any time.' Dr Shirabe pointed out that 'Dr Barnettt, a pediatrician who was a member of the US Atomic Bomb Casualty Investigation Commission visiting Omura Naval hospital, said such things could never happen. He maintains radiation is momentary and says no effect will be felt by anybody going to the sort [sic] after the explosion as there will be no more radioactivity then. But I rather think the radiation remained for some time in Urakami. I think it is not impossible.'

Dr Ishikawa told the group that 'I heard that in Hiroshima some deaths occurred among the people who went to help their relatives or members of fire brigade or youth association who assisted in the disaster after the explosion of the atomic bomb. The people from the US denies [sic] the possibility, but the symptoms are similar.' Dr Shirabe agreed: 'Of course some felt no effect at all, but there are also some who stayed for some time and showed radiation sickness symptoms.' Then Dr Yamazaki from the ABCC said:

> *Recently I took a history from a young woman who stated that she was in the country at the time of the bombing and returned to Urakami the day after the bombing to look for members of her family. She returned to Urakami each day for six days following her first visit and on the 15th of August she finally found the surviving members of her family. Her search took her across the hypocenter in an area 1000 to 1500 metres north and south of the hypocenter. Vomiting developed about the 12th day. About one month after the atomic bomb, she developed gingivitis with bleeding, followed by sloughing of her gums. Petechiae appeared on the skin of arm and thorax. Fever developed about this time. These signs and symptoms persisted for about a month.*

Mr Kawamoto recalled 'The wind changed from south to north for about an hour in Michinoo side. It may have been due to the fire.' Dr Shirabe commented 'A good amount of radiation rays may have been blown to Nishiyama side, with the dusts. Some Americans mentioned this too.' Dr Shee said 'I hear the dust in an eavestrough of a house in Nishiyama was found to contain a considerable amount of radioactive material.'

At the conclusion of the meeting Dr Shirabe asked 'Aren't they carrying out studies on the treatment of irradiated patient [sic] in the United States? Something must have been achieved by now as a therpy [sic] for radiation sickness.' Dr Yamazaki said he thought 'many investigations are now in progress.'

Dr Shirabe had conducted close observations of the survivors in Nagasaki from October through to December 1945 and his report was available in English from at least 1950 since its editing and translation been undertaken by the ABCC.[2] He found that in Nagasaki concrete effectively shielded against heat and blast but was insufficient protection against the large amounts of radiation. There was an inverse relationship between the mortality rate – a function itself of thermal and external injuries as well as radiation injury – and the distance from the hypocentre. Fatalities dropped off markedly beyond the 1.5 kilometre zone. Natural features, such as topography and structural shielding, were determining factors in the mortality rate. Wooden houses beyond 1.5 kilometres gave some protection. Dugouts, although flimsily constructed, were in a large number of cases surprisingly effective in shielding the occupants.

The Professor of Surgery at Nagasaki Medical College observed that within 1 kilometre the presence of thermal or mechanical injuries did not alter the mortality rate, while beyond 1 kilometre the death rate was highest in those persons who had received flash burns. The incidence of flash burns was inversely proportional to the amount of shielding, people in concrete buildings having the lowest incidence and those in the open the highest. Distance was also a determining factor but needed to be interpreted in relation to the amount of shielding. Flash burns frequently involved extensive areas of the body, even at distances of 3 to 4 kilometres. There was no significant difference in the extent of the burns between survivors and victims, again suggesting radiation injury as a common factor.

Professor Shirabe, that is, observed in the first weeks after the detonations that external injuries were much more frequent among people shielded in concrete and wooden buildings while those in the open sustained fewer injuries. The most frequent injury was from flying glass. The manifestations of radiation injury, including nausea, vomiting, diarrhoea, fever, haemorrhage, epilation and oropharyngeal lesions, were related to distance from hypocentre but this relationship was influenced by the shielding.

Starting in 1948, the Atomic Bomb Casualty Commission instituted a clinical and pathological survey to attempt to identify abnormalities which might have been induced by the radiation exposure. Again, like the first round of genetic studies which came to such an inconclusive end, the approach was primarily observational and epidemiological. Despite circumstantial evidence such as that reported at the 1950 meeting, these clinical and pathological studies were conducted on a sample constructed on the same principles as that for the genetic studies – primarily distance from the hypocentre, with some attempt to correct for self-reported shielding on assumptions about the shielding qualities of various building materials.

Patient Contactors employed by the ABCC brought groups of survivors from their homes or schools to the ABCC clinic where their medical and 'radiation' histories were taken. The subject was then given a physical examination by a Japanese doctor under the supervision of American doctors. The examination took about two and a half hours and included a haematologic study (complete blood count, differential count, haematocrit and sedimentation rate), urinalysis, stool examination for ova and parasites, chest X-ray, dental examination and serologic test for syphylis. Those under twenty years old were also checked for growth measurements and X-rays were taken of the left wrist for bone age determination. They were also given a vision test. About forty people a day were being given the full tests in 1955 and another forty were given special tests in relation to abnormalities.[3]

But there was a steady attrition of subjects from these studies. In one programme by June 1952, 4238 subjects had been examined; at the second annual examination the total dropped to 2967. Inquiry into the reasons for the decrease revealed that twice as many unexposed as exposed had moved away, and that twice as many exposed as unexposed had died. A further complication was that older survivors moved back to their village homes to end their days.

In 1950, 1951 and 1952 the incidence of leukaemia had definitely increased. A total of 153 cases had been identified; 92 among exposed, 61 among 'unexposed' individuals. The exposed group contained no children in this series.

Nineteen fifty-four was a difficult year for the Atomic Bomb Casualty Commission. The irradiation of 23 Japanese fishermen and more than two hundred Marshallese at the time of the *Bravo* test at Eniwetok in March greatly alarmed the Japanese and was increasing the attrition rate at the ABCC studies. Several of the ABCC clinical staff had gone to Tokyo to advise on the treatment of the fishermen.

At the 20th meeting of the Committee on Atomic Casualties in October 1954[3] the clinical programme at Nagasaki was referred to as a gesture. Dr Connell reported that he was worried that, on the one hand, the heavy work load of the pathology staff might be wasted because the size of the sample might not be adequate to produce statistically significant results; but that on the other hand 'The answers which we seek will not wait indefinitely for us to harvest at our convenience'. He estimated the attrition rate over recent months at approximately 17 per cent. In the Adult Medical Program about a third of the subjects had not come in when requested over the past six months.

Another consultant, Dr Morton, recommended that the ABCC should be phased out. He detected a lack of central policy of investigation laid down in the US resulting in little continuity in the research programmes. There were personnel problems; the diagnostic ward was a godsend to professional morale but through lack of nurses it could not be kept open on a seven-day-a-week basis. The main problem was the lack of any treatment programme for the Japanese who came to the ABCC. But another consultant, Dr Gordon, argued that the central inquiry of interest was to establish if the life span of A-bomb survivors had been shortened and if so, whether this was a radiation or a disaster effect. This study could be conducted without treating the subjects; in fact, there was a school of thought which felt that treatment would confound the studies and obscure the natural course of what were assumed to be radiation-induced diseases and conditions.

There was still serious doubt about the value of the ABCC and its scientific enquiries. Dr Warren reminded his colleagues that negative data would be of enormous importance – but 'it is not thrilling to obtain; it perhaps gives no satisfaction to the investigators but to the world at large it will be of much importance'. Other committee members such as Mr Eisenbud felt that the antagonism which some Japanese felt towards the United States was itself a powerful reason for staying. 'To pull out would create a vacuum. After leaving, any number of pseudo-scientific positive findings might well be reported in the literature that we could no longer refute. Once out of Japan we could never return.' Another committee member pointed out that no matter what ABCC did, it would be damned: 'If we work we will be accused of using people as guinea pigs. If we pull out we will be accused of not caring.'

Dr Warren mentioned that a major advance in the laboratory approach had occurred recently when Furth's Greenhouse mice were held beyond the duration of the standard experiment and were allowed to live out their lifespans. A longer period of observation of humans might show similarly interesting results. Dr Wearn pointed out that if the death differential between exposed and non-exposed was real, a reorientation of the programme might be required to discover the reasons for it. He argued that much more intensive clinical and pathological screening methods were required rather than epidemiological statistical studies. The Committee began to consider ways in which it could begin to offer treatment to the survivors in order to keep them participating in the studies. The American physicians were not licensed to practise in Japan and the insurance problems were seen as insurmountable, so there was now – nearly ten years after the detonations – a consideration of how treatment could be provided by Japanese physicians under the direction of the ABCC.

The Committee agreed on the importance of allaying fear in Japan, and it was increasingly apparent that an active clinical programme was necessary in order to answer the criticisms of the use of the atomic bombs, including the suggestion that it had been inhumane because of serious late radiation effects in the survivors. But the ABCC only had eight beds and this clearly could not provide a treatment facility.

There was also a reconsideration of the use of what were assumed to be lightly exposed residents of the two cities as controls for the studies of the long-term effects of radiation. Dr Taylor explained to the advisory committee of the ABCC in 1954 that a change had been made when analysis of the original Adult Medical (ME-55) group revealed that a marked difference in racial, economic and disease background existed between the urban residents of Hiroshima and Nagasaki and the rural and repatriate population who took up residence in the cities after the bombing. A lightly exposed person was now defined as one who survived the A-bombs between 3000 and 3500 metres of the hypocentre. It was pointed out that the differential in death rate showed up only when exposed were compared with unexposed. It was not clear whether this was a disaster effect – a consequence of being so close to the centre of the bombing – or a radiation effect. It would be necessary to use not merely lightly but completely unexposed controls to establish this. Dr Neel noted that the racial background of the exposed population of Hiroshima and Nagasaki was far from homogeneous. He felt dependence upon lightly exposed controls alone was dangerous. Dr Warren now felt much the same – that from standard animal experiments he would not want to regard a lightly exposed person as synonymous with unexposed. He noted the striking differences between radiologists (all of whom are lightly exposed) with the medical population as a whole in respect of leukaemia. 'Everyone who has worked with radiation is impressed that sublethal doses of radiation do things to living organisms that show up later in the life span.' Dr Stern asked about the amount of radiation received at 3000 metres. Dr Dunham replied not much. Lt Col Tessmer, however, was not so sure. He pointed out that authentic cases of epilation at 3000 metres were too numerous to ignore. The intensity of radiation did not decrease gradually from the hypocentre in a perfectly uniform fashion. He hoped that the question of fission products would be revived. He felt study of the unexposed group to be important and agreed that lightly irradiated persons in the 3000 to 3500 metre zone were unsatisfactory controls. As the minutes of the 20th meeting of the Committee on Atomic Casualties of the Atomic Bomb Casualty Commission noted somewhat offhandedly of this major sea change in the ABCC's understanding of the potentially confounding role of radiation beyond its assumed distance of effect, 'It appeared to be the sense of the Committee that dependence upon lightly exposed persons alone for control purposes was undesirable'.

In July 1954 Robert D. Holmes MD had taken up the Directorship of the Atomic Bomb Casualty Commission. He reviewed the research agenda and administrative organization of the ABCC in a letter[4] to his superior, Dr Cannan, in February 1955. He wondered whether the organization was truly meeting the terms of the Presidential Directive creating the ABCC to study the late effects of radiation on the A-bomb survivors. He even questioned the real value of the genetics studies. 'No one, apparently, doubts the scientific value of these findings. It is well, however, to emphasize their intrinsic temporal factor and to note that this negativity in certain areas could be ephemeral. There are well founded reasons for stressing this point.' The new director therefore urged that 'Much caution is now indicated in minimizing the late effects of radiation' until the analysis of the Death Certificate studies could be completed to see the effect of the injury on ageing and death and until the clinicopathologic data were collected on the survivors and examined in the light of Furth's recent work which had studied what happened to irradiated mice if they were left to die naturally after the injury. The natural history of the survivors had to be followed for many more years before conclusions could be drawn. Already the Death Certificate Study of 9000 deaths in Hiroshima in the period 1950–54 was showing about a three-fold increase in death rate among the heavily exposed survivors. There also seemed to be a definite exposure–distance relationship but 'This finding is presented with the utmost caution and for careful additional analysis. It is potentially a very explosive observation, at least in Japan'.

Dr Holmes urged that a hundred-bed hospital be provided in Hiroshima and an eighty-bed facility in Nagasaki 'in order to attract and concentrate in one place all the heavily exposed survivors and controls for the purpose of clinical examinations, treatment when necessary, whether surgical or medical, and autopsy when death intervenes.' He even went so far as to propose that the ABCC be transferred to United Nations control because he was apprehensive that the Japanese would urge its transfer to their control, or some other form of internationalization, during the 10th anniversary of the bombings which was now only a few months away.

Dr Holmes restated his views to the February 1955 meeting of the Committee on Atomic Casualties.[5] He urged a more collaborative relationship with the Japanese physicians in order to circumvent their efforts to develop independent research and treatment initiatives that would compete with the ABCC. The Japanese physician Dr Tsuzuki had raised $250,000 with a Christmas card levy and was planning to divide the money between hospitals at Hiroshima and Nagasaki. The Hiroshima hospital would be built alongside the Red Cross Hospital. Dr Nakaidzumi had proposed a plan for a national radiobiological institute. There had been overtures from the Japanese to both Unesco and WHO

to internationalize the research programme. The Japanese wanted a supply of radioisotopes and the Committee thought that these could be
made available in a way which complemented the needs of the ABCC.

At this meeting, Dr Brandt reviewed the progress of the Death
Certificate study. He called attention to the fact that if any two groups of
normal people were studied the death rate would not come out exactly
the same. If the two groups contained several million people, a difference
in the death rates could be quite small but still be alarming. Conversely,
if the groups contained only a thousand people, a rather large difference
in rates might be observed without any cause for alarm.

However, it should be possible, if a radiation effect on death rate in the
Hiroshima and Nagasaki survivors existed, to demonstrate a difference in
the death rates of people at 0 to 1999 metres from the hypocentre, 2000
to 3999 metres, and 4000 metres and over – since Dr Brandt was still
assuming that dose was more or less inversely proportional to distance
from the hypocentre and that dose determined injury. But when he sepa-
rated the survivors into two groups by distance from the hypocentre – 0
to 1999 metres and 2000 metres and over – and compared the death rate
by year from 1950 to 1954 for the age groups 10 to 19, 20 to 29 and so on
to 60 and over, and then for all ages, he found a significant difference in
only one year (1952). Moreover, in this particular year, the death rate per
thousand survivors in the under 2000 metres group was 10.6 and in the
2000 metres and over group it was 13.4 – which was precisely the opposite of what had been predicted by the linear distance–dose–injury
hypothesis.

This provoked considerable discussion of the possibilities of bias by the
Committee. Dr Brandt felt that conclusive evidence of a radiation effect
was lacking but he felt just as strongly that it was too early to say that the
data said nothing. Dr Neel said that while he and Dr Schull had not had
time for a detailed analysis of the Death Certificate data, he could not but
be impressed that while the results were not clear cut there was a certain
consistency in the data. He noted that for the males all but two points on
the curve and for the females all but three points on the curve were in the
direction of support for the hypothesis of an adverse radiation effect upon
life span. In regard to the genetics study, Dr Neel told the 1955 meeting
that while in the preliminary analysis sex-ratio had been determined for
only two categories, exposure and non-exposure, when radiation exposure categories were redefined the significance of the early findings was
lost. There was still a difference in the right direction but it did not
approach the level of statistical significance. The implications of this finer
examination of the dose–distance–injury relationship did not seem to be
taken by the Committee on Atomic Casualties. Dr Holmes did point out

to his advisory committee that 'the program as it now stands is inadequate in both clinical and pathological fields if the natural history of the A-bomb survivors is to be established.' Even if a difference in mortality rate among the survivors were established by the epidemiological methods of the Death Certificate Study, 'we still would not know its cause'. Clearly there was an urgent need for a hospital facility; equally clearly the *quid pro quo* for the cooperation of both survivors and Japanese physicians in the clinical studies and the greater access to autopsy material would be the necessity to offer some form of treatment to the survivors.

The current clinical programme was only a long series of physical examinations, which was 'hardly a program to attract men of training and quality' as Dr Lawrence put it to the Committee. Dr Lawrence asked if the promise of medical reactor might be used as a lever to get the hospital proposed by the Japanese located closer to the ABCC. Dr Holmes felt that location of the hospital might still be open to negotiation and that the prospect of a radioisotopy laboratory and reactor would exert considerable influence in moving the hospital over to the Hiroshima Medical School. Such a hospital would provide the means to make an all out effort to obtain clinical histories on individuals who eventually came to autopsy and many clinical studies could be undertaken. Dr Bugher, formerly Director of the Division of Biology and Medicine of the Atomic Energy Commission and now Director for Medical Education of the Rockefeller Foundation, thought there was a distinct possibility of getting foundation funds to support medical education at the Hiroshima and Nagasaki Medical Schools.

Notes

1. Round Table Discussion by the Survivors of the Nagasaki Medical College Relating their Personal Experiences with Atomic Bomb Victims in Nagasaki, Nagasaki Medical College, June 7, 1950, found at Bowers ACC 93–73: ABCC:1 dated 1/5/82.

2. 'Medical survey of Atomic Bomb casualties', by Raisuke Shirabe, Professor of Surgery, Nagasaki Medical School, found at Bowers: ACC 89–73:ABCC:1 in pamphlet form, no date, but annotated J. Z. Bower, Hiroshima October 19, 1981 and published in *Military Surgeon*. Noted in the pamphlet format that 'This paper is sponsored by the ABCC, NAS. Edited and prepared for publication by Drs William S. Adams, Stanley W. Wright and James N. Yamazaki.' Another reference to Raisuke Shirabe, '1950 medical survey of Atomic Bomb casualties' translated by Kazuo Hamasaki and edited by W. S. Adams, S. W. Wright, and J. N. Yamazaki. ABCC, Nagasaki.

3. Minutes of 20th Meeting of the CAC, dated 30 October 1954

4. Letter from Robert H. Holmes to Dr Cannan of the National Research Council on 10 Februry 1955 at Bugher 2:1:10:113.

5. Minutes of the 21st Meeting of the CAC, dated 26 February 1955

Twelve

In the wake of the 10th anniversary of the bombing of Hiroshima and Nagasaki a high-powered review group arrived in Japan in late October 1955 consisting of Dr R. Keith Cannan of the National Research Council, Dr A. B. Hasting, Dr Thomas Francis Jr, Mr Felix Moore, Mr S. Jablon and Dr Charles H. Burnett. After reviewing the work of the Atomic Bomb Casualty Commission for two and a half weeks Moore, Jablon and Francis issued what came to be known as the Francis Committee Report.[1]

Keith Cannan, chairman of the chemistry department at New York College of Medicine, had become Director of the Division of Medical Sciences of the NAS–NRC earlier in the year. He selected Thomas F. Francis Jr to undertake a review of the activities of the ABCC. Francis had graduated from Yale Medical School in 1925 then worked at the Rockefeller Institute on influenza. In 1938 he had become professor and Head of Bacteriology at New York University where he became friendly with Cannan. In 1941 he had gone to the University of Michigan School of Public Health as Professor of Epidemiology.

They were almost universally critical of the achievements and management of the ABCC. The clinical and pathological studies were yielding little apparent information, not least because the statistical analysis was lagging far behind the data collection. Perhaps the few, relatively early and relatively demonstrable – predictable – effects of radiation had already been detected and the delayed effects were going to be more difficult to observe clinically or pathologically. The staff had lapsed into a view that their primary responsibility was to collect data for someone else to review eventually. 'This view has resulted in a lack of interest in the primary objective, loss of initiative, or diversion of interests into other medical or scientific areas.'[2] There was no overall scientific programme which could be implemented despite the frequent staff changes that were the bane of the ABCC. The lack of scientific leadership and appalling staff morale were the most vivid impressions the group took away with them. 'With few exceptions, existing professional personnel have emphatically stated that they would not, under any circumstances, renew their contracts. Several have stated that, if possible, they would shorten existing contracts if they could.'

The Francis Committee Report noted that 'Whatever the blueprint or plan of operation originally provided, it seems either to have become indistinct or has been lost in the successive changes of staff, lack of indoctrination, and varied motivation.' But the Francis Committee also questioned whether that original 'blueprint' or research design had ever been adequate to the goals of the project. 'There is little of the research attitude'.

To redress this situation, the Francis Committee – Moore, Jablon and Francis, all epidemiologists – proposed that what was required was a Unified Study Program of scientific investigation. They did not concern themselves too deeply with the content of this programme; they were more concerned to identify the sample of survivors to be studied given the enormous problems of logistics and attrition now that a full decade had passed since the bombings. The Department of Internal Medicine of the ABCC was reporting massive attrition throughout 1955 – approximately one third of the adults refused to be re-examined and together with those who were unavailable for re-xamination for other reasons the attrition rate was running close to two-fifths of the sample. In the pediatrics programme the attrition was running between 29 per cent and 35.4 per cent.[3]

The Francis Committee proposed to limit future studies to a 'Master Sample' of survivors who lived in Hiroshima and Nagasaki. This involved 'the transferring of the focus of attention from the shifting, somewhat unstable population of exposed people who happened to be residing in Hiroshima or Nagasaki, to a carefully-defined, fixed population which is to be followed as completely as possible.'[4] According to the Biostatistics Department's interpretation of the intentions of the Francis Committee:

> *Fundamental to the Unified Program is a closed or 'fixed' sample. The philosophy involved is that an accurately-defined, accurately-known group of people is to be the base upon which all major future studies of ABCC are to be based. It is felt that by employing such a fixed sample and following the members of it, as far as possible, it may be possible to avoid most of the errors inherent in a study based upon a population which is continually shifting as members of it move in and out of the city of study.*

The Francis Committee proposed to base the Master Sample on the list of exposed people compiled during the 1950 National Japanese Census as resident in Hiroshima or Nagasaki on 1 October 1950. The Master Sample would consist of two groups – the exposed and the non-exposed.

Although there had been some effort to determine the impact of shielding on exposure, this work was far from complete and 'For the present, it seems clear that distance and symptoms serve adequately as a first approximation of exposure and will be useful in population stratification for sampling purposes.'[5] That is to say, the long-standing assumptions of the earlier ABCC researchers were to be carried over into the new research design, a decade after the bombings.

The definition of exposed and non-exposed survivors was in principle widened by the Master Sample in as much as exposed were defined as those who had been within 10 kilometres of the hypocentres and non-exposed those beyond 10 kilometres.

But the exposed category was then further divided into Proximal (near) and Distal (far) exposed groups. The Proximal Exposed group in Hiroshima were assumed to be all those exposed at a distance of less than 2500 metres from the hypocentre who were listed on the October 1950 National Census as resident in Hiroshima City. In Nagasaki the Proximal Exposed were considered to be those at a distance of less than 3000 metres from the hypocentre and listed in the October 1950 Census as resident in Nagasaki. The 500 metres difference in the two classifications was because the number of survivors in Nagasaki was very small.

The Distal Exposed group was a random sample of those people listed on the October 1950 census as being beyond 2500 metres at the time of explosion in Hiroshima or beyond 3000 metres in Nagasaki but less than 10,000 metres, and resident in the cities in 1950. Because this group was larger than the Proximal Exposed group, a random selection was made.

Anyone who had entered the city shortly after the bombing was classified as 'possibly exposed to residual radiation' but was considered as non-exposed in the sampling procedures. People known to be of non-Japanese ancestry – for example, Koreans, or Australians and Americans who had come into the cities after the bombings, or Indonesians who had remained in Japan after the war – were excluded from the sample.

The Master Sample would thus consist of a total of 97,000 people including 30,000 non-exposed for Hiroshima and 42,600 including 10,000 non-exposed for Nagasaki; there were 47,600 proximally exposed and 20,000 distally exposed in the Hiroshima sample and 24,300 proximal and 8300 distal in the Nagasaki sample.

The Francis Committee discussed the 'Considerations of Survey Design in Relation to the Process of Inference' as an addendum to the report. They argued that 'It is natural to suppose that any effect of radiation would vary in frequency or intensity of manifestation according to the dosage of radiation. This seems to be true for at least the majority of effects which have already been identified.' Nevertheless, it would be 'extremely desirable to consider also the possibility that there may be effects which, at least over the dosage range with which we are concerned, are substantially independent of dose in their probability of appearance.' Such a situation, they noted 'is consistent with the preliminary results of the mortality studies, and while further work may radically alter the present indications it should not, at this stage, be taken as axiomatic that it is impossible for a relationship to be of this character.' Moreover, 'It should not be forgotten in this connection that knowledge of the radiation dose received by exposed persons is quite incomplete. The shielding studies are but well begun; the residual radiation which may have been received by persons who were exposed far from the hypocentre but quickly went into heavily contaminated areas is not known.' It had taken a decade for these possibilities to enter the research designs of the Atomic Bomb Casualty Commission.

Although the Francis Committee was proposing three categories of exposure – heavy, light and non-exposure – it was still closely predicated on distance. Proximal (near) exposure was still assumed to result in heavy dosage; distal or more distant exposure was presumed to result in low dosage. The distance for non-exposure had been moved out to 10,000 metres, but this was still an arbitrary decision since the research designs of the ABCC had not in fact established the range of dosage nor even the presumed linear relationship in the first decade of its existence. It was understood by now that distance itself would have to be considered in relation to shielding but such shielding information as the AEC had been able to develop was still classified and unavailable to the ABCC.

The Francis Committee considered that 'It is primarily desirable to study a group of persons who were heavily exposed to radiation. It is plainly not possible to provide true "controls", and groups for comparative study must be accepted which would not satisfy the requirements of good design in a planned experiment. On the basis of careful review, it is believed essential that both lightly exposed and non-exposed groups should be used for comparisons.' So essentially they were reverting to the old methodology, of comparing those people closer than 3000 or 2500 metres to the hypocentre with the rest on the same assumptions about the aetiology of radiation injury. As the staff statistician, Mr Raoul Simon, commented in a memo responding to the Francis Report[6] 'The terms "lightly exposed" and "heavily exposed" should apply only to such cases where the relative dosage of radiation is fairly evident from radiation symptoms and radiation history', not be presumed from distance alone. While the proposed Master Sample would probably help to detect

123

effects which decreased with exposure and those requiring a heavy dose, it would not necessarily facilitate detection of those effects caused by radiation but not influenced by dosage if the so-called exposed group was grossly compared with the assumed non-exposed group. 'The detection of such effects may require special selection of the exposure group to be determined by the analyst according to the data available at the time of the study.' Already the Pathology Department had observations which 'raise important questions which deserve close attention in the future'.[7] Several cases beyond the 2000 metres had radiation symptoms. Two similar cases had been noted in 1954: 'With further increases in the autopsy material, other instances of exposure beyond 2000 metres and symptoms of radiation disease may reasonably be suggested.' The pathologists on the staff of the ABCC themselves pointed out three possible reasons for these apparent discrepancies. Either the information contained in the radiation symptoms questionnaire was unreliable, or the symptoms of acute radiation syndrome were similar to the symptoms of severe systemic diseases not necessarily connected with radiation, or the data indicated development of true radiation symptoms beyond the 2000 metre radius of the hypocentre.

The Francis Committee met with the long-term advisory committee members of the ABCC in Washington on 27 November 1955.[8] Dr Francis explained forcefully how he felt that a Unified Study Program of a closed population would focus the work of the various departments of the ABCC while leaving room for special studies to be performed on an *ad hoc* basis. Dr Warren defended the work of the ABCC since 1947 by saying that while 'in the past the investigating groups in Japan have had to devise methods to define the acute radiation syndrome, the immediate genetic effects, and certain other late radiation effects. These studies have been successful. The accomplishments of the ABCC should not be under-rated.'

Dr Brandt still considered that the non-exposed group should be dropped from the clinical studies of the new Unified Study Program since he knew of no animal experiments concerning late radiation effects by which it had been shown that an 'all or none' effect existed. For this reason, plus the fact that it was tedious for the clinician to study these patients, Dr Brandt did not believe that this group was necessary. It would be better to 'sharpen up' the distance classifications rather than dilute them with studies of those assumed to be non-exposed. Mr Jablon responded that before he had visited Japan he had thought that an intrinsic control group was sufficient. 'In Japan he had learned that regardless of the distance from the hypocentre, the incidence of acute radiation symptoms never fell below 2 per cent. This may be due to fallout or residual radiation. Therefore, any group that was in the city may have gotten some radiation.'

Jablon also pointed out that although the non-exposed post-war immigrants into the two cities probably were not comparable to the exposed, American insurance studies had shown that mortality differentials between groups selected on medical grounds tend to disappear after about five years. The subjects for the Unified Study Program's Master Sample were taken from those living in Hiroshima and Nagasaki at the time of the 1950 national census. 'Thus, it can be hoped that by now, differences in mortality data for the exposed and non-exposed groups have been equalized, unless exposure to the bomb has had an effect on mortality.'

In response to a question by Dr Brandt on the type of late effect that might be demonstrated by an extrinsic control group but not by an intrinsic control, Mr Jablon said that the difference in mortality was more noticeable when the heavily exposed group was compared with the non-exposed. Dr Brandt suggested that the non-exposed population might be controlling something that was not due to radiation. Dr Francis suggested that it was highly desirable to match non-exposed to lightly and heavily exposed to cover the possibility that an effect might exist which was not proportional to the dose of radiation but occurs once a certain threshold of irradiation had been exceeded.

The review meeting concluded that the Death Certificate Study was the most important single component of the new Unified Study Program but the morbidity, clinical and pathological programmes should not be neglected and the cooperation of Japanese physicians was essential to their development.

The senior staff of the ABCC had a chance to respond to these recommendations in December 1955. G. L. Laqueur, Chief of the Pathology Department, wrote to Dr Cannan with a long defence of the performance of his unit against the criticisms – implicit and explicit – of the epidemiologists of the Francis Committee.[9]

He pointed out that it was being suggested that all one had to do was:

Establish a final diagnosis, let us say tuberculosis, put it on the card, and run it through the IBM machine at the proper time with a similar batch of cards. An answer will come out.

To this argument I would raise immediately strong objections because the mere fact that a patient dies with tuberculosis does not mean at all that he died of tuberculosis. None of us knows what the late effects of radiation may be, if any. It becomes an absolute necessity, therefore, to make each case an object of scientific investigation. If we assume for example that fifteen years from now unusual incidences of variants will be found among the heavily exposed, would we not want to know what preceded this occurrence, in brief its pathogenetic background. We most certainly would and hence our present job is to do our work as detailed as time and personnel allow.

Dr Laqueur reminded the Committee that a great many assumptions were being made about the nature of the data they were trying to establish:

I should also like to point out that each one of us must exert a most critical attitude toward all the statements which have been made that a single exposure to atomic radiation produces all the diseases which have been incriminated, and I, for one, am not even fully convinced in the cases of leukemias which most people accept that they are the results of the single exposure. The time between exposure and today is relatively short, indeed. Only ten years. Having worked with animals and men for the past twenty years, I am not impatient about the scarcity of results at present. If there are any, they will show up in due course of time. Our objective is to keep our eyes open and be critical.

The senior pathologist also remarked:

I also have felt that most of our reviewers thought that radiation injury was something very distinct and that we should pick it up. Dr Francis once asked me whether I thought our methods of examination could pick up unusual occurrences. As I remember it, I told him that we might pick them up provided they documented themselves morphologically on a recognizable level and that this was the reason that I insisted on careful autopsy procedures. I also told him that the most important information which might come from pathology might be differences in the incidence of diseases or a prevalence of diseases at an age where they do not normally occur.

In fact, suggested the senior ABCC pathologist:

It would seem to me that if one wants to study the effects of radiation on the basic processes of life that this might be done much better in acute experiments. The information already available today on the effects of radiation on cells and enzyme systems within cells is abundant. But such studies should be done and continued in experimental laboritories [sic] where procedures and equipments are available. Certainly, the ABCC has nothing of that nor do I understand it to be its primary purpose.

These reservations about the epidemiological research assumptions that underlay the Unified Study Program proposed by Francis and his colleagues were shared by the Biostatistics Department of the University of Pittsburgh. Another external reviewer of the ABCC Program, Thomas Parran MD, was Dean of the Graduate School of Public Health at Pittsburgh and he referred the problem to his colleagues in Biostatistics. They responded:

> *That no clinical entity is found for the complaint does not mean that the person is not ill but simply indicates our ignorance of disease processes. The Francis Committee suggests apparently that some of these complaints may be prodromal symptoms of certain of the chronic diseases and that if such is the case, by following up the individuals with a variety of complaints, one may see emerge a pattern which precedes a certain clinical entity. While reasonable we believe [sic] that this approach is not too profitable especially considering the efforts and money that would be expended. Suppose that one did observe after a few years that all persons who developed coronary heart disease had had a complaint of chest pain some time in the past. Then one would have to determine how the chest pain in these individuals differed from the chest pain reported by persons who did not develop coronary heart diseases. But, by this time it would be too late to learn this.*[10]

Nevertheless on 20 December 1955 Charles L. Dunham, MD, Director of the Division of Biology and Medicine of the United States Atomic Energy Commission, wrote to Dr Detlev W. Bronk, President of the National Academy of Sciences to transmit and endorse the recommendations of the Francis Report as appraised by the Washington meeting. He noted that that meeting had recommended a high-level conference to consider the future sponsorship and management of the ABCC in order to implement the Unified Study Program. Dr Dunham wrote 'I cannot but agree with this idea especially in the light of my several years of contact with the ABCC and its many vicissitudes which have in great part stemmed from too narrow and limited an approach to the radiation problem.'[11]

But even so when the British medical journal *The Lancet* published correspondence[12] arising from an international medical commission to investigate the medical and biological effects of atomic explosions which had met in Tokyo, Osako, Kyoto, Hiroshima and Nagasaki in May 1955, the data reported by researchers not associated with the Atomic Bomb Casualty Commission was dismissed with contempt. The Acting Executive Director of the National Academy of Sciences–National Research Council sent a copy of the correspondence to Dr Bugher of the Rockefeller Foundation (a long-standing member of the Committee on Atomic Casualties) at the end of 1955 as Dr Bugher was preparing for

a visit to the ABCC. A British pathologist, S. Sevitt, reported the findings of Professor Hayashi of the Nagasaki Medical School on the 887
neonatal necropsies he had performed in Nagasaki from 1949 to 1953.
Dr Hayasaki had divided the infants into two groups and compared the
incidence of major congenital malformations among those whose parents
(one or both) were exposed to the A-bomb with those whose parents
had not been exposed. The definition of exposure was residence within
ten kilometres of the hypocentre. The results showed an incidence of
18.9 per cent major congenital malformations among the exposed with
11 per cent among the unexposed. Dr Sevitt related this finding to the
work of Macht and Lawrence[13] who found that congenital malformations
were 24 per cent higher among the children of radiobiologists as compared to the children of other doctors. Dr Sevitt also worried about the
continued effects of experimental H-bomb explosions in the Marshall
Islands since March 1954 and their long-term genetic effects.

Dr Miller sent this *Lancet* discussion to Dr Bugher with a note[14] to the
effect that:

> *Dr Tsuzuki was prominent as a sponsor to the conference. Neither the*
> *Japanese government nor any medical society sponsored the meeting. Its*
> *financial backing has never been made public and at least one of the few*
> *non-communist members (the Belgian representative) professes not to*
> *know where his tickets and invitation came from. Most of the members*
> *came from communist countries. Some representatives of non-communist*
> *countries appear to be at least pink. None, including Dr Sevitt, appears to*
> *have been critical of the material presented by the Japanese. Sevitt's use of*
> *Hayashi's hodgepodge autopsy figures appears typical of other reports ema-*
> *nating from the conference.*

To prepare him for his visit to the ABCC Dr Miller also sent Dr
Bugher some thumbnail sketches[15] of members of staff whom he would
be appraising during his visit. The Biostatistics Department was run by
45-year-old Lowell A. Woodbury who was described as carrying a heavy
burden 'and is presently a key man in the whole operation. Has a good
mind, works hard but has some insecurity that bedevils him from time to
time.' The person in charge of biostatistics at Nagasaki was a young
Australian named Ken Noble who was described as having less than a
high school education but a very high IQ. 'In charge of biostatistics at
Nagasaki. Initiates many promising new investigative studies. Is a most
unique individual. Wants to come to USA to complete his basic education and study demography. He needs good counsel on his future.'

Notes

1. Memo of the Ad Hoc Committee for Appraisal of ABCC Programme, submitted to Dr R. Keith Cannan, Chairman, Division of Medical Sciences, NAS-NRC, 6 November 1955, at Bugher 1:2:9:101.

2. Memo from Charles H. Burnett MD to Dr Keith R. Cannan on Survey of ABCC from 20 October to 9 November 1955, Bugher 1:2:9:101.

3. Reports of Department of Internal Medicine and Department of Pediatrics of ABCC for 1955, at Bugher 1:2:11:114.

4. Report of Biostatistics Department of ABCC for 1955–56 at Bugher 1:2:11:114.

5. Memo of Ad Hoc Committee for Appraisal of ABCC Programme (Francis Committee Report)

6. at Bugher 1:2:9:101.

7. at Bugher 1:2:11:114.

8. Minutes of the Ad Hoc Conference on the Francis Committee Report, at Bugher 1:2:9:101.

9. Letter dated 19 December 1955 from G. L. Laqueur MD to Dr Keith R. Cannan, at Bugher 1:2:9:101.

10. at Bugher 2:1:10:113.

11. at Bugher 1:2:9:101.

12. *The Lancet* 23 July 1955.

13. S.H. Macht, and P.S. Lawrence, *American Journal of Roentgenology* 1955, 73.

14. at Bugher 1:2:9:101.

15. at Bugher 1:2:9:101.

Thirteen

Ten years after the bombings of Hiroshima and Nagasaki, the studies of the genetic and somatic effects of exposure to the radiation emitted by the bombs was still proceeding in the absence of any real understanding of the amount or nature of radiation to which the population had been exposed. The two bombs were made of different ingredients; precisely what they had been composed of was not clear to either the physicists or biomedical researchers. Work proceeded on understanding the injuries caused by them on the assumption that the differences in the composition of the two bombs would not make that much difference, or, if it did, the differences would be detectable.

In the absence of information from the physicists, the biomedical epidemiologists of the Atomic Bomb Casualty Commission thought that they could approximate individual doses for the survivors they were studying by working back from their linear assumptions about the relationship between distance from the hypocentre, amount of radiation or dose received, and injury likely to be suffered. They thought that the best way to develop this retrospective information was to take information (self-reports) from the survivors themselves about where they had been at the time of the explosions. Gradually through the late 1940s and early 1950s they realized that the nature of the shielding which the individual had been protected by must also have some impact on the dose received. Work was proceeding in the Marshall Islands and then in the Nevada Proving Grounds to try to establish the factors that would indicate the nature and amount of radiation received by the people of Hiroshima and Nagasaki. But the work of the ABCC could not wait for those studies to be completed, and the researchers in Japan seemed to be particularly isolated from the work in the other agencies.

In February 1956 Dr Bugher, one of the most senior members of the Committee on Atomic Casualties and party to most of the work going on in radiation studies of the Atomic Energy Commission, noted in his report[1] on his visit to Japan on the need for 'more accurate statement of individual radiation exposures'. He encouraged the ABCC to place more emphasis on the 'shielding studies'.

> *I had discussed the latter subject in 1952 with Dr Woodbury and Dr Taylor, and we concluded at that time that we would need a statement of total shielding in the line of sight between the bomb center and the person together with a better calculation of the radiation field with distance from each of the two bombs. A reasonably good statement of the character of shielding should be possible from the very detailed protocols which have been made in past years for many thousands of people. We were aware as a result of the greenhouse tests at Eniwetok that the computation of the neutron flux and the range of neutrons as given in 'The Effects of Atomic Weapons' were seriously in error. In 1954, at my request, a preliminary recomputation on the basis of the then recent Nevada tests was made by members of the Los Alamos staff.*

By 1956 Dr Bugher recognized that there was a need for both longitudinal studies of those assumed to be highly exposed, but also a 'broad screening' of those present in the two cities at the time of the bombings. However, he concurred with the Francis Committee's proposed Master Sample – he found no problem with a closed sample even though it was still not clear what in fact the study was trying to detect or observe. He was pleased that in 1956, a decade after the explosions, 2000 self-reports on shielding had been collected at Hiroshima and Nagasaki.

> *It is important that as soon as possible work be started with this material in relation to the more accurately computed radiation field in order to determine the radiation dosage from both gamma and neutron components received by each individual. This is a major study in itself and will require the closest cooperation between the people working in Japan and the weapons experts in the US.*

Dr Kurokawa, employed by the ABCC, restated the same assumptions in a conference presentation in February 1956.[2] 'The severity of radiation effects depends on the distance from the hypocenter and the shelter, if any, at that time.' According to the data already collected, 'In epilation, an early symptom of radiation effect, there is a distance factor of 700 meters between the rates of epilation of a patient in a concrete building and one in an open place at the time of the bombing. That is, the persons who were in a concrete building at a distance of 800 meters and who were in an open place at a distance of 1500 meters showed a similar rate of epilation.'

The official report of the ABCC issued in January 1956[3] cautioned that 'Distance from the hypocenter alone is not a satisfactory measure of the degree of radiation exposure since the individual may have been shielded by structures which diminished the radiation dosage he received.' Scale drawings in three dimensions were being made of each subject's location at the time of the explosion, according to his or her own report. 'From these and other data, it is possible to translate in each case to the equivalent of the shielding mass in terms of centimeters of water. This study may contribute to the solution of problems concerned with the measurement of radiation dosage and to a more exact knowledge of the biologic effectiveness of ionizing radiation. This information should aid in the further definition of the maximum permissible exposure to this physical agent in the peaceful use of atomic energy and to civil defense planning.' The ABCC report mentioned that only the industrial valley of Nagasaki was destroyed by the bomb. Three-quarters of the city was shielded from its effects by the hills enclosing the industrial area, but it was not explained how these topographical features were being accounted for in the shielding studies, or in the comparisons with the information coming from Hiroshima.

On the eve of the 1956 meeting of the Committee on Atomic Casualties, the senior biostatistician at ABCC, Dr Woodbury, wrote to Dr Cannan in Washington[4] that he had heard that a group of experts were to be sent to Japan in April 1956 'with the object of establishing actual dosages of radiation for each person within a certain distance of the hypocenter'. Dr Woodbury strongly recommended that 'the group bring with them a small neutron source and, if such a thing exists, a source of gamma radiation with the gamma energies in the range of those coming from the atomic bomb and also the necessary measuring instruments' so that the Japanese housing materials could be measured *in situ* rather than being shipped to Nevada. 'Physicists well acquainted with the interaction of radiation and matter and with special knowledge of the quantity and quality of the radiation given off by atomic bombs of both the Hiroshima and Nagasaki type would be most useful in such a group. A further useful person would be a biologist especially trained in radiation or drug-dose–response techniques and evaluations.'

Dr Woodbury hoped that the visiting experts could spend several days in both Hiroshima and Nagasaki.

> *After that they would serve a most useful purpose, at least as far as the ABCC is concerned, by making on the spot measurements of the absorption characteristics of the major shielding materials. Once these measurements are made and reduced to usable form then calculations of dosage in roentgens can be made. People who were exposed in the open or with extremely light shielding can have their dosages computed immediately but*

the number of such survivors is small. Most of the people surviving were shielded by a mass of matter varying from an equivalent of two inches of concrete up to as high as 4 metres of concrete. We have been computing our final shielding summary in terms of cms of water equivalent as we have lacked information of the type of radiation given off by the bomb and the absorption characteristics of the materials. Lacking this information we have based out [sic] attack on relating distance, shielding mass and the percentage occurrence of the major radiation symptoms.

Dr Woodbury also asked for any information on residual radiation that the group could bring with them. 'Dr Warren, during his last visit here gave us some information on the amount of residual radiation and this information was much appreciated. He gave us one reference to a report on the fallout area in Nagasaki and this reference is badly needed in connection with a proposed research project on the people who live in the fallout area.'

The day after this letter was written from Hiroshima, Dr Miller outlined the shielding studies to the Committee on Atomic Casualties.[5] Two thousand shielding histories had been obtained in Nagasaki and 1100 in Hiroshima. The Nagasaki data included the information for all those who were within 1000 metres of the hypocentre, all those who were *in utero* at the time of the bombing, and all those who had been studied for the presence of radiation cataracts as well as 23 of the 30 survivors who had developed leukaemia. Dr Dunham remarked that there was renewed interest in this work because there were now much better estimates of the yields of the two atomic weapons and great strides had been achieved in the understanding of neutron dosimetry. Dr Neel questioned relying on the accuracy of the subjects' memories for their locations at the time of such a catastrophe, especially since a decade had passed during which they could build a story in which they believed implicitly. The shielding histories obtained during the genetics studies had been poor. An attempt had been made to set up radiation categories based in part on this information, but it seemed that it made little difference whether the subject was in the open or in his house as far as the development of radiation symptoms was concerned. This might be explained by the hypothesis that individuals outside were, unknown to them, shielded by one or more houses. A difference of five feet might make a crucial difference in the amount of radiation received.

Dr Francis suggested that the self-reports were often corroborated by individuals named by the subject as having been nearest to him at the time of the explosion. Dr Neel said that in the genetics study there was a clear difference for those who had been shielded by concrete, but there was almost no difference between those who were in Japanese houses and those who were in the open. Many of the people who said they were out in the open should have suffered flashburns if this were true, but they did not, so they could not have been out in the open. An 'analysis of sorts' had been made about the changes over time of self-reports from the survivors and the fact was that answers did change both in terms of position at the time of the bomb and in terms of reported symptoms. Dr Miller told the Committee that another study of changes in reported histories in the five years after 1945 had shown a decrease in the percentage of patients who described symptoms: 'This may in part be the consequence of a difference in history-takers rather than in the subjects studied'.

The shielding studies were well underway by the end of 1956. According to the end-of-year Biostatistics Report,[6] specially trained field technicians were visiting the various patients and by means of maps and aerial photographs determining where they had been at the time of the bombing. If the building was still standing, as was the case with the Fukuya Department Store in Hiroshima, blueprints were used to reconstruct the shielding potential of the structure. According to the report, 'If the building was destroyed in the blast or aftermath, a reconstruction can frequently be made because of certain standard features of the Japanese house.' The actions of the person immediately preceding the blast were also recorded, and from the combination of the aerial photographs, maps and house reconstructions scaled drawings were made. From these 'the mass of shielding material is computed'. About one a day of these reconstructed histories could be compiled by each technician and by the end of October 1956 there had been 2080 collected in Hiroshima and 2813 in Nagasaki.

As part of the Francis Unified Study Program the study of radiation-induced cataracts was stepped up in the middle of 1956. A draft research design for the study of Lenticular Changes in Survivors of the Hiroshima and Nagasaki Atomic Bombs[7] was circulated in August 1956. It noted that 'several semi-quantitative studies have been made in an attempt to relate the percentage of people showing lenticular changes or abnormalities to the distance from the bomb or to a combination of distance and the amount of shielding material. These studies have indicated that the frequencies of lenticular change is a function of the distance from the bomb in both Hiroshima and Nagasaki.' However, 'The circumstances of the studies were such that no direct comparison of the cities was possible and an evaluation of relative effects of the two bombs cannot be made. Since the relationship of lenticular changes to distance from the bomb is well established the remaining point of interest is a comparison of the relative effects of the two bombs.'

It was noted that the two bombs differed in strength, altitude of detonation and composition of emitted ionizing radiation. The radiation from the Nagasaki bomb was mainly gamma rays, while the Hiroshima bomb emitted mainly neutrons and gamma rays. The Nagasaki bomb was estimated to have emitted only a tenth as many neutrons as the Hiroshima bomb. Neutrons were known to be considerably more likely to cause cataracts than gamma rays. The proposed research would try to establish the relationship between dose and cataract injury. There was reference in this research design to the fact that 'in the past exposure has been measured rather crudely as simple distance from the hypocenter or presence or absence of radiation signs.' The hope now was that the formation of cataracts could be ultimately used as a sort of biological dosimeter of dose–response to ionizing radiation. But the subjects for this study would only be drawn from those exposed at less than 2000 metres since it was still assumed that 'beyond this distance the possible dosage of radiation is too small to be of concern'. In fact, 'The low percentage of cataracts to be expected at the 1800–1999 distance zone and the large number of patients required to make this a reliable figure suggests that after a preliminary study to check the correctness that consideration should be given to dropping this distance zone from the study. The same recommendation applies to the 800–999 meter group. This would decrease the estimated number of patients required to 1590.'

The Committee on Atomic Casualties had been reconstituted as the Advisory Committee and met in this form for the first time in January 1957. Dr Francis was now a full member of the advisory committee which was monitoring the implementation of his Unified Study Program proposal. Mr Jablon reviewed[8] again the need for reintroduction of an unexposed control group – a population that had not been in the city at all at the time of the bombings. The argument against its inclusion was that there was no guarantee that they would be biologically similar to those who had been present at the time of the bombings. But it was also not known what actual exposures to radiation had taken place to those who had been in the cities. Although an individual's distance from the hypocentre was generally known with some assurance, this – Mr Jablon pointed out to the advisory committee – told nothing of his exposure to residual radiation or to fallout.

Moreover, life insurance studies had indicated that the effects of medical selection at a given point in time gradually wore off as the years went by. Mortality rates between differently selected populations gradually approached one another provided there were no continuing sociological differences between the two groups. He thought that sociological status could easily be checked in the ABCC studies.

Dr Francis suggested that some of the effects among the radiation-exposed group could be the result of disaster conditions in general such as the severe typhoon which struck Hiroshima a few weeks after the bomb was dropped. For this reason it would be advantageous to have a non-exposed group. Dr Firth pointed out that the ABCC was concerned to study radiation effects incidental to the environment, and the best group for comparison would seem to be those who had been subjected to the same environmental influences and differed only in radiation exposure. Dr Warren said that from his own experience of the Hiroshima typhoon in mid-September 1945 it was his impression that after the typhoon the general situation of the people was not much worse than it had been before. There was already a great deal of distress, shortage of food and so on. He thought the typhoon was a rather minor episode in comparison to the bomb. He also restated his conviction – still held more than a decade after the bombings – that there was no residual radiation of biological significance in either of the cities. Dr Francis asked about the significance of the black rain in Nagasaki. Dr Warren said that it had no relation to radiation. It was simply the cloud of dust that had been picked up in the stem of the cloud, and had been precipitated when it had come into contact with moisture downwind. The measurements of the areas in which these rains had fallen were not of biological significance. It was important not to expect mysterious happenings in response to radiation levels that were no greater than those which existed in a large number of places.

Dr Dunham pointed out to the advisory committee that the nearly 5000 shielding histories that had been so laboriously compiled by late 1956 were meaningless unless an estimation of the physics of the exposure was known. Some of the information relating to gamma and neutron flux had recently been declassified but it was still necessary to assess the actual shielding properties of the various materials in the buildings in the Japanese cities. As soon as the weapons testing programme in Nevada would permit, it was planned to do further field studies on this. It was proposed to assign a health physicist to the shielding studies at the ABCC.

A major effort was being put into the Death Certificate studies of the people in the Master Sample to see if there was an identifiable shortening of life among those assumed to have been exposed to radiation. Again, those so-called 'non-exposed' survivors were used as the control group.[9] The study protocol did not expect to be able to distinguish between those who had been present in the cities at the time of the bombings and those who had moved in since the war. It noted as a possible source of bias 'fallout from the bomb – the question of whether there was significant fallout from the atomic bomb in Hiroshima is probably not subject to a definitive answer. There is some indication that a percentage of the people entering the city after the bomb explosion and remaining for several days later developed signs and symptoms similar to those of the radiation syndrome. One the other hand, typhoid, dysentry and other diseases were epidemic at that time and may have caused these signs and symptoms. The evidence is inconclusive.' The proposal did acknowledge that 'If there was significant fallout, a number of people now resident in Hiroshima who are classified as not exposed to radiation, i.e. non-exposed, will in fact have had some exposure. A possible result would be to increase the death rate in the non-exposed group and thereby reduce the magnitude of any increase in exposed death rates as contrasted with the control.' The research protocol acknowledged that 'It may or may not be possible to allow for this factor in the analysis of the results.' As for Nagasaki, 'one group of people is known to have been exposed to a significant amount of fallout and still others may have been. This group should certainly be studied in detail if possible.'

There was also, twelve years after the bombings, some rethinking of the assumptions about distance and dose. 'It is customary to use the distance of the exposed person from the hypocenter as a crude measure of the dose of radiation and within limits this is justified as one may say that on the average the further a person was from the hypocenter the smaller the dose of radiation received.' Unfortunately, however, 'this does not hold true within the 1000 meter zone. Within that area, distance alone bears little if any relation to dosage.' A person exposed at 600 metres in a heavy concrete building may have received much less radiation than a person exposed at 1200 metres in a Japanese house. Many people less than 1000 metres from the hypocentre received lethal doses; on the other hand, some received none – or none detected up to now. It was now beginning to be realized by the ABCC researchers that the shielding factor constituted a source of bias in the simple assumptions of a linear distance–dose–response relationship for ionizing radiation in a war situation.

In November 1957 the Advisory Committee[10] was brought up to date on the Ichiban dosimetry project being carried out by the Oak Ridge National Laboratory. Now in its third year, the first phase had involved measurement of the angular distribution spectrum of the radiation from atomic weapons; measurements had been made in Nevada in the summer and were now being analysed. Dr Snyder of Oak Ridge pointed out that the two weapons used in Japan were different and it was hoped that some time in the future, perhaps in 1960, a series of tests could be conducted with weapons made to the same or similar specifications so that more precise information could be obtained.

The second phase of the Ichiban Project was to determine through actual tests which features of Japanese architecture affected the dose received and to measure the amount of shielding they provided. Two houses had been set up in Nevada during the past summer, but the budget for this work had been severely cut and most of the work remained to be done. The third phase would be to calculate the air doses at various distances from the weapons, and the final phase would be to apply all this information to the shielding histories obtained in Japan and calculate the doses received by individuals. Given sufficient funds he hoped that the project would be completed in another two years or so.

Dr Snyder commented on the shielding histories and building studies being carried on by ABCC. Even using aerial photographs, it had been estimated that these would take another 25 years to complete. Simpler methods had been worked out in the hope of reducing this projection. Dr Snyder urged that the peripheral population be taken into account. He thought as a health physicist that this might be an important group to study to determine the effects of low dosage.

Dr Langmuir asked if it was possible to estimate the degree of error in the figures on dose in relation to distance that Dr Neel had used in his book on pregnancy termination. Dr Snyder thought that the physical data, taken from *The Effects of Atomic Weapons*, were the best figures available even now; they had been based on the first tests conducted in Nevada several years ago. He himself had no definite opinion of their accuracy, but some associated with the Ichiban project believed that they might be in error by a factor of two or more. Dr Wald pointed out that Dr Neel had used some biological criteria as well as physical measurements in estimating the doses received by the people in his five exposure categories.

Dr Bugher asked Dr Warren whether this sharpening of the data might not provide a basis for improving the studies which he and Dr Oughterson had conducted for the Joint Commission. Dr Warren felt sure that this would be the case, and there would be opportunities for a good deal of valuable retrospective work. He pointed out, however, that even in those days when eyewitnesses were available it had been difficult to differentiate between the effects of radiation and those of blast and heat in causing early deaths. Dr Warren argued that it was better to aim for an 80 to 90 per cent accuracy in reconstructed shielding histories after more than twelve years but Dr Cronkite felt that the factor of error was far larger than this. For instance, in the case of the relative biological effects of neutrons it had been taken as 1.6 whereas in fact it was probably 0.1

Notes

1. at Bugher 1:2:10:112.

2. Presentation by Dr Kurokawa of the Atomic Bomb Casualty Commission to the Conference on the Advancement of the Use and Study of Radioactive Isotopes, 14 February 1956, at Bugher 1:2:9:104.

3. at Bugher 1:2:10:112.

4. Letter of Lowell A. Woodbury, PhD, Head, Biostatistics Department of ABCC to Dr R. Keith Cannan, 12 March 1956, at Bugher 2:1:10:113.

5. Minutes of the 22nd Meeting of the CAC, dated 13 March 1956.

6. Periodic Report from Dr Holmes dated 7 December 1956, at Bugher 2:1:9:104.

7. Drafts of the Lenticular Changes in Survivors of the Hiroshima and Nagasaki Bombs, August 1956, at Bugher 2:1:9:104.

8. Minutes of the 23rd Meeting of the Advisory Committee on the Atomic Bomb Casualty Commission, dated 5 January 1957.

9. Outline of proposed 'Study of Deaths of People Exposed to the Atomic Bomb', at Bugher 1:2:9:101.

10. Minutes of the 24th meeting of the Advisory Committee on the Atomic Bomb Casualty Commission, dated 13 November 1957.

Fourteen

The growing attrition of subjects from the studies conducted by the Atomic Bomb Casualty Commission and the change of emphasis from epidemiological to more clinical and pathological studies a decade after the bombings of Hiroshima and Nagasaki meant that the American researchers began for the first time to value collaboration with the Japanese working in the same area.

As Director, Dr Holmes was more disposed to cultivate good relations with the Japanese clinicians and biomedical researchers than his predecessors had been. He took the initiative in forming the Japanese Advisory Council for the ABCC which met for the first time in November 1955.[1]

The ABCC was under constant scrutiny and criticism from the left wing of the Japanese press. Japanese parliamentarians were pressing for the Commission to become more transparent in its dealings with the survivors and to offer treatment to those people it wished to study. There was increasing pressure for joint ownership and operation of the ABCC facilities.[2] A Member of the House of Councillors, Gishin Yamashita,[3] wrote to Director Holmes in January 1956 noting that 'Although thousand of citizens of Hiroshima have often undergone various inquiring diagnoses since ABCC was established, yet very few of them have received medical treatment at your center.' In February 1956, two members of the influential A-Bomb Sufferers' Association with a membership of almost 2000 survivors who had been in the 2000 metre range called on Dr Holmes and requested the right to apply directly to ABCC for treatment without referral by a Japanese physician. Dr Holmes replied that non-Japanese nationals at the ABCC did not have a licence to practise medicine and the ABCC had a full patient load with its existing Japanese staff.[4]

The Japanese Advisory Council to the ABCC met for the second time in that February.[5] The main item of business was the appraisal of the Francis Committee proposals. The Japanese advisers were asked to assess the feasibility of the proposed morbidity studies. Dr Tsuzuki, who was closely involved in the plans to build a hospital for the A-bomb sufferers, noted that a study similar to that envisaged by the Francis Committee Report was being undertaken by Dr Shiota. He told the ABCC that 'it is necessary for ABCC in making a long term epidemiological study to have a "channel" available for treatment, when necessary, though the '"channel" itself may be small in scale.' He also warned that 'Ten years have elapsed since the A-bombing and most patients are considered to have recovered to such degree [sic] that, if examined as out-patients, the findings for this epidemiological study will be probably all negative. Here arises the need to hospitalize some patients for five or six days so that their response to a given stress can be closely observed.'

Dr Kikuchi noted that a study of this type was already being done on a small scale in Nagasaki and argued that 'Treatment need not necessarily be done at ABCC alone, but should be done in close cooperation with other treatment organizations in Hiroshima and Nagasaki. If ABCC extends assistance to outpatients of these treatment organs, including the proposed Red Cross hospital, by making available ABCC's data and medical consultation, the citizens' feelings against ABCC will be improved.'

Dr Yamaguchi thought people who came to the ABCC should be compensated for the time they had to take off work. He said the A-Bomb Treatment Council had sent a morbidity survey questionaire to approximately 10,000 survivors in the autumn of 1955 and so far about 3000 had responded.

Dr Morito, President of Hiroshima University, thought that the ABCC should cooperate with both the A Bomb Treatment Council and the Institute for the Fundamental Research of Radiation and Medicine proposed by the Japan Science Council. This would require a medical reactor. He agreed that the ABCC should have a medical centre, perhaps in association with the hospital that the Medical School was planning to establish in Hiroshima.

The Dean of Nagasaki Medical School, Dr Kitamura, reported that 5000 health cards had been issued in Nagasaki in an epidemiological study funded by the Welfare Ministry. 'In 1953', he said, 'we conducted an investigation in Nagasaki which revealed that three out of every five persons investigated had not been examined at ABCC. There is a tendency for ABCC to repeatedly examine the same patients and we have found that there are many patients who have not been examined at all.' His study had seen 3000 patients and expected to double that number.

Dr Kikuchi, a Professor at Kyoto Medical School, was studying survivors who were now living in Kyoto and Osaka and Dr Tsuzuki reminded the ABCC that not all the survivors were still living in Hiroshima and Nagasaki. Together with Dr Nakaidzumi, Professor of Radiology at Tokyo University, he was studying survivors in Tokyo and there were also studies underway in Kyusha.

The next month, March 1956, the Japanese press reported[6] that a thirteen-year-old girl who had been playing in front of her house in Furutamachi over four kilometres from the hypocentre on the day of the A-bomb had been diagnosed as suffering from acute myeloid leukaemia – 'an A-bomb disease, caused by secondary radiation due to the "black rain"'. In May it was reported[7] that Dr Watanabe and his Pathology Department at Hiroshima University Medical School had succeeded in an experiment to induce leukaemia with isotopes. 'It is already known that leukemia may be caused by roentgen rays but this is said to be the first such experiment using isotopes. This experiment has proven to some extent that leukemia may occur even by indirect A-bomb exposure (for instance, when radioactive dust is inhaled etc.).' Dr Watanabe was reported as saying 'Leukemia may develop later not only when the body receives a small amount of external radiation but also when radioactive material enters the body. I feel I can say that even in the case of the A-bomb it has been proven to some degree that leukemia may occur when radioactive material is absorbed into the body.'

Dr Tsuzuki, who was now director of the Red Cross Central Hospital, was reported in the press[8] two days later commenting on the recently released international document on permissible limits of radioactive materials. He said 'If the radioactive products produced by nuclear explosions were scattered evenly throughout the entire world, we might be able to concur with the optimistic view held by Dr Libby of the US Atomic Energy Commission that it would be safe to explode 500 Bikini H-bombs. However, this view would be utterly different should the fall-out products and radioactive material concentrate themselves to certain localities.' Japan was in a region that had experienced many such explosions. Dr Tsuzuki pointed out that the potential genetic effects of a whole population being exposed to even low level radiation could be quite different than would follow from the exposure of a small group of workers. It was still necessary to study how long radiation exists and what the radioactive elements actually are before statements could be confidently made about permissible doses.

In mid-1956 the atomic bomb sufferers' associations federated into a more powerful voice. Not only did these associations advocate the interests of the survivors, but any organization such as the ABCC that wanted access to the survivors would have eventually to work through them. Dr Holmes reported to Dr Cannan in Washington in May 1956[9] that 'the

Treatment Council has been reorganized. This has come about in a devi-ous manner but, in brief, has been maneouvred through some of our friends.' A professional advisory committee was soon to be appointed which would be chaired by Dr Nakaidzumi, who was now an Associate Director at the ABCC. Also President Shirai of the Hiroshima Chamber of Commerce and Industry was proving to be friendly to the ABCC and was one of the people who were very interested in obtaining a reactor for Hiroshima. The next day Dr Holmes informed Dr Cannan that Dr Tsuzuki had been pressing for all the genetics data collected by the ABCC to be made available through the United Nations. He added, 'I should mention one other facet of the conversation: Doctor Tsuzuki wanted to know if ABCC was going to present any of Doctor Hiyashi's work in the Genetics Review. Doctor Hiyashi is one of the Professors of Pathology at Nagasaki and his publications, from autopsy data at ABCC, leave much to be desired.'[10]

The central question put to the Japanese Advisory Council by the ABCC staff in November 1956 was whether they would facilitate the cooperation of the survivors in the medical programme of the ABCC. The ABCC urgently needed the help of the Japanese doctors in Hiroshima and Nagasaki in monitoring the proposed closed sample envisaged by the Francis Report in order to make possible 'a continuing medical surveillance of indefinite duration'.[11] The ABCC was now proposing that a centralized information pool be established in each of the cities into which would flow information from physicians, welfare agencies and medical institutions including the ABCC. The ABCC would contribute substantially to the cost. It was hoped that the Japanese doctors and the A-Bomb treatment Councils of the two cities would help to develop and implement this comprehensive system of epidemio-logical control. In return Dr Cannan proposed that the ABCC would 'negotiate with the appropriate agencies in the two cities, a program of medical care for members of the fixed populations of the the ABCC pro-gramme in one or more of the larger hospitals. This program shall be such as to be consistent with Japanese medical ethics and such as will be accepted by the people concerned as an attractive reward for loyal coop-eration in the program of the ABCC. It will be subsidized by ABCC.' Dr Cannan went on, 'I will make myself clear. We acknowledge the princi-ple that in return for the access to the patients in whom we are interest-ed we have a responsibility to contribute to the cost of their care and hospitalization. For the details of this we need the advice of the experts on welfare and health care in Japan.'

The Japanese advisers were quick to see that the ABCC was primarily interested in the new closed sample – the Master Sample – of survivors within the 2000 metre range. This amounted to only about 25,000 of the 175,000 survivors in the two cities. In effect, as the Japanese colleagues observed, the ABCC was asking them to facilitate the preferential treatment of the survivors who had been within 2000 metres of the blasts so that they could be studied more closely.

Dr Tsuzuki also asked for 'information concerning the exact dosage of the energy released by these atomic bombs dropped on Hiroshima and Nagasaki,' which he pointed out was essential to the studies of the survivors. He asked for the US to release this information to all researchers. Dr Cannan told the Japanese advisers that a health physicist was expected to join the staff of the ABCC soon who would be part of a group trying to find out exactly what the spectrum of the two bombs had been.

Dr Kikuchi told the group that from 1945 to 1947 he had conducted a haematological study of approximately 3000 survivors. Later there appeared to be an increase in leukaemia among the exposed. 'I contacted the ABCC to check whether they had discovered any cases of leukemia among the 3000 survivors whom I had studied, so that I might be able to correlate the early haematological findings with the subsequent findings because this would make a very interesting study. It was to my great regret that Dr Moloney reported that none could be found in the 3000 survivors I had studied.' Dr Holmes and Dr Cannan agreed that Dr Kikuchi must come and consult with the ABCC researchers.

Dr Cannan had been in Japan in response to increasing tension between the Director's views of the mission of ABCC and those views held in Washington. He returned to the US in late November and wrote to Dr Bugher, 'the major administrative difficulties between the Academy and the Director in the field were resolved, and real progress was made in our plans to implement the Unified Study Program of the Francis Report, and encouraging steps have been taken to secure more active participation in the program by the medical institutions and welfare agencies of the two cities.' Dr Cannan had also come to terms with Dr Holmes about a transition period of six or so months after which he would be replaced as Director. Dr Cannan himself planned to return to Hiroshima for the first few weeks of 1957 to ensure that things remained on an even keel.

Since 1947 the Atomic Energy Commission had invested $10,900,000 in the Atomic Bomb Casualty Commission. Approximately $900,000 of this money had gone to the National Academy of Sciences in overhead costs for the management of the programme.[12] But there was continual tension between the Washington office of Dr Cannan of the NAS–NRC and the Hiroshima headquarters of the ABCC. It had been impossible to find a scientific director of stature on whom the advisory committee could agree. It was hard enough even to attract or hold staff of any seniority or calibre in the programme. Dr Bugher wrote to Thomas Parran, one potential candidate for Scientific Director, after he had visited the ABCC in discussing the administrative and scientific malaise that every visiting fireman noted about the ABCC; 'As Shields [Warren] remarked when telling me about the results of the conference [on the Francis Unified Study Program] the real underlying reason is that the NAS-NRC has done a poor job, and Det [Bronk] recognizes it, and in the last analysis he is responsible' as President of the Academy.[13]

After ten years and ten million dollars, for instance, there was only one copy of much of the data that had been collected, and that one copy was kept in Japan and not in fireproof quarters.[14] The analysis of the data had long lagged behind its collection, which many observers felt, in the absence of a Scientific Director, had been unsystematic. By 1956 most consultants were arguing that the ABCC should have a much closer liaison with the universities, major radiobiological laboratories, schools of public health, the United States Public Health Service and the defence weapons laboratories in order to make sure it was not operating at the fringes of both biomedical and radiobiological research.

By September 1956 Dr Bugher was writing to Dr Parran that the ABCC was now in real danger of complete disintegration.[15] The Japanese were becoming more determined to take over the programme and properties of the ABCC. Bugher, who had served on the Committee on Atomic Casualties and on the Advisory Committee to the ABCC throughout the past decade, was now warning 'Some of the charges made have been of such serious character that some official notice will probably have to be taken of them, since they bear on the question of gross mismanagement.'

But Holmes had his supporters, and Bugher was one of them. In August 1956 when Holmes began to threaten to resign over his disagreements with Cannan, Bugher offered him a post at the Rockefeller Foundation. On 30 November of that year Dr Bugher wrote to Dr Cannan, 'I am particularly pleased that you were able to work out an arrangement by which Bob Holmes would stay in this assignment.'[16] But in fact Holmes went on leave for the most of the first half of 1957 and his resignation took effect in June. Dr Cannan spent much of that time in Japan as Acting Executive Director of ABCC.

One of Dr Holmes' disagreements with Washington concerned relations with the A-bomb survivors' groups. He saw them as 'potentially one of our better contacts with all the survivors'[17] and argued that they should be supported in some way in order to counteract the communist and other left-wing influence on the survivors. One way to both reach survivors and help support the organizations that were amenable to ABCC influence would be to hire twenty members of the preferred organizations at Patient Contactors. 'They would work for a period of three months, and then another group would be selected, and so on. We can't beat 'em, so this way we join 'em or, better, they join us. The period of employment is too short to allow the labor union to claim them, and too short to qualify them for termination allowance. The more they become a part of ABCC the less they can afford to criticize.' But Dr Cannan did not agree to this proposal.

This was particularly frustrating to Dr Holmes who was largely responsible for trying to stem the tide of patient attrition from the ABCC studies and for trying to trace and log in the 100,000 subjects of the new Master Sample. The Japanese physicians and researcher were now well mobilized to build a new hospital specifically for A-bomb sufferers. They were even being supported in this by individual American philanthropists such as Mrs Howard-Scripps who had been brought to Japan to meet Dr Tsuzuki and his colleagues by Howard Cousins, the American journalist. Cousins had taken up the case of the Hiroshima Maidens, the young women of marriageable age whose severe keloid scars could be treated by plastic surgery. While these keloid scars were more likely to be a result of the blast and burn injuries they had suffered rather than radiation, the Hiroshima Maidens had come to symbolize the A-bomb suffering. Their trips to the United States for surgery were being paid for by public subscription.

Dr Holmes had from the time he took up the job of Field Director of the ABCC been advocating that the ABCC have its own 25-bed medical ward with complete attached clinical laboratory facilities and X-ray.

> This ward would be organized as a clinical research unit with diagnosis and treatment as necessary by-products. The patients would be selected from our statistically desired population groups. Due to certain political and ethical pressures we would have to accept some referral cases from the local doctors that had defied their diagnosis. This would not comprise a great problem. Diagnostic workup could be given and the patient returned to the referring physician. No long-term or convalescent care is anticipated. Autopsy and surgical pathology should also logically complete the setup. Terminal cases which had received proper clinical study would then be more likely to come to autopsy. It is discouraging to do a rather complete clinical survey for several years and then miss the autopsy.[18]

In June 1956 Dr Tsuzuki announced in the press that he was starting to build a hospital in Hiroshima and in Nagasaki to treat all A-bomb survivors regardless of their distance from the hypocentre and that a large-scale research programme would also be undertaken in these facilities. The hospitals should open in August 1957, little more than a year hence. As Dr Holmes commented[19] 'In substance, the program would largely duplicate our clinical program, plus the patient attraction of treatment.' Dr Holmes warned his immediate boss that 'I must confess candidly that I am concerned as to what such a large hospital could do to our volunteer patient-participation program.' He was very concerned about what he called the 'expanding Cousins-Howard-Tsuzuki combine'. 'It would seem highly desirable to try to divert the Cousins' energy and funds to help the new medical school in Hiroshima.' Holmes could 'visualize this hospital as a good thing for long-term convalescent care, with ABCC doing its pathology, especially autopsy service, but the medical school and ABCC together should more properly carry out the clinical work and the investigative work. ABCC does not have a suitable medical ward and the school has no hospital.'

The resources of the American Embassy in Tokyo were brought to bear on the problem, as were those of the Rockefeller Foundation. Robert Murphy, Deputy Under-Secretary of the US Department of State wrote to the President of the National Academy of Sciences, Detlev Bronk in July 1956:

> You will note that there is a possibility that the work of the Atomic Bomb Casualty Commission may be impaired unless some action is taken in the near future in connection with the construction of hospitals at Hiroshima and Nagasaki by groups friendly to the United States. Hospitals at Hiroshima and Nagasaki under the control of the Medical Schools of the Universities there would aid and assist our continued research efforts in those cities. On the other hand, a hospital in Hiroshima under the control of an individual unfriendly to the United States might well dissipate the good will that had been built up today through the work of the ABCC.[20]

This letter was copied to Dr Bugher in his capacity as Director of medical education funding for the Rockefeller Foundation. The State Department was also closely monitoring the activities of Norman Cousins and Mrs Howard in relation to Dr Tsuzuki's fundraising drive. The Counsellor at the Tokyo Embassy for Economic Affairs advised Washington in June 1956 that 'the research under Dr Tsuzuki's direction would not be dependable and the inaccurate diagnoses of death or illness (made either through ineptness or malice) could be used to fan the flames of resentment against the United States.'[21] By the end of the year, Shields Warren was proposing to the Department of State that $350,000 be made available for the Hiroshima and Nagasaki Medical Schools. 'The operating costs for these units would be met from the budget of the Atomic Bomb Casualty Commission and the facilities would be used for the intensive study of patients essential to their research program.'[22]

Notes

1. Memo of first meeting of Japanese Advisory Council to the ABCC, at Bugher 1:2:11:114; also at Darling 770:111:70:775.

2. The Chuguko Press, 17 January 1956, at Bugher 1:2:9:102.

3. at Bugher 1:2:9:102.

4. at Bugher 1:2:9:102.

5. Minutes of second meeting of Japanese Advisory Council to the ABCC, 20 February 1956, at Bugher 2:1:10:114: also at Darling 770:111:70:775.

6. 19 March 1956, at Bugher 2:1:9:101.

7. Asahi Press, 14 May 1956.

8. Asahi Press, 16 May 1956.

9. Letter from Robert S. Holmes to R. Keith Cannan, dated 15 May 1956.

(10 Letter from Robert S. Holmes to R. Keith Cannan, dated 16 May 1956.

11. Minutes of meeting of Japanese Advisory Council to the ABCC, November 1956, at Bugher 2:1:2:9:106.

12. Letter from Charles L. Dunham MD, Director, Division of Biology and Medicine to Dr Detlev W. Bronk, President, National Academy of Sciences, dated 25 April 1956, at Bugher 2:1;9:103.

13. Letter from John C. Bugher to Thomas Parran, Dean, Graduate School of Public Health, University of Pittsburgh, dated 13 April 1956, at Bugher 2:1:9:103.

14. Letter from Shields Warren to Detlev Bronk and R. Keith Cannan, dated 18 April 1956, at Bugher 1:2:10:112.

15. Letter from John C. Bugher to Thomas Parran, dated 13 September 1956, at Bugher 2:1:9:104.

16. Letter from John C. Bugher to R. Keith Cannan, dated 30 November 1956, at Bugher 2:1:9:104.

17. Letter from Robert S. Holmes to R. Keith Cannan, dated 2 August 1956, at Bugher 2:1:9:104.

18. Letter from Robert S. Holmes to R. Keith Cannan, dated 27 June 1956, at Bugher 2:1:9:103.

19. Letter from Robert S. Holmes to R. Keith Cannan, dated, 29 June 1956, at Bugher 2:1:9:101.

20. Letter from Robert Murphy, Deputy Under-Secretary, US Department of State to Dr Detlev W. Bronk, President, National Academy of Sciences, dated 9 July 1956, at Bugher 2:1:9:103.

21. Letter from Frank A. Waring, Counsellor of Embassy for Economic Affairs, American Embassy, Tokyo to Noel Hemmendinger, Acting Director, Office of Northeast Asian Affairs, Department of State, Washington DC, dated 27 June 1956, at Bugher 2:1:9:103.

22. Letter from Shields Warren to George Spiegel, Department of State, Washington, dated 15 November 1956, at Bugher 2:1:9:104.

Fifteen

One of the commentators on the Francis Committee Report in late 1955 [1] had indicated that while he was particularly enthusiastic about the use of fixed samples for the study of certain specialized problems, such as repeated physiologic studies of organ systems, he should point out that the whole approach of the Unified Study Program would be biased in favour of epidemiological research rather than clinical and pathological findings. In this sense the report was:

> both incomplete and biased. The report is biased because of the very qualities of the committee who made the survey and wrote the report. This is not a criticism; it neither implies nor means more than the fact that any critical survey must follow channels familiar to those doing the analysis. The report then does not reflect a specific type of approach to the problem. It is an epidemiological and demographic 'blueprint' for solution of the problems confronting ABCC. I wish to state again, most emphatically, that I do not consider this wrong. I consider this an inescapable conclusion. It does, however, represent bias.

He felt the report amounted to an 'impulsion by the members of the Francis Committee to determine and to propose only broad scientific outlines for action' the problems of implementation would be left up to others.

This commentator, Clarence Tinsley, also warned that 'Without exception, every one of the Japanese physicians or staff members feel "absolutely certain" that this plan is completely impossible; that it has no chance of working.' There was still too much anti-American feeling in the two cities and this had been hardened by the feeling that the Atomic Bomb Casualty Commission 'does nothing but experiment on patients and has as its ultimate goal an autopsy of each patient contacted'. The Japanese he had talked with felt it most unlikely that their countrymen would discuss their 'family secrets', their reproductive outcomes with anyone freely, least of all researchers from the ABCC.

But just as the Michigan geneticist James V. Neel had prevailed over reservations about his epidemiological research design, so the Unified Study Program proposed by the Professor of Public Health at the University of Michigan, Thomas Francis Jr, was accepted with very little critical comment by the Advisory Committee of the Atomic Bomb Casualty Commission.

The Master Sample which would comprise the fixed sample for the various studies of the Unified Study Program would consist of 100,000 survivors still resident in Hiroshima and Nagasaki. Constructing the Master Sample itself was a time-consuming and laborious task which would take nearly two years to complete – and a decade had already passed since the bombings.

But the radiation spectra of the two bombs was not yet known, nor the shielding properties of the building materials that might complicate the simple linear distance–dose assumptions about exposure. It was hoped that the information from the radiation physicists would become available at much the same time as the Master Sample had been identified so that the morbidity and mortality rates of the fixed sample could begin to be quantified in the second decade after the bombings.

Despite the fact that the worlds of radiation medicine and radiation physics were both made up of very small groups of researchers in the 1950s and 1960s, the researchers at the Atomic Bomb Casualty Commission seem to have been very isolated from the most recent developments and information coming from the Marshall Islands or the Nevada Proving Ground. This was perhaps understandable at the level of the scientists and doctors working in Hiroshima and Nagasaki, both still considered hardship posts. But it is less easy to understand the lack of communication between the men who served on the Advisory Committee of the Atomic Bomb Casualty Commission, each of whom was a distinguished member of the elite of radiation researchers in the United States at that time and each of whom served on more than one major committee of the Atomic Energy Commission and increasingly on international bodies.

One major boundary between the various researchers was the disciplinary one. Was the study of the long term effects of radiation on human beings – the remit of the Atomic Bomb Casualty Commission – a matter for biomedical researchers or physicists? The newly emerging field of health physics was only beginning to bridge this divide.

Security also of course played a significant role in limiting the circulation of the information emerging from the various post-war experimental studies into bomb emissions and laboratory – the curious fact is that even the most senior members of the Advisory Committee did not seem able to get access to the necessary information. When the importance of the shielding studies began to be appreciated in 1953, for instance, the Field Director of the ABCC wrote[2] somewhat plaintively to his Washington Director, 'As for the correspondence to other agencies concerning Japanese homes and shielding studies, I can only state that Dr Ham and Dr Corsbie promised to inform you completely on this project and we have no other contact. The communication with the Embassy was on a verbal basis and I was simply told that the project would be handled by another agency and that it apparently would be handled in a very hush-hush manner, and that there was no reason why ABCC should be involved. I accepted this with the provision that you and Dr Corsbie would be informed through the State Department in Washington.' Even in this correspondence, Dr Holmes was decidedly cautious; 'The information they gave me was of such a nature that it precludes discussion in open correspondence.... I am simply the middleman at present, with impotence extending in both directions. State probably has its reasons for handling it in this way, but I am unable to fathom it.'

In 1956 Dr Holmes was circulating copies of correspondence between himself, Dr Cannan and his Chief of Biostatistics, Dr Woodbury to members of the Committee on Atomic Casualties regarding the proposed Shielding Survey because 'I believe we could be on the verge of making a big error'.[3]

The Shielding Survey group was proposing to limit the study to people who were either in buildings of light construction or were out in the open at the time of the bombings. Those who were in concrete buildings, air raid shelters and other situations that were difficult to evaluate would be excluded from the Shielding Survey because it was thought that it would be too difficult to establish the doses they had received even with the new developments in dose determination. This would amount to excluding 10 per cent of the people who had been studied in the Hiroshima genetics studies and 20 per cent in Nagasaki, which had more concrete buildings and natural shielding.

Dr Holmes felt strongly[4] that those showing signs and symptoms of biologic effects of radiation should not be excluded from the study. Simple considerations of distance and shielding should not be allowed to prevail over the principle of studying the entire survivor population within 2000 metres at least. While he thought that the notion of studying only those cases 'on whom there is hope of dosage determination' was 'a refreshing concept', he reminded Dr Cannan that 'We have three factors before us: distance, shielding and biologic effects. I realize fully that a determination of dosage is primarily a resultant of considerations given to distance and shielding, but I frankly cannot concede that those showing biologic effects on whom distance is also known should be given up because a shielding history appears to be unreliable.'

Dr Bugher, on the other hand, thought[5] that the only thing wrong with the proposed Shielding Survey was that the proposed sample was too large. 'The problem is to establish the radiation field with a sufficient number of individuals as to permit a rough correlation between the physical situation and the survivors' subsequently presenting signs and symptoms. Once this correlation is established, it should be realized that the biological system of man is itself a sensitive dosimeter. The problem has been to calibrate this biological system so that it may be effectively utilized.' He was 'inclined to feel that a thousand such carefully determined instances should be more than adequate for the purpose, combined with the recalculation by the Los Alamos staff of the radiation field which must have been established by the two bombs.'

Dr Bugher was one of the most senior and long-serving members of the Committee on Atomic Casualties and its successor Advisory Committee to the Atomic Bomb Casualty Commission. He had taught bacteriology and pathology at the University of Michigan from 1922 to 1937 then joined the Rockefeller Foundation as a member of its field staff from 1937 to 1951. In 1951 and 1952 he was consultant for nuclear affairs to the Rockefellers, and then served as Director of the Atomic Energy Commission's Division of Biology and Medicine from 1952 to 1955. He returned to the Rockefeller Foundation as Director for medical education and public health from 1955 to 1959 then left for a post in the new Puerto Rico Atomic Energy Agency. He played a pivotal role in the funding – and the conceptualizing – of much of the early work in radiation studies through these roles and his memberships of several international committees and commissions.

Dr Bugher's views about the nature and causes of radiation injury were very influential on the ABCC as mediated through its advisory committee. But Dr Bugher, like so many other researchers working in this newly emerging field of knowledge, was as susceptible to long-standing disciplinary assumptions about the way scientific and even biomedical research should proceed as others in the field.

Professor Thomas Francis Jr, who conceptualized the Unified Study Program based on a closed or fixed Master Sample, was a very distinguished researcher in the field of communicable diseases, particularly influenza and poliomyelitis. In late 1957 he was appointed President of the Armed Forces Epidemiological Board (AFEB), which had been established under Department of Defense Directive 5154.8 of 8 October 1953, to serve as a consultant body to the three Military Departments on technical aspects of the prevention and control of diseases. According to a memo titled 'Justification for the Armed Forces Epidemiological Board' submitted by its Executive Secretary, Captain R. W. Babione MC USN in May 1958[6] 'It serves both an advisory function and a participating one through research and field investigations done at the request of or in active cooperation with the various military agencies'. Each of its twelve Commissions met at least once a year to consider assigned problems and to review progress made in its sponsored field and laboratory research. In its first five years of operation, the Armed Forces Epidemiological Board had conducted basic studies of streptococcal infections, influenza, poliomyelitis, adenovirus, typhoid fever, tetanus, diptheria, smallpox, cholera, plague, Q fever, typhus fever and dengue fever. The AFEB conducted field and laboratory studies of parasitic diseases such as malaria, schistosomiasia, filariasis, amebiasis and various helminthic diseases. It also studied environmental hygiene and did some of the earliest coordinated work on reduction of losses due to accidental trauma. As well, the AFEB advised the Surgeon General of the Army in carrying out his responsibilities in respect to the defensive aspects of biological warfare. In this 1958 memo the AFEB's Executive Secretary noted that 'greatly increased attention has recently been given to the hazards of ionizing radiation, especially those aspects affecting disease and immunity under long-term and low-level exposure, for example, that which is likely to result fromfall-out from nuclear explosions or to industrial accidents.'

The dilemma was how best to go about establishing the aetiology and best treatments, perhaps even prevention, of radiation injury. In his work with the Atomic Bomb Casualty Commission Professor Francis had been able to develop the epidemiological basis for what was expected to be a series of studies of the somatic effects of radiation injury. But there was still an important sense in which the researchers were working in the dark, looking not only for a needle in the epidemiological haystack (which they had already reduced by settling for a closed Master Sample) but also not even being sure if it was a needle they were looking for. Did they really know what signs and symptoms they were looking for, setting aside the other logistical problems of finding them with any validity among the survivors of the bombings of Hiroshima and Nagasaki more than a decade after the detonations?

The poverty of knowledge about 'acute radiation syndrome' was apparent in a study reported in 1952 based on nine known cases[7] that had occurred in the Atomic Energy Commission since its inception. In his preface to this report, Shields Warren claimed that the data showed 'that an individual can be exposed to a large dose of radiation and still return to a productive vigorous life. The data presented in this article supplement the information gained at Hiroshima and Nagasaki, particularly for the period shortly after exposure when the Japanese observations were meager.' He did, however, acknowledge that the nine cases reported 'are peculiar to a nuclear reaction on a limited scale and unaccompanied by biologically significant amounts of heat and blast.'

The authors noted that while the nine cases were similar to 'the uncomplicated acute radiation injuries observed in Japan' there were certain dissimilarities between those injured at Los Alamos and those injured in Hiroshima and Nagasaki. 'The differences are largely the result of the inequality of radiation absorption in the medium through which the radiation passed before reaching the individuals. In the case of the Japanese explosions, the radiation traversed several thousand yards of moisture-laden air. In the Los Alamos accidents, in contrast, the radiation had a short course in shielding materials and a negligible pathway in air.'

In September 1958 C. W. Shilling, MD, Acting Director of the Division of Biology and Medicine of the United States Atomic Energy Commission invited[8] Dr Francis to a meeting on how best to determine the environmental effects of atomic radiation upon the people of the United States. 'There have been' Dr Shilling noted, 'many claims and counter-claims concerning both the somatic and genetic effects.' The AEC was 'under great pressure to at least undertake further studies aimed at an answer.' This pressure was coming from the United Nations, the US Academy of Sciences and the World Health Organization. Dr Shilling told Dr Francis that 'It is our thought to assemble, as a first step, as much information as possible from existing "ready-made" experiments in human radiobiology.' By this he meant a comprehensive review of the work being done on the radium dial painters, the accident cases, the inhabitants of radioactive areas, miners of radioactive ores, patients who had received thorotrast, the patients who were given radium salts to cure arthritis and mental disease. They would also review the progress of those who had been exposed *in utero* in pelvimetry X-rays, those who had received extensive X-ray therapy for gastral and duodenal ulcers and those who had received thymus X-ray treatment. There were also the Marshallese who had been irradiated during the *Bravo* tests, and the people of Hiroshima and Nagasaki. Dr Shilling indicated that 'as part of the plan for answering the total problem, and as a second step, we would like to consider the feasibility of carrying out extensive studies on the populations of four American cities at different altitudes in the United States to ascertain the presence or absence of effects of cosmic ray and terrestrial background exposure.'

By the late 1950s, several of the researchers – including the geneticist William J. Schull, now of the University of Michigan – associated with the ABCC were also working with other groups studying 'radioepidemi-ology' and other aspects of health physics. The summary of a meeting of the Radioepidemiology Study Group of the Argonne National Laboratory from February 1959[9] found in the files of Professor Francis discussed several ways of detecting and quantifying possible somatic effects of low-level, chronic exposure to very low intensity radiation. One approach was the animal experiments conducted in laboratories or during weapons tests. At the other extreme were the large-scale epidemi-ological studies of whole populations such as those at Nagasaki and Hiroshima, or communities with a high degree of natural background exposure to radiation. There was also the 'exploitation of ready-made human experiments such as dial painter studies' those workers who had ingested radium when painting watches in New Jersey in the 1930s. Dr Schull, largely responsible for the epidemiological studies of exposure to high levels of radiation in Japan, argued against using the epidemiological approach to establish whether or not incidences of leukaemia increased with very low differences in yearly exposures because of the magnitude of the populations that would be required to get statistically significant results. Dr Casarett of the University of Rochester emphasized the diffi-culty of testing the 'linearity' and 'threshold' hypotheses in a human epi-demiological study, pointing out the great advantages of large-scale ani-mal experiments. The consensus of the meeting 'seemed to be that a large scale study of populations was scientifically uninviting' for several reasons. The Argonne National Laboratory studies of the radium dial workers were then discussed, as were the problems of establishing the effects of very low ingested doses. It was noted in passing that 'Some patients in the Elgin State Hospital who were injected with radium are being studied in an effort to gain more accurate information on the time and dose-rate relationship in order to make more accurate estimates of lifetime dose.' It was not clear if these were patients receiving therapy or subjects being experimented upon. Nor was it clear whether or not they had consented in an informed manner to the procedures.

There had been reference at the opening of the study group's meeting to the discussion a few months earlier of 'some 17 human experimental possibilities'. At the 1959 meeting Dr Marinelli 'presented estimates of possible bone sarcoma cases from the radium-water drinkers, the Travancore population, the thorotrast patients, the dial painters, and the Elgin State Hospital patients as compared to the entire State of Illinois, Chicago and Boston as controls and under various assumptions as to dou-bling dose and percentage of "natural" bone sarcomas due to radiation.' After extensive discussion, 'opinion seemed unanimous that studies such as those involving radium containing water, thorotrast, and dial painters were important and much more promising than proposed large-scale population studies with slight variations in background radiation levels. and that they should be pursued with energy.'

Institutions such as the New York University Institute of Industrial Medicine submitted research proposals to the AFEB and other agencies for funding. The Institute of Industrial Medicine was affiliated with the Health and Safety Laboratories of the Atomic Energy Commission, and proposed to 'establish a facility for measuring with extreme sensitivity whole body radioactivity' which would help to establish a definition of internal dosimetry by surveying the internal radioactive burdens in particular groups, such as clinical cases of osteosarcoma and leukaemia and people with possible exceptional body burdens from occupational exposures such as the surviving radium dial workers.[10]

During 1958 Dr Francis received a proposal[11] from Dr Donald M. Pillsbury of the Department of Dermatology of the University of Pennsylvania to 'determine short- and long-term effects of ionizing radiation on the human skin, under conditions of strict control'. Dr Pillsbury noted that most of the studies on late effects of ionizing radiation were entirely retrospective 'with incomplete and inaccurate data on the amount of radiation which had been given to the skin'. He proposed to 'give careful calibrated ionizing radiation in varying amounts to small areas of skin in human subjects. The size of the areas would be such that surgical excision could easily be accomplished later if any permanent untoward effects were noted.' The subjects to be used 'principally would be idiots and feeble-minded children permanently committed to a home in New Jersey. An excellent rapport with the institution has been established and a number of experimental studies have been carried out there without incident and with the full cooperation from the authorities in charge of the institution.' Dr Pillsbury noted that 'In these individuals, observation would be possible for indefinite periods of time.' It was possible that subjects at Holmesburg Prison would also be used but the likely period of observation for these inmates was closer to two years. One of the short-term studies proposed was the determination of the protective effects of melanin pigment in respect to superficial radiation. It would also be possible to study the comparative methods of treating the burns arising from the irradiation. Tests would be conducted on the biologic defence mechanisms, using antigens such as tuberculin, deep fungi and 'simple chemical contact allergens'. Various pharmacologically active compounds such as atropine, acetylcholine and histamine would also be experimented with 'both during the acute reaction and later'. Dr Pillsbury believed 'that these studies could be carried out with complete safety to the general health of the subjects concerned' and would have 'the very distinct advantage of being done on human tissue'.

It is not clear if the AFEB funded this proposal, although Dr Francis' file copy is annotated, 'Babione had already sent forms'. In a letter in December 1958 to the Executive Secretary of the AFEB[12] Dr Pillsbury noted 'I have had a certain amount of correspondence with Dr Francis' regarding the studies which might be done on the effects of irradiation upon the skin and upon immune mechanisms. In this December letter he informs the AFEB that 'I have recently discussed the problem again with Dr Albert M. Kligman, of our staff, who has established a very satisfactory rapport with the Woodbine State Colony in New Jersey, which is an institution for mental defectives. A number of studies have been carried out quite successfully there with no untoward incidents whatever.' Dr Pillsbury argued that:

> There is no satisfactory study which has dealt with irreversible and long-term changes produced by known varying quantities of gamma rays. The precise doses required to cause permanent damage to such appendages as hair, sweat glands, sebaceous glands, and to blood vessels and connective tissue are merely guesses. There is still much controversy as to whether or not the sequelae after divided doses of irradiation are likely to be more severe than if the irradiation is given in one dose. Obviously these defects in our knowledge have implications in respect to possible reactions to radioactive isotopes. One may find statements on all these matters in the medical literature, but opinions are at variance, and there is no body of solid experimental evidence.

Dr Kligman and Dr Pillsbury felt that 'such experiments could be carried out safely at this institution. There would be no concern about the possible genetic effects; these individuals will never reproduce.'

Dr Pillsbury had trained in dermatology and syphilology. He was chairman of the Department of Dermatology at the University of Pennsylvania Medical School from 1945 to 1965 and was a consultant to the Surgeon General of the US Army from 1946 until his death in 1980.

Notes

1. Letter from Clarence M. Tinsley MD to Robert H. Holmes,18 November 1955, at Francis:39.

2. Letter from Robert H. Holmes to R. Keith Cannan, dated 3 July 1953, at Bugher 2:1:2:9:103.

3. Memo, dated 2 August 1956, at Bugher 2:1:9:104.

4. Letter from Robert H. Holmes to R. Keith Cannan, dated 2 August 1956, at Bugher 2:1:9:104.

5. Letter from John C. Bugher to R. Keith Cannan, dated 23 August 1956, at Bugher 2:1:9:104.

6. Memo for Brigadier General Sheldon Brownton USAF (MC), Office of the Assistant Secretary of Defense (Health and Medical), Department of Defense, Washington DC from R. W. Babione, Captain, MC USN, Executive Secretary Armed Forces Epidemiological Board, dated 22 May 1958, at Francis:29.

7. Louis H. Hemplemann, Hermann Lisco, and Joseph G. Hoffman, 'The acute radiation syndrome: a study of nine cases and a review of the problem', *Annals of Internal Medicine* 36:2: February 1952.

8. Letter from C. W. Shilling, Acting Director, Division of Biology and Medicine, United States Atomic Energy Commission to Dr Thomas Francis Jr, School of Public Health, University of Michigan, dated 4 September 1958, at Francis:29.

9. Summary of Meeting of Radioepidemiology Study Group, Argonne National Laboratory, 2–3 February 1959, at Francis:29.

10. 'Radiation Hazards from Internal Burdens of Radioactivity', at Francis:29.

11. Letter from Donald M. Pillsbury to Thomas Francis Jr, dated 20 May 1958, at Francis:29.

12. Letter from Donald M. Pillsbury to Robert W. Babione, Executive Secretary, Armed Forces Epidemiological Board, dated 5 December 1958, at Francis:29.

MANAGING MEGA SCIENCE

A morbidity detection program as outlined by Francis et al. will do little or nothing to cut down patient attrition and, on the contrary, if not handled with utmost care, could actually increase the attrition. An interrogation of a survivor who is ill, without a means of administering to his illness, will not do much to win his favor; it could antagonize.

John C. Bugher to R. Keith Cannan, 24 August 1956

Sixteen

Although the Ad Hoc Conference of the Atomic Bomb Casualty Commission had strongly endorsed the Francis Committee Report with its proposed Unified Study Program of research in November 1955, much of 1956 was spent in defending this vision of the work of the ABCC both in Japan and in Washington. It would be almost the end of the decade before the new research designs would actually begin to be implemented.

The Francis Report provided a broad blueprint for focusing the work of the ABCC. The problems arose when the relevant departments began to try to understand their role in the unified programme. On one hand the official report of the *ad hoc* committee[1] 'recommended that the Death Certificate Study be recognized as the most important single component of the Unified Study Program which must not be sacrificed'. On the other hand, the pathologists at the ABCC from the head of department on down felt that using death certificates for a study of the causes of death was unreliable even in studies of known disease aetiologies and sequelae.[2]

The reviewing committee of the Francis Report also acknowledged that 'The Unified Study Program emphasizes the statistical and epidemiological approach because this is the need of the moment. It is fully recognized that the success of the program depends upon the excellence of the clinical, pathological, radiological and laboratory observations. If this has not been emphasized in the report it is because it is an elemental fact that was taken for granted.' But it is also recognized that there were major organizational and intellectual issues to be resolved in the field before the various departments could be harnessed to a common enterprise.

It was now more than a decade since the bombings; the problems of patient attrition were also apparent to all the external reviewers. The Ad Hoc Conference recommended the urgent appointment of a Scientific Consultant of stature and the extension of the diagnostic medical ward. Subjects should be paid for their time spent attending the ABCC but the greatest incentive for participation in the studies would be greater access to medical care. Relations with the Japanese physicians in the two cities should be cultivated even further and those who worked with the ABCC in the studies should have the opportunity to continue their studies in the United States. It may be that the ABCC itself should be more widely sponsored in order to overcome some of the apparent problems in recruitment and staffing – the committee recommended that the President of the National Academy of Sciences call a top-level conference of appropriate government and private agencies who 'might be interested in supporting the exploitation of the unique opportunity presented at Hiroshima and Nagasaki for long-term medical and sociological studies of populations for whom extensive health data have already been amassed and for whose support extensive clinical and laboratory facilities are available'.

These reservations about the performance of the ABCC a decade after the bombings were not reflected in the Newsletter of the Division of Medical Sciences of the NAS-NRC in January 1956[3] where the results of the Francis Committee's review were reported to the membership of the élite academy of American science. The origins of the ABCC in 1946 and 1947 under the auspices of the Atomic Energy Commission were rehearsed. 'Investigating units were established at Hiroshima and Nagasaki and studies got under way. In the beginning, the major emphasis was on a carefully designed systematic genetic program. This was continued according to plan until the field work was terminated early in 1954, by which time the panel of geneticists that had designed the study had determined that the point of diminishing returns had been reached in the accumulation of data on the first generation offspring of the survivors of the bombs.' The data were now being analysed and would be available in the summer of 1956. 'The results of this study are awaited with great interest. They derive from an investigation of some 70,000 infants – undoubtedly the largest and most complex study in human genetics that has ever been undertaken. It will remain a permanent monument to the work of ABCC.'

Alongside these genetic studies was 'a series of short-term medical and pathological studies designed to answer a number of specific questions'. After the 1950 census became available, 'a systematic medical-pathological study of the survivor population and a group of matched controls was initiated in 1950 and has been prosecuted, with some modification in design, up to the present.' The major finding so far 'has been the establishment of a significant increase in the incidence of leukaemia in the two cities.' One hundred and five cases had been detected. 'There has also been an increased incidence of cataracts which are probably attributable to radiation.' Among the individuals *in utero* at the time of the bombs, 'there have been found a few cases of small head circumference accompanied by some degree of mental retardation. Susceptibility to this effect is related to the distance from the hypocenter and gestational age of the subject at the time of the bomb.'

The Division of Medical Sciences of the NAS-NRC noted that these results were consistent with the results of animal experimentation and the data on accidental exposures. 'The major problem that remains is to determine whether evidence will be found in man of those more remote responses to radiation which have been observed in animals – notably accelerated ageing, and an increased incidence of cancer and other degenerative diseases. This may prove to be a long and frustrating task.' It was also 'becoming increasingly difficult to maintain statistically significant samples in the face of the progressive attrition which is inevitable in a volunteer population.'

According to the Division, 'As the long-term nature of the undertaking has come more clearly into focus' it had become apparent that the ABCC was embarked on a broad community health survey of large dimensions and indefinite duration. 'We therefore concluded that the program must receive a more critical epidemiological appraisal if its full potentialities were to be realized.' Dr Francis and his colleagues had undertaken that review and outlined a Unified Study Program of research 'designed to place the current studies on a sounder statistical basis'. This proposal 'represents an extended and intensified program for the detection of abnormalities and the study of their pathogenesis in a fixed population containing exposed and unexposed persons. The program retains the valuable features of present procedures but seeks to provide greater coherence and to increase the sensitivity of detection at every level of observation.' It would depend on a morbidity detection programme which would amount to a long-term community health survey which would provide information 'of tremendous value to the whole field of medicine' and one which, indeed, would add 'a new dimension to preventive medicine'.

Not everyone was convinced. Dr Holmes, the Field Director of the ABCC in Hiroshima and Nagasaki, and Dr Woodbury, Head of the Biostatistics Department – two crucial players in the successful implementation of the Unified Study Program – were both critical about the prospects for a long-term morbidity detection survey or community health study on the scale proposed. They were lobbying Drs Parran, Bugher and Warren on the Committee against the proposals.[4] Seymour Jablon, one of the Francis Committee, wrote to Dr Francis in February 1956, 'It seems fairly clear that Woodbury and Holmes don't much care for the Morbidity program. I suspect that, if permitted, they will, while professing sympathy for the objectives, find all kinds of reasons why it won't work, or will be too expensive or should not be undertaken until later or anything else which will excuse a failure to make an honest and enthusiastic effort to make it work.'

Dr Francis responded to criticism of his proposals by threatening to withdraw from any further participation in the work of the ABCC. He took the position that he had had the vision of the Unified Study Program; it was up to the field force to implement it and to the senior administrators such as Dr Cannan to ensure that they did so efficiently and faithfully.[5] Dr Cannan took this as a personal challenge. But he needed Dr Francis' continued participation as a consultant to carry the day against the objections to the Unified Study Program. Throughout 1956 he wrote letters imploring Dr Francis not to act on his threat to withdraw from the review committee's deliberations. In March 1956 he wrote[6] 'It is becoming quite clear that we face a showdown on the questions of an aggressive prosecution of the Unified Study Program and of the need for a strong scientific leadership at ABCC.... So here is my plea that you make just one more appearance in order that the real opportunity that ABCC offers may have a fair chance of realization. Frankly I never conceived the possibility of this roadblock but here it is.' Dr Francis told him to put his house in order first. He was not prepared to attend meetings to foist something that was considered undesirable or impracticable on a reluctant ABCC. He was not going to be put in the position of defending his report. 'It was made in good faith and our confidence in its desirability is unchanged... if the Committee should decide it wants to play along with the present organization as it is, I would have no interest whatever in the setup nor could I encourage any others to be interested in it.'[7]

The gauntlet was dropped. Dr Cannan had to choose between Holmes and Woodbury – who were actively criticizing the shielding surveys at the same time as they were lobbying against the Unified Study Program – and the eminent consultant, Dr Francis. It was to be almost two years before Dr Cannan could write to Dr Francis that, 'The malcontents have all been liquidated. The new heads of departments are full of enthusiasm, recognize the "unified" nature of the task and hold each other in mutual respect.'[8]

While Dr Holmes was sceptical of the capacity of the ABCC to implement the large-scale epidemiological health survey required for the morbidity studies, he recognized the urgency of increasing access to clinical and pathological material. He thought that the problems of the ABCC – recruiting both high calibre staff and enough subjects for them to study –

could be largely solved by offering treatment to the survivors who continued to participate in the ABCC studies. In February 1956 he wrote to Dr Cannan:

> *A stimulating clinical service with modern, orthodox pathologic correlation is simply fundamental to the satisfaction of a professional staff of proper caliber. This is a good argument in favor of an expanded medical ward. Such clinico-pathologic correlation is also essential to the collection of data related to the possibility of premature ageing, shortening of life span, increased neoplasia, and increased degenerative disease. This involves an expanded treatment policy but could be controlled and directed primarily at the exposed population. Such a program would lessen considerably the criticism of the Japanese and other nationalities, including some of our own. It would also favorably influence the attrition rate. Improvement in staff morale would naturally lead to an increase in scientific yield.*[9]

The Field Director of the ABCC felt that 'The cry for treatment and the guarantee of treatment is a frequent political note capitalized upon by emotional scavengers'. But the real reason why treatment of the survivors was now necessary 'is that it is simply *necessary to accomplish our scientific objective*' (his emphasis). 'It is necessary to get the patients to come back again and again, so that we can accumulate the clinical and pathologic data that are essential for valid biostatistical analysis.'

Dr Holmes was working with the American Embassy in Tokyo to negotiate with the presidents of the Hiroshima and Nagasaki universities about the funding of hospitals that would be treatment centres that could be used by the ABCC. In May 1956 Ambassador Allison put forward a proposal for funding to Washington which argued:

> *This proposal is not submitted to assuage any feeling of guilt in connection with the atomic bomb which doubtless saved countless thousands of lives, by bringing the war to a speedy termination, or in a spirit of maudlin sentimentality for innocent survivors. Rather it is a hard-headed business proposal designed to accomplish two objectives: (1) silence an increasingly vocal resentment which can impair Japanese–American relations by giving a propaganda tool to the communists, and (2) make more effective the research already undertaken through enhanced opportunity for cooperation between improved university treatment centers and the ABCC.*[10]

Dr Holmes' contract ran out in mid-1956 and at the end of August a reorganization of the ABCC in relation to the NAS-NRC was announced.[11] The executive office of the ABCC was transferred from the Division of Medical Sciences of the NAS-NRC to the office of the President of the Academy and Dr Cannan was appointed as full-time

Executive Director. The Committee on Atomic Casualties of the Division of Medical Sciences was replaced by a reconstituted committee to be known as the Advisory Committee. While many long-serving members such as Dr Bugher remained on the new advisory committee, senior consultants such as Dr Francis were now appointed to the committee which would advise on the implementation of the Unified Study Program. This new committee would advise the President of the Academy on scientific and technical matters but 'will not be burdened with those distracting administrative matters that have occupied so much of the time of the Committee on Atomic Casualties in the past.'

Dr Holmes submitted his resignation and Dr Cannan announced that he would be going to Japan for several months until a new Field Director could be recruited. Five days after this announcement, Warren Weaver of the Rockefeller Foundation telephoned Shields Warren of the Committee on Atomic Casualties to sound out the suitability of Robert Holmes for a job with the Foundation. According to a memo of the conversation which was apparently dictated for the files by Dr Bugher[12] Weaver said that Holmes' strongest point was the relationships he had developed with the Japanese medical scientists. 'He seems to understand their point of view, does not treat them as attractive children but as colleagues and [ ] he has really excellent working relationships.' Weaver asked Warren how he would rate Holmes' intellectual capacity. 'He started out by saying that he would probably say "upper average", but then went on to say (probably this does not involve any contradiction, coming from Boston) that at Harvard he would doubtless have been in the low one-third of his class. In terms of organizing ability, and ability to get along with the Japanese, SW [Shields Warren] would put him in the top one-third. He says that he would certainly never be an outstanding scientist.' Warren suggested that Holmes had difficulty with his American colleagues, particularly Dr Cannan. But 'Keith Cannan is well known to be a pretty stiff person.' Holmes was also not liked by his predecessor Grant Taylor, but this was put down to policy disagreements and Warren thought Holmes' judgement in these areas was the better of the two men. Warren warned Weaver that Holmes was known to be 'having a very active affair with Ambassador Allison's secretary' and that Cannan had suggested he had a drinking problem but Warren 'had never seen him do anything at all foolish in this connection'.

Dr Holmes had been working closely with Dr Bugher and the Rockefeller Foundation to set up fellowships in the US for promising Japanese doctors and scientists as one way of attracting them to work with the ABCC and promoting their professional development.[13] He had also demonstrated that he understood the broader mission of the

Rockefeller Foundation in Japan when he sent a clipping about the participation of the Zengakuren student union at the Afro-Asian Conference in Bandung in May 1956. He promised Dr Bugher in his cover note[14] that 'My Gestapo will give me the names of the students who will represent Japan at Bandung. In view of your interest in educational affairs, it may come in handy some day' since Zengakuren was considered to be a Communist-front organization.

But there were other critics of the Unified Study Program and particularly of its construction of the Master Sample. Dr Alexander Langmuir, an epidemiologist and member of the Advisory Committee, was very worried by the size of the samples for the Death Certificate Study and the morbidity studies and expressed his views forcefully at the January 1957 meeting of the Advisory Committee.[15] Dr Langmuir pointed out that the animal experiments suggested that general body breakdown rather than the collapse of specific organ systems seemed to be the consequence of irradiation. It was necessary and sufficient to establish differentials in mortality rates between exposed and non-exposed populations. But what size of sample would be required to establish the differentials if they existed? A mortality rate of 1 per cent per year was expected in the exposed group; over a decade it was expected that 10 per cent would die. If there was a failure to follow 5 to 10 per cent of these the results might be off by as much as 100 per cent. It was important that 98 per cent to 99 per cent of the deaths should be followed; if the design of the mortality study was properly conceived, the clinical studies should be built around this sample. But it was proposed to study the death certificates arising in a population of 100,000 in Hiroshima and 30,000 in Nagasaki; this population would be too large to conduct comprehensive morbidity studies on. It was more important to achieve 98 per cent follow-up on 20,000 people than 98 per cent follow-up on 100,000. Dr Francis argued that the 100,000 sample was necessary to generate sufficient death certificates for the mortality study, while the morbidity studies were planned on a sample of only 18,000.

Dr Furth questioned reliance on two apparently contradictory views of radiation; that there were no specific delayed effects of radiation, and that findings drawn from the studies of male radiologists in the US provided a good basis on which to predict mortality and morbidity rates in the Japanese survivors.

Dr Francis responded to these challenges by reminding the committee that attrition had been a major consideration and in the first half of 1956 more than half the sample in the adult medical programme had refused to be re-examined. In the event only 38 per cent of those on the roster for that period had been examined. It would be another year before the roster of 100,000 subjects for the Master Sample had been completed. Clinical data was being collected but on an almost random basis of those who chose to come to the ABCC. They were not representative of the survivors, exposed or non-exposed. Dr Bronk noted that when the committees of the Academy and the Research Council and those of the British Medical Research Council were engaged a year earlier in a study of the effects of radiation on human beings they had frequent recourse to the information obtained by the ABCC. 'The committee here this day should recognize that its members were serving as trustees of a population which offered many significant scientific opportunities, and that guidance from this advisory group was very greatly needed in selection and elimination, so that the program was not hindered by trying to do too much.' The President of the National Academy of Sciences reminded the advisory committee that:

> We have to learn to live a double life, a life of hope and a life of caution. Caution can be built on knowledge. To this end the committee should be one more group which would spend a little time thinking about the danger which faces us, doing everything that could be done to avoid that danger and at the same time considering what could be done biologically to reduce the consequences that might befall in a period.

The Advisory Committee was also informed[16] that while the ABCC's own ward was far too small to meet the needs of a study of 15,000 to 18,000 people, the Medical School of Hiroshima University was about to return to the city after its relocation in Kure. The school had applied to the US Embassy for funds to build a ward and there was a gentleman's agreement that the ABCC would be invited to participate in the operation of this ward if the funds were obtained. 'Any relation that may be worked out will certainly involve some sort of Blue Cross plan whereby ABCC contributes materially to the hospital care of patients in whom it is interested. This is in no sense to be regarded as an undertaking to treat A-bomb survivors. It should be considered simply to be a proper research cost of the study of selected patients and indirect reward for their loyalty to the program.' Relations with Nagasaki Medical School had always been much better than those with Hiroshima and it was expected that there would be no major obstacle to increased clinical studies in Nagasaki. The Red Cross Hospital now had an A-bomb memorial wing with a hundred beds and an outpatient clinic handling 800 patients a month. But it still had not been possible to appoint an Associate Director at ABCC who would have responsibility for the conduct of this expanded clinical and pathological study.

Dr Francis was furious at the criticisms levelled by Dr Langmuir at the

January 1957 meeting. Dr Langmuir wrote to Dr Cannan apologizing for the level of tension but pointed out that the committee had not taken the time to resolve the differences that were apparent. 'We took "unanimous" votes without really knowing what we were endorsing.'[17] Dr Cannan, in forwarding a copy of this letter to Dr Francis, remarked 'We probably all agree that considerable confusion was evidenced at the meeting on January 5 as to what are the basic epidemiological principles of the Unified Study Program.'[18] He was afraid that there would be procrastination in implementing the new proposals in the field 'should the opinion spread that there is disagreement on basic principles' and proposed a meeting of the major players at the Cosmos Club over dinner on 1 February 1957.

Dr Francis responded[19] that his 'first thought when Alex Langmuir proposed that we would have to have another meeting was to tell him that I would not engage in any further discussions of the program.' He had been so distressed by the 'morning performance' that he had barely been able to attend the afternoon session of the Advisory Committee. 'I am interested to know that subsequently several others of the committee said this seemed just like three years ago, or ten years ago.' In his opinion, the Francis Report was clear in its intentions; Dr Langmuir could not have been fully conversant with it. Moreover, 'I believe that what went on in that morning's meeting so clearly played into the hands of Holmes that any scientific director would be in an untenable position in trying to lay down on the spot the plan because he would be immediately encountered [sic] by the statement that the committee itself did not agree on what should be done.'

According to Dr Francis, 'The death certificate study obviously is not part of the unified examination program; it is primarily a statistical and clerical job.' Equally it was necessary to find some way to keep track of people otherwise 'you may as well fold both your medical and pathological programs'. A great deal of ground had been lost to Holmes; 'My feeling is that you are going to have to do something firmly and strongly in support of the scientific plan, even if some of it has to be modified in operation. Otherwise, I think the ship is sunk.'

Notes

1. Recommendations of the Ad Hoc Conference on ABCC held at the Academy Research Council, 27 November 1955, at Francis:39.

2. For example Letter from Edward S. Murphy to Thomas Francis Jr, dated 21 November 1955, at Francis:39, 'I found myself in agreement with all that was said there, [at the Ad Hoc Conference], with the possible exception of the use of death certificates for a study of the causes of death. In that respect I am in agreement with Dr Laqueur, who feels that they are so inaccurate that no good could be obtained from such a study.' Murphy also refers to five alumni of Michigan being at that meeting.

3. The Division Newsletter No. 5, January 1956 of Division of Medical Sciences, National Academy of Sciences-National Research Council, at Francis:39.

4. Letter from Seymour Jablon to Thomas Francis Jr, dated 20 February 1956, at Francis: 39.

5. For example, Letter of R. Keith Cannan, Chairman of the Division of Medical Sciences, National Academy of Sciences-National Research Council, to Thomas Francis Jr dated 13 February 1956 at Francis:39

6. Letter of R. Keith Cannan to Thomas Francis Jr, dated 15 March 1956, at Francis:39.

7. Letter of Thomas Francis Jr to R. Keith Cannan, dated 22 March 1956, at Francis:39.

8. Letter from R. Keith Cannan to Thomas Francis Jr, dated 17 October 1958, at Francis: 39.

9. Letter from Robert H. Holmes to R. Keith Cannan, dated 15 February 1956, at Bugher 1:2:9:103.

10. Memo from John M. Allison, Embassy of the United States, Tokyo, dated 1 May 1956, at Bugher 2:1:2:9:103.

11. Letter from R. Keith Cannan to John C. Bugher dated 29 August 1956, at Bugher 2:1:9:105.

12. Memo dated 4 September 1956, at Bugher 1:2:29:503.

13. For example, letter of Robert H. Holmes to R. Keith Cannan, dated 29 June 1956, at Bugher 2:1:2:9:103.

14. Memo from Robert H. Holmes to John C. Bugher, dated 18 May 1956, at Bugher 2:1:2:9:103.

15. Minutes of the 23rd Meeting of the Advisory Council to the Atomic Bomb Casualty Commission, 5 January 1957.

16. 'The current and the projected program of ABCC: a report prepared for the meeting of the Advisory Committee on the Atomic Bomb Casualty Commission to be held on Saturday, 5 January 1957' at Bugher 2:1:2:9:106.

17. Letter from Alexander D. Langmuir to R. Keith Cannan, dated 14 January 1957, at Francis:39.

18. Letter from R. Keith Cannan to Thomas Francis Jr, dated 16 January 1957, at Francis:39.

19. Letter from Thomas Francis Jr to R. Keith Cannan, dated 25 January 1957, at Francis:39.

Seventeen

In 1957 the interim Executive Director of the Atomic Bomb Casualty Commission, R. Keith Cannan, who had been associated with the studies from their outset, achieved a consensus around a modified version of the Unified Study Program and its Master Sample. Now it was agreed that 'the Proximal Medical Sample is restricted in that it comprises only those within 2000 m of the hypocenter for who major signs of acute radiation sickness have been recorded. It is presumed that this restriction has been accepted because the biological evidence of exposure to significant radiation is held to be more dependable than current estimates of radiation dose based upon distance from the explosion and degree of shielding. Those who were within 2000 m of the bomb but recorded no symptoms are excluded from the medical program' unless they belonged to the small group carried over from earlier studies. In other words, the study of long-term effects was to be confined to those who had manifested short-term effects in a manner detected by the ABCC's earlier studies.[1]

These plans were set back by the discovery that the 1950 Census list of 'non-exposed' persons had been destroyed.[2] Seymour Jablon and Felix Moore, the two members of the Francis Committee who reviewed progress on the Unified Study Program in March and April 1957, revised the samples to those exposed at less than 2500 metres and those exposed at more than 2500 metres – the proximal and the distal exposed. The 'non-exposed' were declared to be those named on the 1950 or 1951 ABCC Sample Census lists or on the 1953 Hiroshima City Census as being a person at that time resident in one of the cities of interest but who had not been resident in either city or within 10,000 metres of the hypocentres at the time of the bombings and who had honseki registrations (municipal registration system) in the two prefectures at some time prior to 1 October 1957. The second two groups, the distal and non-exposed, would consist of samples matched to the proximal exposed as to age, sex, location of *honseki* [municipal registration] and number of persons included.

A new Director had finally been appointed. Dr George Darling, Professor of Human Ecology at Yale University, had agreed to go to Hiroshima. Professor Darling had begun his career in Public Health in the Department of Health in Michigan in 1927. Five years later he joined the Kellogg Foundation as its Executive Director and subsequently President.

There was another major new development in the Japanese scene. From 1 April 1957 the survivors of the bombings of Hiroshima and Nagasaki would have extensive health coverage. As Dr Cannan explained to the Advisory Committee in June 1957[3] this development seriously prejudiced the proposal that the ABCC develop its own health care programme for its sample population since it clearly could not compete with a national programme. However, relations with the Japanese physicians and social welfare officials undertaken by Dr Holmes had progressed a long way, and the Japanese Advisory Committee was not opposed to facilitating increased patient referrals to the ABCC now that it was offering more extensive clinical reviews. The future of the ABCC now lay in being perceived by the Japanese agencies as a cooperating partner rather than a competitor in Hiroshima and Nagasaki.

In canvassing for their support for the new research agenda of the Francis Committee Report, Dr Cannan told the Japanese Advisory Council in April 1957[4] that:

> In the design of the genetic program it was realized from the very beginning that the most refined statistical control of observations would be necessary if significant conclusions were to be reached on the effects of radiation in the first generation of children of exposed parents. The final report on the genetics studies which was published this year bears eloquent testimony to the statistical care with which this program was conducted.

But the conduct of the medical programme had until now rested upon quite a different conception. It was based on the assumption that the delayed effects of radiation would manifest themselves as striking increases in the incidence of a few specific anomalies in the exposed populations.

> Consequently, exacting epidemiological control of the medical surveillance of the people was not insisted upon. Uncertainties as to the precise composition of populations under investigation and inadequacies in follow-up were tolerated in the belief that they would not obscure such important effects of radiation as might exist.

The justification of this programme was that it had, despite these shortcomings, demonstrated significant increases in anomalies such as leukaemia and cataracts. These might be described as the 'early delayed effects' of radiation. But attention now had to turn to effects which might still be latent and not manifest themselves clinically until late in the lives of the persons affected. Animal experiments had resulted in observations of a reduced life expectancy which appeared to be due not to the aggravation of one or two specific diseases but rather to an acceleration of the degenerative processes which constitute the major causes of death.

> *It is now generally agreed that the future medical program of the ABCC should be so designed as to be able to demonstrate whether or not a similar situation obtains in man. That is to say, the program should be one that is capable of establishing what may prove to be small quantitative differences in the incidence of a wide spectrum of diseases. It follows that there is now required a precision of epidemiological control of the population under study far exceeding that which has been practised in the past.*

Dr Cannan was confident that this could be achieved. In the first years after the war the populations of the two cities had been in flux, but now the cities had been rebuilt and the populations were relatively stable. Censuses were available, the workforce and the social services sector were both highly organized 'and ABCC has come to be recognized as an integral part of the community'. It was now possible to 'contemplate careful long-term epidemiological studies of the sort clearly needed to fulfil the mission of ABCC' but this would rely on the cooperation of the medical and welfare agencies in the two cities. This was both prompted and facilitated by the new health insurance laws. It was hoped, for instance, that the pathology centres in the two cities could now be united 'in an effort to bring to autopsy as many as possible of the cases of death in the Master Sample'. These new insurance laws 'removed the last vestige of motivation on the part of the population to cooperate in the ABCC program (a free examination is no longer a strong inducement) but at the same time provided a mechanism which would be made to serve the needs of the Unified Program in obtaining information on the state of health of the samples.'

In the research design discussions that now took place around the mortality and ageing studies, there was explicit recognition of potential sources of bias in studies to be conducted twelve or more years after the bombings. An early outline proposal[5] listed six potential sources of bias including the role of fallout and of preferential treatment in confounding the distinction between exposed and non-exposed. But from these earliest discussions, people of non-Japanese origin, such as Koreans, were excluded from the studies and the status of early and later entrants to Hiroshima and Nagasaki after the bombings was never very clear. The major confounding element was thought to be the general disaster effect. It was acknowledged that the best way to address this problem would be to compare the fates of the populations of Nagasaki and Hiroshima with another city such as Kure which had received extensive conventional bombing. But by the later 1950s the prospect of the ABCC conducting a major study in Kure met with as little enthusiasm as it had in the late 1940s.

Preferential treatment of those showing radiation symptoms was now – a decade after the bombings – acknowledged to be developing into a potential bias in itself. On the one hand, the greater access to treatment may have decreased the death rate in what were presumed to be the most heavily exposed – those with the most severe symptoms. On the other hand, some of that treatment involved X-ray exposures which may have compounded the problems of those already irradiated.

A review conference on the proposed research designs for the ageing and mortality studies was held in Washington in November 1957.[6] The reviewers were trying to find a way of quantifying any shortening of life-span or acceleration of the ageing process but they were doing so without a substantial hypothesis about the somatic processes that might be involved. Do organisms whose lives are shortened by radiation pass through the same sequence of senescent changes? Are irradiated and senile changes similar? If radiation shortens life span, does it do this by striking off specific increments of life span, or by compressing the life span that would be otherwise expected, in a way that could be detected statistically? Would such radiation-induced ageing necessarily progress at the same rate for different organisms and tissues? Is such ageing linearly related to dosage? Would it be comparable across species – would the indications from animal experiments predict the rate and quantity and type of changes to be seen in humans? What would be the biochemical explanation of such changes? What role would mutations play in these processes? Would the changes be irreversible? What role does natural radiation play in normal ageing? What other agents cause ageing? Is there a threshold for recovery from radiation-induced injury and ageing? What happens at the molecular level?

By November 1957 the Advisory Committee was also receiving more substantive reports from the studies of leukaemia in the two cities. The leukaemia studies had been very influenced by the British work in this field and the data had been collected reasonably systematically. But the data had been reviewed again more independently of the British data which was too dependent on studies of patients who had been treated with radiation for ankylosing spondylitis. The new tabulations were reported to the Advisory Committee at the end of 1957.[7]

The data from 1950 to 1956 indicated that the incidence of leukaemia among those exposed within 2000 metres of the hypocentre was at first substantially higher than among the other groups of survivors. From a peak of 39.39 per 100,000 in 1951, however, it had fallen to 6.6 per 100,000 in 1956. The decline had continued but in 1956 there had been a surprising increase among those exposed *beyond* 2000 metres. The incidence of 8.0 per 100,000 in 1956 equalled the total of the previous five years. The minutes of the Advisory Committee noted 'While the series was too small to give these trends statistical significance, and while additional cases originating during these years might still be identified, this finding demanded closer study.'

It was also found that while susceptibility to radiation-induced leukaemia was greater among younger persons, the incidence among those more than 2000 metres from the hypocentre was found to increase with age at the time of the bombing, especially in the case of chronic granulocytic leukaemia. It was acknowledged that the assumptions about dosage for these studies were based simply on distance from the hypocentre.

A striking difference between the two cities in the incidence of acute leukaemias was apparent by 1959.[8] There were more acute than chronic leukaemias in Nagasaki and this was thought to relate to the differences in neutron flux in the two bombs. The total number of cases under 1000 metres in this 1959 report was sixteen but the total number between 1000 and 1499 metres was thirty. There were eight cases detected from 1500 to 1999 metres and nine cases beyond 2000 metres. There was no comment in the discussions of the haematologists to whom these data were reported of the lack of linear correlation between these data and similar data presented exactly four years earlier. In a report published in *Science*[9] two ABCC researchers, Moloney and Kastenbaum, had reported an incidence of fifteen cases of leukaemia under 1000 metres, twenty-four cases from 1000 to 1499 metres, five cases at 1500 to 1999 metres; two cases at 2000 to 2499 metres and four cases over 2500 metres.

The 1955 researchers had claimed that their data indicated that the incidence of leukaemia was high at distances close to the hypocentre whether or not the survivors had presented severe early radiation complaints but that it approached the normal at distances beyond 2500 metres. Their categories of survivors (and level of radiation complaints) were based on the observations made by the ABCC's genetics departments on 19,675 Hiroshima survivors of child-bearing age in relation to the ABCC's 1949 radiation census and the Japanese National Census of 1950. This resulted in estimates of the numbers of survivors in Hiroshima of 1200 below 1000 metres, 10,500 in the next 500 metres, 18,700 in the next 500 metres and 67,700 over 2000 metres. The linearity, therefore, was as likely to be a function of the number of survivors as the number of leukaemia sufferers – a potential fallacy that was to be brought to the ABCC's attention by Dr Alice Stewart in the 1980s.

In February 1959 Morihiro Ishida and Gilbert W. Beebe of the ABCC Departments of Epidemiology and Statistics proposed a research plan for a joint study between the ABCC and the Japanese National Institute of Health on the longevity of the A-bomb survivors.[10] This research design claimed to implement two central tenets of the Francis Report – to bring epidemiological and clinical-pathological studies into complementarity, and to rationalize the sample to be studied by observing cohorts at the different distance levels in numbers amounting to those available at the minimum level – that is the approximately 2000 survivors who were closer than 1000 metres to the hypocentres. Ishida and Beebe acknowledged the need for a control group but argued that since it was now understood that the confounding of the disaster effects meant that really only an external group such as the Kure population constituted a true control, and since it would be too difficult to mount that study, 'no such comparison is intended in the present study'. Even so, 'To sample the non-exposed population is more difficult. By the time it became generally recognized that the non-exposed population required representation in the mortality sample, the original 1950 National Census schedules had been destroyed.'

But this 1959 research design did have a more sophisticated definition of exposure to radiation. It referred to 'exposure *per se*, distinguishing between immediate radiation as the bomb burst and later radiation from fallout, activated particles etc.' as well as the influence of shielding against radiation and distance from hypocentre. It also introduced another category – exposure subsequent to the burst, although this group was still effectively dismissed.

> *Continuing exposure from fallout particles or otherwise activated objects is a subject for debate. If for a period of days after the bombs radiation persisted to any appreciable extent, one would need to map the course of each individual through the ruins and integrate exposure on the basis of physical observations. It is palpably impossible to require such detailed information as a basis for sampling. It is not believed that such information, even if available, would greatly augment dosage estimates based solely upon the instantaneous dose. However, it is possible to segregate, as a special group, a set of people who were not present when the bombs actually fell but who entered one or the other within any fixed interval thereafter. Inclusion of this group in the non-exposed sample with a special label 'possible exposed to residual radiation' does not deny that residual radiation existed and sets the stage for any appropriate special investigation.*

Ishida and Beebe still held that 'Distance from hypocenter and shielding determined the instantaneous dose received by anyone in Hiroshima or Nagasaki at the time of the A-bomb.' But they argued that as it would be too difficult to get reliable shielding histories to rely on as the primary criterion, 'it has seemed better to choose the sample on the basis of distance, and then to obtain good shielding histories on the patients actually selected and exposed within, say, 2000 m. In this way distance plus shielding will eventually be transformed into estimated dosage *after* the sample is drawn and will become the basic independent variable of analysis.'

Ishida and Beebe proposed the terms 'inner proximal' for those closer than 2000 metres and 'outer proximal' for those from 2000 to 2500 metres. The distal exposed would be those exposed beyond 2500 metres. They noted that there was a disproportionate number of males exposed in Hiroshima because of 'a large military component that scattered after the termination of the war and thus was not enumerated in Hiroshima at the time of the 1950 National Census. However, the sampling plan itself can hardly cope with a problem of this nature.' Similarly, while they acknowledged that it was possible that exposed individuals not resident in the city of exposure in 1950 differ as to life expectancy from those residing in the city, 'it seems impractical to design the present study to include exploration of this problem.' The study would be limited to those with residence in the city of exposure at the time of the census from which they were drawn, whether it be the 1950 National Census or the June 1953 Hiroshima Daytime Census. 'In the interests of homogeneity and ease of long-term follow-up' the 11,000 foreign nationals, mostly Koreans and Chinese, listed in the 1950 National Census in the two cities would also be excluded from the longevity studies.

The Director of the Atomic Bomb Casualty Commission, George B. Darling, wrote to *The Japan Times*[11] on the eve of the thirteenth anniversary of the bombings in August 1958 that 'ABCC is continuing the laborious and methodical comparison of a large number of survivors in Hiroshima and Nagasaki, with an equal number, matched for age and sex, of people in the same cities who were not exposed to determine if possible any delayed effects of radiation from the bombs. The study of acute conditions was of course completed long ago. This work, carried out cooperatively by the Japanese National Institute of Health and ABCC, is unspectacular and results will take a long time to obtain.'

The Japan Times asked Dr Darling, 'Because atom-bomb victims often give birth to abnormal children atom-bomb diseases are thought hereditary. For this reason fewer and fewer people want to marry men and women of Hiroshima. It is feared Hiroshima citizens will soon find themselves a "segregated group" in Japan. How do you react to this social problem?' Dr Darling replied, 'Ever since 1946 ABCC has been concerned with the question of determining possible hereditary effects of the atom bombs. A careful study of children who were conceived after the bombing included 70,000 families and took six years to complete.' While he acknowledged that damage did occur to those who were *in utero* at the time of the bombings, the Director of ABCC in 1958 insisted that 'The cold clear facts of this study are that no genetic effects attributed to radiation were demonstrated'. While he conceded that 'From a scientific point of view this answer is incomplete due to the complexity of the problems of human genetics and the little that is known about the subject. From a human point of view, however, this is reassurance of a high degree. Fortunately the fears we all held can be discounted.'

Notes

1. Memo 'The medical program in Hiroshima', undated, found at Francis:39.

2. Memo to Dr R. Keith Cannan from Seymour Jablon and Felix E. Moore, Review of the Unified Program, March–April 1957, dated 1 May 1957, at Francis:39.

3. Memo dated 7 June 1957, at Bugher 2:1:2:9:106.

4. Cover note to document 'The future program of ABCC', dated April 1957, at Bugher 2:1:2:9:106.

5. Outline of proposed 'Study of deaths of people exposed to the atomic bomb' at Bugher 1:2:9:101.

6. Ad Hoc Conference on the ABCC Program of Studies on the Effect of Radiation on the Ageing Process, 11 November 1957, at Bugher 1:2:9:101.

7. Minutes of the 24th Meeting of the Advisory Committee of ABCC, 13 November 1957.

8. Discussion of Haematology Material from Japan and Great Britain, Conference at the Armed Forces Institute of Pathology, 18 February 1959, at Bugher 2:1:9:105.

9. William C. Moloney and Marvin A. Kastenbaum, 'Leukeogemic effects of ionizing radiation on atomic bomb survivors in Hiroshima City', *Science* February 1955: 121:25:308–9,

10. Morihiro Ishida MD and Gilbert W. Beebe PhD, 'Draft research plan for joint NIH-ABCC study of longevity of A-bomb survivors', 16 February 1959, at Francis:39.

11. Letter from George B. Darling to Mr Kenji Arai, *The Japan Times*, dated 1 August 1958, at Francis: 39.

Eighteen

In contrast to his reservations about the Francis Unified Study Program, Dr Bugher was one of the strongest supporters of the Shielding Studies. He wrote to Dr Holmes in May 1956, 'I talked with Bob Corsbie on Saturday after his return from the Pacific and also listened to his report to our [AEC] Advisory Committee for Biology and Medicine on the shielding study and its value to general radiobiology and US civil defense. I am sure that if you had heard his report and the comments of the committee you would have special citations prepared for Dr Woodbury and his staff, who have done such a remarkably fine piece of work.'[1]

But the work proceeded very slowly. Three years later, in May 1959, even though the ABCC was now committed to the limited Master Sample, it was still proving very time-consuming to take the 'shielding histories' – the location of the survivor in terms of both distance and protection from building materials or natural environment from the hypocentre. It was thought that the shielding factor on the dosage of any individual survivor could be calculated by establishing his or her whereabouts within the topography of the cities (which themselves had to be reconstructed from maps, aerial surveys, and on-the-ground surveys of buildings), and the individual's location inside or outside buildings of particular construction. The building materials divided broadly into two categories; heavy, such as concrete, and light, such as the paper and wood fabric of most Japanese houses at the time. While the early radiation measurements from late 1945 were used in these calculations, it was also found necessary to try to calibrate the shielding factors of these materials by erecting two medium-sized single-storey Japanese houses in the Nevada desert during the Plumb Bob series of tests in 1957.

In July 1951 the first 'non-medical radiation histories' were taken by the Field unit of the Statistics Department in Nagasaki. These included a sketch map of the area showing the location of exposure with respect to at least two landmarks and a cross-sectional drawing showing all intervening material between the individual and the hypocentre. A total of

319 such histories were taken in the first six months of the studies.

On the basis of these data together with the distance and estimated 'backscatter' of radiation, Mr Noble and Mr Wright of the ABCC calculated the dosages for seven surviving physicians from the Nagasaki Medical School. Their calculations were based on the air-dose curves and straight line attenuation in concrete given in *The Effects of Atomic Weapons* – themselves guesstimates. By thus combining the various factors – manifested early symptoms of seven survivors, their distances from the hypocentre, assumptions about the shielding value of the buildings they were in, and the early assumptions about air-dose curves of the two bombs – 'dosages' were calculated by these two laymen.[2]

These early 'dosage calculations' were not dismissed by the scientists and other researchers even though they came from untrained sources. Ken Noble seems to have commanded a certain grudging respect from his colleagues in the Atomic Bomb Casualty Commission. Dr Holmes, the Field Director of ABCC wrote of him to Dr Cannan in 1956:

> *He is an adolescent with a good mind and fox-like ability. His market value is far less than his personal estimate, and even this lies in the unusual circumstances of necessity that have vaulted him into a position beyond his thinking or potential. He is clever and knows the city of Nagasaki, as certain characters world-wide tend to know certain cities. In this instance that knowledge is of considerable value ... He is outstandingly adept at commiseration and with a certain dominance of personality that tends to overcome his weaker seniors. In spite of this he has held the fort and deserves well-earned praise. He would make a good second man in Nagasaki for a strong and capable first man.*[3]

However, it gradually came to be realized that the calculation could not be done simply in terms of straight line radiations from a known hypocentre. On the one hand, it came to be understood in the early 1950s that the two bombs had emitted neutrons and these 'would diffuse, like a cloud of smoke, through openings such as doors, windows, and thin walls no matter where the openings were in relation to the bomb direction: A person in a deep slit trench might be adequately shielded from gamma rays but only partially from neutrons.'[4] On the other hand, it was realized that the locations of the hypocentres were not actually known.

> *A precise determination of the point of burst of the A-bomb exploded over Hiroshima and also over Nagasaki is one of the most fundamental parameters in the dosage estimation for survivors of the A-bombs. However, a search through the ABCC files shows that a good documentation of the*

hypocenter is nowhere available. The assumed location of the ABCC Hiroshima hypocenter appears to be fairly accurate but the location of the Nagasaki hypocenter does not have adequate substantiation.[5]

In 1959 E. T. Arakawa was studying the 3000 measurements taken of the shadows cast by the thermal rays of the bomb in Hiroshima held in the Hiroshima A-bomb Museum to try to confirm the hypocentre. He estimated that at 1000 metres, every 5 metres error in hypocentre location would introduce a +−2.7 per cent error in dose.

In Nagasaki in 1954 there were six technicians attempting to take the histories of all survivors under 2000 metres. They had daily lectures and field training for a month as well as studying trigonometry. They developed three-dimensional scale drawings of exposure information 'and from this, the straight line shielding is converted to equivalent thickness of water' which was the convention used at the time for measuring radiation penetration. However, by 1959 it was noted 'The equivalent water thickness is not calculated and recorded at present because recent information has revealed that radiation does not arrive at a point in a straight line but approaches from all directions.'[6]

Nevertheless the shielding studies continued despite the labour intensity of the task. In April 1956 a Shielding Survey Team visited Japan from the US and included Robert Corsbie, the architect who was in charge of the building materials studies for the AEC. Corsbie had been part of the initial armed forces team into Hiroshima and had contributed to and edited *The Effects of the Atomic Bomb, Hiroshima, Japan 1945*. Corsbie believed[7] that estimates of civilian casualties in an urban nuclear or atomic blast were much too high in the 1950s and 1960s: 'Not enough thought is given to the protective layout, to the high buildings and close proximity in the cities'. Criteria of damage, he argued, had been developed on 'open field' (i.e. Nevada) assumptions rather than the protective qualities of cities. He also believed, as he told the US Congress, that 'there has never been *one* fallout victim, including the two Japanese blasts and all the Nevada and Pacific tests.' In 1961 he was still defining 'fallout of principal concern' as 'contaminated matter descending from the sky within 24 hours after having been sucked up by the atomic bomb explosion.' This did not include the initial massive 'bomb radiation' which last but a minute or two during the actual explosion. As an architect advising the US Government on civil defence procedures, Corsbie was far more concerned with the thermal and blast damage he had observed in the first few weeks in Hiroshima and Nagasaki.

The main outcome of the 1956 visit of the Shielding Survey Team to Hiroshima and Nagasaki was a simplification of the three-dimensional drawing taken by the investigators, and the dropping of the 'psychologi-cal trauma' statements as being irrelevant. Even so, it was estimated in 1957 that it would take another sixteen years to complete the 24,000 shielding histories on the Hiroshima Master Sample alone, during which time it was expected there would be at least a 50 per cent attrition of informants from the study. At a January 1958 conference on ABCC Dosimetry and Shielding Studies held at the Oak Ridge National Laboratory[8] it was recommended that the shielding histories at ABCC 'be pursued in some random sequence which would permit an unbiased estimate of dose for population bases even before all of the histories have been completed.' It was also agreed that 'declassification of the most recent air dose curves, house attenuation factors and angular distribution results is essential.'

The Plumb Bob tests in Nevada in the summer of 1957 had generated new information on the air dose for the neutron and gamma rays which had been calculated along lines developed by Captain Edward York.[9] It was still thought that 'A parameter of vital importance in assessing the total attenuation of Japanese houses is the angular distribution of the incoming radiation'[10] although it was found in studies of both gamma ray dose and fast neutron dose that 'the angular distribution was observed to be rather insensitive to the type of weapon and to the distance from burst point.' However the 'attenuation of radiation by light frame structures' was also tested in the two simulated houses in the Plumb Bob tests and in both cases 'the dose correlated reasonably well with a very simple parameter – name-ly, the distance measured along the ray path from the first point of entry into the house to the dosimeter (house penetration distance).' So in the late 1950s, the researchers were working with T-57D – Tentative 1957 'doses' – calibrated from the simulations in the Plumb Bob series which they then extrapolated to the survivors who had reported themselves as being in lightly built Japanese houses. The air-dose was determined by the use of York's air-dose curves and the known location of the survivor, and the attenuation factor was assigned by reading the house penetration dis-tance from the ABCC shielding records. Self-reported information, fre-quently uncorroborated, taken often a decade after the trauma of the explosions, was thus factored with data taken from a small simulation in the Nevada desert to arrive at the T-57 'doses'. Work was confined to those who had been in Japanese housing rather than concrete buildings because it was still too difficult to develop 'attenuation factors' for other than light building materials.[11] There was now an awareness that the amount of X-ray treatment that the most injured survivors were receiving might be confounding the individual dose calculations and this was being monitored in the ABCC clinic and other medical facilities in Hiroshima.

By mid-1959 too it was increasingly accepted – at least outside the Advisory Committee to the ABCC – that there had been significant residual radiation in the two cities and that there had been decidely non-linear dispersion of the fallout by rain. In June 1959 a Symposium on Late A-Bomb Disturbances was held in Hiroshima sponsored by the Prefectural and City Offices of Hiroshima and the Treatment Panel of the Hiroshima A-Bomb Casualty Council with the support of the Japanese Welfare Ministry, the Nagasaki Prefectural and City Offices, the Nagasaki A-Bomb Casualty Council and the Hiroshima Prefectural and City Medical Associations.

Dr Ishida, who had been assigned to the ABCC by the National Institute of Health in cooperation with the Hiroshima City Medical Association, reported[12] data from investigations begun in May 1957 on malignant tumours in Hiroshima under the auspices of the Hiroshima City Medical Association in association with the ABCC. He reported the incidence of cancer among the survivors was approximately 1.4 to 4.6 times higher than among non-exposed people. While the overall incidence of cancer for non-exposed people was 280 per 100,000, for those under one kilometre from the hypocentre in Hiroshima it was now 1287 or 4.6 times the expected rate, and for those in the next 500 metres (to 1500 metres) it was 524 per 100,000 or 1.9 times the normal and 383 per 100,000 at 1500–2000 metres or 1.4 times the expected rate. There were no differences in incidence between males and females in the area up to 1500 metres radius from the hypocentre and the increased cancer incidence was not merely an acceleration of age of onset but an absolute increase in incidence regardless of age. Dr Gensaku Oho of the Hiroshima City Medical Association concluded that the mortality rate of the exposed people from all cancers was running about 20 per cent higher than that of the non-exposed. The mortality rate and the incidence rate were both very high.

At this symposium, too, Assistant Professor Naomi Shono of Hiroshima Jogakuin University, Professor Kiyoshi Sakuma of Hiroshima University and Mr Michio Hirofuji of the Hiroshima Memoral Hospital reported on residual radiation in Hiroshima. They maintained that strong residual radiation remained for ten days in both cities and since the number of neutrons which caused induced radiation Hiroshima was ten times greater than in Nagasaki, radiation in Hiroshima was ten times greater than in Nagasaki at ground zero. They noted that heavy rains called 'black rain' had fallen in the northwestern part of Hiroshima City immediately after the explosion and this has resulted in a fallout of 0.4 r in areas where the rain fell and 0.2 r in the areas where it did not fall. In Nagasaki there had been a northeasterly wind and residual radiation in the area around the Nishiyama Water Reservoir was abnormally high. Measurements taken on 2 October 1945 had indicated that the fallout would cause a person to receive 60 r of radiation were he or she to remain there for 1000 hours.

The lines of research that the ABCC was pursuing fifteen years after the detonations were meant to demonstrate the linearity of the distance–dose–response relationship by demonstrating that symptoms that were assumed to be induced or accelerated by radiation increased directly in relation to the distance of the sufferer from the hypocentre at the time of the explosion, regardless of his or her later behaviours. For at least the first decade of these studies, it was assumed that residual radiation and fallout could be discounted. The drawing of the samples was deeply influenced by the logistics and practicalities of working in the two cities in the immediate post-war years. The samples progressively shrunk to those survivors still reasonably easily accessible in the two cities demonstrating symptoms who had been closer than 2000 metres to the hypocentres. Patient attrition combined with the progressive 'closing' of the study samples meant that by 1958 only 43 per cent of those who had been nearer than 2000 metres in the two cities were being studied.[13] Under the Master Sample of the Francis Unified Study Program, 2153 adults who had been seen by the ABCC in earlier years were now excluded including 863 who had presented with radiation symptoms.

At the same time as the studies were 'closing in on themselves' in Hiroshima and Nagasaki, the assumptions and consequent research designs of the ABCC were now increasingly deviating from the mainstream of health physics studies. While other researchers were trying to understand the effects of low, chronic doses of radiation from naturally occurring radiation, workplace hazards, or from what was now appreciated as the accumulating increase in atmospheric radiation from weapons tests, the ABCC scientists and epidemiologists were trying to reconstruct the experience of a massive dose of what they thought of as instantaneous exposure to bombs with differing ingredients which were not precisely known. They were still very ready to dismiss any complications that might arise from residual radiation or randomly dispersed fallout, whether immediate or longer term.

There was a school of thought which argued that the two research agendas must be directly connected. If radiation injury was directly related to the dose received – the more radiation, the more injury – then it would be possible to develop a linear picture of the relationship that went from the lower to the higher levels of exposure/injury. It was presumed that the distance-dose-injury relationship would hold steady from the lowest to the highest doses, even if on a proportional basis. Many scientists believed – or hoped - that there would be established a 'threshold' below which no injury occurred from, for instance, chronic low-level natural exposure or medical exposure. If that threshold could be detected, then the safety guidelines for human exposure to atomic and nuclear energy could be established in order to guide military and civilian and medical uses.

As the Chairman of the Ad Hoc Committee on Somatic Exposure of the US National Committee on Radiation Protection and Measurements, H. L. Friedell pointed out at a Munich conference of experts in 1959[14] 'If we understood the exact mechanism of the interaction of physiological, and morphological effects leading to the final effects, we could extrapolate back to very low doses and make confident estimates of the extent of human damage to be expected from such a dose. Lacking this information, we must rely on the character of the dose-effect curve at higher doses and estimate the effects of changes in intensity and spacing of the dose.' But while there were indications of linearity at detectable doses of radiation, the instruments were not yet available to detect low, chronic doses. It would be mere supposition to presume that there was a threshold below which humans could safely tolerate radiation. The chairman of this subcommittee on somatic and genetic effects of radiation exposure of the US National Committee signalled very clearly in 1959 that:

> the present evidence is not sufficient to establish the dose-response curve for somatic effects at low doses. In the absence of such information, the committee has chosen to make the cautious assumption [his emphasis] that there is a proportional relation between dose and effect and that the effect is independent of dose rate or dose fractionation. On this, or any other non-threshold assumption, it follows that even the smallest dose is associated with some risk. Under these circumstances, the exposure of the population to any increase in radiation should not occur unless there is reason to expect some compensatory benefits.

As John Keosian put it in an article in *Science* in 1955, 'The question of maximum tolerance dose of radiation for man has not been satisfactorily determined. There has been a downward revision of this value over the years, and it may well turn out that the value is zero – all high energy radiation, even of low intensity and brief duration, must be considered as potentially dangerous to the exposed individual.'[15]

Shields Warren, Stafford Warren, John C. Bugher and Curt Stern were members of significant committees of the US National Committee on Radiation Protection and Measurements in the late 1940s.[16] In a guest editorial in *Health Physics* in 1981, the long-time chair of the NRCP,

Lauriston S. Taylor, acknowledged that:

Our entire permissible dose structure of today is based upon our inability to observe any deleterious or other effect at the permissible dose levels which have been in vogue since 1934. There is an unbroken chain of derivation in today's protection standards even though [sic] there has been no observation of effect of radiation exposures within the permissible dose limits.

It was also Lauriston Taylor who wrote at the same time that:

It is well past the time that we should have stopped trying – for whatever reason – to read into later incomplete or reworked statements concepts that could not have prevailed at the time the original ideas were developed. Let us stop trying to reconstruct history. Let us record it as it was, and from that draw separately any sociological or subjective judgements and opinions that may be deemed to be useful. But when they are judgements or opinions, clearly identify them as such.[17]

But as two historians attached to the US Nuclear Regulatory Commission in Washington DC commented in 1984[18] although the biological consequences of exposure to heavy radiation doses were apparently clear, scientists remained uncertain about the effects of low-level radiation and the degree of risk it posed. Most agreed with the AEC that bomb tests had not raised levels of radiation enough to be harmful, but some believed that the Commission was too complacent, especially about the genetic implications of fallout. The AEC therefore commissioned a panel of scientists to study the question, and this work was funded by the Rockefeller Foundation. In 1961 John C. Bugher's successor at the Rockefeller Foundation, Virgil C. Scott, wrote to Bugher in his new post as Director of the Puerto Rico Nuclear Center asking for clarification of some earlier funding decisions.

I am confused at the moment by the number of agencies both national and international which are concerned with the biological effects of radiation, radiation hazards etc. You will recall that The Rockefeller Foundation has been supporting studies of this general type being carried out by the NRC, the American College of Radiology, and there are probably others. I believe that similar or related studies are being done by WHO, the AEC, and probably one or more of the armed forces.[19]

Bugher replied[20] that there were various national committees on radiation protection in the US including the NRCP and International Commission of Radiation Protection, but none of them had any formal authority. 'These organizations, which are closely linked, concern themselves with the principles of radiation protection, formulate standards of such protection which are published as recommendations.'

Then there were the United Nations-affiliated organizations such as the UN Scientific Committee on the Effects of Atomic Radiation (UNSCEAR) and organizations functioning under World Health Organization sponsorship. There were also the official scientific organizations such as the American College of Radiology, the National Academy of Sciences, the National Research Council and various technical societies concerned with specialized aspects of nuclear energy. The National Research Council committees 'are an important means of achieving a reasonable degree of coordination between the various research programs so that such overlapping in research as occurs may be generally beneficial.'

In respect of the particular grant to the NAS-NRC, Bugher told his colleague:

> The program was trustee initiated in 1955 because of the general concern with fallout from nuclear weapons testing. The general theme in the beginning was that there should be an objective survey by independent scientists of the AEC program with the object of making an authoritative statement to the public concerning the dangers of environmental contamination from weapons testing. Det Bronk soon uncovered a most significant fact that practically all of the competent radiobiologists in the country were already working in the AEC program and that there did not exist a sufficient body of competent scientists without AEC relationship to conduct the requested study. The studies which were conducted by a series of panels were actually manned by persons who had some connection with the AEC program.

Nevertheless, Dr Bugher felt that 'The NAS-NRC program is one of the most significant contributions the Rockefeller Foundation has made in recent years. The fact that it is conducted without government support has given it greater authenticity in the minds of many people than would have been the case had government funds been used.'

Notes

1. Letter from John C. Bugher to Robert H. Holmes, dated 29 May 1956, at Bugher 2:1:9:101.

2. E. T. Arakawa, 'Health Physics Division of the Oak Ridge National Laboratory and the Atomic Bomb Casualty Commission Liaison Pool Activities' for period from 5 January 1959 to 30 April 1959, dated 27 May 1959, at Francis:39.

3. Letter from Robert H. Holmes to R. Keith Cannan, dated 27 March 1956, at Bugher 1:2:9:102.

4. Research Project Outline ST-70, October 1952, quoted in Arakawa *op cit.*

5. Arakawa *op cit.*

6. Arakawa *op cit.*

7. Unsourced biographical article dated April 1961 attached to John C. Bugher's copy of Robert L. Corsbie's Statement on 'The effects of nuclear explosions' before the Military Operations Subcommittee of the Committee on Government Operation of the House of Representatives, dated 4 August 1961, at Bugher 1:2:14:195.

8. Arakawa *op cit.*

9. ORNL-CF-57-11-144, 'Dose calculations for Hiroshima and Nagasaki', Lt Col M. Morgan, FSWC to Mr G. S. Hurst, ORNL; Payne S. Harris, 'Biological effectiveness of nuclear radiations from fission weapons', LA-1987, August 1955 and G. S. Hurst *et al.*, 'Techniques of measuring neutron spectra with threshold detectors – tissue dose determinations', *Review of Scientific Instrumentation*, 27:3:153, March 1956.

10. Typescript document 'Dose calculations for Hiroshima and Nagasaki survivors' prepared in Health Physics Division, Oak Ridge National Laboratory, stamped 'Rec'd June 4 1958' at Francis:39.

11. 'Abstract summary of ABCC Project – April 1959', at Bugher 2:1:9:105.

12. Morihiro Ishida, 'Epidemiological observations of malignant neoplasm among exposed survivors in Hiroshima', presented to Symposium on Late A-Bomb Disturbances, Hiroshima, June 1959, reported in Abstract of Newspaper Reports on Symposium on Late A-Bomb Disturbances, at Francis:39.

13. Status of the ABCC Program, April 1958, at Bugher 2:1:9:105.

14. Paper by H. L. Friedell given to International Committee on Radiation Protection 'Meeting with Experts on Somatic and Radiation Effects, Munich 1959', at Bugher 100 Int'l:1:2:Projects:9:66.

15. John Keosian, 'Speculations on hazards of exposure to radiations', *Science*, September 1955: 30:536–7.

16. See Committee lists in Lauriston S. Taylor, 'Brief History of the National Committee on Radiation Protection and Measurements (NRCP) covering the period 1929–1946', *Health Physics* 1958:1:3–10

17. Lauriston S. Taylor, 'Technical accuracy in historical writing', *Health Physics*, May 1981: 40: 595–9.

18. George T. Mazuzan and J. Samuel Walker, *Controlling the Atom: The beginnings of nuclear regulation 1945–1962*, (University of California Press, 1984) 44.

19. Letter from Virgli C. Scott MD to John C. Bugher, dated 21 February 1961, at Bugher 1.2:200 US:98:850.

20. Letter from John C. Bugher to Virgil C. Scott dated 28 February 1961, at Bugher 1.2: 200 US:98:850.

Nineteen

In order to improve the T-57D – the Tentative 1957 dose assessments – the Oak Ridge Laboratory health physics group developed a series of tests on seven simulated Japanese-style houses in the Operation Hardtack test series in Nevada in 1958. The atomic bomb was simulated by an unshielded nuclear reactor which was mounted on the hoist car of the 1527-foot tower. Further measurements were made in 1961 of the angular and spatial distribution of the radiation in Operation Bren which resulted in air-dose curves which were thought to be superior to those calculated by Captain York in 1957. Meanwhile Japanese researchers at the Japanese National Institute of Radiological Sciences at Chiba were estimating the dose by irradiating reinforced rods in concrete walls, bricks and tiles with neutrons and gamma rays. They applied a formula which included nine parameters such as the number of storeys of the building and the number of walls inside combined with the air-dose for an estimation of exposure dose. These studies relied on the earlier work of Kenneth Noble and others at ABCC as the first 'possibly accurate estimates'.[1]

Another complication arose in the early 1960s. What was the effect of the thermal burns and blast injuries on the radiation injuries? How could this be accounted for in the dose estimates? These questions seem to have first arisen in late 1959 among the researchers at the Oak Ridge National Laboratory who were trying to develop the dose-estimate formulae. Animal experiments conducted in the course of the Bikini and then the Nevada tests as well as in Oak Ridge and other laboratories, were alerting the biomedical researchers to the role of wounds and burns in influencing both early mortality and the subsequent course of radiation sickness and injuries. As Dr Bugher wrote to Robert Corsbie[2] in recommending Dr Herman Pearse, Professor of Surgery at the University of Rochester, to carry out studies of the combination of thermal, blast and radiation injuries, 'All of the problems studied by ABCC, which in the beginning seemed simple, have turned out to have numerous complications.' A study of 1000 Japanese cases in the records of the Oak Ridge Laboratory revealed that 200 had also received thermal burns but their significance could not be evaluated because in 87 per cent of the cases the information in the record was insufficient to assess the severity of the burns.[3] Dr Robert Conard of the Brookhaven National Laboratory, director of the studies on the Marshallese who had been irradiated during the *Bravo* test, commented in the ABCC Advisory Committee discussion of these problems in May 1961 that of 82 Marshallese with severe systemic effects, 90 per cent had developed skin ulcerations which had healed rapidly, and the burns which were due to fallout contact on the skin had healed rapidly. The problem was, as Dr Shields Warren pointed out, that it was difficult to distinguish flash burns from thermal burns and many survivors had both. Dr Darling, the Director of ABCC, invited suggestions as to how to account for these issues in the current research designs.

> *While everyone agrees that we wish we had more and better information (including for instance a medical classification of burns as first, second or third degree) so far no suggestions have been forthcoming as to how to overcome this lack after fifteen years. In Japan, there is no enthusiasm for reopening the issue by new introspective history taking. No medical opinion is available. It would be necessary to ask the patients for it and their information would be of a low level of confidence on this subject. Also, each time the experiences are re-dredged, new anxieties are created, and another bias in the survivors is introduced.*

Another aspect of the burns suffered by the survivors that was beginning to worry the researchers in the early 1960s was their incidence in unpredicted locations. Robert L. Corsbie told[4] a Congressional Committee in August 1961, sixteen years after the bombings, that 'The interiors of shelters with open doors near points of detonation may become hot enough in high pressure regions to cause burns. In Japan burns were received by sheltered persons who could not be seen by the fireball. The phenomenon was also observed in biomedical shelter tests at the Nevada Test Site. The mechanism is not completely understood'. He thought that this effect was somewhat less with surface bursts but still believed that 'The surface burst is the source of the early fallout which is the principle delayed effect against which we must defend in nuclear war.'

The narrowness of understanding of the implications of radiation injury was not confined to the senior advisers of the ABCC. In February 1958 Dr Francis wrote a memo[5] to his file about a conversation he had had with a colleague, Dr G. Hoyt Whipple Jr, about how best to advance the study of radiation injury for the Armed Forces Epidemiological Board and the ABCC. 'He has not been engaged in animal work and does not have a very high opinion of what has been done. He states that too many of the men will talk indefinitely, but always retreat to this own special position.' Whipple 'thinks it would be almost smarter to get some good biologists to talk about the problem and consider the radiation men as assistants who would carry out that part of the study under direction.' He suggested bringing together 'a group of thoughtful persons' who should be able to produce some good clear questions which could be put to some of the 'radiation biologists' but he wondered if 'the best plan still would be to frame some clear and unambiguous experiments, and then farm them out to competent workers'. He also commented that 'one still does not know what an irradiated animal dies of.'

At much the same time, Norton Nelson, Professor and Chair of the Institute of Industrial Medicine at New York University-Bellevue Medical Center pointed out to Dr Francis that 'virtually all the work on the relationship of radiation to the immune response has been done with external radiation and very little with internal deposited radioactive isotopes.'[6]

But John C. Bugher – pivotal to so much funding and information exchange with the small network of radiation injury researchers for more than two decades – was still able to suggest in 1960 (in a conversation with a behavioural scientist):

> that one element in the situation that leads to difficulty is the oversimplification of a highly complex biological problem. In order to make what seems a clear explanation to people who are interested, but not scientifically informed in the radiobiological sense, we find that these oversimplifications tend to get taken as the complete and correct statement and used as a basis of further reasoning on the part of scientific people who are competent in specialized fields unrelated to the question at hand.[7]

Dr Bugher gave as a good example of this process 'the tendency to compute numbers of cases of leukemia and bone sarcoma ultimately resulting from minute amounts of fission products from weapons testing.' According to Dr Bugher, 'there is actually no evidence at all on which to base such calculations which are, in fact, little more than childish examples in arithmetic. Over-simplification of a problem may defeat the purpose of the explanation.'

By the early sixties, the Master Sample – with all its exclusions of difficult categories – had been codified and work could now begin. But the research designs of this decade perpetuated the assumptions that had influenced the work of the ABCC from the beginning.

A joint NIH-ABCC research plan for Pathology Studies in Hiroshima and Nagasaki[8] was based on the recommendations of Dr Francis and his committee. It was initially drafted by Drs L. J. Zeldis and Y. S. Matsumoto and then 'extensively reviewed' in the United States and Japan by both organizations and individuals including the National Research Council Advisory Committee on ABCC, groups representing local governments, medical schools, medical associations and hospitals in Hiroshima and Nagasaki, the Joint Japanese–American advisory committee to the Director of the National Institute of Health and 'the entire professional staff, Japanese and American, of ABCC'. It was one of the earliest ABCC documents to be published simultaneously in Japanese. According to the preface, 'Many suggestions resulted from these review procedures and the present protocol thus represents the work of many minds.' The sample to be used for the pathology studies was directly selected from the Master Sample. It was not a random sampling. 'It was a specific recommendation of the Francis report that the sample for mortality study be chosen so that: Exposed subjects may be divided as to apparent dosage or distance from the hypocenter, permitting study of any apparent effect as a function of dose or distance; Exposed individuals may be compared with non-exposed and effects judged to be real to the extent that they distinguish these two groups.' In other words, it was a highly pre-selected sample from a Master Sample which itself had already been drawn up partially on criteria of distance, dose and symptoms – the presumed linear relationship between which factors these studies were supposed to be testing.

This protocol did acknowledge that 'Since the Life Span Study cohort is composed of exposed and non-exposed persons who were alive and resident in Hiroshima and Nagasaki in 1950 or at specifiied times thereafter, it is likely that the sample differs from the original surviving population. The implication of course is that findings among the present study may only with reservation be extrapolated to the period prior to 1950.' Early and undetected fatal effects of radiation may have radically altered the nature of the survivor cohort; migration in the post-war years may have biased it irredeemably. 'Satisfactory investigations of these problems is scarcely possible so they must be recognized as defining one limit of the scope of late effects studies.' Even the autopsies that were coming to the ABCC were unrepresentative of the survivor group after 1950 as many social factors intervened.

Nevertheless, the consensus reflected in this research protocol in 1962 was:

The independent variable of interest in the study of late effects is ultimately radiation dose. Estimates of dose require knowledge of the radiant ener-

gy yield of the bombs, attenuation factors for air and other shielding materials, and detailed shielding histories for the survivors. From the studies of prototype weapons, air-dose curves for neutron and gamma components, together with estimates of probable limits of error have been provided ABCC by the US Atomic Energy Commission. Attenuation factors for various Japanese building materials have also been provided. (...) For approximately 90 per cent of survivors under 2000 meters who are known to have been exposed either in the open or in Japanese-style buildings, detailed shielding histories are being obtained and will eventually permit estimations of dose. Since air-dose beyond 2000 metres was probably less than 18 rads in both cities estimation of dose in other than the proximal exposed survivors is not regarded as an urgent matter. For the 10 per cent of proximal exposed individuals shielded by other than light building materials satisfactory dose estimates may not be possible since attenuation factors for heavier shielding are not available.

The attenuation factor data that this statement was relying on was that provided in Neel and Schull's 1956 report on 'The effect of exposure to the atomic bombs on pregnancy termination in Hiroshima and Nagasaki'. But 'Pending completion of shielding histories and dose calculations, exposure status must continue to be stated indirectly in terms of distance from the hypocenter, perhaps with consideration of type of shielding.'

The research protocol for the joint NIH–ABCC Adult Health Study drafted by J. W. Hollingsworth and G. W. Beebe and reviewed in the same way as the Life Span Study protocol was also released in May 1962.[9] It began by stating that

The successful integration of atomic energy into modern life requires that its attendant hazards to man be fully known in relation to type of radiation, total dose, duration and rate of radiation exposure, part and volume of body exposed, sex, age at exposure and other biologic, social and environmental factors. Not only the early, acute effects but also the late effects must be known. Further, these effects must be quantitatively understood, for the absolute elimination of radiation hazard we now know will never be possible.

In Dr Bugher's copy of the protocol the next sentence was crossed through with a heavy line: 'the most we can hope for is to control exposure within biologically tolerable limits'.

The survivors of Hiroshima and Nagasaki 'provide the great bulk of existing human data on early effects, and hold in their subsequent experience potentially more information about late effects than the rest of humanity combined.' So every effort should made 'to identify such effects as do occur as a part of the rational therapy of exposed survivors'. But there was another purpose to the studies. 'Because of the many understandable fears of thousands of people regarding possible long-range consequences it is very important to rule out any justification for such fears whenever possible. This means that negative findings of careful research have great importance, especially to the survivors and their families.'

But equally 'One wants a study plan to provide an efficient route to the end in view.' Another sentence crossed out in Dr Bugher's copy of this protocol then read 'In the present instance the end can only be dimly perceived, and it is necessary to adopt a very broad strategy if one is to avoid unknown risks of failing to find particular effects.' Certainly a longitudinal study was required, despite the difficulties.

These researchers were 'mindful that survivors represent a truncated sample and that selective host factors may have played a part in both survival and the likelihood of acute radiation symptoms.' But they still expected to be able to make 'adequately strong negative statements when competent examination of the data has shown no evidence of a particular effect. We cannot hope to prove a negative case by the inductive logic of statistics, but can specify in probability terms the limits within such effects might be. These confidence limits are inversely proportional to the square root of the sample size. Such statements are important not only to the investigator but also the victims of the bombings.'

The authors did reflect that 'Statistical calculations of power, or sensitivity, of comparisons are often made with ease, but the price one pays is having to grind into the calculations so many assumptions that one must be in a well-structured investigative situation before the calculations provide anything more than a *tour de force*.' They felt they were in such a well-structured situation since 'The Francis Committee adopted the position that the samples should be made as large as possible, and advocated taking all *eligible individuals with symptoms* [my emphasis] exposed under 2000 meters, matching the other groups to this size. Subsequent discussion has brought no change in this thinking and it has been adopted for the present subsample.'

They acknowledged that the 'topography of the two cities differs materially, creating different problems in the area of dosimetry. Also the hypocentres differ in relation to the character of city life, so that at comparable differences environments differ in the two cities.' They conceded that 'The problem of defining satisfactory "controls" for the exposed, or of devising other means for inferring the existence of late effects of radiation, is so great as to create the risk of false inference based on purely local phenomena.' But they maintained that this risk would be reduced by the replication of the study in both cities. This study of the adult morbidity would use the same dosimetry data that had been gathered for the Life Span Study. As in that study Hollingsworth and Beebe insisted that 'To be fully credited, effects must be demonstrable functions of dose.' Instead of demonstrating those functions, the research design presumed them *a priori*.

The Francis Unified Study Program was now being implemented despite increasingly vocal criticism that the survivors under 2000 metres were being given all the attention.[10] The Master Sample prevailed even though it was now realized that the autopsy data from the period from 1948 to 1959 was drawn from individuals of whom only one-third were listed in the Master Sample; the remainder were drawn for the most part from non-exposed people who had entered the cities only after the bombings or from a small group of exposed and non-exposed who had been excluded from the Master Sample 'on epidemiologic grounds'.[11]

Dr Francis himself was increasingly detached from the implementation of his 1955 Report and Unified Study Program. In 1960 he wrote to Dr Cannan[12] that he was feeling over-extended and that he really preferred to be engaged in active work. 'I have less confidence in my advisory abilities when these are not backed up by some form of study. My hope for the next few years is to return to the status of a student and to reduce my poobah activities.' He had been trying to withdraw from the ABCC Advisory Committee ever since he took on the presidency of the Armed Forces Epidemiological Board in late 1957.[13]

Moreover the Atomic Bomb Casualty Commission was under continuous threat of closure throughout the 1960s. As Director, Dr Darling spent at least as much time preparing for closure of the programme – with all its administrative, financial and research implications – as on implementing the Francis Unified Program studies. From the outset, there were discussions within the ABCC about how soon the Adult Health Study just initiated could be terminated.[14] It was hoped that three cycles of data collection – to see if the sample were reporting increased sickness over the years – could be completed over the next three or four years in Hiroshima but Nagasaki might be restricted to two cycles of data collection. The Nagasaki staff would be absorbed as far as possible in the Hiroshima field office. But both the Japanese National Institute of Health (NIH) and the relevant trade unions were not advised of these contingency plans since 'premature disclosure or discussion of these contemplated steps could create a real simulation [*sic*] of chaos in short order.' In June 1962 Dr Darling cabled to Dr Cannan in Washington that the proposed budget cuts would only infuriate the trade unions further – and they were already calling one and two hour strikes which were severely disrupting the work. Handbills were being handed to patients urging them to suspend cooperation until the wage negotiations were successfully concluded. Dr Darling feared violence would be the next step.[15]

Dr Darling saw the answer – as increasingly did his Washington superiors – in negotiating closer involvement of the Japanese National Institute of Health and other agencies in the Adult Heath Study and other research programmes with a view to their eventual assumption of full responsibility for them, and their funding. But the Japanese researchers were unhappy about the restriction of the ABCC studies to the 2000 metre mark. In 1962 the Japanese Ministry of Health and Welfare extended its medical care programme to 3000 metres and Dr Darling warned Dr Cannan[16] in May that this increased the pressure on the ABCC to extend its studies to 3000 metres, and he was looking into the logistical implications of doing this. He commented:

> *Certainly no new evidence suggests a change in our thinking in relation to the probable dosimetry factors and the arguments for the exclusion of the 2000 to 3000 meter group built on dosimetry are probably as sound today as they were originally. I think we are all more confident, however, that there is less of an impact 'borderline' radiation in this zone that was previously theoretically assumed in the design of the population. I think if we were building the ME-200 population today I would include them without question since the value of a common medical care program would far outweigh in my mind the reasons for their exclusion. This is a good example of how a change in the social factors revises the ecological equation!*

There was talk in Washington of transferring sponsorship of the Atomic Bomb Casualty Commission from the Atomic Energy Commission to the Public Health Service. Cannan and Darling considered that this could also be the time to negotiate new protocols of closer collaboration with the Japanese with a view to the eventual transfer of the ABCC to Japan. While this process proceeded well with the Japanese NIH and the Ministry of Health and Welfare in 1962, the trade unions continued to use strikes and other pressures to bargain for better wages and conditions for the Japanese employees of the ABCC. Dr Darling suggested to Mr Masunosuke Sumida, Chairman of the Nagasaki City Assembly in August 1962[17] that the labour unions were presuming unwisely on the willingness and capacity of the United States to pay ever-spiralling labour costs for the nearly one thousand Japanese employees of the ABCC. Although Dr Darling could not say so to the Japanese, Dr Cannan was having difficulty in ensuring the continuity of the NAS-NRC commitment to the ABCC; he was actively looking for a new sponsor for the work. Yet at the same time the Americans who were managing the affairs of the ABCC were very concerned that 'the loss of face of American science would have been irreparable'[18] if the ABCC had been forced to give up by financial considerations or passage of the new Japanese health care legislation for atomic bomb survivors. Both Dr Cannan and Dr Darling knew they were on borrowed time; they had to arrange for the transfer of the ABCC's research agenda to the Japanese while at the same time trying to maintain control of that agenda.

Notes

1. Typescript of John Z. Bowers at Bowers:ACC 89–73:ABCC:1. Bowers refers to T. Hashizune, T. Maruyama, A. Shiragii, F. Tanaka, M. Igawa, S. Kawamura, and S. Nagaoka, 'Estimation of the air dose from the atomic bombs in Hiroshima and Nagasaki', *Health Physics*, 1967:13:149–161 TR 6–67 , K. B. Noble, (ed.) *Shielding Survey and Dosimetry Plan, Hiroshima–Nagasaki* and Roy C. Milton, and Takao Shohoji, 'Tentative 1965 radiation dose estimation for atomic bomb survivors, Hiroshima-Nagasaki', TR 1–68

2. Letter from John C. Bugher to Robert L. Corsbie, Civil Effects Tests Operations, Division of Biology and Medicine, USAEC, dated 21 March 1961, at Bugher 1:2:15:195. See also Proposal from Herman E. Pearse, Professor of Surgery at University of Rochester, to Division of Biology and Medicine of AEC, dated 23 September 1960, at Bugher 1:2:15:195 and letter from Robert L. Corsbie to John C. Bugher, dated 10 March 1961, at Bugher 1:2:15:195.

3. Minutes of the 27th Meeting of the Advisory Committee of the ABCC, 18 May 1961.

4. Statement by Robert L. Corsbie on 'The effects of nuclear explosions' before the Military Operations Subcommittee of the Committee on Government Operations of the House of Representatives, dated 4 August 196l, at Bugher 1:2:14:194

5. Memo to file dated 20 February 1958, at Francis:29.

6. Letter from Norton Nelson to Thomas Francis Jr, dated 7 May 1958, at Francis:29.

7. Memo to file by John C. Bugher dated 10 February 1960, at Bugher 1:II:15:206.

8. Joint NIH-ABCC Pathology Studies Hiroshima and Nagasaki Research Plan, dated 16 May 1962, at Bugher 2:1:2:10:109.

9. Joint NIH-ABCC Adult Health Study Hiroshima and Nagasaki Research Plan, dated 16 May 1962, at Bugher 2:1:2:10:109.

10. Progress Report on ABCC dated 18 May 1961, at Bugher 2:1:2:10:108.

11. L. J. Zeldis MD and Y. Scott Matsumoto PhD, 'Second draft for technical report, provisional research plan for pathology studies of atomic bomb survivors in Hiroshima and Nagasaki', dated 1 July 1961, at Bugher 2:1:2:10:108.

12. Letter from Thomas Francis Jr to R. Keith Cannan, dated 12 January 1960, at Francis:39.

13. Letter from Thomas Francis Jr to R. Keith Cannan dated 28 August 1957, at Francis:39.

14. Memo for the Record, dated 13 March 1962, at Darling 770:1:5.

15. Cable from George B. Darling to R. Keith Cannan, dated 18 June 1962, at Darling 770:1:6.

16. Letters from George B. Darling to R. Keith Cannan, dated 2 and 10 May 1962, at Darling 770:1:6.

17. Letter from George B. Darling to Masanosuke Sumida, dated 24 August 1962, at Darling 770:1:7.

18. Letter from George B. Darling to R. Keith Cannan, dated 5 June 1963, at Darling 770:1:10.

Manufacturing error?

The ABCC program, which has been in existence here for 20 years, as with all programs at the AEC, and all fields of research, not only biology and medicine but also in the physical sciences, has been reviewed by various bodies which are advisory to the AEC. Now I would like to mention that some of these reviews which have taken place in the past are of considerable significance to us because of the stature of the bodies which advise the AEC. The Surgeon General of the United States and his office have concluded, as others which I will mention, that the basic scientific information being accumulated here is of great importance for everyone and for basic science throughout the world.

In addition, the advisory committee on Biology and Medicine has similarly endorsed the program, the committee of the NAS, the President's Scientific Advisory Committee to the AEC which is a statutory, that is established by law, whose members are presidential appointees, have reviewed the program, and of course, the Congress of the United States which has the responsibility for authorizing the funding of the AEC, the joint Committee on Atomic Energy has likewise reviewed as it does all our programs and commented favourably on the basic information being generated.

Spofford E. English
Assistant General Manager for
Research and Development of the AEC
18 June 1969

Twenty

The story of the Atomic Bomb Casualty Commission, Dr Cannan – now Chairman of the Division of Medical Sciences of the National Academy of Sciences-National Research Council – told the members of the NAS-NRC in early 1962[1] is a tale of two cities and their people. 'It is the story of a Cause in search of its Effects. Specifically, it is the record of an attempt to learn all that can be learned of the late effects of ionizing radiations on man from a long-term study of the health of those who survived exposure to the atomic bombs exploded over Hiroshima and Nagasaki in August 1945.'

Dr Cannan told his colleagues that it was now thought that the Hiroshima bomb contained about one kilogram of Uranium 235 and the Nagasaki bomb about a kilogram of Plutonium 239. It was estimated that about half the energy released by the bombs – equivalent to 20,000 tons of TNT 'appeared as thermal energy'. Another 35 per cent was transmitted in the shock wave.

> *Only 15 per cent of the energy was radioactive and two-thirds of this was in the form of residual radiation. The latter will not be further considered here because it consisted of radioactive products of the atomic fission that were so finely disintegrated in the fireball that they would have been carried up into the stratosphere by the shock wave which was reflected from the ground. The conclusion that there was little local contamination of the area is confirmed by Japanese observers who found only small ground activity in surveys made a few days after the event.*

Dr Cannan conceded that there had been some reports of 'black rain' in some areas of the cities 'but these have not been well documented and could not have affected any considerable number of people.' The medical problem, the Chairman of the NAS-NRC Division of Medical Sciences told his colleagues in 1962, was therefore 'the identification of the late effects of an instantaneous whole-body exposure to the gamma rays and neutrons radiated in the process of fission.'

The earliest researchers in the two cities had observed that the area within a radius of 2000 metres of the two hypocentres had been flattened by the shock wave and gutted by fire. Over the years three areas encircling the hypocentres had been delineated – the Proximal Zone within 2000 metres, the Intermediate Zone between 2000 and 3000 metres, and the Distal Zone beyond 3000 metres. Dr Cannan told his colleagues that 'it will become evident that these three zones will be helpful in categorizing the hazards of injury, not only thermal and mechanical, but also those to be attributed to radiation.'

Tentative air-dose calculations had been made for the two bombs. At 1000 metres it was estimated to be about 900 rads; at 1500 metres, about 120 rads; at 2000 metres only 15 rads. These estimates were given for both cities although it was noted that the neutron component was a considerable fraction of the dose in Hiroshima but a minimal component in Nagasaki. Nevertheless the median lethal dose – the dose at which half the exposed would be expected to die – was thought to be 450 rads of whole body irradiation. So 'it is evident that the radiation hazard to the survivors was confined to the Proximal Zone.'

The ABCC had begun its work in 1947 under very difficult conditions and 'Apart from special local circumstances that made possible a well-controlled search for genetic effects in the offspring of exposed parents, only broad screening procedures designed to disclose major changes in medical patterns were feasible in the early years.' But in 1955 the Unified Study Program was initiated. The foundation of the unified study was the Master Sample of 100,000 people on which all major studies of the ABCC were now focused. 'It is a closed population, that is to remain unchanged with time, comprising the majority of the survivors in the Proximal Zone who were recorded in the 1950 Census as residents of one city or the other, together with two comparison groups matched by number, age and sex. One of the latter groups is composed of individuals who were in the Distal Zone at the time of the bomb and, therefore, though they did not receive significant radiation, were subject to the physical and psychological stresses of the event.' This work was still being carried out.

Sixteen years after the bombings, the Chairman of the Division of Medical Services of the NAS-NRC told the membership that there had been two areas of investigation that had yielded significant results. The incidence of leukaemia among survivors at 1000 metres was thirty times the normal and there had been demonstrated an increased incidence of leukaemia who were exposed in the Proximal Zone to a degree inversely related to the subject's distance from the hypocentre.

The other area where 'definite results of real significance' had been detected was the genetics studies, the 'well-controlled follow-up of all pregnancies in the two cities' between 1947 and 1953. 'Some 72,000 pregnancies came under review *in about 10 per cent of which* [my emphasis] one or both of the parents had been exposed in the Proximal Zone. No increase was found, in the latter group, in the incidence of abortions, stillbirths or major malformations.' There were no significant differences from the comparison groups in the weights at birth or nine months of age of the infants born to exposed parents; the mortality rates in the nine month period were not enhanced.

> *These conclusions immediately raise the question of the significance of negative results. All that can be said is that the sample was of such size that a doubling of the rates of the abnormal conditions examined should have been detected had it occurred. That some genetic influences were operating is indicated by the fact that changes in the sex ratio of births were found whose direction depended on whether it was the father or the mother that [sic] had been exposed and that the direction of these shifts in ratio were consistent with genetic hypotheses.*

But this reassuring report from the senior liaison officer of the NAS-NRC and the Atomic Bomb Casualty Commission to the membership of the funding body in 1962 was barely published when Dr Darling wrote from Hiroshima to Dr Cannan that 'You can well understand that the article contributed by Paul De Bellefeuille of Ottawa in the July and August 1961 issues of *Acta Radiologica* titled 'Genetic hazards of radiation to Man' may create quite a stir here ... I am sending out for Dramamine myself!'[2] Dr Darling assumed that Dr Cannan had received comment and perhaps rebuttal from Neel and Schull and others to Dr De Bellefeuille's critique of their work.

Dr De Bellefeuille, of the Department of Paediatrics at the University of Ottawa, announced in the opening paragraph of his two articles[3] that 'a new analysis of the data gathered by the official US Commission of enquiry in Hiroshima and Nagasaki compels one to question its generally negative conclusions.' He reviewed the work done on mutations since Muller's pioneering work in the 1920s, and suggested that the consensus lay with researchers such as Dobzhansky [4] that 'As far as genetic effects are concerned, the only safe dose of high energy radiation is no radiation'. But equally it was now generally agreed that 'It is a classical finding in Drosophila and in lower life forms (bacteria, bacteriophage) that the relation between dose and effect is "linear" and cumulative; a given dose of radiation produces the same total effect, whether given at low intensity over a long period or in one large dose, and the linearity of the dose–effect holds so constantly that no lower limit, or threshold, can be set for the mutagenic effect of roentgen rays.' While some researchers questioned extrapolating from fruit flies and mice and other animal experiments to humans, it was now held that 'the only limitation to inferences from the animal to the human lies in the question of dosage'. Indeed, Haldane had argued 'sadly'[5] that the experimental work on mice that might have given the answers to the threshold and other questions could have been done by now for a fraction of the cost of one H-bomb.

De Bellefeuille reviewed the work done by Macht and Lawrence on US radiologists' reproductive outcomes[6] and the French work on the genetic change in the offspring of people who had been medically irradiated in the pelvic area[7] together with epidemiological studies of communities living amid high levels of natural radiation in America and India. This work was still too unsophisticated to give a baseline against which to evaluate the Japanese experience.

In considering the methodology employed in the ABCC Report[8] De Bellefeuille refers to 'their rather complicated system of correcting the distance from the hypocenter by the amount of shielding (light, moderate or heavy) which may have protected the exposed person' which the authors themselves acknowledged was 'conservative' and had the effect of 'relegating to class 2 (exposed lightly) many individuals who must have suffered appreciable radiation effects.' Neel and Schull had noted in their preliminary report in 1953[9] a significant effect of maternal exposure (without shielding correction) on the sex-ratio; but in 1956 they stated that the 'improved' system of exposure categories erased this effect. De Bellefeuille pointed out that this 'improved' categorization was not applied to the studies of microcephaly following prenatal exposure or of leukaemia and results in both these correlated well with distance from the hypocentre. De Bellefeuille pointed out that 'one may thus well ask if the shielding correction constitutes an improvement for any reason other than it affords a more reassuring view of the long-term effects of atomic bombing'.

De Bellefeuille also pointed out that the ABCC Report measured the statistical weight of the exposure of one parent without taking into account whether the other parent was exposed or not which resulted in a dilution of the exposure factor in both exposed and unexposed; 'this is undesirable, in view of the genetic hypothesis that germ cells of both sexes are subject to mutagenic influences, and especially serious in the case of the sex-ratio, upon which exposure of father and mother are expected to act in opposite directions.' He also noted the significant differences between those who had been in the city at the time of the bombings and those who had come subsequently and who were being used as (partial) controls, particularly the significantly different mean maternal age and parity in the exposed and unexposed.

When De Bellefeuille corrected the data as much as he could along the lines he had indicated, he found 'a well-marked trend in the direction of the genetic hypothesis [of radiation induced mutagenesis] in 7 of 8 comparisons involving one-parent exposure, and in the 3 the difference is statistically significant: for maternal exposure toward the sex-ratio and the incidence of stillbirths, and paternal exposure toward the incidence of neo-natal deaths.'

The Canadian researcher also commented that the data of the ABCC Report are 'given in such a way that offspring showing a given accident are removed from the group to be considered for the next accident.... Thus, each child who might constitute an indicator of genetic factors is considered but once. But if the 'reproductive failures' are totalled, 'the statistical evaluation of this summation yields a result which is highly significant in favour of the hypothesis of a genetic ill-effect of radiation.'

Dr De Bellefeuille also placed far more value on the autopsy data reported[10] by Professor Hayashi, Professor of Pathology at Nagasaki University, than Dr Holmes and his colleagues at the ABCC had. The Nagasaki data of Hayashi, based on twice as many cases as the ABCC studies in Hiroshima, showed a strong statistical suggestion in favour of the mutagenic effect of atomic radiation while the Hiroshima data failed to show an effect of radiation. It was possible that the different types of two cities – more gamma, fewer neutrons in Nagasaki – and the different climatic conditions at the time of the two explosions might account in part for the disparity.

> *Nevertheless, the authors of the ABCC Report, who claim to have records on 363 autopsies in Nagasaki (which they fail to publish), question the validity of Hayashi's data and suggest, rather gratuitously, that a bias may create a spurious correlation. They claim, for instance, that the control figure (11.0 per cent) for the incidence of abnormal bodies from unirradiated parents is too low. However, it is a simple matter to compute from Hayashi's data the incidence of abnormal bodies in relation to distance from the hypocenter; the comparison, which excludes the unexposed controls, yields a significant difference at the 3 per cent level. This would seem to dispose of the doubts referred to above.'*

Dr De Bellefeuille reviewed the current understanding of the impact of fallout from test detonations of nuclear weapons in 1960 (his articles were submitted to *Acta Radiologica* in December 1960 and published in July and August 1961; they seem to have been first read in the ABCC in Japan in March 1962). It was now understood that 'Fallout from test detonations of nuclear weapons consists of a large number of radio-nuclides liberated into the atmosphere. These present a two-fold genetic danger. External radiation comes to the gonads from the ground; internal radiation is due to isotopes which are incorporated into human tissues.' Some of these are bone-seekers and cause leukaemia and bone sarcomas; others are ingested. The total thirty-year gonad dose from fallout products, both internal and external, was estimated in the 1958 United Nations Report[11] at 0.01 r if the tests stopped in 1958, but could reach as high as 0.12 r if the tests continued at the same rate. 'Thus the expected hazard from fallout lies between 0.3 per cent and 4 per cent of the hazard from natural radiation.'

Some scientists took this conclusion as a reason for minimizing the danger from fallout in the 1960s and 1970s. But others such as Dr De Bellefeuille were also concerned about the continuing exposure of patients to pelvic radiography – indeed, X-rays had been used by some doctors to stimulate fertility in some patients. The Medical Research Council of Great Britain had recommended[12] that the maximum permissible dose of man-made radiation to the gonads from conception to age 30 be set below 6 rads. A few X-rays would bring a patient over this limit and Dr De Bellefeuille warned that 'present practices do, in fact, approach the danger point for the population as a whole. Strictly, from the genetic viewpoint, all radiation is unsafe, and it may well be that even the tolerance just cited is too lax.'

Dr De Bellefeuille acknowledged that there was still much to be learned about the impact of radiation on humans but he concluded his review of the ABCC data published in 1956 by commenting that 'It is misleading and unwarranted to make statements on the inexistence [sic], or the insignificance, of a genetic hazard of radiation to man.' The rush to reassure the survivors about their genetic prospects was premature on the data available. As the British radiobiologist Peter Alexander put it, it was not possible even with the fruit fly to demonstrate mutagenic action by

> *mere inspection of the individuals of the first generation, and only exact genetic methods, which cannot be applied to man, will reveal these. In the case of the Japanese bomb victims the genetic damage will be spread rapidly over large sections of the population as a result of intermarriage with partners who have not been exposed, and no conspicuous permanent damage will be found which can be ascribed to the bombings.[13]*

The geneticists Neel and Schull had begun a second phase of studies in Japan in 1958, on the outcomes of consanguineous marriages and the impact of ionizing radiation on children of such matings. These studies had been planned at the University of Michigan over two years with the aid of two Japanese scientists. The funds were supplied by the Rockefeller Foundation and the Crippled Children's Association as well as the US Atomic Energy Commission[14]. The ABCC supplied office space and data processing. Schull oversaw these studies, and returned to the ABCC in 1964 to continue the studies on the island of Hirado. Schull found the physical plant of the ABCC much improved in the 1960s but he was less sure about the directorship of George Darling who had been in post since 1957.

> *An affable, portly, deep-voiced man with a cultivated, courtly manner, a sense of drama, and a flair for binational sensitivities, he was nonetheless accepted by his more scientifically oriented associates with some reservation. Presumably they expected not only an adroit administrator but a scientific father-figure, and George was not this. He delegated that role to his successive chiefs of research and to the heads of individual research departments. He intervened little or not at all in the Commission's research program. His function, as he saw it, was to adjudicate policy and to provide the bridge to the lay and scientific Japanese communities, a function at which he was exceptionally adept.[15]*

Schull acknowledged that Darling was 'an important transition figure' preparing for the transfer of the ABCC to Japanese control over the next decade. But he was less admiring of the new climate at the ABCC.

> *Research at the institution became increasingly bureaucratized. Each proposed project had to be carefully described, its budgetary implications identified, and a schedule for completion drawn up. These protocols were reviewed, generally with the Commission; but occasionally outside authorities were consulted. Program reviews occurred with intimidating regularity, and each encounter induced its own turmoil. Summaries of progress on existing studies had to be prepared and future activities defined and planned. Although these steps were essential to a properly managed scientific program, each took time that might have been better spent on further work. Moroever, most of us were unaccustomed to institutional research and the constraints it necessarily imposed. We were used to designing our own research, implementing the experimental strategy, describing what we had done, and then awaiting peer acceptance or approval.[16]*

Moreover in the new climate of close cooperation with Japanese researchers and authorities, there was a diplomatic necessity to obtain the approval of institutions such as the Japanese National Institute of Health and Japan Science Council to new studies such as Neel and Schull planned in the area of consanguinity. Dr Darling was closely involved in negotiating these agreements. That the relationship between Dr Neel and the ABCC was somewhat strained in the 1960s is apparent from a letter from Dr Darling to Herbert Gardner of the National Academy of

Sciences in 1963, which remarks, 'While I did not blame Dr Neel at the time, nor do I now, widespread statements in the United States and in Japan that he could not afford to associate his study with ABCC because of ABCC's performance and reputation still have an impact here'.[17]

For his part, Dr Darling admitted that he was feeling stressed. He referred more than once in his 1962 correspondence to the suspicion that he himself was suffering from 'radiation-induced ageing'; in 1963 he wrote 'I find the strain of leaning over backward, which has to be the natural posture of the director, difficult to sustain'.[18] As Schull commented[19] 'Directorship of the Commission has always been a thankless lot, torn between a sometimes militant union and mounting Japanese sense of self-esteem, a distant National Academy of Science, and the financial shortfalls in the budgets of the Atomic Energy Commission and its successors, the Energy Research and Development Administration and the Department of Energy, where a research institution in Japan had few advocates in a Congress dominated by local interests.'

And in Japan the left-wing critics of the ABCC frequently joined with the trade union militants to lend an air of siege to the premises of the ABCC. Dr Darling regularly reported to Washington about the picketing and clenched fists; sometimes it got the better of him and he wrote in June 1962[20] 'we are still here but I honestly do not know why we should fight for the privilege'. A week later he wrote[21] 'At present the effort spent each day to maintain an outward calm results in something closely resembling a universal muscular spasm. If I could only be sure that it would not be accompanied by similar mental rigidity!' He had taken a holiday in India in January 1962 but was so busy with labour strife, audits and other aggravations that he did not get his thank-you letters written to his hosts until September.

However, in July 1962 Dr Darling succeeded in getting the first of the joint research protocols presented to US Ambassador Reischauer for signature. It had been a long process of peer review.

Fortunately most of the discussion has revolved around expression rather than substance, but no one will be able to say that the protocols did not receive full consideration! I have now written comments also of almost all the professional members of the ABCC staff. There are still a few Japanese physicians to be heard from. As you know, part of this is for staff education but I am quite sincere in wanting to give all concerned an opportunity to improve these protocols or record their reservations. Under the circumstances I think this is an important policy. I just hope that someone some day will not say 'never have so many contributed practically nothing to so little'.[22]

Notes

1. R. Keith Cannan, 'The Atomic Bomb Casualty Commission The first fourteen years' *News Report*, National Academy of Sciences-National Research Council, January–February 1962: XII:1:1–7.

2. Letter from George B. Darling to R. Keith Cannan, dated 20 March 1962, at Darling 770:1:5.

3. Dr Paul de Bellefeuille, 'Genetic hazards of radiation to Man', Part I *Acta Radiologica* 56:65–80; Part II 56:145–59.

4. Thomas Dobzhanski, 'Genetic loads in natural populations', *Science*, 126:1957:191.

5. J. B. S. Haldane, 'The genetic effects of quanta and particles of high energy', *Science and Culture* (India) 24:1958:16.

6. S. H. Macht and P. S. Lawrence, 'National survey of congenital malformations resulting from exposure to roentgen radiation' *American Journal of Roentgenology* 73:1955:442.

7. R. Turpin *et al.*, 'Sur la necessite de limiter l'exposition aux radiations ionisantes,' *French Archives of Paediatrics* 14: 1957: 1055.

8. *Effect of Exposure to the Atomic Bombs on Pregnancy Termination in Hiroshima and Nagasaki*, National Research Council Publication 461 (Washington, 1956).

9. J. V. Neel and W. J. Schull, 'The effect of exposure to atomic bombs on pregnancy termination in Hiroshima and Nagasaki (preliminary report)', *Science*, 118:1953: 537.

10. I. Hayashi, 'Pathological research on influences of atomic bomb exposure upon fetal development', *Research in the Effects and Influences of the Nuclear Bomb Test Explosions 2: Part VIII.* (Medical Sciences, Japan Society for the Promotion of Science, Tokyo, 1956).

11. United Nations, 'Report of the United Nations Scientific Committee on the effects of atomic radiation,' United Nations General Assembly (New York, 1958).

12. Medical Research Council (UK), *Hazards to Man of Nuclear and Allied Radiations*, (HMSO, London, 1956).

13. Peter Alexander, *Atomic Life and Radiation*, (Pelican, Harmondsworth, 1957, revised 1965) p.181.

14. Minutes of the Advisory Committee of the ABCC, 27 March 1959.

15. William J. Schull, *Songs of Praise*, (Harvard University Press, 1990) p.220. See also James V. Neel *Physician to the Gene Pool*, (John Wiley and Sons, 1994) Chapter 6.

16. Schull, *ibid.* p.222.

17. Letter from George B. Darling to Herbert N. Gardner dated 14 December 1963, and Letter from George B, Darling to James V. Neel dated 26 July 1963, at Darling 770:1:5, and cables dated 27 November 1963.

18. Letter from George B. Darling to Herbert N. Gardner dated 14 December 1963, at Darling 770:1:5.

19. Schull *ibid.* p.222.

20. Telegram from George B. Darling to R. Keith Cannan dated 22 June 1962, at Darling 770:1:1:6.

21. Letter from George B. Darling to R. Keith Cannan dated 29 June 1962, at Darling 770:1:1:6.

22. Memo from George B. Darling to R. Keith Cannan dated 8 March 1962, at Darling 770:1:1:5.

Twenty-one

In his annual memorial greetings throughout the 1960s the Director of the Atomic Bomb Casualty Commission would reassure the survivors and others who were worried about the long term effects of the bombs on the people of Hiroshima and Nagasaki that:

> *The results of these studies make possible more accurate diagnoses of the ills of the living and, consequently, more effective medical care and treatment. The knowledge thus gained helps to substitute the certainty of established truth for the fear of the unknown. Through the wisdom and understanding of their surviving relatives those whose memory we honor today were able after death to make a special gift to the living.*[1]

But these reassurances provided little comfort to those individuals who were stricken with leukaemia or other diseases that may have been radiation-induced. Dr Darling wrote to an American ex-servicemen, Lt Col Frederick Dykstra, sixteen years after the bombings:

> *As you have correctly deduced from the reports you have read, we have no evidence which would support the idea that your leukemia was related to your service in Nagasaki. The amount of induced and residual radiation in Nagasaki either as measured or theoretically computed is believed to be far below the values that would have had to have been reached if a cause and effect relationship could be postulated.*[2]

Dr Darling also responded to an inquiry from the British Legion about the possibility that one of its members who been at Christmas Island during British tests there suffered radiation-induced leukaemia. Dr Darling sent the General Secretary of the British Legion several official ABCC technical reports about leukaemia and dosages and commented[3] 'As you will see we have as yet only an increased statistical incidence among those exposed to significant amounts of radiation as a positive finding of our studies. There is still no way to tell which cases were "naturally occurring" and which ones were perhaps triggered in some way by exposure to radiation.' While he acknowledged that 'We are not yet able to convert distance from the hypocenter to dose with real confidence' and he had no knowledge of the dosimetry of the Christmas Island tests, Dr Darling suggested that if the serviceman in question – a Mr William Morris – had received over 50 rads of air entry dose 'I think you could say that our studies would suggest that the leukaemia might have been associated with his exposure, if less – probably not.' But 'If his body dose depends upon absorption from induced radiation or fallout then we have no pertinent evidence since the nature of weapons used at Hiroshima and Nagasaki and the height of the air bursts reduced these factors to relative unimportance in our studies.'

Dr Darling was asked for advice about the proposed studies of communities living on the monazite sands of the Malabar coast of India who were thought to be subjected to chronic low doses of natural radiation. He responded[4] that his Japanese experience led him to warn against undertaking such studies.

> *Here we have one of the best systems of vital statistics in the world, machinery for documenting births and deaths, an alert medical profession, and death certificates restudied by autopsy in a fair percentage. Sample populations, including the exposed and matched controls, are selected with great care. Even so we have the greatest difficulty in discriminating between chance and possible causal relationships.*

At the same time, Dr Darling was writing to the Director of the Japanese National Institute of Radiological Sciences[5] that 'We have some unresolved problems concerning those who entered the area after the explosion'. But the Oak Ridge National Laboratory was working to refine the T-57 doses and he hoped that the new dose estimates would be available within eighteen months. In fact, it was 1965 before the new 'T-65D' – Tentative 1965 dose – estimates became available. Dr Darling invited the National Institute of Radiological Sciences to join the ABCC in the furtherance of the dosimetry studies. There was talk in 1963 in Washington and Nevada of a 'repeat firing' of the Hiroshima bomb but Dr Darling advised Dr Cannan[6] that he had 'grave doubts as to whether refiring of the bomb would actually add sufficient new information to the problem to in any way compensate for the adverse effect upon Japan and world opinion.'

In April 1965 two assistant professors from Kyoto and Nara presented data to the Japan Applied Physics Society on their studies of roof tiles collected from Hiroshima and Nagasaki. They had identified tiles which had been present at the times of the explosion and subjected them to a 'thermo-luminescent' method of measuring the trapped electrons remaining from the gamma irradiation. They postulated an estimated gamma dose in Hiroshima at 400 metres from the hypocentre of 6000 roentgen and 370 roentgen at 980 metres. The estimated dose at the Hiroshima hypocentre was 13,000 roentgen. In Nagasaki, gamma dose at 100 metres was 25,600 roentgen and even at a point 1000 metres away, the dose was 1000 roentgen. Estimated dose at the Nagasaki hypocentre was about 28,000 roentgen, 'which shows that the Nagasaki type released more than four times the amount of radiation than the Hiroshima type.'[7] The Ichiban Project at Oak Ridge Laboratory was still working on what were to become the T-65D and at the end of 1963 Dr Darling wrote to Seymour Jablon that 'I am still in kind of a fog about the Oak Ridge data but I am sure it will lift in time'.[8]

It was now twenty years since the bombing of the two cities in August 1945 and the Presidential instruction to the National Academy of Sciences-National Research Council to establish the Atomic Bomb Casualty Commission. But inflation in Japan was increasing the wage bill of the ABCC by at least 10 per cent each year during the 1960s. The United States Government was trying to protect the gold flow between the two countries. The Atomic Energy Commission had many other projects and was growing ever more wary of the annually increasing budget of the ABCC which was becoming harder and harder to defend in Washington. But there was a considerable fear of American loss of face, particularly among the scientists, if the research programme of the ABCC were to be suspended abruptly. Politically, the United States could probably walk away from the survivors of Hiroshima and Nagasaki, but scientifically the commitment to study the long-term effects of whole body irradiation on a human population was just beginning to enter the period when the life-shortening effects – if any, and the animal experiments all demonstrated some – should begin to become apparent.

Dr Darling and Dr Cannan spent much of their time lobbying for the continuation of US commitment to the Atomic Bomb Casualty Commission past the second decade. At the same time, they were negotiating closely to prepare for transfer of the physical assets and the research responsibilities to Japan within a decade.

The AEC Scientific Representative wrote to the United States Ambassador in Tokyo in July 1967 arguing the value of the ABCC.

So far, radiation has not produced any new human disorders, but it often accelerates the appearance of familiar diseases; hence, the clinical study program requires maintenance of an accurate medical history on a large statistical sampling of the exposed survivors as well as a comparison group who

*live in approximately the same environment and who differ only in the
amount of radiation received.... Some projects, such as radiation dosimetry,
are now being phased down, after the radiation dose received by the survivors has been accurately determined by mock-up experiments and analyses. ABCC research proposals are carefully documented in both Japanese
and English, and are subject to rigorous review by the multi-disciplined bi-
national staff, using outside advisor consultants wherever necessary.*

*... In addition to its contribution of a small basic research staff, the
Japanese Ministry of Health and Welfare is providing certain treatment
and relief programs to A-bomb survivors. Likewise, the ABCC has provided treatment, upon referral by Japanese physicians, and for a number of
years has been able to say that no member of their 20,000 cooperators in
the clinical study group with known medical problems has gone without
treatment. The ABCC achieved their contribution to the treatment program not only through their modest treatment facilities, but also through
obtaining American grants to Japanese University Hospitals that have
resulted in important increases in Japanese treatment facilities, such as 140
beds at the Hiroshima University Hospital and a research building in
Nagasaki which released sufficient space for 130 beds at Nagasaki.[9]*

The Ambassador was advised that the ABCC programmes were under
review by a Special Problem Panel of the Japan Science Council with the
stated objectives of reviewing the research activities of ABCC and the
question of the 'return' to Japan of the research facilities. The ABCC had
long been under attack from the Asahi Press for alleged secret and sinis-
ter activities relating to military affairs such as survival in nuclear warfare;
the failure to return 1500 autopsy specimens to Japan from the US
Armed Forces Institute of Pathology; and past criticisms of ABCC by
atom bomb survivors and researchers of the methods of investigation and
lack of treatment and relief. 'The campaign for "return" of the facilities
and research program is based on the simple argument that the "assailant
should not be permitted to research or analyze the victim".' The AEC
Scientific Representative advised that 'If the US effort is phased down
and there were no corresponding pickup of the program by the Japanese
agencies, then I expect the loudest outcry would come from the Labour
Union rather than the scientists. I believe that it would be far more
appropriate for the US to continue seeking better operating efficiency in
this program, with phase-down occurring as a natural consequence of
project completion.'

Dr Darling was engaged in regular consultations with the Japanese
authorities about the implications of a gradual phase-down of the
research projects as a prelude to US withdrawal from the ABCC through

the late 1960s.[10] Dr Darling was looking for 'non-jeopardizing economies' in the motor vehicle pool, laundry services, janitorial costs, and guard services without provoking the Japanese labour unions any further than he had to.[11] His conclusion was that it would be better to make a complete withdrawal over three years if the unions would not cooperate with a gradual phase-down.

While the future of Washington's commitment to the ABCC was precarious, Dr Darling was also told in 1968 that the Japanese Foreign Ministry could not locate any documents from the 1940s authorizing the establishment of the agency in Japan.[12] All they could find was the *Note Verbale*. The ABCC was reminded that it was only allowed to operate in Japan on the sufferance of the Japanese Government. Minor irregularities such as the fact that the Director was serving food imported through US military services to Japanese doctors in the staff dining room led to a warning from the American Embassy that the Government of Japan could expel the ABCC on this ground alone.

In his introduction to the 1966–7 annual report of the ABCC, Dr Darling issued an even-handed warning to the two governments. He suggested:

> It is possible that some US policy decision makers (who perhaps forget that Japan participates to the maximum in every other way) will mistake unreadiness by Japan to increase its financial contribution for apathy toward the study and its results which are admittedly quite as meaningful for Japan as for the rest of the world. Japan may assume that the United States will carry on anyway, but there is always the danger that the United States interpret such lack of action as evidence that Japan believes that most of the useful information has already been garnered. In that case it is possible that the US will lose confidence in its own position, doubt the wisdom of its advisors, and begin a graduated withdrawal.

The Division of Biology and Medicine of the Atomic Energy Commission prepared a report on the future of the ABCC which was circulated to the relevant funding agencies in July 1967.[13] Although it was labelled a 'Special Analytic Study', this report was completely uncritical of the ABCC. It put the studies of the 50,000 survivors in Hiroshima and Nagasaki in the context of the other available studies of human irradiation – there were approximately 35 cases of men surviving accidental virtual whole body exposure in the nuclear energy industry; the data on the lifespans of radiologists; 1983 cases of patients exposed to whole body irradiation as part of their therapy; the 133 Marshallese and 22 surviving Japanese fishermen from the 1954 *Bravo* incident/accident. Of these, 'The ABCC study is clearly the largest, best controlled and most precisely organized of all these studies.' It was now possible to provide a radiation dose for nearly every subject with a confidence of ±30 per cent for Hiroshima and ±15 per cent for Nagasaki 'in place of having to resort to the radial distance from ground zero which though crude did serve as a measure of relative radiation dose.' It was now understood that 'the total radiation doses at the same ranges from ground zero differ in the two cities and that the neutron to gamma ray ratios also differ for the two cities. These differences will be taken into account in analyzing the biomedical data; the relative carcinogenicity of neutrons versus gamma rays may become apparent.' The 'classic study' carried out by Neel and Schull 'demonstrated that in 76,626 pregnancy terminations there was no statistically valid indications of genetic effects in the offspring.' All in all, the AEC reported of its daughter programme, 'The ABCC has a record of solid achievement as a medical research organization. Its basic long-term epidemiological programs are progressing smoothly and are capable of achieving its long-term goals, namely, an evaluation of the delayed and long-term effects of *"flash" whole body irradiation of a population*' [emphasis mine]. These data were already of immense value to evaluating hazard to workers in the nuclear energy industry, and their bearing on workmen's compensation claims and claims under third party liability.

The AEC also reassured its funders that 'ABCC has maintained scientific objectivity toward its subjects, the program and the data, and consequently its findings are accepted nearly everywhere at face value. Contributing importantly to this acceptance is the inclusion of equally meticulous data from the carefully matched control population.' This was particularly important because 'Provision for such massive control procedures has been fortunate since it has prevented blaming radiation for the incidence of diseases which were merely a part of the shifting pattern of disease associated with Japan's change to a different way of life.' The ABCC was carrying out 'a well-planned, unique, very useful study in a competent, professional manner. The data and scientific reports are published in recognized biomedical journals.' The negative findings were as important as the positive results.

This internal evaluation of the ABCC was supported by letters urging continuation of funding from all the major relevant organizations. It was the consensus of these authorities that the work should continue until more than 50 per cent of the exposed population died – which was expected to occur around 1990. As the Surgeon General of the United States put it:

I realize that there are some who may feel that the Atomic Bomb Casualty Commission may not have contributed as much as was expected over the years. However, it should be apparent that this particular study of a human population is one that requires time and careful observation through an extended period of years in order to enter the phase of major return in terms of scientific achievement.[14]

Frederick Seitz, President of the National Academy of Sciences, one of the governing agencies of the ABCC, wrote[15] to the Chairman of the AEC testifying to the fact that 'The national and international bodies charged with establishing standards of radiation safety have relied heavily on data from ABCC'.

In his testimony on behalf of continuation of the ABCC research programme the Chief of the Health Physics Division of the Oak Ridge National Laboratory – responsible for the dose estimates – pointed out[16] that 'most of the guesses of the dose-effect relations for man for external and for internal exposure are shaky extrapolations that are made for the most part from animal experiments'. But the survivors of Hiroshima and Nagasaki provided a unique population of 'thousands of exposed persons who received relatively uniform total body exposure and the individual absorbed doses are being calculated by our health physics group in Oak Ridge. We are making use of the data that has been painstakingly collected by the ABCC staff in Japan together with data we have collected from weapons tests and numerous field studies.' This work was critical not only to the survivors but also to the nuclear energy industry since:

The health physicist must know the uncertainties as well as the accuracy and adequacy of the MPE (Maximum Permissible Exposure) he recommends through the ICRP, NCRP and FRC and decisions in which he plays a major role. Likewise, he has deep concern for the validity of these values which he applies and enforces in his day-to-day operations. The research programs associated with the ABCC offer what I believe is our best opportunity to assure a wise choice of exposure levels.

The Advisory Committee on Biology and Medicine of the AEC expressed the opinion[17] that 'The lack of numerous large, startling differences between the exposed and non-exposed samples should be regarded as valuable scientific findings.' At the same time, it warned, 'If positive differences between the exposed and non-exposed populations should be demonstrated *after our withdrawal* [their emphasis] of participation, our withdrawal could be a costly political error.' The Acting Country Director for Japan at the Department of State in Washington put it most bluntly, that the ABCC

has done much to demonstrate American concern for the victims of the atomic bombings, thereby forestalling the development of adverse attitudes that would have seriously hampered our post-war relations with Japan. The scientifically documentable information obtained through the ABCC program has also provided us with irrefutable grounds to counter hostile charges which might have been made concerning the effects of the bombing.[18]

Notes

1. Memorial greetings, 23 September 1961 from Director of the Atomic Bomb Casualty Commission, at Darling 770:1:1:4.

2. Letter from George B. Darling to to Lt Col Frederick Dykstra, dated 21 August 1961, at Darling 770:1:1:3, and letter from George B. Darling to Richard W. Petree, American Consul Fukuoka, dated 21 August 1961, at Darling 770:1:1:3.

3. Letter from George B. Darling to D. E. Coffer, General Secretary, British Legion dated 17 August 1961 at Darling 770:1:3

4. Letter from George B Darling to Reverand [*sic*] Father Patrick P. Murry, Chairman, Division of Mathematics and Natural Sciences, University of San Diego, College for Men, dated 12 October 1962, at Darling 770:1:7.

5. Letter from George B. Darling to Dr Kempo Tsukamoto, Director, National Institute of Radiological Sciences, dated 2 August 1961, at Darling 770:1:3.

6. Letter from George B. Darling to R. Keith Cannan, dated 5 June 1963, at Darling 770:1:10.

7. Translation from Yomiuri Press, dated 9 April 1965 'Atomic bomb secret to be elucidated on 21st year following detonation', at Francis:39.

8. Letter from George B. Darling to Seymour Jablon, dated 9 December 1963, at Darling 770:1:1:13.

9. Memo to the Ambassador: 'Subject: Briefing on ABCC', dated 14 July 1967 from Whittle J. McCool, AEC Scientific Representative, at Darling 770:III:70:773.

10. For example, see Talking Paper on the 20th anniversary of ABCC of talks between the two governments, dated 5 February 1969, at Darling 770:111:70:773.

11. For example, see ABCC Budget Reduction Estimates, dated 13 July 1968, at Darling 770:111:70:775.

12. *ABCC History of Efforts to Increase Japanese Participation*, ABCC report for Dr C. L. Dunham, 13 July 1968, at Darling 770:111:70:775.

13. *Report on Future of the Atomic Bomb Casualty Commission*, (Special Analytic Study No. 67–7), prepared by AEC Division of Biology and Medicine, July 1967, at Darling 770:11170:773.

14. Letter from Surgeon General to General Manager, USAEC, undated. Appendix A-2 of *Report on Future of the Atomic Bomb Casualty Commission*, July 1967.

15. Letter from the President of the National Academy of Sciences to the Chairman of the US Atomic Energy Commission, dated 18 July 1967, Appendix A-5 of *Report on Future of the Atomic Bomb Casualty Commission*, July 1967.

16. Extract from a letter of Dr K. Z. Morgan, ORNL, dated 14 June 1967, 'Supporting the Atomic Bomb Casualty Commission', Appendix A-6 of *Report on Future of the Atomic Bomb Casualty Commission*, July 1967.

17. 'Item from the Advisory Committee on Biology and Medicine Report to the Commission, dated 9 June, 1967, expressing opinion on the ABCC', Appendix A-7 of *Report on Future of the Atomic Bomb Casualty Commission*, July 1967.

18. Letter from Richard W. Petree, Acting Country Director for Japan, Department of State, Washington to Mr James Clark, Chief, International Division, Bureau of the Budget, dated 18 December 1966, Appendix A-9 of *Report on Future of the Atomic Bomb Casualty Commission*, July 1967.

Twenty-two

Formal agreement that all data obtained through the ABCC[*] studies belonged equally to Japan and the United States was accomplished in a memorandum of understanding signed in Tokyo on 1 December 1970 between the Directors of the Japanese National Institute of Health and the Atomic Bomb Casualty Commission.[1] Since his Annual Report in 1967–68 Dr Darling had been signalling a staged transfer of the studies and the physical assets of the ABCC to the Government of Japan.

The studies were now entering their second twenty-year cycle. The Unified Study Program was in place and the first results were beginning to become available. The Director of the Division of Medical Sciences of the Atomic Energy Commission, Dr Charles L. Dunham, told an audience in March 1969 that:

> *Some 40,000 pregnancy terminations involving both irradiated and non-irradiated populations in the cities of Hiroshima and Nagasaki were studied [by Neel and Schull]. There was not observed any statistically significant increase in congenital defects among the irradiated as compared with the non-irradiated in either of the two cities. The data are still being massaged from time to time in the light of newer knowledge concerning the genetic effects of high dose rate exposures in experimental animals but, so far, the original conclusions stand.*[2]

Data on the thyroid glands from 3067 consecutive autopsies from the Master Sample had been reviewed. The prevalence rate of thyroid cancer in 1096 persons with (presumed) zero radiation exposure was 17.9 per cent compared with comparable US material where the prevalence ranged from 1 to 4 per cent. In the 50 rad or more (presumed) exposure group, the prevalence was 24 per cent giving a relative risk of 1.4 per cent. In only 5 instances was thyroid cancer the cause of death.

But in the same month, March 1969, Seymour Jablon, one of the original members of the Francis Committee and now Chief of the Department of Statistics at the ABCC, wrote to Dr Gilbert Beebe at the

NAS-NRC in response to his inquiry about the prospects for 'milking' the first five cycles of the Adult Health Study, one of the central components of the Unified Study Program. Mr Seymour advised Dr Beebe that:

> *ever since 1960 when I first became familiar with how the Adult Health Study was going, I have been discouraged because of the emphasis on what was clearly the softest of soft kinds of data (the diagnoses) to the almost total exclusion of obtaining hard, objective, reproducible laboratory measurements of physiologic state. I believed then, and still believe, that we would have done far better to have obtained a couple of liver function tests on a routine basis over the years that to attempt to diagnose liver disease clinically.*[3]

He was very distrustful of the diagnoses because they were made by a wide range of physicians of varying training and skills; there was moreover no standardization of diagnostic criteria, and a 'serious incompleteness' of the information on each illness. How now to 'milk' these data? 'It is very hard to know just which piece of this elephant to grab hold of.'

Meetings were continuing on a regular basis between both the scientific and diplomatic negotiators with a view to transferring the ABCC to Japan, but the Japanese were linking this negotiation to the reversion of Okinawa (which was achieved in 1972).[4] The United States had spent $50,000,000 on the ABCC to this point and was offering to commit twice that amount over the next 25 years. But the budget for Fiscal Year 1971 was projected at $3,636,385; there had been a four-fold increase of staff during Dr Darling's fifteen years as Director. These levels could not be sustained unless the Japanese Government was willing to contribute to the funding.

Like the statisticians, the pathologists were increasingly critical of the data coming from the studies after 25 years and $50,000,000. In a symposium reviewing the pathological findings to 1970 published in *Human Pathology* in December 1971, Robert E. Anderson, MD, Professor and Chairman of the Department of Pathology at the University of New Mexico School of Medicine at Albuquerque who had been a Visiting Research Scientist at the ABCC, contributed several papers critical of the early research designs and data collection.

> *The posture of the ABCC has changed considerably during the past 25 years, In the initial several years it became obvious that some forms of leukemia were rather markedly increased in prevalence among members of the surviving population, and much effort during the subsequent ten years was expended in a search for other diseases with similarly altered prevalences. During this period the unfortunate assumption was made by many*

of the involved personnel that the altered incidence of additional radiation-related disease entities would be comparable to that documented with leukemia and therefore strict adherence to epidemiologic principles was not necessary.

…Prior to 1961 effort with respect to autopsy procurement continued to be somewhat unstructured with primary emphasis on specific disease entities. A large volume of case material from hospital deaths with almost no representation of deaths occurring at home led to many unanswerable questions about possible biases in the earlier studies based on autopsy findings.[5]

Professor Anderson was also critical of the approach to dosimetry.[6] From the first days of the Joint Commission the studies:

related a variety of acute effects to distance from the hypocentre at the time of the bombs. Definition of exposure groups solely by distance was clearly a sub-optimal approach to the problem and ignored the attenuation provided by man-made and natural objects. However, division of the surviving population by distance gradients allowed comparisons between groups that on the average received varying magnitudes of exposure. More recently it became convenient *[my emphasis] to divide the survivors into those who in general received biological significant amounts of radiation and persons more distally located who received dosages* thought *[my emphasis] to be of little or no biologic significance.*

The distance selected for this arbitrary division, Professor Anderson pointed out, differed and depended upon the effect under consideration but was generally in the 1400 to 1600 metre range. Oak Ridge Laboratory developed the T-57 dose estimates 'based largely on theoretical considerations', but 'Subsequent usage of these curves was complicated by the presence of numerous survivors with dose estimates in excess of 600 rads; other experience suggests that survival in this range is unlikely. *Therefore many investigators reverted to distance gradients as an interim solution to the dosimetry problem.*' (my emphasis)

In another paper, Professor Anderson returned to the problem of leukaemia and related disorders.[7] He considered that there were several unresolved issues: Is there a threshold phenomenon? Is the apparent discrepancy with respect to incidence of leukaemia between Hiroshima and Nagasaki survivors real or artifactual? Are radiation induced leukaemia and related disorders identical to the spontaneous variety? Did the information accumulated so far with respect to leukaemia and related disorders assist in an understanding of the biologic behaviour of these diseases? The Nagasaki data were suggesting a threshold phenomenon, which was not evident in comparable information from Hiroshima. 'The size of the sample in the low dose levels, and particularly the number of leukemia cases in this region of the curves, makes it unlikely that a definitive answer to this question will be forthcoming from the ABCC data. '

It was tempting to combine the Hiroshima and Nagasaki data and thereby increase the statistical strength of the sample; however, 'there appears to be a considerable reservoir of uncertainty as to the validity of combining data from the two cities'. The radiation spectrum emitted by the two bombs differed significantly and 'radiation modality greatly influences the pattern and incidence of subsequent malignant tumors'. Professor Anderson also warned that 'it should also be emphasized that the available data neither support nor refute the concept of a threshold dose.'

The inter-city discrepancies were now becoming apparent in the data on the incidence of malignant lymphoma. Dr Anderson noted that[8] the previously suspected relationship between highly exposed persons and the subsequent development of lymphoma was apparent in the Hiroshima survivors but not in the Nagasaki data.

> *An interesting related observation is that the one year survival rate appears to be greater in persons exposed to more [my emphasis] than 1 rad than in individuals exposed to less than this amount....The presently available evidence suggests that there is an increased prevalence of malignant lymphoma in highly exposed >100 rads Hiroshima survivors. Proximally located males who were less than 25 years of age at the time of the bomb appear to be particularly susceptible. Similar relationships are not mirrored in the Nagasaki experience, and the definition of these intercity discrepancies forms one of the most intriguing and perplexing problems facing ABCC scientists at the present time.*

Dr Anderson considered that 'there is strong reason to suspect that the described differences are not artifactual but rather related to known discrepancies between the radiation spectra of the two bombs or biologic differences between the two populations at risk.'

Robert W. Cihak, a surgeon with the US Public Health Service's Bureau of Radiological Health, who had been assigned to the ABCC, considered the data available from the two cities on lung cancer in this symposium. He concluded[9] that '*When distance and dose estimation figures were applied* [my emphasis], an interesting effect was noted. No oncogenic effect was noted until dose levels in excess of 128 rads were reached. Therefore, although no linear relationship between incidence and dosage could be obtained, a "threshold" effect was suggested. However, no significant increase in any one histologic type of carcinoma could be documented.' He considered the survivors of Hiroshima and Nagasaki to have been subjected only to a single dose of radiation; 'Radiation from activation of ground material and from fallout generally is felt to constitute an insignificant proportion of the total dose received. Thus, the study of this group differs intrinsically from the earlier investigation of miners who were chronically exposed to radioactive particulate matter.' But in reviewing the various approaches to ageing induced by radiation Anderson concluded bluntly:

> *A number of biochemical and morphologic parameters have been applied to the populations under study at the ABCC. Thus far only one such study has shown a significant discrepancy between the various segments that would suggest the possibility of acceleration among this group of persons. Alternative explanations for this finding are discussed, and it is concluded that the parameters employed may not be sensitive enough to detect changes of the magnitude expected.[10]*

In his summary of the symposium, Dr Anderson pointed to the 'possibility of a prolonged latent period, particularly in connection with neoplasia and degenerative change, and the critical importance of continued surveillance of this unique population.'

In 1974, the year that the Atomic Bomb Casualty Commission was finally transferred to Japanese control and reconstituted as the Radiation Effects Research Foundation (RERF), the eminent Japanese researcher Susumu Watanabe published[11] an overview of the findings to date relying primarily on Japanese sources. Watanabe began by describing the explosion at Hiroshima:

> *At the instant of explosion, there was a bluish-white flash in the sky followed by a sound like that of thunder. The sun was almost instantly obscured and the sky was covered with yellow, white and brown smoke for about 20 minutes, and then the rain (chiefly in the northwestern area of the city) began to fall 20 to 60 minutes after the explosion, and lasted until the evening near the hypocenter (the spot on the earth's surface vertically under where the atom-bomb exploded). The rainwater was black for the first 1–2 hours and then gradually became clear…. The heavy rainfall which occurred in Hiroshima was not recorded in Nagasaki.*

In more than 100 pages, citing nearly a thousand references, the majority of them Japanese studies conducted outside the auspices of the ABCC, Watanabe reviewed the findings of the first 25 years, and the areas of differences between the Japanese and American researchers.

Although Watanabe acknowledged the presence of the rain in Hiroshima, he still thought that the two detonations 'provides an unparalleled opportunity to investigate the nature of the leukemogenic effect of *a single, instantaneous radiation exposure* [my emphasis] on human beings.' He too accepted the prevailing assumption that the doses of radiation varied 'from low to supralethal levels according to the distance from the hypocenter and shielding conditions'. Yet he reported significant Japanese findings of radiation injury among the 'early entrants' – those who had entered the cities *after* the '*instantaneous*' irradiation of the communities.

It was estimated that more than 25,000 people entered Hiroshima alone in the first three days after the bombing. As Watanabe described it:

> *Shortly after the detonation thousands of people went into the parts of Hiroshima where the damage was greatest, and they stayed there doing rescue work, ground cleaning, or to search for their relatives. Large unknown variables render estimation of the radiation doses received by these people is [sic] almost impossible, and there is tendency to ignore the existence of appreciable residual radioactivity in the city. There are various possible modes of uptake of radioactivity by the human body... Concerning the types of irradiation which may give late effects to early entrants, we have emphasized the importance of the deposition in the tissues (especially in the bone through inhalation and ingestion) of radioactive isotopes induced by the explosion. In fact, it has been noted that some of the early entrants showed various acute radiation syndromes such as hemorrhagic diathesis and epilation. Therefore, we also investigated the incidence of leukaemia among these early entrants. According to our survey, no leukaemia had developed among these people until 1950. Ever since then, however, leukaemia began to appear sporadically among those living in and outside the city, and no clear peak of the incidence has been observed.*

Up to the early 1970s, 75 cases of leukaemia were recorded among those entering the city within two weeks of the detonation and 62 of these cases were among people who had entered Hiroshima within three days of the explosion.

In the case of thyroid carcinoma, Watanabe accepted the prevailing view that there was a linear correlation between the incidence of this injury and the distance of the survivor from the hypocentre. 'It was quite high among the survivors exposed within 1500 m from the hypocenter. It decreasd to one half among those exposed between 1500 and 3000 m and further decreased to two-thirds of this among those exposed between 3000 and 5000 m. These data clearly indicate the correlation between radiation dose and development of thyroid carcinoma.' The survivors were suffering from thyroid carcinoma at a rate ten times that of the non-exposed beyond 5000 metres. But there were also ten cases of thyroid carcinoma among those who had entered the city after the bombing, nine of whom had arrived within a week of 6 August Watanabe notes:

> It is known that Marshallese people who had been exposed to the test explosion of hydrogen bomb in 1954 also developed thyroid carcinoma. The development of thyroid carcinoma among them was due probably to the radioactive fallout. However, not only the effects of external irradiation but also of internal irradiation should be considered. As in the case of leukemia, we have found for the first time in this study that all the early entrants who developed thyroid carcinoma entered the city shortly after the explosion (within one week), and two-thirds did so immediately after the explosion (within three days).

Similarly, in the case of lung cancer, Watanabe reported early Japanese findings of 31 cases of primary lung cancer among 32,276 survivors who presented at the Hiroshima Atomic Bomb Hospital from September 1956 to September 1961. Fifteen cases were exposed within 2000 metres; two between 2000 and 3000 metres; four between 3000 and 4000 metres and ten cases were among the early entrants, nine of them having entered withn four days of the bombing. In another study seven of 41 cases had entered the city within ten days of the bombing.

In 1975 the Japan Radiation Research Society published a review of Thirty Years Study of Hiroshima and Nagasaki Atomic Bomb Survivors.[12] It made no mention of Watanabe's review of the Japanese findings. In large part, the review supplement was an extended argument for the need for at least another twenty years funding. After thirty years of work 'Major contributions include estimates of risks of ionizing radiation for human populations, of great practical importance in the coming era of atomic energy,and the multifaceted effect of exposure to the ionizing radiations of the A-bombs.' The knowledge accumulated was vast, but 'this review affords us pause for consideration of the amount of work that lies ahead'.

J. A. Auxier gave[13] an account of the Oak Ridge Laboratory studies that led to the T-65D estimates of individual doses received by the survivors. After their visit to Japan in 1956 the survey team had returned to the Oak Ridge National Laboratory in Tennessee and created what was termed the Ichiban Project. They built two replicas of typical Japanese houses. 'The only variations from the detailed specifications were omissions of thin glass and paper doors and windows; materials were imported from Japan'. During Operation Plumb Bob in 1957 these two houses were exposed to the radiations.

Data from Plumbbob indicated that radiation fields in Japanese houses might be related, in general, to a few identifiable parameters such as house size, orientation, mutual shielding, proximity of walls and windows, etc. The basic program provided a description of the angular distribution of radiation, especially for fast neutrons, and shielding information on building materials. The greatest uncertainties in the dose–distance distributions involved the gamma radiation.

From these two mock-up houses exposed in the desert 'a summary of all dosimetry information applicable to the survivors was prepared and submitted to the shielding group in ABCC. Designated, T-57D, this tentative dosimetry information served as a guide to the establishment of techniques for determining dose values from the shielding "histories" of the exposed individuals; also, it provided an estimate of dose which supplanted the use of distance as the correlative factor for observed responses.'

After the Plumb Bob tests, Auxier reports that laboratory studies of the shielding coefficients of Japanese and domestic building materials were conducted. Cement-asbestos board which was commercially available in large sheets in the US 'was found to be suitable as a substitute for the mixture of clay, oyster shells, and seaweed wall plaster and for the mud and tile roofs of Japanese houses for both neutron and gamma rays.' The wood framing used in Japan also 'fitted well with the substitution of cement-asbestos board'. 'Consequently,' Auxier wrote in 1975, 'it was planned to use radiation analogs of Japanese houses for any further field experiments.'

In the Operation Hardtack II tests series in late 1958 'radiation analogs constructed of cement-asbestos board in wood framing typical of Japan' were used to determine 'radiation fields as a function of house size, orientation, and position relative to its neighbor'. Seven of these 'radiation analogs' were built, six of which were repaired and used three times and the seventh was used twice. Auxier wrote in 1975 under the auspices of the Japan Radiation Research Society, 'With all the data available after Hardtack II, it was possible to compute the neutron dose at any point in a Japanese house for a large number of typical configurations.' From seven simulated Japanese houses lined up in a row in the American desert, the Ichiban Project researchers felt confident of producing equations which would represent among other things the penetration distance of the direct radiation through the house, the number of interior walls shielding the survivor from the front, the number of interior walls shielding the survivor from the side, the lateral shielding exterior to the house of the survivor, the frontal exterior to the house of the survivor, the height above the air–ground interface, and the distance from an open window in the direction of the hypocentre. These calculations would of course be based upon the account of the survivor, sometimes ten or fifteen years after the cataclysmic event, of the configuration of the building in which he or she was caught by the blast.

These equations were correlated with other data on reconstructions of the air-dose curves and the spectra of the two bombs including new verifications of their yields. The British scientist, Lord Penney, for instance, recalculated his yield estimates 'based on photographs and distance measurements supplied by the ABCC and ORNL'. 'By 1968,' wrote Auxier, 'the uncertainties were generally eliminated, and the "T" from the T-65D could be dropped, although it is generally kept from habit.' In 1975, Auxier noted, further studies were being conducted on the 'black rain exposures'.

But not everyone accepted that these 1965 values were valid ways of calculating the radiation doses of thirty years earlier. In December 1977 the report of a team of scientists called the Natural Science Group organized by the Geneva-based International Peace Bureau were published.[14] More than twenty scientists, half of them Japanese and including the dissident British atomic scientist J. Rotblat and the eminent American Nobel prize-winning biologist George Wald, drew particular attention to the 37,000 people who had entered the cities after the explosions and who may have been subjected to significant residual radiation. They noted that 'an enhanced incidence of leukaemia has been found in persons who entered Hiroshima within a week after the bombing, when there was no neutron irradiation and when the calculated cumulative doses from residual radiation were well below 100 rads.' The Nishiyama district of Nagasaki was also beginning to present chronic myeloid leukaemia. The issues of threshold tolerances and latency in injury needed to be considered thirty years after the events. This international panel of scientists urged that an effort be made to work out the dosimetry of people exposed only to residual radiation, the internal dosimetry of those who were in the fallout area of the plutonium products and a full comparative study of those who were exposed directly during the explosions and those exposed only to the residual radiations.

A team of Nagasaki-based researchers reported in 1978[15] that fallout deposits were still measurable in the Nishiyama district of the city. Although the Nishiyama district was 3000 metres from the hypocentre and thought to have been shielded to a large degree from the explosion by Mount Kompira, some 400 metres in height, these researchers found the Caesium 137 content on the west side of Nishiyama reservoir to be approximately three times that of the sediment of other reservoirs. While there was no difference in the Caesium 137 content of soil and uncultivated land between Nishiyama and other districts at depths of more than 20 centimetres, there was more Caesium 137 in the soil of Nishiyama district at depths less than 20 centimetres, particularly to the west.

The researchers concluded that the increased Caesium 137 content of Nishiyama residents was being maintained by constant replenishment from ingested contaminated farm products. In a related study[16] soil samples from the Nishiyama district had ten times the Plutonium 239 content of those from Nagasaki and other comparison areas. This finding was important in substantiating that the elevated Caesium 137 contents of the Nishiyama subjects were due to the A-bomb fallout, since the bomb was a plutonium device. Plutonium 239 has a half life of 240,000 years.

Despite this accumulating evidence that the ABCC may have overlooked important factors in its three decades of work, Shields Warren told the American Philosophical Society in 1977:

> *The Atomic Bomb Casualty Commission, staffed by American and Japanese investigators, produced many useful reports as to the effects on the survivors. These helped to provide basic facts for the committees of the National Academy of Sciences concerned with biologic effects of atomic radiation and were also of great help to the United Nations Scientific Committee on the Effects of Atomic Radiation, providing basic material for their reports.*

Notes

1. ABCC Inter-office Memo from LeRoy R. Allen MD to Dr Darling, dated 24 September 1971, at Darling 770:111:70:777.

2. Speech typescript, dated 10 March 1969 by Charles L. Dunham MD titled 'Atomic Bomb Casualty Commission', at Darling 770:111:70:777.

3. Letter from Seymour Jablon to Gilbert W. Beebe, dated 26 March 1969, at Francis:39.

4. Conference of Chairman, NAS-NRC Medical Division with Director, Japanese National Institute of Health *in re* ABCC, 27 July 1971, in Washington, at Darling 770:111:70:777.

5. Robert E. Anderson, 'Establishment of ABCC', *Human Pathology*, 2:4:December 1971:485-6.

6. Robert E. Anderson, 'Study populations, dosimetry and pathology study program', *Human Pathology*, 2:4:December 1971:487–93.

7. Robert E. Anderson, 'Leukemia and related disorders', *Human Pathology*, 2:4:December 1971:505–14.

8. Robert E. Anderson 'Malignant lymphoma', *Human Pathology*, 2:4:December 1971:515–19. See also R. E. Anderson *et al.*, 'Geographic aspects of malignant lymphoma and multiple myeloma, select comparisons involving Japan, England and the United States', *American Journal of Pathology* 61:85–97.

9. Robert W. Cihak, 'Radiation and lung cancer', *Human Pathology*, 2:4: December 1971:525–28.

10. Robert E. Anderson, 'Ageing', *Human Pathology*, 2:4:December 1971:567–71

11. Susumu Watanabe, 'Cancer and leukemia developing among atom-bomb survivors', in E. Grundmann (ed.) *Handbuch Der Allgemeinen Pathologie, Geschwaltse, Morphologie, Epidemiologi, Immunologie* (Berlin, Springer-Verlag 1974):460–577.

12. *Journal of Radiation Research, Supplement* 1–11, 1975.

13. J. A. Auxier, 'Physical dose estimates for A-bomb survivors: studies at Oak Ridge, USA', *Journal of Radiation Research, Supplement* 1–11, 1975.

14. 'The physical and medical effects of the Hiroshima and Nagasaki bombs' and 'The continuing body count at Hiroshima and Nagasaki', *Bulletin of the Atomic Scientists*, December 1977:48–56.

15. Shunzo Okajima *et al.* 'Radioactive fallout effects of the Nagasaki Atomic Bomb' *Health Physics*, 1978: 621–32.

16. M. Sakanooue and T. Suji 'Plutonium content of soil at Nagasaki', *Nature* (Japan) 1971:234: 92.

17. Shields Warren, 'Hiroshima thirty years after', *Proceedings of the American Philosophical Society*, April 1977:121:2.

Twenty-three

A central area of research of the ABCC/RERF was the investigation of the ageing or life-shortening effects of the two detonations in 1945. The Adult Health Study and Life Span Study were two ways of attempting to identify and quantify radiation-induced injury which would shorten life or induce premature ageing.

After thirty years of data collection, it should have been possible to come to some preliminary conclusions about whether the exposures had adversely affected the life expectations of the survivors. The hypothesis that there would be radiation-induced life-shortening was premised on studies begun in the immediate post-war period on American and British radiologists and other medical specialists using radiation therapies.[1] But the results of these studies were inconclusive and the researchers themselves could not agree on appropriate statistical methodologies for establishing whether or not there was a significant effect.

Underlying the methodological difficulties was a lack of agreement on the very definition of and therefore the appropriate ways of measuring ageing. As well as this, the problem was posed in the early 1970s by the British epidemiologist Dr Alice Stewart and the former atomic scientist R. Rotblat that the very sample that was being examined in the case of the survivors of Hiroshima and Nagasaki was skewed because of the 'healthy survivor' factor. This is the proposition that in a cataclysmic trauma such as the two bombings, the weakest victims will die, and die first. The survivors will be those who were best able to survive the trauma – the healthiest victims. Dr Stewart and her colleagues argued that the data from Hiroshima and Nagasaki were skewed in several ways including the 'healthy survivor effect'. They also argued that the studies undertaken in the first two decades of the nuclear energy industry of the longevity of nuclear power workers were also biased by a 'healthy worker effect' – job applicants are screened for their fitness, just as armed forces recruits are, and those employed or recruited are not typical of the population as a whole.

Put another way, the studies of longevity of the survivors in Japan or the nuclear industry workers were themselves based on 'intrinsic controls' since they were not able to be truly compared to the longevity rates of the general population. Whatever evidence of life-shortening which was found in either of these closed samples would be an under-estimation of the true life-shortening effect of radiation injury since in the case of the Japanese survivors those who survived after the first few weeks were probably atypical of those who had been killed by the first effects of the exposures. Those early deaths, Dr Stewart argued, themselves constituted a selection effect which was not being taken into account by the studies of the longevity of the survivors.

Dr Stewart also raised the issue of over-reliance on cancer and especially leukaemia as the major clearly identifiable cause of premature death among the survivors. She was concerned that the latency of marrow damage was being overlooked and that the degradation of the immunological system by the initial insult would lead to delayed but still premature morbidity and mortality even among the healthy survivors. Dr Stewart never questioned the linearity of the dose–distance–response assumptions of the Hiroshima and Nagasaki data; her criticisms were made within that article of faith.

Dr Stewart was warning[2] that the conclusion that was being drawn from the Hiroshima and Nagasaki studies that 'we can expect early warning of any cancer hazard for radiation workers, and that this will take the form of extra deaths from myeloid leukaemia' was misplaced. Yet 'This interpretation of the mortality experiences of A-bomb survivors has held sway for many years and is still the basis of all safety recommendations approved by the International Commission on Radiation Protection.' It was relying on the findings of the studies that the effects of the two explosions were largely exhausted after six years. This was based, as we have seen, on studies which only began in 1950, a full five years after the exposures. They assumed – and now the IRCP was assuming – that 'late effects of atomic radiation are always the result of mutations and never the result of damage to bone marrow and other blood-forming tissues'[3] or delayed consequences of the damage to the person's immunological system which may have partially repaired but still be responsible for premature death.

Dr Stewart's own studies of the health and longevity of workers at the Hanford Plant in Washington State had brought her into direct confrontation with the nuclear energy industry and its regulators since she had found a much higher level of morbidity and mortality than the researchers of the ABCC/RERF were reporting. Yet it was the Japanese data that were being institutionalized as the basis for health and safety regulations by the ICRP. 'Therefore', as she and her co-worker G. W. Kneale noted in 1985[4] 'if there has been faulty interpretation of the Japanese data there will be many ramifications.'

Dr Stewart and her co-workers accepted the assumption that the studies of the Hiroshima and Nagasaki survivors were primarily studies of people who had received instantaneous whole body exposure of varying doses. The workers in the nuclear power plants were exposed to low level doses over time. The findings of Dr Stewart, and her colleagues G. W. Kneale and T. F. Mancuso, of higher incidences of cancer and non-cancer injuries among the Hanford workers than was being predicted from the Japanese data after thirty years, brought them directly into confrontation with the very influential nuclear power lobby. The implication of their findings was that there was not a threshold dose below which human beings could safely tolerate irradiation of a single or chronic exposure – there was no area of low level dosage that could be declared a safe margin for workers or military personnel or even medical workers. These researchers were concluding that 'there could be late effects of the A-bomb radiations that (a) were extremely difficult to recognize; (b) masked the prevalence of all cancers by causing premature infection deaths; and (c) provided ideal conditions for mutations of haemopoetic stem cells to cause an early epidemic of acute myeloid leukaemia.'[5]

Yet 'In spite of these possibilities, both analysts and assessors of RERF data have continued to find the normal non-cancer death rate reassuring rather than puzzling.' The RERF position that 'all non-cancer effects of two explosions which all but destroyed two large cities were so short-lived that in less than five years the slate was wiped clean' was now being used to argue that radiation workers exposed to low doses were not at risk. As Dr Stewart wrote in 1985, 'These opinions have been repeated so often and over such a long period that very few scientists are prepared even to consider the possibility that the reason why there is incompatibility between MSK [Mancuso/Stewart/Kneale] risk estimates and ICRP recommendations is because official interpretations of RERF data are seriously flawed.'

The nuclear hierarchy was arguing that the risk for low level exposures could be extrapolated back from the 'linear' data generated by the ABCC and the RERF. Dr Stewart and Dr Kneale warned again in 1987[6] that 'the present method of risk estimation for low-level radiation (by linear extrapolation of high dose effects) is grossly under-estimating the true cancer risks. Consequently, present directives (which are based on ICRP recommendations) are probably under-stating, not only the cancer hazards of radiation workers and nuclear hazards, but also the contribution made by natural background radiation to cancer mortality.' It had become 'accepted practice both to base risk estimates for small doses of radiation upon linear extrapolation of high dose effects, and to regard RERF data as one of the best sources of these effects.'

In 1970 Dr Stewart had published the results of her Oxford Study of Childhood Cancers, a twenty year study of the consequences of X-raying foetuses. She and her colleague G. W. Kneale found that the risk of childhood cancer was doubled if one rad of X-rays were given before birth. As one commentator[7] noted, their 1970 report[8] 'has, in spite of considerable resistance, transformed a once-standard practice into an unusual one, and established beyond doubt the high sensitivity of the foetus to radiation-induced cancer.' Nevertheless, the findings of Stewart, Mancuso and Kneale on the impact of radiation on healthy workers in the nuclear energy industry have not met with acceptance, and in fact they claim to have been victimized by the loss of research contracts controlled by the scientific and biomedical establishment.[9]

By the early 1980s, there was sufficient data emerging from the studies now under the auspices of the Radiation Effects Research Foundation for the statisticians to be able to reflect on the statistical modelling techniques that they were utilizing. A conference on 'Atomic Bomb Survivor Data: Utilization and Analysis' was funded by the Department of Energy and convened by the SIAM Institute for Mathematics and Society in Philadelphia in 1984. The statisticians were interested in the possibilities for developing mathematical models of risk analysis, and felt that the data being generated from the RERF was being under-utilized. 'The time seemed ripe for gathering a small group of current RERF scientists, veteran US statisticians and epidemiologists and others with more recent entry into the field of radiation biology' to plan for further development of the data but also to provide 'a useful critique of their scope and quality'.[10]

The strongest reservations came in the discussion of how the dosimetry values had been arrived at. The introduction to this section notes that 'Every phase of the present (T-65) dosimetry system is being subjected to a thorough re-analysis by scientists in the United States and Japan', and warned 'An important message from this series of papers is that even if the systematic components of the air-dose curves and shielding factor models become highly specified and accurate there will remain important sources of random variation in individual survivor dose estimates that, unless quantified and accommodated in dose response analyses, will produce misleading inferences in respect to radiation risk.'[11]

Seymour Jablon, an original member of the Francis Committee in 1955 and now an employee of the National Academy of Sciences, now conceded[12], almost thirty years later, that 'Inadequate attention has been given in the past to possible problems arising from errors in radiation doses assigned to A-bomb survivors in Hiroshima and Nagasaki'. These errors, he thought, were of two kinds. Systematic errors which result from mistaken values for such characteristics as bomb yield or atmospheric attenuation of radiation, and individual errors such as mis-reporting of location and shielding of a survivor. 'Recent studies have demonstrated substantial systematic errors in the T-65 dosimetry system which has been used by RERF for analyses of radiation effects upon the health of the survivors during the decades after the bombings.' All aspects of the T-65 dose estimates were now being revised.

How had these errors come about and been perpetuated for thirty years? Mr Jablon suggested three reasons. The early researchers had been over-whelmed with the problems usual to survey studies, especially in places as difficult as Hiroshima and Nagasaki after the bombings. A second reason, he suggested, was 'a failure of communication between physicists and statisticians. The physicists produced a black box, and out of that box flowed numbers, called 'kerma" or "doses", and these were handed out to the statisticians. There were, to be sure, inquiries made of the physicists as to how accurate they considered the doses to be – to which the answer came that they were accurate to plus or minus 30 per cent, or 50 per cent, and the statisticians were, perforce, contented with that.' The third reasons for not taking account of the uncertainties in dosimetry, suggested Mr Jablon, 'is that we don't really have a good methodology for doing so'. In summary:

The three reasons that so little attention has been paid to errors in dosimetry are that we had our hands full with other important problems that were more traditional and that we thought we knew how to address, if we worked at them; that we didn't know the characteristics of the uncertainties that affect dosimetry estimates; and, finally, that we didn't have any established way mathematically of dealing with the enormously complex set of problems inherent in the system.

Although Mr Jablon acknowledged that the measurements made in Nevada were made from bombs that were not replicas of the Hiroshima and Nagasaki weapons, and were made in dry desert air rather than in 'the moist August air in Hiroshima and Nagasaki', he claimed that the shielding factors for light Japanese housing arrived at by the Ichiban Project were well grounded. 'An elaborate experimental system was used to develop the nine parameter formula. Models of Japanese houses were built at the Nevada test site and were irradiated experimentally, with dosimeters outside and at several points inside the houses.' However,

'Unfortunately, it turned out that much of the gamma radiation measured inside the houses resulted from neutron interactions with the building materials themselves, so the so-called shielded values for gamma radiation were seriously mis-estimated.' However, 'If a linear dose-effect model is assumed' Mr Jablon felt in 1984 that the estimates of cancer risk per rad are only likely to change by a factor of about two.

Arthur V. Peterson, Jr of the Department of Biostatistics at the University of Washington in Seattle spelled out the nine components of A-bomb dosimetry.[13] They included the location of the epicentre, the bomb yield, the source neutron spectrum, the behaviour of the fission product cloud and emission of delayed gamma radiation, the attenuation of radiation in air, and, for each survivor, the location at the time of the bomb of each survivor, the amount and configuration of the shielding available to each survivor, and, lastly, the assessment of residual radiation from fallout and induced radioactivity. Virtually all of them were currently – forty years after the event – under reassessment. Not even the actual epicentres of the two bombs, it was now realized, were known with the degree of precision required to premise the simple linear assumptions of radiation which had underlain all the work of the Atomic Bomb Casualty Commission and then the Radiation Effects Research Foundation for four decades. The differences between the bombs that were detonated at Hiroshima and Nagasaki were now increasingly understood to have resulted in different radiations.

Dr Peterson pointed out that the linear assumptions of the mathematical and statistical models that had been developed were premised on circular symmetry around the epicentres – they had assumed that the bombs exploded in a vertical position from which the radiation had radiated in straight lines. This assumption itself rested on four conditions – that the estimated hypocentre be accurate; that any asymmetry in prompt radiation exposure at the distances of interest be negligible; that the rising fire ball remain directly above the estimated hypocentre during the first ten seconds with no appreciable lateral displacement; and the residual radiation exposure from fallout be negligible. All the ABCC and RERF data of the past forty years had been premised on these assumptions.

In fact, Peterson acknowledged, the data of the Japanese researchers had demonstrated the existence of residual radiation, there was no firm knowledge of the tilt of the weapons at the moment of detonation and there was increasing evidence of asymmetry in the cancer data. As E. S. Gilbert showed in the next paper at this 1984 meeting of statisticians,[14] if one divided each city into octants from the presumed epicentres, there were very clear differences in the incidence of cancer which were not reconcilable with the notion of a simple linear circular radiation.

What could be done, forty years after the event, about these biases? Dr Peterson suggested several strategies.[15] The end point data – the actual statistics on cancer mortality, for instance – could be used to compare Hiroshima and Nagasaki and individuals could be compared between the types of shielding they reported in order to see if this real information correlated with the mathematical models for shielding and dose that had been developed. In other words, data that were now considered 'random' or anomalous because they did not conform with the models which had been built up from so many assumptions should be looked at again. Dr Peterson also urged a more careful investigation of the differences between prompt radiation, delayed radiation and residual radiation rather than the assumption that had prevailed for forty years that all radiation emitted from the two bombs was similar and instantaneous.

Gilbert Beebe made another point in a private letter to John Bowers, who in 1982 was writing a history of the Atomic Bomb Casualty Commission.[16] Beebe noted that whenever there had been talk of eliminating one city from the two-city study over the years, it had always been assumed that Nagasaki would be sacrificed. One reason for this was that when the sample was decided upon for the Adult Health Study under the criteria of the Francis Committee, it resulted in a sample in Nagasaki that was only half the size of the Hiroshima sample. However:

Although we still don't know just what the admixture of neutrons is in the Hiroshima dose, the nearly complete absence of neutrons from the Nagasaki dose gives the Nagasaki sample a very decided advantage. We may never be able to assess the contributions of the neutrons in Hiroshima data and the Hiroshima data may be of use to us mainly in contrasts with the Nagasaki data.

Dr Beebe also reflected in the early 1980s that

ABCC was organized in the traditional way, as you know, and without regard for the fact that it was the effect of radiation that was the object of research. This was not too bad as long as the task had to be defined in terms of identifying effects, a classificatory phase, as it were, but in time the lack of personnel who knew the radiation biology literature, who knew what was really wanted by the international community of scientists interested in these matters, and who knew what to look for in the data, contributed to a lack of focus in the work being done there.... We should have had a direct pipeline into the thinking of UNSCEAR, ICRP etc.

In 1981 two physicists from the Lawrence Livermore National Laboratory had published[17] serious reservations about the T-65 dose estimates developed by Auxier and the Ichiban Project. This provoked the

Department of Energy to convene a meeting of 120 scientists at the old Atomic Energy Commission building in Germantown, Maryland to consider what should be done. John Auxier attended the meeting and 'Even though he occasionally felt an impulse to speak up for his old research', he said, 'I have tried to keep quiet for the last year' because it seemed proper for younger scientists to refine the work he started. 'We knew at the time that the answer we had [in 1965] wasn't good enough,' he said, 'but we had an answer, and the funding dried up.'[18]

A decade earlier, the journal that reported this remark, *Science*, had published a commentary on the status of the Hiroshima and Nagasaki studies[19]. Philip M. Boffey reported that 'Survivors have been interviewed to determine just where they were and what shielding they were behind; replicas of Japanese houses have been tested for shielding effects at the AEC's Nevada test site; and the epicenter of the explosion has been determined as precisely as possible by studying thermal ray shadows burned into gravestones and other granite objects.' Boffey acknowledged that the yield of the Hiroshima bomb had been recalculated down from 20-kilotons of TNT to 'probably only 12.5'. 'The upshot of all this refining and recalculating is that Oak Ridge National Laboratory has developed sophisticated equations for estimating the dose of gamma and neutron radiation actually received by any given individual. There are considerable disagreements over how accurate the estimates are in any individual case, but on a statistical basis the errors are believed to cancel out.' These data and their results, he said, 'are expected to be particularly helpful in establishing the maximum radiation exposure which can be safely tolerated by man.'

But in 1984 a senior RERF consultant was reminding his colleagues that:

> The current emphasis on the adaptation of newer multivariate statistical methods to the analysis of RERF data is an entirely wholesome development, one to be encouraged. At the same time it must be recognized that complex models simplify analyses in part by making strong assumptions, that the assumptions underlying a model may be more influential than the data to which it is applied, that statistical models do not always fit the data well, and that communication with the target audience may be hampered unless the impact of highly abstract and complex models is mediated by parallel presentations of a more concrete nature.[20]

Notes

1(a) L.I. Greblin and M. Spiegelman 'Mortality of medical specialists 1938–1942, *Journal of American Medical Associations*, 1948:137:1519–24.

(b) L.I. Greblin and M. Spiegelman 'The longevity and mortality of American physicians, 1938–42' *Journal of American Medical Associations*, 1947:134:1211-1215.

(c) Warren, S. 'Longevity and causes of death from irradiation in physicians' *Journal of American Medical Associations*, 1956:162:464–8.

(d) C.B. Braestrup 'Past and present radiation exposure to radiologists from the point of view of life expectancy', *American Journal of Roentgenology*, 1957:78:988–92.

(e) R. Seltser and P.E. Sartwell 'Ionizing radiation and longevity of physicians' *Journal of American Medical Associations*, 1958:166:585–87.

(f) R. Seltser and P.E. Sartwell 'The influence of occupational exposure to radiation in the mortality of American radiologists and other medical specialties' *American Journal of Epidemiology*, 1965:81:2–22.

(g) S. Warren and O.M. Lombard 'New data on the effects of ionizing radiation on radiologists' *Archives Environmental Health*, 1966:13:415–21.

(h) W.M. Court-Brown and R. Doll 'Expectations of life and mortality from cancer among British radiologists ' *British Medical Journal* 1958:2:181–7.

(i) G.M. Matanoski, R. Selster, P.E. Sartwell, E.L. Diamond and E.A. Elliot 'The current mortality rates of radiologists and other physician specialists: Deaths from all causes and from cancer' *American Journal of Epidemiology*, 1975:101:188–98.

(j) K.P. Duncan and R.W. Howell 'Health of workers in the UK atomic energy authority' *Health Physics*, 1970:19:285–91.

2. A. M .Stewart, 'Delayed effects of A-bomb radiation: a review of recent mortality rates and risk estimates for five-year survivors', *Journal of Epidemiology and Community Health*, 1982:36:2:80–6.

3. A .M. Stewart, G. W. Kneale, 'Mortality experiences of A-bomb survivors', *Bulletin of the Atomic Scientists*, 1984:40:5:61–2

4. A. M. Stewart and G. W. Kneale, 'Non-cancer effects of exposure to A-bomb radiation', *Journal of Epidemiology and Community Health*,1984:38:108–12.

5. A. M. Stewart, 'Detection of late effects of ionizing radiation: why deaths of A-bomb survivors are so misleading', *International Journal of Epidemiology*, 1985:14:1:52–6.

6. A. M. Stewart, G.W. Kneale, Correspondence, 'Late effects of A-Bomb radiation: risk problems unrelated to the new dosimetry', *Health Physics*, May 1988:54:5:567–9.

7. John Valentine, *Atomic Crossroads: Before and after Sizewell* (London, The Merlin Press, 1985) p.167.

8. A. M. Stewart and G.W. Kneale, 'Immune system and cancers of foetal origin', *Cancer Immunology and Immunotherapy*, 1982:110–16 summarizes these findings.

9. John Valentine, *Atomic Crossroads: Before and after Sizewell* (London, The Merlin Press, 1985) pp. 161–71.

10. Ross L. Prentice and Donovan J. Thompson, *Atomic Bomb Survivor Data: utilization and analysis* (SIAM Philadelphia, 1984) Introduction.

11. Prentice and Thompson, *ibid.* p.142.

12. Seymour Jablon, 'Characteristics of current and expected dosimetry', in Prentice and Thompson *ibid.* pp.143–52.

13. Arthur V. Peterson, 'Use of cancer mortality data in Hiroshima and Nagasaki to assess various aspects of the radiation dosimetry', in Prentice and Thompson, *ibid.* pp.153–69. The report of the British Medical Association's Board of Science and Education, *The Medical Effects of Nuclear War*, 1983:58, also notes that 'The convention of representing the zones affected by blast around a nuclear explosion as perfectly circular assumes absolutely flat ground. The same applies to the areas exposed to a given level of thermal radiation. In practice the shape of hills and val-

leys would create shadows, modifying the ranges of damage – although in ways which would be hard to predict in detail.'

14. E. S. Gilbert, 'The effects of random dosimetry errors and the use of data on acute symptoms for dosimetry evaluations' in Prentice and Thompson *ibid.*, pp.170–82.

15. A. V. Peterson, in Prentice and Thompson, *ibid.*, pp.165–6.

16. Letter from Gilbert Beebe to John Bowers, dated 20 February 1982, at Bowers: ACC 89–73:ABCC:1.

17. W. E. Loewe and E. Mendelsohn, 'Revised dose estimates at Hiroshima and Nagasaki', *Health Physics*, October 1981:41:4:663–6.

18. 'Japanese A-Bomb data will be revised', *Science*, October 1981:214:2:31–2.

19. Philip M. Boffey, 'Hiroshima/Nagasaki, Atomic Bomb Casualty Commisson perseveres in sensitive studies' *Science*, 8 May 1970:679–83

20. Gilbert W. Beebe, 'RERF agenda for radiation-induced cancer', 1984.

SECTION VI

Setting Standards

Our entire permissible dose structure of today is based upon our inability to observe any deleterious or other effect at the permissible dose levels which have been in vogue since 1934... There is an unbroken chain of derivation in today's protection standards even though [sic] there has been no observation of effect of radiation exposures within permissible limits.

... It is well past time that we should have stopped trying – for whatever reason – to read into later incomplete or reworked statements concepts that could not have prevailed at the time the original ideas were developed. Let us stop trying to reconstruct history. Let us record it as it was, and from that draw separately any sociological or subjective judgements or opinions that may be deemed to be useful. But when they are judgements or opinion, clearly identify them as such.

Lauriston S. Taylor, Guest Editorial, 'Technical accuracy in historical writing', *Health Physics,* **1981:40:595–9**

Twenty-four

As early as the mid-1950s, there was considerable disquiet at the self-confirming ways in which the Atomic Bomb Casualty Commission and its daughter projects such as the Atomic Energy Commission were functioning.

Representative Chet Holifield chaired a Congressional Special Radiation Subcommittee which was as well informed as anyone outside the AEC could be about the agency which was both developing and policing civilian and military uses of nuclear energy. The Congressman wrote an article for public interest in the *Saturday Review* in August 1957,[1] the twelfth anniversary of the bombings of Hiroshima and Nagasaki. Since then, more than 120 nuclear weapons had been 'tested' – about one a month.

Like the scientists who testified before his subcommittee, Representative Holifield thought that air bursts were relatively safe.The detonation created a

> *seething cloud [which] as it reached the upper air, soon became strewn out into tiny invisible particles. High altitude winds buffeted and blew them around the world. This was really quite fortunate, for the stratosphere acted like a kind of isolation ward. The floating particles continued to emit powerful radioactive rays, but these hurt no one as long as they remained in the upper air. If all of them were to be suspended indefinitely in the stratosphere, perhaps an unlimited number of big bomb tests could be conducted without causing global contamination. But what goes up unfortunately must come down. As a result, we have the phenomenon of global fall-out.*

He was aware that the 1954 *Bravo* shot had contaminated 7000 square miles of ocean territory and that the islands there were 'still so radioactive that they are above the permissible safety level for normal land use'. He was also aware from his committee's hearings of the reports on the amounts of Strontium 90 that were being measured in milk after test shots in the Nevada Proving Grounds.

But, he wrote for a wide public in 1957, 'As a layman I was somewhat shocked to find out how much the experts admitted they did not know. In fact, when I thought over how little is known for sure, I wondered how some government officials could be so positive that bomb tests were so safe.'

The Congressman did not put much confidence in laboratory experiments where:

> the effects on heredity of various radiation doses are being conducted on fruit flies, mice, dogs and monkeys. It is of course not practical to experiment on human beings; anyhow, the human lifespan is too long to furnish the knowledge we need now on genetic or hereditary effects. We can only try to extrapolate the effects of radiation on insects and short lifespan mammals, and consider these effects as we think they would apply to human beings. The element of error in this extrapolation is admitted by all scientists.

The Chair of the Special Radiation Subcommittee of the Joint Committee on Atomic Energy of the United States Congress was very frank in his comments on the AEC even in the security-conscious 1950s.

> It has been my experience that a Congressional investigation is often the only way to make the Atomic Energy Commission come out into the open. We literally squeeze the information out of the agency. Except for the Congressional hearings, the AEC would withhold some important information that the public should have. Then, too, when the Commission releases information on its own initiative it comes in forbidding technical form or in driblets through speeches of commission members or other high ranking personnel. Even skilful newspaper reporters, not to mention the layman on the outside, have difficulty piecing together the information or understanding its significance.

He charged AEC officials who testified before the Congressional hearings of adhering to

> a party line – 'play it down'. As custodian of official information, the AEC has an urgent responsibility to communicate the facts to the public. Yet time after time there has been a long delay in issuance of the facts, and oftentimes the facts have to be dragged out of the agency by the Congress. Certainly, it took our investigation to enable some of the Commission's own experts to break through the party line on fall-out.

Congressman Holifield detected a conflict of interests: 'Is it prudent to ask the same agency both to develop bombs and evaluate the risk of fall-out?'

Reservations about the conflict of interests evident in the AEC were expressed from other quarters, such as the journal *Science* in 1971.[2] In a feature article titled 'Radiation standards: are the right people making decisions?', Philip M. Boffey wrote that 'It was not until 1959, after the advent of the atomic age had aroused public fears over fallout from nuclear weapons, that the government suddenly realized that it was relying primarily on private organizations to determine acceptable radiation protection standards. As a result, a new governmental organization, the Federal Radiation Council, was established to promulgate "official" guidelines.' The FRC became the Environmental Protection Agency in the late 1960s.

Boffey noted that there was a remarkable consistency in the radiation protection standards issued by the relevant agencies. But, he observed:

> *The significance of this unanimity can be looked at in two ways. Officials of the standards-setting organizations argue that the unanimity underscores the validity of the existing standards, for different bodies of the world's leading radiation experts have all looked at the relevant scientific literature and reached essentially the same conclusions as to allowable exposure levels. However, critics of the standards charge that the various groups are so similar in outlook and have such overlapping memberships that they are merely different parts of the 'nuclear energy lobby' wearing different hats and rubberstamping each other's decisions.*

Boffey also observed that 'As far as can be determined by the public record, the scientists have not really tried to perform a quantitative risk–benefit analysis in developing the standard. The various standards groups have refused to get involved in "the numbers game" of estimating how many deaths might result if the public received the radiation allowed by the standards. Nor have they tried to quantify the presumed benefits of atomic energy. Thus the public is left with little more than an assurance that the risk is "acceptable".' Boffey thought that 'it would seem highly desirable that some way be found to assure the public that its fate does not lie solely in the hands of a small group of scientists meeting behind closed doors.'

There were two central areas of disagreement among the scientists and biomedical researchers. One was the significance of hazards from fallout, and the other was whether or not there existed a safe, permissible dose of radiation – a threshold of exposure below which it would be safe for humans to be irradiated for medical, industrial or military purposes.

The remarkably slow perception of the hazard of fallout is apparent from the memoirs of Merril Eisenbud, one of the earliest radiation safety experts in the United States who directed the New York Operations

Office of the AEC during the 1950s, became Professor of Industrial Safety at New York University and served as Environmental Affairs Commissioner for the City of New York. While Eisenbud is generally credited with having insisted to the AEC that it take fallout seriously as a hazard, even in 1990 he could write that:

> *Dangerous fallout of radioactive particles occurs when a nuclear bomb is exploded so close to the ground that particles of soil and other materials are sucked into the cooling fireball as it rises. When bombs are exploded at greater altitudes, the debris takes the form of fine particles that settle to the ground, usually with rain or snow, at great distances from the explosion, after most of the short-lived radionuclides have decayed. The two bombs dropped on the Japanese cities were exploded high in the air, which tended to minimize fallout, but rain showers shortly after the explosions did result in slight, but measurable levels of fallout in both Hiroshima and Nagasaki.*

Eisenbud had been alerted to the fact that the Eastman Kodak photography company had detected fallout in Rochester, New York in the early 1950s after test detonations in Nevada. He notes:

> *At the time of the Rochester fallout there was little appreciation of the fact that some of the nuclides present in the bomb debris were capable of being absorbed by plants and animals and could eventually find their way into food and the human body. Such information was available from studies that had been conducted at Hanford and other nuclear centers, but the information was still secret in 1951 and at HASL [Health and Safety Laboratory, NY] we didn't know it existed.'*

Eisenbud too was extrapolating his understanding of nuclear explosions from vulcanology. He remembered that at the time of the first thermonuclear blast at Eniwetok in the fall of 1952:

> *There was much thoughtful discussion about the possible consequences of such an explosion: Some scientists believed that the force of megaton explosions would drive the radioactive dust into outer space! Our staff was less optimistic, and predicted that dangerous levels of fallout could occur for hundreds of miles downwind of the explosion. During those months I spent a considerable amount of time reading about the dust produced by volcanic eruptions, which were more violent by far than thermonuclear explosions [my emphasis]. I was impressed by the fact that the dust was injected high into the stratosphere where it remained for years and affected the coloration of sunsets around the world. In addition to high levels of fallout that would occur within hours after an explosion in which*

*the fire ball touched the ground, it was highly likely that fallout of small
particles would 'dribble' from the stratosphere for many years.'*

It was the *Bravo* test of 1 March 1954 that vindicated Eisenbud's fears
about fallout. 'The fallout of March 1 had proved that we were correct in
our belief that massive fallout covering large areas of land would be a
consequence of nuclear war.' But as recently as October 1952, he and his
colleagues had understood so little about fallout that he recalled a flight
over an ocean to measure the fallout after a detonaton when:

*there were a number of times on that flight when my instrument reading
began to drift upscale. I interpreted these reading as the result of instabili-
ties in the instrument, which was only recently off the drawing board. The
instrument was in fact behaving properly and was recording radiation from
fallout in the water. It had not occurred to me that the radioactive materials would remain near the surface long enough to be detectable, even with
the effect of shielding by the water.*

One reason for the ignorance on the part of one of the country's
senior radiation hazards specialists was because information was dispensed
on a 'need to know' basis. 'The trouble with the system was that one
might not know what one needs to know! This was particularly true of
our group because we were not part of the regular weapons testing organization and did not really understand how the classified information related to what we were doing, and therefore did not know what report to
ask for or what questions to ask.' Curiously, Eisenbud particularly notes
that John C. Bugher – Director of the Division of Medicine and Biology
of the AEC and a pivotal member of the Committee on Atomic
Casualties of the Atomic Bomb Casualty Commission, and who was to
direct Puerto Rico's nuclear programme in the 1960s – was very supportive of his work. According to Eisenbud, Bugher was trained as a
physician and as a physicist. Yet he seems, despite his pivotal roles in the
work of the AEC in the first thirty years of its life, to have been ineffective in networking information between his different colleagues and
organizations.

In 1990 Eisenbud still believed that air bursts did not create significant
local fallout, and that Hiroshima and Nagasaki had been air bursts even
though they were detonated at the height of the Empire State Building
in New York. But he did note a change in the consensus about whether
or not there existed a threshold below which radiation was safe for
humans. In the early days 'It was then believed that there was a "threshold dose", below which no delayed effects of radiation would occur.
This is no longer believed to be true, as least so far as cancer and genetic

effects are concerned, but until the late 1950s the concept of threshold dose prevailed.'

He explains:

> *Until the late 1950s it was generally accepted that a threshold radiation dose existed, below which there would be no effects from exposure. However, new laboratory and epidemiological research suggested that there might not be a threshold and that it would be prudent to assume that the risks of producing cancer or causing genetic effects are increased by all radiation exposure, however small the dose. It was further suggested that the dose–response relationship is linear, ie a strict proportionality exists between the dose received and the health effects produced. Thus, for every increase in radiation exposure, there is a corresponding increase in risk. At very low doses, of the order of the natural radiation background, the increased risk is exceedingly small but finite nevertheless. This being the case, there is no 'safe' dose of radiation. The risks associated with radiation exposure could no longer be based on the answer to the question What is the safe dose? If there is no threshold, there is no such thing as a safe dose. This made it necessary to pose a new question, How safe is safe enough?, a question whose answer has eluded consensus to the present time.*

After a lifetime spent largely working for government agencies, Merril Eisenbud concurred with Congressman Holifield and Philip Boffey in their concerns about how information is controlled by big science and the uneasy relationship between politicians and the projects for which they vote funds:

> *Elected officials are expected to reflect what the public wants, however ill-informed the public may be. This in turn has an influence on decisions made by the agencies charged with responsibility for environmental matters. The agencies are expected to adopt policies that are consistent with the wishes of both the public and the legislators who represent them. An agency must avoid taking issue with the legislators, because to do so would jeopardize the financial support that only the legislators can provide. For this reason, a scientist who disagrees with a proposed agency position is not likely to be appointed to either its staff* or advisory committees [my emphasis]. *The scientists cannot be picked on the basis of their competence, but primarily on whether they support the policies the agency wants to develop. This explains why the scientists become polarized. The 'ins' continue to support the policies of the agency, whereas the 'outs', who may be capable, are likely to be sought as industry consultants. In the process, the agency loses its independence.*

Eisenbud recalled that when he visited the ABCC in 1951, it was in great turmoil and dire danger of being terminated but General MacArthur intervened because 'it was important for political reasons to continue the ABCC studies because if they were terminated, it would create a scientific vacuum into which investigators of uncertain scientific credibility would be drawn. Moreover, some of the investigators might be so influenced by political factors as to affect their scientific objectivity.' But, according to Eisenbud, MacArthur's intervention 'because of the political considerations' he had identified meant that the ABCC survived and 'The information that has been gathered in the two cities now contributes uniquely to our understanding of the delayed effects of radiation *and serves as the basis of many of the radiation protection standards* [my emphasis].'

Eisenbud's recollections of the growth of understanding about the probable non-existence of a safe threshold below which humans could be exposed to radiation concur with another Congressional committee report. In August 1980, the thirty-fifth anniversary of the bombings of Hiroshima and Nagasaki, the Subcommittee on Oversight and Investigation of the US House of Representatives was told :

> *at the start of the continental nuclear testing program in the 1950s, a precautionary attitude had already developed among government officials as well as within the scientific community regarding the health risks of radiation exposure for the general population. The pervasive damage sustained as a result of the atomic blasts at Hiroshima and Nagasaki alerted the entire nation to the immediate threat of atomic weaponry. Even at this initial stage of our development of nuclear technology, scientists were suggesting that no safe threshold level existed below which radiation would have no carcinogenic effect.*[4]

The Congressmen were told that at a seminar on low level radiation on 19 February 1978, conducted by the Environmental Policy Institute/Environmental Study Conference, Dr Victor Bond of the Brookhaven Laboratory had reminded his audience that 'it was way back in the late 1940s and early 1950s that the ICRP and NCRP made a very important change in philosophy from a[n]... essentially threshold concept to a non-threshold concept. This was spelled out clearly in NRCP Handbook 59 published in '54 but was agreed formally in 1951.' Certainly, Lauriston S Taylor, a founding member of both the International Commission on Radiology Protection and the National Council on Radiology Protection and Measurements, had reported to the United Nations as early as 1958[5] that the Maximum Permissible Dose was being *decreased* by a factor of 3 over those promulgated in 1950 and 1953 in April 1956.

Notes

1. Chet Holifield, Chairman, Special Radiation Subcommittee, Joint Committee on Atomic Energy, 'Who should judge the atom?', *Saturday Review*, 3 August 1957, 34–7.

2. 'Radiation standards: are the right people making decisions?', *Science* 26 February 1971:171:780–3.

3. Merril Eisenbud, *An Environmental Odyssey* (University of Washington Press, 1990).

4. 'The forgotten guinea pigs: a report on the health effects of low level radiation sustained as a result of nuclear weapons tests program conducted by the US Government', Report prepared for the Use of the Committee on Interstate and Foreign Commerce, United States House of Representatives and its Subcommittee on Oversight and Investigation, August 1980.

5. Lauriston S. Taylor, 'The influence of lowered permissible dose levels on atomic energy operations in the United States' , *Proceedings of the Second United Nations Conference*, 1958: 211–14.

Twenty-five

Although the first round of genetics studies had been terminated in 1954, James Neel and William Schull continued to collect data in related studies. In 1966 Neel told a University of Michigan audience in the prestigious Russel Lecture[1] that the control city of Kure had been dropped within the first year of the first studies because 'it was discovered that half of the current inhabitants of Hiroshima and Nagasaki had not been there at the time of the bombings, so that there were adequate internal controls, and a control city became unnecessary'. According to this 1966 statement, 'By the end of 1953 "complete" information had been collected on the outcomes of 71,280 births in the two cities of Hiroshima and Nagasaki, and an extensive statistical analysis was undertaken. Although 71,280 sounds like a goodly number, only 9686 of these births were to parents one or both of whom had received a "substantial" amount of irradiation.'

Nevertheless, 'the decision was reached to terminate in 1954 the extensive and expensive clinical program concerned with the study of congenital defect but to continue to collect data on the sex-ratio, and also to set up a long-range program on the death rate of children born to survivors. This decision was based on the fact that the number of children born to the more heavily irradiated parents was falling off year by year, as older individuals completed their reproductive period *and younger ones migrated from the city* [my emphasis]; it could be demonstrated statistically that it was highly unlikely that even another ten years of work would substantially alter the picture with respect to those indicators showing no effect.'

What did Professor Neel make of his findings as early as 1966? Although the consensus of scientific opinion, as we have seen in the previous chapter, had moved strongly away from the assumption of a threshold below which there would be a permissible dose of radiation exposure well before the mid-1960s, Professor Neel remarked 'Negative conclusions are seldom intellectually satisfying – fortunately, there is a more positive context in which we can employ the data. They can be used to set upper limits to the sensitivity of the human genetic material to radiation'. Because he had assumed that exposure to such massive ionizing radiation as occurred in Hiroshima and Nagasaki must cause injury to humans as it had to animals and fruit flies in laboratory situations, Neel was arguing not that his methodology was too crude to capture the damage but rather that it indicated that the parameters of exposure that would injure humans was not as low as the non-human experiments had suggested. Against the stream of scientific and biomedical thought, which was progressively reducing the permissible limits of human radiation exposure throughout these years, Neel was arguing for the existence of a threshold, and at a *higher* level than had been thought.

Professor Neel said, for instance, in this 1966 address that 'our studies on sex-ratio and death rates extend back to the first children conceived following the bombings. They thus include the data most appropriate to demonstrating the production of mutations.' Yet he himself had not entered the Japanese cities until fifteen months after the bombings – a period during which no data on births, much less conceptions, had been collected by American researchers. Even when he did get his research programme up and running, he was relying on reported pregnancies which had survived to at least five months by building his sample from the ration rolls. There was no data collected by the ABCC on the pregnancies lost before five months until 1949. Even then, they were confounded by new government policies of 'abortion literally on demand'.

Neel remarked in 1994, 'The frequency of induced abortion so complicated our effort to study spontaneous abortion that after several years we abandoned the undertaking. Our data [*on genetic consequences of the bombs*] pertain only to children who survived through the fifth month of pregnancy.'[2]

Neel had to argue the superiority of his data over the laboratory experiments which were producing values for injury at variance with his lack of results in the Japanese survivors. Neel and Schull had always had their differences with the 'experimentalists' such as H. J. Muller who had from the beginning had reservations about their research design and methodology. For instance, Neel and his colleagues wrote in a defence of their approach to monitoring human populations for mutation rates and genetic disease :

> It is not sufficient to limit studies to experimental animals and then extrapolate the results to man. Species may differ in their susceptibilities to mutagenic agents, rates and mechanisms of repair may differ among species, and the data on experimental organisms may be obtained only

years after human exposures have been initiated.... No experimental ani-
mal population can be a satisfactory indicator in real time of the sum total
of the panoply of potential mutagens to which man is subject.[3]

In his autobiography[4] Neel later remarked on the irony that his men-
tors were people such as Salvador Luria during his time at Cold Spring
Harbor when Neel was 'simultaneously fumbling with thoughts of
bringing Drosophila-type rigor into genetic studies of that most
intractable of all organisms, man.' But in designing his work on the
Japanese survivors, he had come up against considerable criticism from
Hermann Muller, in particular, and he was very concerned to get 'the
appropriate endorsements' for what he knew could come to be known as
'Neel's Folly'.[5] But the epidemiological study he designed and directed
(from Michigan) failed to produce laboratory-type experimental results.

But that very failure could be used to reassure the survivors. 'Since...
we found very little in the way of a genetic effect of the A-bombs, the
principal tangible result of our study has been to dispel nasty rumors, to
provide reassurance.'[6]

Twenty years after the bombings, cytogenetic techniques for assessing
chromosomal changes became available to Professor Neel and other
researchers in the two cities. By 1980 he and his team had conducted half
a million locus tests still using as controls children born during the study
period (ie from May 1946 to 31 December 1958) to distally exposed parents, one or both of whom were within the city at the time of the bombing but more than 2500 metres from the hypocentre 'and therefore
received essentially no radiation.'[7]

Despite the controversies surrounding the dose reconstructions –
which were repeatedly revised every decade or so as we have seen – Neel
and his colleagues wrote in a 1980 report on the cytogenetic studies that
'Based on meticulous histories of survivors' locations at the time of the
bombings and the physical facts concerning the atomic bombs, an effort
has been made to assign a body surface dose to each survivor ...' They
were also still assuming that the exposure had been only of the instantaneous type, despite the increasing evidence that there had been radiation
effects from residual radiation in the cities.

In a 'reappraisal' of the data on genetic effects of the atomic bombs
published in 1981,[8] Schull and Neel noted that 'Children born to individuals one or both of whom were within 2001 to 2500 m of the
hypocenter were excluded from the study because of difficulty in accurately evaluating the very low doses received at this distance.' They also
note in passing that 'the exact position of the hypocenter in Nagasaki was
not resolved until late 1978.' They were still working on the T-65 doses.

After thirty years of study they concluded:

> *Extensive experimental evidence attests to the genetic effects of radiation; thus there can be no doubt that some mutations were induced in the survivors of the bombings. The chromosomal damage seen in the survivors also suggests that this is the case, as, given the correlation between carcinogenic and mutagenic exposures, do the data on increased incidences of leukemia and other malignant neoplasms in the survivors. Under these circumstances, since the effect may be presumed to exist, it seems permissible even in the absence of statistically significant results to use these data to generate an estimate of the effect. The most convenient way to phrase this estimate is in terms of the genetic doubling dose of radiation.*

The next year, 1982, C. Satoh and colleagues who included Neel wrote:

> *Beginning shortly after the bombs were dropped [i.e. fifteen months], and continuing down to the present time, a major effort has been mounted to develop distance–surface dose relationships for exposure to the bomb, relationships that also made appropriate allowance for the attenuation of dosage that resulted from the physical setting of the individual at the time of the bombings. This required an effort to reconstruct the precise position and shielding of each individual within the zone of appreciable direct radiation, thought to be described by a radius of 1600 m from the hypocenter in Hiroshima and 2000 m in Nagasaki. Separate gamma ray and neutron doses have been assigned each survivor. The errors of the individual surface doses assigned survivors are thought to amount to almost 30 per cent plus or minus, largely because of the difficulties in reconstructing a survivor's precise shielding, but no systematic biases for these estimates have been recognized.*[9]

Nevertheless, they were now prepared to suggest the range in which the doubling dose for an endpoint such as untoward pregnancy outcomes would be. And this range – the point at which a threshold of injury would occur – would be much higher than the laboratory researchers were suggesting. Although they were preliminary,

> *Even at this point in time, however, the estimates are consistent in pointing to a higher doubling dose for these important endpoints than the average figure derived from various endpoints in experimental studies on the mouse. Thus, the unweighted average of our estimates is 250 rem, whereas the figure frequently applied to the human risk on the basis of experiments with mice has been 40 rem.*

They assumed that:

The estimate of doubling dose that we have generated is for acute radiation. Extensive experiments with the mouse indicate that the genetic yield from low-level, chronic exposures to radiation is approximately one third that from acute radiation. Guided largely by that finding and the mouse-based estimate of 40 rem mentioned earlier, the most recent report of the Committee on the Biological Effects of Radiation of the US National Academy of Sciences suggests that the genetic doubling dose for humans subject to chronic radiation is 100 rem. The present data suggest a substantially higher figure.

The implications were considerable.

Should our estimate be validated, then it will forever testify to the difficulty in extrapolating from findings using select indicators in experimental mammals to the human situation. Clearly there is a major role for animal experimentation in indicating potential human hazards, but equally clear now is the requirement for human data in setting human risk estimates. These comments delivered in the context of radiation risk are equally applicable to the evaluation of the risk to human [sic] of exposure to the chemical mutagens, where too standards are being set for human exposure in the absence of human data.

The advent of the revised 1986 doses did not cause Neel and Schull to revise their interpretation of the data. Neel reflected in 1994:

Over the decade of the 1980s, Jack [Schull] and I began to develop a new perspective on these data. In the early years, as noted, we had felt the conservative and responsible course of action was to limit our conclusions to what the data could exclude in the way of effects, with no speculations as to what else the data might imply. But as the data accumulated and none of it suggested a statistically significant effect of radiation, even at doses that were being accepted as sufficient to double the mutation in the mouse, a line of thought began to take shape. Perhaps this total lack of statistically significant findings was suggestive that the doubling dose of radiation for humans was actually considerably higher than had been projected from the mouse data, ie perhaps humans were more resistant to the genetic effects of radiation than was being assumed on the basis of extrapolation from experiments with mice.[10]

He saw as a difficulty in developing this thesis the scientific tradition 'that one does not draw conclusions concerning effects unless one has a statistically different [sic] between the "treated" and the controls.'

'But then,' Professor Neel continues, 'I realized that this approach applied to hypothesis testing. We were not in Japan to test the hypothesis that radiation induced genetic damage. There was an enormous literature to that effect, on a wide variety of organisms.' Forty years after he began the studies, Neel wrote 'Our challenge could be restated: take all our data at face value, as the most appropriate data for calculating the genetic effects on humans of exposure to ionizing radiation to be available in this century and see where a proper analysis led us.'

Data collected on the basis of one hypothesis were now to be looked at to demonstrate another hypothesis – that the doubling dose for mutations of ionizing radiation in humans was much higher than predicted from laboratory studies.

As Professor Schull recalled in 1990:

> *Some forty years after the initiation of the first studies of the children of the survivors of the atomic bombings of Hiroshima and Nagasaki – a program that would embrace the physical examination of over 75,000 infants and the surveillance of mortality in an even larger group – the following is clear: we can exclude a doubling of the risk of birth defect or premature mortality under the circumstances of exposure that obtained in Hiroshima and Nagasaki. We can also show that these children are not conspicuously more likely to develop childhood cancers or to die in early childhood. This should be reassuring to prospective parents who may be exposed to ionizing radiation, wittingly or unwittingly, for clearly there has been no epidemic of birth defects, malignancies, or early mortality among the survivors' children.*[11]

From this initial conclusion, Professor Schull like Professor Neel draws a secondary conclusion:

> *We believe that some genetic damage has occurred, largely based on experimental investigations, and accept the human data as the best evidence available to us for estimating the mutagenic risk. Although these latter data alone would not satisfy the usual evidential requirements of science, we argue that even if there was no experimental data on humans, every other well-studied animal and plant species exhibits a deleterious effect of exposure to ionizing radiation, and there is no compelling biological reason to believe that the human species would be different. [From this he concludes] If one takes at face value the observations at Hiroshima and Nagasaki, then in terms of those mutations that are measurable by epidemiological means, the mutability of human genes is not greater, indeed may be somewhat less, than that seen in experimental animals.*

In the 1990s, research reports arising from the work of the Atomic Bomb Casualty Commission and the Radiation Effects Research

Foundation continue to be published at the rate of nearly one a week. The data and results have also been widely used as baselines against which other exposures to ionizing radiation have been assessed.

For instance, a group studying the relationship of leukaemia risk to radiation dose following uterine cancer conclude[12] 'In the low dose range, where dose was protracted and delivered at relatively low dose rates, the leukemia risk appears lower that that projected from risk estimates derived from the instantaneous whole-body exposures of atomic bomb survivors.'

A study of lung cancer among women who had been treated for breast cancer commented[13] 'Breast cancer radiotherapy regimens in use before the 1970s were associated with an elevated lung cancer risk many years following treatment. The estimated risk coefficients are lower than those reported for atomic bomb survivors.'

But at the same time, the premises on which the ABCC/RERF results have been developed have continued to be questioned. One group, which included Seymour Jablon, reviewed the causes of death stated on the death certificates of over 5000 autopsies carried out on the survivors. They examined the death certificates for accuracy of disease categories and assessed the effect of potential modifying factors on agreement and acccuracy. The overall percentage agreement between death certificate and autopsy diagnoses was only 52.5 per cent. Almost a quarter of cancers had been missed even though neoplasms had the highest detection rate. 'Since the inaccuracy of death certificate diagnoses can have major implications for health research and planning, it is important to be aware that their accuracy is low and that it can vary widely depending on cause, age, and place of death.'[14]

Another aspect of the data that was becoming evident in the late 1980s and early 1990s was the appearance of conditions which may have lain latent for forty or more years. A study[15] of the mortality rate experienced by over 23,000 A-bomb survivors in Nagasaki between September 1945 and 1950 based on the data of the ten-year House Reconstruction Survey was reported in 1994. 'As expected, these data show an increasing mortality rate with increasing proximity to the hypocenter of the bomb. What was not anticipated was higher mortality rate in the 1400–1699 m band than in the closer distance interval of 1200–1299 m. This suggests a possible selective survival among the A-bomb survivors. Whether this affects the cancer risk estimates has not yet been determined.' It might also suggest, rather than a selective survival rate, that the initial premises of linearity based on distance from the hypocentre were misplaced.

Other questions are still being raised about the assumptions on which the doses have been estimated over the past fifty years. Japanese researchers from the Department of Physics of Nara University of Education reported in 1992[16] their findings using thermoluminescence techniques on tile samples. The readings at 2.05 kilometres were 2.2 times larger than the corresponding DS-86 estimate. 'These results and those in the literature show the DS-86 estimate is 50 per cent or less of the measured value 2.05 km from the Hiroshima hypocenter.'

Researchers from the Applied Nuclear Physics Unit of the Faculty of Engineering at Hiroshima University studied the level of radionuclides still present in the Atomic Dome – the nearest metal structure to the hypocentre that survived the blast. They reported in 1992 that:

> *Detailed measurements of 60 Co and 152 Eu activities for samples col-*
> *lected from various locations of the Dome show almost no directional*
> *dependence whether the sample faced to the epicenter or not, nor vertical*
> *height dependence between 17 m height and ground level. In addition,*
> *152 Eu was not detected in the sample collected from the basement. It has*
> *been shown that the present 60 Co activity value, the nearest steel one to*
> *the hypocenter, as well as other short-distance data are systematically lower*
> *than the calculated values based on the neutron fluence of the DS-86.*[17]

Another group, from Kanazawa University, has continued to study the radionuclide levels in the 'black rain' areas in Nagasaki and Hiroshima which remain consistently higher.[18]

Amid all this questioning of the premises on which forty or more years of work has been conducted, and on which the American researchers were now willing to premise universal standards of risk assessment for ionizing radiation, a group of researchers from the Department of Internal Medicine at Nagasaki University School of Medicine have found[19] after studying the records of the 66,276 Master Sample for Nagasaki, and conducting a statistical analysis of the incidence of skin cancers by age, gender, histology and latency period, that 'the results showed a high correlation between the incidence of skin cancer and distance from the blast hypocenter, and that the incidence of skin cancer in the Nagasaki suvivors *appears now to be increasing with exposure distance*' [my emphasis].

Meanwhile, extensive work still continues in the Marshall Island to study the residual radiation from the *Bravo* test of March, 1954. The displaced islanders are still unable to return to their atolls forty years later. American researchers have developed sophisticated models for studying exposure pathways through the food chains, inhalation and drinking water in order to try to design ways of cleaning up or at least covering over the residual radiation of Rongelap and other atolls.[20]

Notes

1. James V. Neel, 'Atomic bombs, inbreeding, and Japanese genes: the Russel Lecture for 1966'.

2(a) James V. Neel, *Physician to the Gene Pool* (John Wiley and Sons 1994) p.86.

(b) M. Susan Lindee discusses the early abortion studies in 'What is a mutation? Identifying heritable change in the off-spring of survivors at Hiroshima and Nagasaki', *Journal of the History of Biology*, 1992:25:2:231–55

3. J. V. Neel and T. O. Tiffany and N. G. Anderson, 'Approaches to monitoring human populations for mutation rates and genetic disease'. In A. Hollander (ed.) *Chemical Mutagens: Principles and Methods for their Detection*. Vol.3 (New York: Plenum Press, 1973).

4. Neel *ibid*., p.19.

5. Neel *ibid*, p.72.

6. Neel *ibid*, p.85.

7. J. V. Neel *et al*, 'Search for mutations affecting protein structure in children of atomic bomb survivors: Preliminary Report', Proceedings of the National Academy of Sciences of the USA, July 1980:77:7:4221–5.

8. James V. Neel, Hiroo Kato and William J. Schull, 'Mortality in the children of atomic bomb survivors and controls', *Genetics*, February 1974:76:311-–26.

9. Satoh *et al*., 'Genetic effects of atomic bombs', *Human Genetics, Part A: The Unfolding Genome*, (New York Alan Liss Inc, 1982) pp.267–76.

10. Neel, *op cit*. 1994:238.

11. Schull, *Songs of Praise* (Harvard University Press, 1990) pp.270–1.

12. R. E. Curtis *et al*.. 'Relationship of leukemia risk to radiation dose following a cancer of the uterine corpus',

Journal of the National Cancer Institute, 1994: 86:17: 1315–24

13. P. D. Inskip *et al*., 'Lung cancer risk and radiation dose among women treated for breast cancer', *Journal of the National Cancer Institute*, 1994:86:13:983–8.

14. E. Ron, R. Carter, S. Jablon, K. Mabuchi, 'Agreement between death certificates and autopsy diagnoses among atom bomb survivors', *Epidemiology*, 1994:5:2:48–56.

15. H. Mori *et al*., 'Early mortality rate of atomic bomb survivors based on House Reconstruction Survey', *International Journal of Radiation Biology*, 1994:65:2:267–75.

16. T. Nagatomo *et al*., 'Comparison of the measured gamma ray dose and the DS-86 estimates at 2.05 km ground distance in Hiroshima', *Journal of Radiation Research* (Tokyo), 1992:33:3:211–7.

17. K Shizuma *et al*., 'Specific activities of 60 Co and 152 EU in samples collected from the atomic-bomb Dome in Hiroshima', *Journal of Radiation Research* (Tokyo), 1992:33:2:151–62

18. M. Sakanoue *et al*., 'A review of forty-five years study of Hiroshima and Nagasaki atomic bomb survivors. Residual radioactivity in neutron-exposed objects and residual alpha radiation in black rain areas.' *Journal of Radiation Research* (Tokyo), 1991:32 Supplement:58–68.

19. N. Sadamori *et al*., 'Incidence of skin cancer among Nagasaki atomic bomb survivors', *Journal of Radiation Research* 1991:32 Supplement: 217–25.

20. For example, see William L. Robison, Cynthia L. Conrado, and Kenneth T. Bogen, *An Updated Dose Assessment of Rongelap Island*, Lawrence Livermore National Laboratory, Health & Ecological Assessment Division, July 1994, UCRL-LR-107036.

Twenty-six

The genetics studies carried out by Neel and Schull and their colleagues over forty years have been remarkably immune from criticism at the elite levels of American science. In 1991 the National Academy of Sciences published a compendium of reprints of their major papers.[1] Yet almost simultaneously the NAS was initiating major reviews of two related areas of American military medicine and research carried out this century.

Fifty years ago, war-related research programmes organized by President Roosevelt under the White House Office of Scientific Research and Development (OSRD) became involved with secret testing programmes concerned with mustard agents (sulphur and nitrogen mustard) and Lewisite involving almost 60,000 military personnel as human experimental subjects.

In 1991, a report on the studies[2] on the health effects of mustard gas and Lewisite was commissioned by the Governing Board of the National Research Council, whose members are drawn from the councils of the National Academy of Sciences, the National Academy of Engineering, and the Institute of Medicine.

The report was externally reviewed and published under the imprimatur of the Institute of Medicine, itself chartered in 1970 by the National Academy of Sciences to enlist distinguished members of the appropriate professions in the examination of policy matters pertaining to the health of the public. This review project or meta-analysis was funded by the Department of Veterans Affairs. The review panel studied 2000 scientific reports and received testimony from thirteen military and civilian experts and 250 veterans. They note that:

The major scientific challenges were the meagre literature on long-term health effects of exposure to these agents and the lack of quantitative exposure data for the veterans who served as human test subjects. The vast majority of the scientific and medical literature was concerned with the short-term, acute effects of mustard agents and Lewisite, because the research priorities of most countries had been placed on treatment of battle-

field injuries and the fact that most investigations of mustard agents and Lewisite have been conducted throughout this century under the control of military establishments. Particularly distressing was the essential lack of information regarding the toxicology of Lewisite.

Nevertheless the review committee felt able – in assessing the relationship between exposure and specific health conditions – to follow the guidelines provided by Hill[3] more than twenty years ago. These guidelines propose six considerations to be brought to bear on judgements of causality. Strength of association reflects the relative risk or odds of an association. A dose–response relationship can reinforce the judgement of causality when the strength of association increases with increase in exposure. Association needs to be temporally correct; the effect should occur in a reasonable or expected time period following the exposure. Consistency and specificity of associations are also important considerations. A consistent association, according to Hill, is one that is found in a variety of studies. If a particular health condition is reliably predicted by a given exposure, then specificity of the association is held to be demonstrated. Finally, for an association to be judged causal – according to the Hill guidelines – it must be biologically plausible or explainable by known biological mechanisms.

But can we be sure that we know all the biologically plausible or explainable mechanisms of injury that we are trying to identify with these principles of establishing causality? Especially in relation to new manufactured hazards such as chemical weapons or ionizing radiation?

The committee reviewing the studies of mustard gas and Lewisite comment that while mainstream biomedical science is 'hypothesis driven' and its interesting results are published in the open literature, critically reviewed by outside experts and available to all, most military research is 'applications driven'.

Priorities are determined on the basis of military needs (eg treatment of acute injuries, development of protective clothing), and results not directly relevant to the original questions are seldom pursued. Such research is commonly classified and is published only for other military groups. The tight controls and restrictions on military research can result in a 'stunted' body of literature that presents major limitations to later assessments in areas that were never pursued – in this case the long-term health effect caused by exposure to chemical agents in general, and mustard agents and Lewisite in particular.

This distinguished review panel commissioned by the National Academy of Sciences and National Research Council also addressed the ethical issues.

The first response of many of the committee members to these discoveries [of deliberate or careless exposure to injury] was to try to understand the actions of the investigators in historical context – it was a war and the experiments were conducted before the Nuremberg Code of 1947 established formal principles to govern the proper treatment of human subjects. However, examination of the treatment and care of WWII chemical warfare production workers, and the conduct of later military experiments with human subjects from 1950 to 1975, demonstrated a well-ingrained pattern of abuse and neglect. Although the human subjects were called 'volunteers', it was clear from the official reports that recruitment of the WWII human subjects, as well as many of those in later experiments, was accomplished through lies and half-truths.

The committee was 'appalled' that no formal long-term follow-up medical care or monitoring was provided for any of the Second World War human subjects, other exposed military personnel, or chemical warfare production workers, despite knowledge available by 1933 that mustard agents and Lewisite could produce long-term debilitating health problems, particularly in those people suffering severe burns and inhalation injuries.

There can be no question that some veterans, who served our country with honor and at great personal cost, were mistreated twice – first, in the secret testing and second, by the official denials that lasted for decades ... the committee believes that any future military research with human subjects should be conducted according to publicly established ethical principles similar to those that apply to civilian research. The Department of Defense should consider including civilian medical experts in reviews of all proposed military research protocols involving human subjects.

The review panel concedes that it may be fair to argue that no formalized set of rules, carrying the weight of law, existed in 1942 to govern the treatment of human subjects. However, a Department of the Army Inspector General's Report[4] in 1975 documented how these patterns of neglect of human subjects, established during the Second World War, continued through the 1950s and 1960s, well beyond the immediacy of wartime concerns

The committee also addressed the issue of the relationship between dose and damage and the possibility of a threshold below which damage would not occur.

If acute pulmonary reactions can identify individuals at risk for long-term sequelae of chemical exposures, can the probability or degree of damage be predicted from the magnitude of the acute response? This question has not

been adequately studied. An association with dose is found for acute as well as chronic responses, which provides support for the association, but not for a relationship between the magnitude of the acute response and the magnitude of the chronic response. If the disease model involved required the acute exposure to cause acute irreversible damage, then one might reasonably expect the magnitude of acute response to predict the magnitude of the chronic response. However, if another disease model is invoked, one in which the acute exposure results in or leads to an alteration in individual risk factors, then it is quite likely that the magnitude of the acute and chronic responses would be unrelated.

They concluded from indirect evidence, based on a review of the relationships between acute and chronic effects caused by other substances, that the likelihood of long-term respiratory effects may not necessarily be linked to the presence of an acute respiratory response.

Review of the evidence does not support a minimum magnitude [threshold] of acute response necessary in order for there to be long-term sequelae. Further, if the disease model requires the acute exposure to cause acute irreversible damage, then the magnitude of acute response might well predict the magnitude of the chronic response. However, if acute exposure led to an alteration in individual risk factors, then it is possible that the magnitude of the acute and chronic responses would be unrelated. Finally, indirect evidence suggests that only an unusual disease model would exclude the possible mechanism of change in individual risk factors so that the absence of an acute reaction would eliminate the possibility of a chronic effect related to an acute exposure. Thus, there is insufficient evidence to conclude that long-term respiratory responses occur only in cases where an earlier acute response has been documented.

Between 1962 and 1971 US military forces sprayed nearly 19 million gallons of herbicides such as Agent Orange over approximately 3.6 million acres in Vietnam. Herbicides were used to strip the thick jungle canopy that helped conceal opposition forces, to destroy crops those forces might depend on, and to clear tall grass and bushes from around the perimeters of US base camps and outlying fire-support bases.

In December 1966 the Council of the American Association for the Advancement of Sciences (AAAS) sent a letter to Secretary of Defense Robert McNamara calling for studies of the short- and long-term consequences of the massive use of herbicides in Vietnam. In February 1967 a second petition signed by more than 5000 scientists, including seventeen Nobel laureates, was delivered to President Johnson requesting that he end the use of herbicides in Vietnam. A Department of Defense official, responding to criticisms regarding the questionable military use of herbicides, stated that 'qualified scientists, both inside and outside the government, have judged that seriously adverse consequences will not occur. Unless we had confidence in these judgments, we would not continue to employ these materials.'

An estimated three million US military personnel served in Vietnam during this period of herbicide use. Of these, only an estimated 5000 to 7000 were women, of whom eight (all nurses) were killed. The report does not concern itself with the health effects on the Vietnamese population except for reference to some studies on birth defects. After a scientific report in 1969 concluded that one of the primary chemical used in Agent Orange could cause birth defects in laboratory animals, US forces suspended use of this herbicide in 1970 and halted all herbicide spraying in Vietnam the next year.

In response to veterans' concerns, the US Congress passed Public Law 102-4, the Agent Orange Act of 1991, directing the Secretary of Veterans Affairs to request that the National Academy of Sciences conduct a comprehensive review and evaluation of all available scientific and medical information regarding the health effects of exposure to Agent Orange, other herbicides used in Vietnam, and their components, including dioxin. The Institute of Medicine undertook this work in 1992 and established the Committee to Review the Health Effects in Vietnam Veterans of Exposure to Herbicides.[5]

The panel convened by the Institute of Health on the same principles as the one that was simultaneously studying mustard gas and Lewisite conducted two meta-analyses – of the potential health effects of exposure to herbicides and to dioxin (2,3,7,8–tetrachlorodibenzo-para-dioxin: TCDD) an unintentional contaminant of some of those herbicides; and a review of the epidemiologic studies. The Agent Orange committee was also guided by the Hill principles for the methodology of establishing causality between insult and injury. However, this committee concluded that a new series of epidemiologic studies of veterans could yield valuable information *if a new, valid exposure reconstruction model could be developed.*

The committee recognized that its recommendations for development of a historical exposure reconstruction model and its use in epidemiologic studies might seem at variance with the conclusions reached by the Centers for Disease Control (CDC), White House Agent Orange Working Group (AOWG) and the Office of Technology Assessment (OTA) in 1986 with regard to the congressionally mandated Agent Orange Study. The committee came to a different conclusion for four reasons. The CDC-AOWG-OTA conclusions were based in large part on serum TCDD measurements, which the committee felt were insufficient taken alone for validating exposure to herbicides used in Vietanm. They felt that arguments underlying the earlier conclusions that individuals in combat units were widely dispersed and that troop movement data are incomplete imply that exposure measurements may be imprecise, not that they are invalid. However, these arguments do suggest that historical reconstruction of exposure will have nondifferential classification errors that will lead to underestimates of the relative risk of outcomes if an association is in fact present. Third, the 1994 committee is proposing the use of more, but less formal, information on exposure than was considered in 1986. This includes the development and use of informal information on perimeter spraying, which might account for more meaningful herbicide exposure than the aerial spraying.

The report also comments on the problem of whether or not there is a threshold beyond which herbicides such as Agent Orange become injurious. They note that scientists hold vastly different opinions about the existence of a threshold effect, about whether there is a point below which no effect of the chemical exists, for the activity of TCDD. There are those who argue that all events that occur up to and including the induction of gene transcription have a linear dose–response curve; others argue that more complex events that require the concordance of two or more events, such as cell proliferation, may have a threshold. 'This seems to be the most favored view, and it is supported by the available data. This does not mean, however, that there is a threshold for the biological effects of TCDD, simply that the response is receptor-mediated.'

But the jury is still out, the committee contends, because they found in their review 'that the weakest methodologic aspects complicating the interpretation of the available epidemiologic studies are the definition and quantification of exposure.' They propose using the established methods of industrial exposure reconstruction to develop a model where spraying records are cross-checked against structured interview reports of location and against serum TCDD measurements together with incidence of health outcomes.

Because of the controversy surrounding the issue of Agent Orange, the committee recommends that a non-governmental organization with appropriate experience in historical exposure reconstruction be commissioned to develop and test models of herbicide exposure for use in studies of Vietnam veterans and the exposure reconstruction models evaluated by an independent non-governmental scientific panel established for this purpose.

This marked a full circle for the National Academy of Sciences as the agent of government-commissoned biomedical research. As the panel on the mustard gas and Lewisite studies had pointed out, the National

Academy had been chartered by President Lincoln in 1863 to serve as an independent scientific advisory organization to Congress and government agencies. Three other components of the Academy complex were added later under the Academy's original charter, the National Research Council in 1916, the National Academy of Engineering in 1964, and the Institute of Medicine in 1970. Each agency works through committees of scientific experts who gather to discuss, share their expertise and make recommendations on scientific policy and issues. A key aspect of all such committees is held to be their independence from outside pressure and influence.

But as the United States mobilized for the Second World War, the level of involvement of NRC committees in the actual research enterprise was dramatically changed. Several NRC committees began to act directly for the government in the supervision of war-related research.

Despite the establishment in 1947 of the Nuremberg Codes regarding the appropriate use and treatment of human subjects in research, the researchers for the study of *Veterans at Risk* reported that no documentation could be found about whether the Army was explicitly bound by the Codes. By 1952 the Armed Forces Medical Policy Council filed a request to use human subjects and suggested that the Nuremberg Codes be used as guidelines. There were many in the Army leadership, not least in the biomedical units, who preferred to rely on the doctrine of sovereign immunity of the Government in its military activities.

Possible guidelines were discussed at a meeting at Edgewood Arsenal in March 1953. It was proposed that any human-use codes based on the Nuremberg Codes should only apply to biological warfare testing, not to chemical or radiological testing but this proposal was rejected. Formalized guidelines were finally issued in June 1953 in a Chief of Staff Memo (MM385). These guidelines represented an official adoption of the Nuremberg Codes (although somewhat modified) and were meant to apply to all types of chemical, radiological and biological warfare testing. They required all projects to be approved by the Secretary of the Army. However, no detailed descriptions of what types of experiments required this approval were included, and researchers into the chemical war agents consider that this was a 'loophole' that permitted 'selective compliance' with the guidelines.[6]

The report on the exposure of US veterans to chemical warfare agents such as mustard gas and Lewisite includes as an appendix a submission[7] from Jay Katz, Elizabeth K. Dollard, Professor of Law, Medicine and Psychiatry at Yale Law School to Dr David Rall, Director, National Institute of Environmental Health Sciences suggesting that the Nuremberg Tribunal 'also constituted a retrospective judgement about conduct by Nazi physician-scientists during the days of the Second World War.' Professor Katz warned the review panel that if they only addressed the 'limited scientific task' of examining scientific knowledge about the relationship between exposure to mustard gas and subsequent physical illness, 'you may be abdicating your responsibility to condemn such studies for 1992 and beyond, even if you wish to excuse them for 1943–45 when supposedly our ethical sensitivities were less developed'.

Professor Katz maintained that the record showed that 'the experiments themselves were conducted in the spirit of cheap availability of human beings for these purposes, and with utter disregard to alternative ways of proceeding (not to speak of giving consideration to the *minimum* number of human subjects required for the conduct of such scientific studies etc) or without regard to the future welfare of the participants.'

Professor Katz acknowledged that no authoritative policies governed such research in the United States at the times these chemical warfare agents were tested on non-consenting US soldiers. But when this defence had been introduced by Nazi physicians at the Nuremberg Tribunal, the Tribunal made short shrift of it: 'Certain basic principles must be observed [in the conduct of research] to satisfy moral, ethical and legal concepts [and one of them is that] the voluntary consent of the human subject is absolutely essential.' He noted that Andrew Levy and Leo Alexander, on behalf of the prosecution, had averred that obtaining consent is the customary practice in American research.

Henry K. Beecher, Dorr Professor of Research in Anaesthesia at Harvard Medical School, broke the professional cabal of silence about uninformed consent in biomedical research in an article published in the *New England Journal of Medicine* in June 1966.[8] 'Human experimentation since World War II has created some difficult problems with the increasing employment of patients as experimental subjects' he wrote, 'when it must be apparent that they would not have been available if they had been truly aware of the uses that would be made of them.' The trouble arises, Beecher suggested, 'in the different areas of experimentation on a patient not for his benefit but for that, at least in theory, of patients in general.' Because, he pointed out, 'Ordinary patients will not knowingly risk their health or their life for the sake of "science". Every experienced clinician investigator knows this.' Yet all ambitious young medical faculty members know that they will not be promoted unless they prove themselves as investigators. Beecher gave 22 explicit examples where he felt that standards of informed consent had not been met.

In discussing the impact that this article had on biomedical ethics, David J. Rothman[9] notes that Beecher's examples were drawn from the mainstream of post-war American biomedical research and could not be dismissed as aberrant. Rothman argues that what had happened was that:

> *the exceptional protocol of the pre–1940 period [had] become normative.*
> *Clinical research had come of age when medical progress, measured by*
> *antidotes against malaria, dysentery, and influenza, was the prime con-*
> *sideration, and traditional ethical notions about consent and voluntary*
> *participation in experimentation seemed far less relevant. A generation of*
> *researchers were trained to perform, accomplish and deliver cures – to be*
> *heroes in the laboratory, like soldiers on the battlefield. If researchers creat-*
> *ed effective vaccines, diagnostic tests, or miracle drugs like penicillin, no*
> *one would question their methods or techniques.*

And of course it was men like Thomas Francis and agencies like the Armed Forces Epidemiological Board (AFEB) which had been at the forefront of this 'military biomedicine'. The subjects used were frequently army conscripts or incarcerated men and women. In the case of the former, it was considered and frequently accepted that any risk involved was tantamount to war injury. In the case of the latter, the jail inmates, it was thought that acceptance of such risks in some part made up for their non-participation in the war effort. The research to understand, prevent and cure radiation sickness was part of this agenda, and the men (and handful of women researchers) who worked for the Atomic Bomb Casualty Commission were working within this framework as they repeatedly examined their Master Sample of Japanese survivors. In the climate of the times, the survivors were viewed as vanquished members of a nation that had launched an unjust war, and it would have been difficult to assert their rights above those of American servicemen or even prisoners as the United States prepared to fight a nuclear war.

William J. Schull, for instance, who had participated in meetings of the Radioepidemiology Group of the Argonne National Laboratory that considered issues of human experimentation in February 1959, wrote in 1990, 'Should we, indeed could we, legally treat the survivors? And if so, what should that treatment be? How could it possibly be more than palliative, when we were not even certain what the effects of ionizing radiation were?'[10]

In early 1994, in response to revelations published in *The Albuquerque Tribune* about experiments on eighteen people who, in the 1940s, were unwittingly injected by government scientists with plutonium to test excretion rates, President Clinton convened an Advisory Committee on Human Radiation Experiments. Within six months, the staff of the committee had unearthed from the files evidence of 600 experiments on humans in the past fifty years where the subjects were ill-informed and/or incapable of giving knowledgeable consent.

Dr Merril Eisenbud, identified as Professor Emeritus of Enviromental Medicine at New York University Medical Center, described one of his experiments to *Newsweek* in December 1993.

> *One of my experiments was to determine the significance in terms of the dose absorbed by a child's thyroid. We used to get the children to come over from a pediatric clinic with their moms. We'd explain what we were doing, sit each child down and – using a scintollometer that didn't even touch him – measure radiation in the thyroid. We'd give the child a lollipop, and that was the end of that. Today you'd have to fill out so much paperwork that it would discourage people from participating in the test.*[11]

Reflecting on the same 'non-invasive' experiments with children in his 1990 memoirs, Professor Eisenbud had written:

> *Nowadays it is much more difficult to do studies that involve human volunteers. Twenty-five years ago it was possible to recruit people of all ages for noninvasive studies such as ours, in which there was literally no physical contact with the subjected* once they were seated in the chair in our shielded room *[my emphasis]. Investigators are now required to obtain signed 'informed consent' forms from the subjects. The complexity of these forms is a deterrent to even the simplest kind of human research.*[12]

But as the son of a woman who had been subjected to such experiments on plutonium excretion and elimination at the University of Rochester's Strong Memorial Hospital in the autumn of 1945 said, 'I was over there fighting the Germans who were conducting these horrific medical experiments. At the same time my own country was conducting them on my mother.'[13]

Notes

1. James V. Neel and William J. Schull, *The Children of Atomic Bomb Survivors: A Genetic Study* (National Academy Press, Washington, 1991).

2. Constance M .Pechura and David P. Rall, (Eds.), *Veterans at Risk: the health effects of mustard gas and Lewisite,* Committee to Survey the Health Effects of Mustard Gas and Lewisite, Division of Health Promotion and Disease Prevention, Institute of Medicine (National Academy Press, Washington DC, 1993).

3. A. B. Hill, *Principles of Medical Statistics* (New York, Oxford University Press, 1971: ninth edition).

4. Johnson W.N. Taylor Jr, 'Research Report concerning the use of volunteers in chemical agent research', DAIG-In-21–75 Washington DC Department of the Army, Office of the Inspector General and Auditor General, 1975.

5. *Veterans and Agent Orange: health effects of herbicides used in Vietnam* (National Academy Press, Institute of Medicine, 1994).

6(a) *Veterans and Agent Orange, ibid*:379.

(b) The doctrine of sovereign immunity in relation to veterans' claims for radiation injury is reviewed in Nancy Hogan, 'Shielded from Liability', *American Bar Association Journal*, May 1994:56—60.

7. Letter dated 16 June 1992 from Dr Jay Katz to Dr David P. Rall, Appendix H of *Veterans at Risk*

8. Henry K. Beecher, 'Ethics and clinical research', *New England Journal of Medicine*, 16 June 1966:274:24:1354–60.

9. David J. Rothman, *Strangers at the Bedside*, (Basic Books, 1991).

10. William J. Schull, *Songs of Praise*: *op. cit.* p.6.

11. 'America's nuclear secrets', *Newsweek*, 27 December 1993:14–18.

12. Merril Eisenbud, *An Environmental Odyssey*, 1990:151.

13. Fred Schulz, quoted in 'A human horror story', *Newsweek*, 27 December 1993:17.

Twenty-seven

The first Allied journalist to enter Hiroshima after the bombing in August 1945 was the Australian, Wilfrid Burchett who managed to get the first eyewitness reports from the city out to the *Daily Express*. When he got back to Tokyo he attended a press briefing given by General MacArthur's staff to discredit his sensational reports of radiation sickness.

> *A scientist in brigadier-general's uniform explained that there could be no question of atomic radiation or the symptoms I had described, since the bombs had been exploded at such a height as to avoid any risk of 'residual radiation'. ... He discounted the allegation that any who had not been in the city at the time of the blast were later affected. The scientist in uniform also said it was impossible that fish should be dying in the stream that ran through the city.*[1]

The first scientists, doctors and biomedical researchers into the two cities in late 1945 were still commissioned in the US Armed Forces. Many of them had been part of the Manhattan District Project which developed the two bombs and the earlier Trinity device. General Groves had been over-all director of the Manhattan District Project and he had attempted to achieve a strict compartmentalization of knowledge about the different facets of the development of the weapons for security reasons. In fact, General Groves frequently said that he – and not the scientific directors such as Oppenheimer – was the only person who knew everything that was going on in the Manhattan Project.

General Groves later testified[2] to the Personnel Security Board of the United States Atomic Energy Commission in the matter of J. Robert Oppenheimer. He acknowledged that the Manhattan Project scientists chafed under his compartmentalization rules. He told the Oppenheimer inquiry that:

> *the scientists – and I would like to say the academic scientists – were not in sympathy with compartmentalization. They were not in sympathy with the security requirements. They felt that they were unreasonable. I*

never held this against them, because I knew that their whole lives from the time they entered college almost had been based on the dissemination of knowledge. Here, to be put in a strange environment where the requirement was not dissemination, but not talking about it, was a terrible upset. They were constantly under pressure from their fellows in every direction to break down compartmentalization. While I was always on the other side of the fence, I was never surprised when one of them broke the rules.

He recalled, for instance, travelling out to Los Alamos in the train with Neils Bohr and discussing classified matters with him for twelve hours or so. But 'within five minutes after his arrival he was saying everything he promised not to say'.

In fact, many of the memoirs of Los Alamos recall most vividly the interchange of ideas among the scientists during hikes and parties as much as in the laboratories. Frederic de Hoffman, for instance, who later became President of the Salk Institute for Biological Studies, was a young theoretical physicist at Los Alamos. Thirty years later he recalled[3] that 'The research groups were really organized in a superb manner, in that the matrix of disciplines and projects was well conceived and smoothly run. Viewed from the inexperience of a nineteen-year-old, it just seemed the natural and logical way to accomplish complex scientific and technical research tasks. It seemed hard to believe that there was any other way.' He also remembered the remarkable lack of an age barrier. 'What counted were ideas and one's willingness to work, not one's age or the position one had previously held.' He thought there had been a wonderful research ambience that was generated by a combination of planned and spontaneous meetings between some of the world's best minds in the camp atmosphere of the former boarding school in the desert.

But within a year of the end of the war – brought about in August 1945 by the two atomic bombings – scientists such as Philip Morrison were worrying about the ways in which science had been mobilized during the war and whether it would ever be demobilized. 'About a year has passed since the war ended; and in that year science has not learned how to demobilize.'4. The Office of Scientific Research and Development – created to manage wartime science – was spending more, not less, and much of this funding was being placed in the universities, binding them ever closer to the research agenda of the government. The Atomic Energy Commission was being born and would prove to be a coeval of the Cold War.

Many scientists such as Morrison urged the creation of a National Science Foundation which would work independently of military interests in adjudicating the funding of big science from government.

Twenty years later, an analyst of the politics of science, Daniel S. Greenberg noted[5] 'There is no American Scientific Establishment. Yet Harvard, MIT, Caltech, and the University of California are its Oxbridge. Two World War II research centers, the MIT Radiation Laboratory and the Los Alamos Scientific Laboratory, of radar and atom bomb fame, respectively, are its Eton. The Cosmos Club in Washington is its Athenaeum, the physicists are its aristocracy. The National Academy of Sciences is its established church, and the President's Science Advisory Committee is its Privy Council.' *Science*, the weekly journal of the American Association for the Advancement of Science (for which Greenberg was a staff writer) was the quasi-official journal of this scientific elite.

In the 1960s the National Academy of Sciences had a membership of nearly 800; the average age of admission was 49.1 and the average age of total members was 61.6. Greenberg observed, 'there are many distinguished young scientists outside the Academy, and regardless of age, there are some rather undistinguished ones inside. On the whole, however, the Academy represents the best of post-middle-age science in America. Election is by a process that rivals the papacy for mystery.' Even so, since 1950 the Nobel Prize had been awarded to nine scientists who had not yet been elected to the NAS; one of them, Jonas Salk, never was.

Detlev Bronk had been elected President in the early post-war period after James B. Conant, inventor of Lewisite and President of Harvard, had been blackballed. While Bronk was President of the Academy, he sat on the President's Science Advisory Committee and also chaired the National Science Board, the top advisory board of the National Science Foundation. He also simultaneously served as president of the Rockefeller Institute for Medical Research and about ten other organizations. He had accepted the Rockefeller presidency with the full intention of retaining his presidency of The Johns Hopkins University, but the Rockefeller board objected. Greenberg suggests that while Bronk was 'perhaps the most multi-hatted of science statesmen' his was not atypical of the pattern of interlocking appointments in those post-war decades.

Despite these perceptions of the interlocking nature of science within the military-industrial complex of the United States (as the former Commander of the Allied Armies in Europe, President of the United States and President of Columbia University, Dwight D. Eisenhower described America's post-war power structure in the 1950s), Greenberg did not see a fundamental flaw in the peer review system by which American science was and is managed. 'Where it does come in for criticism is on the grounds that it encourages orthodoxy, permits back scratching and discriminates against the young. But these are criticisms of its operation, not the fundamental premise on which it is founded.'

273

Yet Greenberg himself cites the case of Michael Polanyi's theory of the adsorption of gases, rejected by Einstein and others in 1914 but which found peer acceptance thirty years later. In 1963 Polanyi himself pondered:

> *Could this miscarriage of the scientific method have been avoided?.... I do not think so. There must be at all times a predominantly accepted scientific view of the nature of things, in the light of which research is jointly conducted by members of the community of scientists. A strong presumption that any evidence which contradicts this view is invalid must prevail. Such evidence has to be disregarded, even it is cannot be accounted for, in the hope that it will eventually turn out to be false or irrelevant ... I am not arguing against the present balance between the powers of orthodoxy and the rights of dissent in science. I merely insist on acknowledgement of the fact that the scientific method is, and must be, disciplined by an orthodoxy which can permit only a limited degree of dissent, and that such dissent is fraught with grave risks to the dissenter.*[6]

We might term such a view by a victim of a miscarriage of professional justice a form of internalization of oppression. But more profoundly, can we accuse whole professions – whole knowledge systems – of being internally oppressed by their own orthodoxies? The problem in Polanyi's formulation of the problem he faced is that he considered his experience on the one hand to be a 'miscarriage of the scientific method' yet on the other hand insisted that scientific method is the defence of orthodoxy until it is finally persuaded by dissenters whom it is ready enough to marginalize of the error of its findings.

P. B. Medawar, Director of the National Institute for Medical Research, Fellow of the Royal Society and Nobel Laureate in Physiology and Medicine in 1960, suggested provocatively in a BBC broadcast in 1964 that there was a sense in which the scientific paper – the results reported in the literature which become the texts of scientific orthodoxy on which peer review is conducted – is a fraud.[7]

'What is wrong with the traditional form of the scientific paper', Professor Medawar told a British public that would soon be able to read the candid realities of scientific discovery in Crick and Watson's *The Double Helix*,[8] 'is simply this: that all scientific work of an experimental or exploratory character starts with some expectation about the outcome of the inquiry. This expectation one starts with, this hypothesis one formulates, provides the initiative and incentive for the inquiry *and governs its actual form* [my emphasis]. It is in the light of this expectation that some observations are held relevant and others not; that some methods are chosen, others discarded; that some experiments are done rather than others. It is only in the light of this prior expectation that the activities the scientist reports in his scientific papers really have any meaning at all.' Moreover, said one of Britain's premier scientists, hypotheses arise from guesswork, they are inspirational in character. What he did not say, was that hypotheses can also be trivial, pedestrian and wrong.

The implications of Medawar's argument were profound for the writing of the history of science, as well as for the self-perception of scientists. If 'the scientific paper is a fraud in the sense that it does give a totally misleading narrative of the processes of thought that go into the making of scientific discoveries' then it cannot be totally relied upon as a source of information about how science is practised. This perception, together with Thomas Kuhn's revolutionary book on *The Structure of Scientific Revolutions*[9], spawned a new field of sociology, the sociology of scientific knowledge.

Now that scientists and the practice of science were coming under a new form of intellectual scrutiny – at the same time, and not fortuitously, that they were coming under the new political scrutiny of the political sea-change of the 1960s – how would scientists react to the interests of non-scientists in their practices, and their ethics?

Eric Larrabee, writing in 1966 about the increasing tension between 'Science and the common reader'[10] argued:

> *Perhaps the time has come for them [scientists] to wonder about why they sometimes jar the nerves and try the patience of non-scientists.*
>
> *The humanist who looks at science from the viewpoint of his own endeavors is bound to be impressed, first of all, by its startling lack of insight into itself. Scientists seem able to go about their business in a state of indifference to, if not ignorance of, anything but the going, currently acceptable doctrines of their several disciplines.... The only thing wrong with scientists is that they don't understand science. They don't know where their own institutions came from, what forces shaped and are still shaping them, and they are wedded to an anti-historical way of thinking which threatens to deter them from ever finding out.*

Many scientists have responded by becoming what Schon[11] terms 'reflective practitioners'. William J Schull, for instance, wrote in 1990:

> *Thomas Kuhn, the famed philosopher of science, in* The Structure of Scientific Revolutions, *has maintained that crises provide the necessary tension for the emergence of novel theories, and notes that creative investigators, like artists, must be able to live in a world out of joint. The anomalies that arise between observation and the conceptual framework that guides investigative activities produce the intellectual and emotional challenges that spur revolutions. Scientists respond to the intellectual tensions,*

the objects of Kuhn's concerns, through modifications or changes in theory, but they cope less well with the more human element, the emotional turmoil. Ultimately, one either rejects science in favor of another occupation or learns to live with its tension ... science is more than the multiplication of instruments; it involves intellectually creative acts. The separation of creativity from the pull of our own wishful thinking, often culturally inspired, that we misconstrue as scientific can be difficult and lead to absurdities, of which even the brightest are guilty.[12]

But Schull also reflected on the realities of practising good science in the difficult conditions of the Atomic Bomb Casualty Commission in early post-war Japan. He pointed out that:

A problem all of us came to know well was how to retain our scientific skills under such tedious circumstances and routines. We had little time for, or access to, current scientific publications ... the journals were always late, issues failed to arrive, volumes published prior to the Commission's founding were unavailable, and timely purchase of new books was virtually impossible. We shared with one another the journals to which we subscribed individually and the books we had brought, or subsequently purchased, from the United States. However, this was a poor substitute for the currency of thought that comes from the frequent perusal of the new.

He expresses the isolation of young men trying to make a career in 'world class science' in the logistical and political backwaters of a defeated country. 'It was a time of ambivalence; one was flooded with different and rewarding cultural stimuli that prompted healthy self-inspection, but there was a gnawing sense of loss of skills that were central to the lives we had chosen for ourselves.'

Even though the managers of the Atomic Bomb Casualty Commission recognized the problem and sought to solve it by trying to establish steady channels of recruitment, they in various ways acknowledged that they failed. Schull[14] wrote of the arrangements set up with the Department of Medicine at Yale, the Department of Pathology at UCLA, the Veterans Follow-Up Agency in Washington, and with the University of Michigan for genetics:

Academic affiliations, if not driven by a sense of the uniqueness of the study and the scientific opportunities it holds, must inevitably wither. They do not acknowledge the impermanence of the staff of departments, including their chairmen, their commitments, nor the nature of the Commission's need. Institutional commitments without overriding personal ones cannot succeed. It is not the immediate return that counts but perseverance and a belief in the long term importance of the undertaking.

In fact, what we have seen in the history of the Atomic Bomb Casualty Commission's investigations into the long-term effects of the atomic bombs on humans has been a series of 'critical closures' that began prior to the first investigators reaching the cities. Not expecting any survivors to be suffering from radiation sickness, the importance of residual radiation was denied. Early entrants into the city could therefore not have experienced radiation sickness or injury and so evidence that they had was dismissed as anomalous. The visible impact of the blast and thermal injury correlated with long-standing predictions in the fifth year of war so the military doctors and scientists who were first into the cities premised radiation injury on the same assumptions. The early data confirmed their impressions, so they dismissed increasingly divergent data as anomalous. The next wave of researchers drew up their sample based on these early impressions. The Master Sample only refined the sample on grounds of convenience and accessibility. The senior officers became managers of post-war science and biomedicine and carried their assumptions with them into their new posts. The senior men who commanded the research designs increasingly commanded the funding. It wasn't long – the early 1950s – before they were also in command positions in the advisory committees that were the daughters of the agencies they designed and developed and managed. Dissidents such as Alice Stewart and her colleagues found that they also commanded the peer review processes. One could go on with the litany of processes by which 'critical closure' was achieved.

The ABCC wasn't alone in this process. Ian Hacking has described[15] what he terms 'the self-vindication of the laboratory sciences' and suggests that 'as a laboratory science matures, it develops a body of types of theory and types of apparatus and types of analysis that are mutually adjusted to each other ... "a closed system" that is essentially irrefutable. They are self-vindicating in the sense that any test of theory is against apparatus that has evolved in conjunction with it – and in conjunction with modes of data analysis. Conversely, the criteria for the working of the apparatus and for the correctness of analyses is precisely the fit with theory.' Hacking confines his comments to science carried out in the laboratory. 'The theories of the laboratory sciences are not directly compared to "the world"; they persist because they are true to phenomena produced or even created by apparatus in the laboratory and are measured by instruments that we have engineered.'

But as we have seen, laboratory work has often not only been extrapolated to predictions (which have been allowed to become self-confirming) about humans, but even to the design of the practice of science or biomedical studies on humans. We have seen the tension between 'the experimentalists' and the epidemiologists as data gathered by observation against protocols which were determined by a combination of criteria from laboratory-derived knowledge and practicality in the field failed to produce statistically significant results according to the experimental predictions.

At the same time, another series of critical closures has been introduced by the problems of 'do-ability' of human epidemiological studies, especially in environments which are initially stressed and traumatized and then rapidly changing. Joan H. Fujimura has investigated how the 'do-ability' of science and biomedical research has influenced cancer research in the laboratory.[16] What we have traced out in the working of the Atomic Bomb Casualty Commission and to some degree its successor the Radiation Effects Research Foundation, which inherited so much of the ABCC's organization and assumptions, is what Fujimura would term the articulation of the alignments of a do-able research programme. But one, I would argue, which compounded its progressive critical closures. Fujimura shows how when the alignments wouldn't articulate because the anomalies became too great to bear – in her case, the fact that the tests showed no specificity – the researchers worked overtime in order to 'move the experimental hoop'. Fujimura notes that when mistakes or other problematic data appear, 'researchers tinker at one or several levels to adjust for the disturbance. Unless resources are unlimited, that attention must be subtracted from other tasks.... Some contingencies, like unexpected results, may prove rewarding as new findings. However, even these new findings have to be woven (articulated) into a new alignment – a new do-able problem – before they can pay off.' She points out – and surely we have seen this happen in the interpretation of the data from Hiroshima and Nagasaki over the past fifty years – that 'Just as unexpected results could lead to the development of a whole new problem given adequate resources, they can also lead to difficulties if demands at other levels require that researchers complete the present do-able problem.'

Andrew Pickering[14] sees scientific practice as 'the creative extension of the conceptual net to fit new circumstances ... the extension of the net is accomplished through a process of modelling or analogy; the production of new scientific knowledge entails seeing new situations as being relevantly like old ones.' This modelling is an open-ended process and can 'plausibly proceed in an indefinite number of different directions; nothing within the net fixes its future development.' So how then is what Pickering terms 'closure' – 'the achievement of consensus on particular extensions of culture' – to be understood? 'The Sociology of Scientific Knowledge emphasizes the instrumental aspect of scientific knowledge and the agency of scientific actors: knowledge is for use, not simply for contemplation, and actors have their own interests that instruments can serve well or ill.' The introduction of the concept of interest helps to clarify the problem of closure in two ways. 'On the one hand, actors can be tentatively seeking to extend culture in ways that might serve their interests rather than in ways that might not. And on the other hand, interests serve as standards against which the products of such extensions, new conceptual nets, can be assessed. A good extension of the net is one that serves the interest of the relevant scientific community best...' To sociologists of scientific knowledge such as Pickering, science is not, or not necessarily, knowledge but 'has to be seen, not as the transparent representation of nature, but rather as knowledge relative to a particular culture, with the relativity specified through a sociological concept of interest.'

Have I committed *lèse-majesté* and assumed vested interest and bad faith where they do not lie? Steve Fuller has suggested:

> *When a philosopher and a sociologist start talking about scientists at work, two stereotypes are immediately conjured up. The philosopher invariably evokes the image of the methodologically steadfast scientist, one who will break the rules of her disciplined pursuit only for the sake of some higher principle of truth seeking. By contrast, the sociologist's scientist is an agile opportunist who will switch research tactics, and perhaps her entire agenda, as the situation requires. Much of the rancor that has accompanied the debates between philosophers and scientists is traceable to this radical difference in the moral psychology of the scientist that the two sides presuppose.*[18]

But what we have been examining has been the *refusal* of researchers to abandon their earliest formulations because they have too much time investment, career projection and perhaps emotional commitment to them as well as a certain intellectual rigidity. As the senior researchers became more aloof from the actual research process, and conducted it at arm's length through their participation in the advisory and review committees, the very insecurity of the short-term junior researchers made them unwilling and perhaps unable critically to review the premises on which they were conducting their tours of investigation.

Notes

1. Wilfred Burchett quoted by John Pilger in Preface to Ben Kiernan (ed.) *Burchett Reporting the Other Side of the World*, (Quartet Books, 1986). See also Richard Tanter 'Voice and silence in the first nuclear war: Wilfred Burchett and Hiroshima' in the same volume.

2. '*In the matter of J. Robert Oppenheimer, transcript of Hearing before Personnel Security Board, United States Atomc Energy Commission*' (The MIT Press, 1971) pp.165–6.

3. Frederic de Hoffman, 'Pure science in the service of wartime Technology', *Bulletin of the Atomic Scientists*, January 1975,41–4.

4. Philip Morrison, 'The laboratory demobilizes ...' *Bulletin of the Atomic Scientists*, 1946:2:5–6.

5. Daniel S. Greenberg, *The Politics of Pure Science: An inquiry into the relationship between science & government in the United States* (New American Library, 1967,1971).

6. 'The potential theory of adsorption', *Science*, 13 September 1963:1010-3.

7. P. B. Medawar, 'Is the scientific paper a fraud?', BBC, *Experiment*, 1964:–1.2

8. Francis Crick and James Watson, *The Double Helix: a personal account of the discovery of the structure of DNA* (Weidenfield and Nicolson, 1968).

9. Thomas S. Kuhn, *The Structure of Scientific Revolutions* (University of Chicago Press, 1962).

10. Eric Larrabee, 'Science and the common reader', *Commentary*, June 1966, quoted in Greenberg, 26.

11. Donald A. Schon, *The Reflective Practitioner: how professionals think in action* (Basic Books, 1983).

12. William J. Schull *Songs of Praise, op cit.* pp.268–9.

13. William J. Schull, *ibid.* p.71.

14. William J. Schull *ibid.* p.222. John Z. Bowers gave a more anodyne view of the relationship in 'Yale and the Atomic Bomb Casualty Commission', *The Yale Journal of Biology and Medicine*, 1983:56:39–45.

15. Ian Hacking, 'Self-Vindication of the Laboratory Sciences', in Andrew Pickering (ed.) *Science as Practice and Culture* (University of Chicago Press, 1992).

16. Joan H. Fujimura, 'Constructing doable problems in cancer research: articulating alignment', *Social Studies of Science*, 1987:17:257–93.

17. Andrew Pickering, 'From science as knowledge to science as practice' in Andrew Pickering (ed.) *Science as Practice and Culture* (University of Chicago Press, 1992).

18. Steve Fuller, 'Social Epistemology and the Research Agenda of Science Studies', in Andrew Pickering, *Science as Practice and Culture* (University of Chicago Press, 1992).

Coming Home
To Roost

All too often, investigators disregard a positive association between exposure and disease, because the confidence interval includes one or because the finding is not statistically significant. A number of authors have eloquently discussed the impropriety of such an approach. A consequence is that negative findings can be guaranteed simply by doing studies of small populations or by stratifying data so finely that it becomes impossible to obtain 'statistically significant' findings unless an extremely strong exposure effect is present. Another common error is to dismiss associations between exposure and disease in the absence of statistically significant dose–response trends. Such an approach tacitly ignores the possibility of trends other than linear that may exist between the exposure and the health outcomes.

Gregg S. Wilkinson, 'Epidemiologic studies of nuclear and radiation workers: An overview of what is known about health risks posed by the nuclear industry', *Occupational Medicine, State of the Art Reviews***, 1991:6:4:715–24.**

This very unusual case involves a 70 year old white male who was within 50 miles of atomic bomb testing in the Mohave Desert and had 56 primary malignancies from 1946 to 1992.... There is a history of repeated contact with fallout material and he believes this exposure may be responsible for his recurrent malignancies.

Ahmed Ghouri *et al.* **'A patient with 56 primary malignancies',** *Iowa Medicine***: 1993:83:2:67-9**

Twenty-eight

In 1971 Robert E. Anderson, Professor and Chairman of the Department of Pathology at the University of New Mexico in Albuqerque (the nearest city to the Los Alamos establishment) had commented, in a discussion of leukaemia and related disorders, that 'The presence or absence of a threshold effect [a point below which ionizing radiation was non-injurious] is clearly an issue of marked socio-economic and political importance as well as of considerable biologic interest. Such disparate groups as utility companies in the United States, conservationists the world over, and several governmental agencies as well as the survivors of the atomic bombs would like to know whether the relationships between radiation and leukaemia is linear at the lower dosage levels.'[1]

In the period from 1947 to 1958, 231 cases of leukaemia had been identified in Nagasaki and Hiroshima, and the rate of incidence within the 1500 metre radius of the hypocentres was running at about fifteen times the normal rate.[2] But Gilbert Beebe pointed out in 1979 that the picture produced by the Atomic Bomb Casualty Commission did not include the early entrants into the two cities, among whom Japanese researchers had identified 'an unduly high incidence of leukemia' even while the ABCC dosimetry research 'suggests that their average exposure was probably not biologically significant'.[3] Beebe recalled that in the mid-1960s the estimated yields of the Hiroshima weapon had been almost halved and in the process only 34 of the 231 cases registered with the Nagasaki Leukemia Registry for the period 1946 to 1974 could be used in analyses based on the Life Span Study (LSS). 'The uncertainty attached to any dose–response analysis of the leukemia cases in the LSS sample for Nagasaki is so great', he warned in the open literature in 1979, 'as to reduce it almost to the level of a *tour de force*, but at present there is no reliable substitute for the LSS sample.' Moreover while the linear hypothesis of dose–response–injury had been 'rather firmly established in radiation protection work in the 1950s', there was now less certainty.

'The force of numerous experimental demonstrations of non-linear dose–response functions for low-LET radiation, combined with the possibly curvilinear dose–response functions for leukemia among Nagasaki survivors, however, has injected a great deal of uncertainty into all discussions of human data, especially as they are employed to estimate low-dose effects.' Nevertheless he notes that in the NAS 1972 BEIR Committee report data coming from the ABCC studies 'were extensively relied upon to produce *low dose estimates on the basis of the linear hypothesis* [my emphasis].

In the early post-war years, the studies of injury arising from low doses of ionizing radiation still concentrated on those immediately involved in radiation-related occupations, especially medical radiologists. British researchers led by W. M. Court Brown and Richard Doll studied the life expectation and cancer mortality of British radiologists.[4] They were sceptical of the results published in a similar study by Shields Warren in 1956[5] because they thought it 'fraught with danger' to compare two groups by average ages at death without ensuring that the samples had simple age distributions, which is to say were reasonably matched. This was a time when the ABCC was postulating a life-shortening effect for those exposed to ionizing radiation and Court Brown and Doll too were looking for reductions in the life expectancy of those occupationally involved with radiation. They could detect in 1958 no non-specific reduction in their sample's expectations of life, but did detect an increased mortality from skin cancer, pancreatic cancer and leukaemia in those who had entered radiological practice in Britain prior to 1921. The eighty women who would have been eligible for inclusion for the study 'were excluded to simplify the analysis of the data' on the 1377 men.

But the 1950s was the decade of British nuclear weapons testing in the South Pacific. Twenty-one atmospheric tests were carried out between 1952 and 1958 at Christmas Island and in South Australia. In 1983 three British researchers, including Alice Stewart, reviewed the health status of 8000 of the estimated 13,000 men who had been present in one capacity of another at those tests. They found that the number of deaths from leukaemia and other reticuloendothelial system neoplasm was already markedly raised.[6] Other researchers pointed out also the high incidence of cataracts, 'Virtually unknown as a spontaneous occurrence in young men, [which] is a strong indication that some of those involved had received radiation greatly in excess of a safe dose.'[7]

But this data did not agree with the data coming out of Hiroshima and Nagasaki from the Atomic Bomb Casualty Commission. During the 1980s, therefore, researchers were concerned to understand how to evaluate the risk from relatively low doses of radiation to what was assumed to have been an instantaneous exposure to very high doses in Hiroshima and Nagasaki. One of the central problems was to find a population in which radiation-induced cancers occurred with sufficient frequency to permit a statistical detection model that would have sufficient power to both detect and predict risk. There was thus increasing research interest – as well as growing public interest – in the fate of people occupationally exposed to radiation in the burgeoning nuclear power industry. Work was also done on patients who had received radiation therapy for anky-losing spondylitis. But in 1986, at a time when the average annual occu-pational dose in nuclear fuel-cycle facilities in the United Kingdom was 4 mSv and the maximum permissible annual dose for radiation workers was 50 mSv, S. C. Darby noted that 'Although several studies of low-dose radiation effects, such as those received occupationally by radiation workers, are under way, it seems likely that cancer risk estimates will continue to be based primarily on extrapolation from populations exposed to much higher doses'[8] – that is, on the ABCC data.

Darby and her colleagues at the Imperial Cancer Research Fund Cancer Epidemiology and Clinical Trials Unit at the University of Oxford published in 1988 the results of a study on 22,347 men who had participated in the British tests between 1952 and 1967. They found slightly enhanced mortality from leukaemia and multiple myeloma than would have been expected from the national values (to which of course, all radiation-induced cancers were now also contributing). But they found 'substantially lower' levels of mortality from these causes among the matched controls (who were also men who had served in the armed forces but had reportedly not been present at the tests). They considered this to be 'the chance occurrence of very low mortality in the controls' and concluded that 'participation in the nuclear weapons test programme did not have a detectable effect on the participants' expectation of life or on their total risks of developing multiple myeloma and leukemia (other than chronic lymphatic leukemia).' They conceded that this was a 'con-fusing finding' and 'on balance we conclude that there may well have been small hazards of both diseases associated with participation in the programme but that this has not been proved. The only carcinogenic agent that has been shown to cause an increased incidence of both dis-eases is ionizing radiation, but we have no evidence that the participants who developed these diseases were exposed to unusual amounts.'[9]

These researchers did not consider the implication of a finding of 51 deaths from diseases acknowledged to be inducable by radiation among the exposed sample as against 28 similar deaths among the presumed unexposed controls in what Stewart would call a 'healthy worker sam-ple'. Recruits to the armed forces are known to be healthier than the general population, since they are screened for fitness, so the finding of a lowered incidence of relevant mortality among the control sample should not be surprising. It should highlight rather than diminish the detection of a much higher incidence among the exposed sample. The assumptions about the amounts or doses of ionizing radiation required to induced such cancers are based on the Japanese data, rather than serving as a check on them.

From 1990, research attention has been focused less on the mortality of exposed adults to ionizing radiation than to the possibility that paternal exposure in the workplace has caused leukaemia in children conceived after such exposure. From the early 1980s there has been apprehension about the incidence of childhood leukaemia detected around nuclear power plants and the British Committee on Medical Aspects in the Environment commissioned studies which confirm the existence of such clusters around the Sellafield and Dounreay nuclear reprocessing plants in England and Scotland.[10] Valerie Beral, Director of the Imperial Cancer Research Fund Cancer Epidemiology Unit, noted in an editorial in the *British Medical Journal*[11] in February 1990 that all three studies had concluded that there was a real excess and that the increases were too large to be accounted for by radioactive discharges from the plants. 'Each report emphasised that alternative – but as yet unknown – pathways of exposure and mechanisms of carcinogenesis needed to be considered.'

Professor Beral was introducing a report of a study conducted under the leadership of Martin J. Gardner on the incidence of leukaemia and lymphoma among young people near the Sellafield nuclear plant in West Cumbria.[12] Gardner noted that the 50 mSv annual dose limit for radiation workers recommended in 1965 by the International Commission on Radiological Protection was still operative in Britain although in 1987 the National Radiological Protection Board recommended a reduction to 15 mSv per year. During 1987 alone some 1100 workers received annual doses above the 15 mSvs; only ten of these were health professionals. In a case-control study of 52 cases of leukaemia, 22 of non-Hodgkin's lymphoma and 23 of Hodgkin's diseases occurring in people born in the West Cumbria health district and diagnosed there in the period 1950 to 1985 under the age of 25 years and of 1001 controls, Gardner and his colleagues concluded that the raised incidence of leukaemia, particularly, and non-Hodgkin's lymphoma among children near Sellafield was associated with paternal employment and recorded external dose of whole body penetrating radiation during work at the plant before conception. This suggested that preconceptual paternal exposure to ionizing radiation was a pathway for childhood leukaemia.

As Professor Beral wrote in her editorial, 'The explanation offered by

Gardner *et al.* is not, however, without its problems. The only other relevant human data available are on the 7400 children of Japanese men [*sic*] who survived the atomic bomb explosions, and these show no hint of an increased risk of leukaemia in the offspring. And the average exposure to external ionizing radiation of the Japanese men was four times higher than that of the Sellafield workers.' But as we have seen, the study of the 7400 children began at least one full reproductive cycle after the bombings and never included conceptions lost before the fifth month. It was also of offspring of parents, *one or both* of whom had been exposed to the bombings, not of fathers alone. The actual exposures of doses in Hiroshima and Nagasaki, as we have seen, were continually being revised *downwards*. Moreover, despite these shortcomings, Shimzu, Schull and Kato noted in 1990[13] that 'Leukemia is the most strikingly elevated cancer among the Life Span Study cohort. The pattern of the effect is well established. An increased risk was apparent one to three years after August 1945, reached a peak about six to seven years after the bombing, and has since declined steadily. It was also demonstrated that the younger subject was ATB, the greater was the risk of leukemia during the early period and the more rapid was the decline in risk thereafter. Acute forms of leukemia are primarily responsible for these trends.'

As Yoshimoto noted in a review of the Radiation Effects Research Foundation Epidemiologic Studies,[14] Kneale and Stewart had suggested as early as 1978 that 'potentially induced' leukaemia cases may have been selectively eliminated from the Hiroshima and Nagasaki cohorts by an increase of infant deaths from infectious diseases among those infants whose reticuloendothelial systems were damaged due to heavy radiation exposure. Yoshimoto commented that 'The RERF data are inconclusive about an association of leukemia risk with paternal radiation exposure in the six months prior to conception because of the few leukemia cases and the limited number of children from May 1945 to December 1946 (ie those presumed to have been conceived during the six months after the bombing, which amounts to about 2 per cent of the sample.' If the Japanese data are relied upon, 'In the context of radiation genetics, the estimated paternal doses to the Sellafield workers are considered to be too low to result in the end point, childhood leukemia.' But only if the interpretation of the Sellafield data relies upon the Japanese data rather than being taken as a potential baseline of dose-injury relationships in itself.

Later in 1990 Morris and his colleagues identified a cluster of three retinoblastomas among grandchildren of workers at Sellafield. None of the children had been born in the nearby dormitory town of Seascale, although their mothers had spent part of their childhood in Seascale. These researchers called for a large-scale study of the incidence of retinoblastoma – which is extremely rare, occurring with a frequency of 1 in 20,000 live births and being ten times less common than acute lymphoblastic leukaemia – in the children and grandchildren of nuclear industry workers.[15]

Reaction to the Gardner *et al.* study's proposal of a 'Gardner effect' of preconceptual paternal exposure to industrial sources of ionizing radiation was sharp and startled. Writing in *Nature,* John Maddox pointed out that if it was accepted that the releases of radiation from the plants are well monitored and 'unambiguously too small to account for the recorded cases of death among young people by the induction of mutations in somatic cells', the data, despite being 'dauntingly inconclusive' challenged the stoical acceptance by the Sellafield workforce that radiation exposure can cause cancer of various causes, but at a low frequency. 'But if it were shown that radiation exposure can cause leukaemia among children, even at a lower frequency hardly distinguishable from that expected naturally, the reaction would probably be out of proportion to the numerical frequencies, whatever they are.'[16] Three weeks later the same journal reported that 'US researchers say the Sellafield results, if confirmed, are surprising enough to change dramatically the science of radiation epidemiology' and was being closely considered by the US Department of Energy researchers studying cancer deaths in 113 counties containing or adjacent to 61 nuclear facilities.[17] A British writer pointed out that Muller had long ago shown that it is the cumulative dose of radiation that is important for heritable effects, not the dose received on a single occasion. 'If I were a parent at Sellafield, I would … be asking for chromosome spreads and the very best that molecular genetics can offer … childhood leukaemias will not be the only dominant mutations. And there are all the recessives.'[18]

But there were highly placed critics of the Gardner study. George M. Watson, formerly Chief, Environment and Public Health Division of the Australian Atomic Energy Commission Research Establishment at Lucas Heights insisted that 'the postulate of a causal relation between parental [*sic*] exposure at Sellafield and leukaemia in progeny is incompatible with what is known of the role of genetic mechanisms in leukaemia, with current views of the quantitative relation between radiation dose and mutagenetic effect, and with observations on the children of people exposed to radiation by the nuclear [*sic*] bombs used in Japan in 1945.'[19]

The Department of Health and the Health and Safety Executive (HSE) of the United Kingdom responded to the Gardner study by immediately commissioning an investigation by a group drawn from the HSE's Nuclear Installations Inspectorate and the Epidemiology Unit of its Health Policy Division. The resulting report[20] was published three and a half years later, in October 1993. Although the study was undertaken to review the 'Gardner effect' which suggested a causal association between paternal irradiation up to six months prior to conception, the HSE review concentrated on the twelve week period prior to the conception of the identified sufferers. One reason for this was that they were also interested to evaluate the suggestion made by another research group, led by Leo Kinlen in Edinburgh, that the undisputed increase of the relevant cancers in the populations around Sellafield and the Scottish plant, Dounreay, might be attributed not to a mutagenetic effect in sperm but rather to a viral infection that was a particular response to what Kinlen termed 'population mixing' when workers came to a new environment to build and staff power plants. To establish the population mixing hypothesis over the paternal preconception irradiation hypothesis would of course exonerate the nuclear energy industry from liability for the childhood cancers.

The HSE endeavoured to keep their review apart from the employers they were investigating, British Nuclear Fuels (BNF) and the Atomic Energy Authority, although they needed to work with them to gain access to the records required on the workers and doses. After publication of the report, BNFL queried the two central conclusions, inconclusive as they were. These were that the association of the childhood cancers with cumulative pre-conception external radiation dose when treated as a continuous variable for those resident outside Seascale at the time of the child's birth, and the weak association that the HSE study had detected with twelve-week preconception external radiation for those resident in Seascale at the time of the child's birth. BNFL successfully challenged the doses attributed to the three employees whose data generated the (albeit weak) statistical significance of the associations reached by the review study. A year later, the HSE issued a revised set of conclusions from their study based on these negotiations with the employer.[21] They sustained their original findings that there was a clear distinction between the incidence of childhood leukaemia and non-Hodgkin's lymphoma in Seascale and elsewhere in West Cumbria, and that the incidence in Seascale of these diseases in the children of Sellafield fathers was some fourteen times the national average.

They did not dispute the strong association for the children of Seascale families between the fathers' cumulative preconception external radiation dose, and the incidence of these diseases together with the concentration of the increased risk solely in the children of fathers who began work in Sellafield prior to 1965. This was complemented by the absence for the non-Seascale subjects of an association with the father's 12-week preconception external radiation dose. But in the absence of any positive association for other cancers with these factors and the absence of any (detected) association with internal radiation dose, they now considered that 'for the non-Seascale subjects there is no indication of any association of childhood leukaemia or NHL with the father's pre-conception external radiation dose, and for those resident in Seascale at the time of the child's birth, the weak association with twelve-week preconception external radiation dose now becomes non-significant (p=0.08).' Their final conclusion was to note that the raised incidence in children of the Seascale fathers 'may in some way, be associated with Seascale's unusually high proportion of in-comers, ie non-Cumbrian born fathers'.

In May 1994 eight families who were suing for compensation from BNFL were denied the right to pursue their claims when the judge ruled that 'on the balance of probabilities'[22] the paternal preconception irradia-tion theory was not to blame.

Meanwhile, Darby and her colleagues were pursuing their study of the men who had participated in Britain's atmospheric nuclear weapons tests and experimental programmes. Their follow-up report on 21,358 ser-vicemen and civilians from the UK who participated in the tests and a control group of 22,333 non-participants was published in December 1993.[23] They thought that by concentrating on the period more than ten years after initial participation in the tests, they could avoid the time when the effect of selecting healthy men into the armed forces would have the greatest impact on their sample, although they studied the inci-dence of leukaemia in the first decade.

They continued to find a lower than expected incidence of leukaemia in the controls and continued to conclude that 'participation in nuclear weapon tests had no detectable effect on expectation of life or on subse-quent risk of developing cancer or other fatal diseases.' They attributed the excess of leukaemia in participants that they did detect in contrast to the lower than expected level in the controls as due to 'a chance deficit' but acknowledged that 'the possibility that participation in the tests may have caused a small risk of leukaemia in the early years afterwards cannot be ruled out.' One of their reasons for minimizing the interpretation of their results was their conviction that the excess of leukaemia detected in Royal New Zealand Navy staff who had observed the Pacific tests[24] seems unlikely to have been caused by the tests since their ships were at least 40 km from the detonations and three of the New Zealand deaths occurred 25 years after the tests 'which would not be expected if they were caused by irradiation at the time of the tests'. They seemed to be unaware of the data on the fallout victims from the Marshall Islands and increasingly from the Nevada Test Site. Veterans' organizations were not impressed with the results. Nicholas Frayling, Honorary Chaplain to the

British Nuclear Test Veterans Association wrote at the time the results came out, 'I was with a veteran two weeks ago whose identity I do not have permission to disclose. He has cancer. His daughter has cancer. His son is sterile. His two other children have already died of cancer. An extreme case, perhaps, but there are many others. I feel deeply ashamed.'[25]

Notes

1. Robert E. Anderson, 'Leukaemia and related disorders', *Human Pathology*, 1971:2:4:505–14.

2. R. Keith Cannan, 'Atomic Bomb Casualty Commission: The first fifteen years', *Bulletin Of The Atomic Scientists*, October 1963:45–8.

3. Gilbert W. Beebe, 'Reflections on the work of the Atomic Bomb Casualty Commission in Japan', *Epidemiologic Reviews*, 1979:1:184.

4. W. M. Court Brown and Richard Doll, 'Expectation of life and cancer mortality of British radiologists', *Proceedings of the Second United Nations Conference*,1958: 179–82

5. Shields Warren, *Journal Of The American Medical Association*, 1956:162. See also R. Seltser and P. E. Sartwell, *Journal of the American Medical Association*, 1958:166:585.

6. E. G. Knox, Tom Sorahan and Alice Stewart, 'Cancer following nuclear weapons tests', letters to the editor, *The Lancet*, 9 April 1983:815.

7. J. W. Boag *et al.*, letter to *The Lancet*, 9 April 1983:815.

8. S. C. Darby, 'Epidemiological evaluation of radiation risk using populations exposed at high doses', *Health Physics*, 1986:51:3:269–81.

9. S. C. Darby *et al.*, 'A summary of mortality and incidence of cancer in men from the United Kingdom who participated in the United Kingdom's atmospheric nuclear weapons test and experimental programmes', *British Medical Journal*, 30 January 1988:296: 332–38

10. Independent Advisory Group, *Investigation of the Possible Increased Incidence of Cancer in West Cumbria* (London, HMSO, 1984). See also Black Report: Committee on Medical Aspects of Radiation in the Environment, *Third Report, Report on the Incidence of Childhood Cancer in the West Berkshire and North Hampshire Area, in which are situated the Atomic Weapons Research Establishment, Aldermaston and the Royal Ordnance Factory, Burghfield* (London, HMSO, 1989); and *Second Report, Investigation of the Possible Increased Incidence of Leukaemia in Young People near the Dounreay Nuclear Establishment, Caithness, Scotland* (London, HMSO, 1988).

11. Valerie Beral, 'Leukaemia and nuclear installations', *British Medical Journal*, 17 February 1990: 300:411–12.

12. Martin J. Gardner *et al.*, 'Results of case-control study of leukaemia and lymphoma among young people near Sellafield nuclear plant in West Cumbria', *British Medical Journal*: 17 February 1990:300:423–29 and Martin J. Gardner *et al.*, 'Methods and basic data of case-control study of leukaemia and lymphoma among young people near Sellafield nuclear plant in West Cumbria', *British Medical Journal*: 17 February 1990:300:429–34. See also M. J. Gardner 'Childhood cancer and nuclear installations', 8th Duncan Memorial Lecture, University of Liverpool, 5 December 1990, *Public Health*:1991:105:277–85. See also the discussion in letters to the Editor, *British Medical Journal*, 10 March 1990:300:676–8.

13. Yukiko Shimzu, William J. Schull, Hiroo Kato, 'Cancer risk among atomic bomb survivors', *Journal Of The American Medical Association*, 1990:264:5:601–4. See also letters to the editor, *British Medical Journal*: 3 March 1990:877–9 particularly that from A. Stewart and E. G. Knox.

14. Yasuhiko Yoshimoto, 'Cancer risk among children of atomic bomb survivors: a review of RERF epidemiologic studies,' *Journal of the American Medical Association*, 1990:264:5:596–600, referring to G.W. Kneale and A.W. Stewart, 'Pre-cancers and liability to others', *British Journal of Cancer*, 1978:37:448–57.

15. J. A. Morris *et al.*, 'Retinoblastoma in grandchildren of workers at Sellafield nuclear plant', *British Medical Journal*, 1 December 1990:1257.

16. John Maddox, 'Sellafield makes news again', *Nature*, 22 February 1990:343:690.

17. G. Christopher-Anderson, 'US response to Sellafield data', *Nature*, 15 March 1990:344:184. The work on developing methodologies for identifying clusters has been advanced by the studies in the 1990s of the populations around nuclear plants in France (eg Catherine Hill and Agnes Laplanche, 'Overall mortality and cancer mortality around French nuclear sites' *Letters to Nature*, 347:1990:755–7) the United States (see *inter alia*, Stevens *et al.* 'Leukemia in Utah and radioactive fallout from the Nevada Test Site', *Journal of the American Medical Association*,1990:264:5:585–91; Wing *et al.*, 'Mortality among workers at Oak Ridge National Laboratory: evidence of radiation effects in follow-up through 1984', *Journal of the American Medical Association*: 1991:265:11:1397–402, and Jablon *et al.*, 'Cancer in populations living near nuclear facilities: a survey of mortality nation-wide and incidence in two states', *Journal of the American Medical Association*, 1991:265:11:1403–8), UK Office of Population Censuses and Surveys, *The Geographical Epidemiology of Childhood Leukemia and non-Hodgkin Lymphomas in Great Britain*, 1966–83, HMSO, 1991 (Studies in Medical and Population Subjects No. 53) and G. J. Draper *et al.* 'Cancer in Cumbria and in the vicinity of the Sellafield nuclear installations, 1963–90', *British Medical Journal*, 9 January 1993:306:89–94. Eva Alberman commented in an editorial in the *British Medical Journal*, 'After Windscale [Sellafield]', 30 May 1992:304:1393–4, that the large amount of research money certainly 'has stimulated the development of new statistical approaches to spatial analyses, which may be applicable to other circumstances. It has also strengthened the validity of what was previously weak evidence on the presence of clusters of cases, even if we have learnt little more about the effects of environmental radiation. Considerably more research is needed, probably on an individual basis, before the causes of these devastating diseases are fully understood.'

18. Guil Winchester, letter to the editor, 'Missing link at Sellafield', *Nature*, 3 May 1990:345:10.

19. George M. Watson, 'Leukemia and paternal radiation exposure', *The Medical Journal of Australia*, 1 April 1991:154: 483–7.

20. Health and Safety Executive, *HSE Investigation of Leukaemia and other Cancers in the Children of Male Workers at Sellafield* (HSE Books, 1993).

21. Health and Safety Executive, *HSE Investigation of Leukaemia and Other Cancers In The Children Of Male Workers At Sellafield: review of results published in October 1993* (HSE Books, 1994).

22. Rosie Waterhouse, 'Families lose fight to sue BNFL', *The Independent*, 10 May 1994.

23. S. C. Darby *et al.*, 'Further follow-up of mortality and incidence of cancer in men from the United Kingdom who participated in the United Kingdom's atmospheric nuclear weapons tests and experimental programmes', *British Medical Journal*:11 December 1993:307:1530–5.

24. N. Pearce *et al.*, 'Follow-up of New Zealand participants in British atmospheric nuclear weapons tests in the pacific', *British Medical Journal*, 300:1990:1161-6.

25. Nicholas Frayling, letter to the editor, *The Independent*, 11 December 1993.

Twenty-nine

Meanwhile, in Scotland, Leo Kinlen and colleagues at the Cancer Research Campaign Cancer Epidemiology Unit at the University of Edinburgh published a study of evidence for an infective cause of childhood leukaemia by comparing a Scottish New Town with nuclear reprocessing sites in Britain.[1] Kinlen suggested that Dounreay and Sellafield were built in unusually isolated places 'where herd immunity to a postulated widespread virus infection (to which leukaemia is a rare response) would tend to be lower than average'. He proposed to test this hypothesis by comparing the incidence of leukaemia in people under 25 years old in 'the only other rural area that received a large influx at the same time, when it was much more cut off from the nearest conurbation than at present'. This was the New Town of Glenrothes, formed in 1948. There Kinlen found a significant increase of leukaemia below 25 years old – 10 cases instead of 3.6 as expected on national averages with a greater excess below age five (7 observed and 1.5 expected).

Kinlen's first assumption, that the observed increases in childhood and adolescent leukaemia could not be explained in terms of radiation, rested on statements by 'three official reports by groups of independent scientists [who] all concluded that the levels of radiation in those areas are far below those necessary on conventional models to account for the excesses'.

Kinlen therefore assumed that the excesses must be caused by some other factor, and he hypothesized an infective process in a situation where there had been a sudden population influx to a formerly isolated rural environment. He was modelling his hypothesis on the possibility that childhood leukaemia is of viral origin because of work done on leukaemia in cats. He therefore contended that 'the obvious test of the above hypothesis is to determine whether there is an excess of leukaemia in other isolated areas which have seen a considerable influx of population but which lack any man-made potential source of radiation.' He settled on the New Town of Glenrothes as fulfilling these criteria for a control for the incidence of leukaemia in Thurso, the town nearest to the Dounreay plant.

Kinlen did acknowledge that while Thurso is 240 miles north of Edinburgh, and indeed very isolated, Glenrothes lies barely twenty miles as the crow flies from Edinburgh. However, Kinlen argued that the area that became the New Town of Glenrothes in 1948 was much more isolated than it has since become with the opening of the Forth Road Bridge in 1964.

Kinlen asserted the isolation of Glenrothes and assumed that the population growth that occurred after 1948 was a matter of incomers joining a new community. The official history of the new town published by the Glenrothes Development Corporation in 1982,[2] however, tells us that in 1954 three-quarters of all households established since 1948 came from the immediate area – the villages around the site for the new housing developments and the town of Kirkcaldy. The figures for the 1960s on the origins of households in Glenrothes are not provided but throughout the 1970s almost exactly half of the community still originated from the immediate neighbourhoods.

A map published in the 1994 Factfile put out by the Glenrothes Development Corporation[3] indicates Glenrothes as a community of 52,000 people who are within fifteen minutes travelling time of a constellation of villages and the town of Kirkcaldy, a total population of 170,000 people. The third ring of the concentric travel-time map shows Glenrothes as being within thirty minutes of the outskirts of Edinburgh and this zone of population is listed as containing 310,000 people. Edinburgh itself is a city of over 400,000 people, the capital of Scotland.

While there was in 1994 a 15 per cent unemployment rate in Glenrothes the workforce is slightly atypical for Scotland in that half of it is skilled manual or higher technical proficiency (another quarter is professional or managerial). The irony is that while Glenrothes was built to provide a dormitory suburb for the expansion of the Frances Colliery, one of the main sources of fossil fuel in Scotland, in fact it is now known from Texas to California as Silicon Glen. The Frances Colliery, far from being expanded, was closed down as the British Government invested in nuclear energy.

The two main employers in Glenrothes are defence electronics and the petrochemicals industry, including the welding of oil rigs and other offshore equipment. As the Fife Regional Council's Structure Plan for Glenrothes and its surrounding communities expressed it[4] 'Fife has a substantial share of total manufacturing employment in "electronics" and within this sector in "defence electronics". Fife also has a high dependence on employment in a range of defence establishments.'

The defence establishments range from Rosyth Naval Dockyard, a base and refitting port for nuclear powered and weaponed submarines fifteen miles down the motorway from Glenrothes, to the Marconi, Hughes Microelectric and other companies in the defence and electronics field. Indeed, the first international company into Glenrothes was Beckman which arrived in 1958, the year Dounreay was opened.

There are almost one hundred sources of ionizing radiation in the Glenrothes area licensed for industrial and medical uses. In 1988 an apparent excess of lymphoid leukaemia in the postcode areas immediately adjacent to Glenrothes was studied. A case-control study of 43 cases diagnosed between 1970 and 1985 in people under fourteen years (at a time when the population of children in the area was falling) identified two apparently distinct leukaemia clusters to the immediate east and west of Glenrothes, around the Rosyth Naval Base and in the town of Kirkcaldy.[5]

Another Edinburgh-based group headed by Urquhart undertook a case control study of leukaemia and non-Hodgkin's lymphoma in children in Caithness near the Dounreay nuclear installation after Gardner published his hypothesis that childhood leukaemias may be explained by paternal occupational exposure to ionizing radiation.[6] This study identified fifteen cases of leukaemia and non-Hodgkin's lymphoma registered in Caithness during 1968–86 in young people below the age of 25 but one case was diagnosed at age 23 and eliminated from the study 'because of difficulties in obtaining reliable information about the preconceptional and early childhood periods after such an extended time interval'. The remaining fourteen cases had been younger than fifteen years at the time of diagnosis. Eight of theses cases were children resident with the 25 kilometre zone around Dounreay at the time of diagnosis. Seven of them had been diagnosed in the period 1979 to 1986. Five of these children had been born within the 25 kilometre zone.

While the researchers acknowledge that 'It must be emphasised that the results from such a small study cannot be used to refute claims of association with risk factors that have been based on studies carried out in other geographical areas', they do conclude on the basis of these eight cases that 'the observed excess incidence of childhood leukaemia and non-Hodgkin's lymphoma in the area within 25km of the Dounreay nuclear installation cannot be explained by any of the risk factors for which evidence has been adduced from earlier studies.' They thus conclude that these eight cases were not caused by either paternal preconceptual exposure or foetal exposure to X-rays, or playing on the beaches around Dounreay.

Black and colleagues who included Urquhart then looked more closely at the incidence of leukaemia and other cancers in those born in the

Dounreay area as compared with children in school in the town of
Thurso to see if they could detect a difference between those who were
born in the area and those who had moved into it as their parents took
jobs at Dounreay.[7] This required a data linkage between the birth records
for the area (which were only computerized in Scotland after 1969) and
the school admissions records. They established a cohort of 2301 children who had been born in the study area and 1641 children who had
attended schools in the area but had not been born there in the period
1969 to 1988. They then checked these cohorts against the Scottish
national cancer registrations. There was a good match with the cases
identified in other studies – eight children, of whom five were in the
birth cohort and three in the schools cohort, both incidences being raised
against national expectations. But the researchers concluded that place of
birth is not a more important factor than place of residence at diagnosis in
the series of cases they identified in the Dounreay area by the computerized record linkage method. They note that the period 1979 to 1983 saw
the diagnosis of six of the eight cases and concluded that 'The most
remarkable features of this series of cases in the Dounreay area remain
their concentration in a relatively short period of time and the common
diagnosis of leukaemia with a complete absence of other types of childhood cancer'.

Kinlen re-entered the debate in a discussion of rural population mixing and childhood leukaemia in the North Sea oil industry in a study
published in 1993.[8] He introduced his study by asserting that 'Evidence
has mounted that the incidence of childhood leukaemia can be increased
by population mixing, particularly in a rural area' but his only citations
for this statement are to his own work. On the premise that the rapid
expansion of the North Sea oil industry had created a considerable
amount of population mixing in formerly isolated rural areas such as the
Sullom Voe oil terminal in Shetland, this study traced the details of more
than 30,000 construction workers in the large oil terminals in Shetland
and Orkney islands to the north of Scotland as well as those working offshore. The incidence of leukaemia and non-Hodgkin's lymphoma in the
children of these workers were compared with communities with con-
trasting numbers of oil workers.

Kinlen and his colleagues wrote 'A significant excess of leukaemia and
non-Hodgkin's lymphoma was found in 1979–1983 in the group of rural
home areas with the largest proportion of oil workers, following closely
on large increases in the workforce.' This included the Dounreay area
which was also identified as a 'rural high oil area'. From this they concluded that their findings support the infection hypothesis that population mixing can increase the incidence of childhood leukaemia in rural

areas and that the recent excess in the Dounreay–Thurso area is due to population mixing linked to the oil industry, promoted by certain unusual local demographic factors.

Of the 17,160 oil workers resident in Scotland whom they studied, there was a marked excess of childhood leukaemias at ages 0–4 of the children of the workers, 31 cancers observed against 16.6 expected of which 27 were leukaemia.

Kinlen and his colleagues term this period 1979 to 1983 the 'early post-mixing period' and feel that their hypothesis has been vindicated. They do not discuss the age of the children (0–4 years) as potentially indicative of preconceptual paternal exposure to ionizing radiation, a resource increasingly used in the oil fields construction industry in precisely the period indicated. They assume, without any explicit discussion of the issue, that workers in the oil construction industry are not occupationally exposed to sources of ionizing radiation, just as it was earlier assumed that the New Town of Glenrothes did not contain radioactive sources.

Kinlen and his colleagues remark that they found an unexpectedly high number of oil industry workers in Dounreay and Thurso. Moreover they acknowledge that 'The 20-year interval between the first influx of nuclear workers in the late 1950s and the cluster of cases near Dounreay beginning in 1979 could not readily be explained since the excesses usually followed fairly quickly on other types of population mixing.' But they then suggest that the influx of oil workers into the Dounreay area caused a *second* excess of childhood leukaemias, the first one being the two cases in the age groups 0–14 years in the period 1951–67. They argue that because the oil workers tended to live in the western part of Thurso alongside the nuclear workers ('the atomics') this accounts for the concentration of cases there rather than in the eastern sector of Thurso. They do not consider the possibility that nuclear and oil construction workers are *both* occupationally exposed to ionizing radiation.

In 1992 an industrial radiographer, William Neilson, who had spent most of his working life at the BP oil refinery complex at Grangemouth on the Forth estuary in eastern Scotland, died of bronchopneumonia, radiation-induced myeloid leukaemia, radiation dermatitis and radiation-induced myelodylsplasia.[9] He had part of his right hand amputated in 1990 after the index finger turned gangrenous. After his death one of his molar teeth was immersed in a pot of carnivorous beetles to strip it of flesh, then sent to Japan where an electronic spin resonance analysis revealed that Mr Neilson had received a cumulative dose over nearly 15 Grays – the equivalent of 15,000 X-rays and the highest human dose ever recorded in Britain.

Mr Neilson became an industrial radiographer in 1974 and received one month's training and a year's practical experience. In recent years he had been using powerful sources of high energy gamma rays – Iridium 192 – to check the integrity of welds in pipe work and pressure vessels at the BP Grangemouth complex across the river from Edinburgh.[10] It was reported in May 1994 that since 1991 more than sixty industrial radiographers received doses greater than the level of 15 mSv (milli-Sieverts) that triggers investigation by health monitors while in the same period only seven workers in the nuclear industry exceeded more than 15 mSv. Chris Wilby, Head of Radiation Safety Policy of the Health and Safety Executive was quoted in early 1994 as saying that 'although radiation doses to workers in Britain have been falling steadily overall, this has not been reflected in industrial radiography. Inadequate controls of industrial radiation sources can lead to substantial exposures to radiographers and we are aware of several such incidents.'

Industrial radiography is not a unionized occupation in Britain, and often paid by piecework. There are 8000 registered industrial radiographers in Britain, and 40,000 workers in the nuclear industry. Because Mr Neilson was inadequately monitored, he received a steady excess dose which accumulated into the highest recorded in post-war Britain. But neither he nor his family received compensation from his employer. The Deputy Director General of the Health and Safety Executive held that his case was an exception even though he acknowledged that there has generally been a sustained reduction in doses since the mid-1980s in both the nuclear and industrial sectors and that this demonstrated the effectiveness of the regulatory system. 'However, we accept the need for greater efforts in the industrial radiography sector, since there had been no equivalent downward trend in this sector.'[11]

The Health and Safety Executive issued a new information sheet about industrial radiography and pointed up the importance of improvement in its newsletter, *The Radiation Protection Adviser*.[12] 'A typical example of poor practice was found by an HSE inspector at a routine visit to an open air fabrication yard associated with the offshore industry. Six thousand radiographs of pipe welds were planned over two months. Radiography was in progress, but no shielded enclosure had been provided. The controlled area had not been adequately restricted by local shielding; it was not properly marked; the control point for radiography was well inside the area giving unnecessary exposure to the operators and there was no effective control to prevent employees of the fabrication company from entering the area. The inspector stopped work until the company's RPA [radiation protection adviser] visited the site. As a result many improvements were made.' The same discussion notes that Mr

Neilson's *recorded* doses 'were not out of the ordinary.' He had not had a high level of reported sickness over the years that would have triggered an HSE investigation; even the severe ulceration to his left hand in 1990 had not been reported to the HSE. Hence 'It was not possible to reach a definite conclusion about how the overexposure had been received, so long after the event(s).'

The survivors of John Jarvis, an oil rig worker who died of chronic myeloid leukaemia at 54, are suing the owners of the North Sea Thistle Alpha platform alleging that his death was due to exposure to gamma radiation used to check welds in pipelines.[13] Affidavits from fellow workers on the platform claim that they regularly worked within 20 to 30 feet of radioactive isotopes being used to inspect the welds. It is reported that the work was particularly intense in the period from 1979 to 1982. Workers recalled that on the rigs, often housing a thousand men at any one time, radiographers would put a tape around the area in which they were working. 'The men referred to this red-and-white plastic tape as magic tape as it was jokingly thought that this would stop the radiation from going beyond this point', said one former safety officer on Thistle Alpha. 'It is possible that John Jarvis and other workmen could have come as close as 20 or 30 feet from the bombing.'

In March 1994 the prototype fast breed reactor at Dounreay was closed down because 'In the run-up to privatisation of the electricity supply industry, neither Government nor private enterprise were willing to pay now for the promise of unlimited energy far in the future'[14] in an era of increased availability of cheap oil and gas from sources such as the North Sea. Dismantling Dounreay is expected to provide work for a thousand people, two-thirds of the present workforce, for the foreseeable future.

In November 1994, the UK Atomic Energy Authority indicated it would conduct an inquiry into unexplained deposits of radioactive metal particles on a beach near the Dounreay plant over the past fifteen years.[15] One hundred and thirty two particles measuring from 1 to 3 millimetres across have been recovered from the foreshore near Dounreay since 1979. The particles are mostly uranium/aluminium alloy and contain radioactive Caesium 137 and radioactive Cobalt 60.

In 1990 routine radiation monitoring detected particles of Radium 226 on the beach at Dalgety Bay which Black and his colleagues describe as 'a small town situated on the south coast of the Fife Health Board area in east central Scotland.'[16] According to these researchers from the NHS in Scotland Information and Statistics Division, 'The contamination is thought to have been due to the disposal by burning of military aircraft in the 1940s. Some of these aircraft were equipped with night vision instruments manufactured using radium-based luminous paint.' Dalgety Bay, they note, 'was made up originally of private housing, built in the 1960s and 70s, designed for commuters to the city of Edinburgh and white collar staff in the growing defence and electronics industries in Fife.' At the time of the 1981 census the population comprised mainly young families of relatively high socio-economic status, which are noted to have higher rates of childhood leukaemia. Black and his colleagues were concerned to study the incidence of cancer in this population that might be attributable to the particles found on the beaches where it might be assumed the children played. Although three cases of childhood leukaemia were found, no general excess of cancer was observed by this study in Dalgety Bay; the observation of raised incidence of pancreas and skin cancer being thought to be likely to be an artefact of the research design. The incidence of childhood leukaemia was not held to be significantly greater than expected even though they were all found in children under four years old.

This study does not mention that Dalgety Bay is part of the penumbra community around Glenrothes (the sort of beach where young families might go to play) and barely five miles down-river from the Rosyth Naval Base opposite Edinburgh on the Firth of Forth, and cheek by jowl with the Grangemouth petrochemical complex where William Neilson worked. Five miles inland, towards Glenrothes, is the Mossmorran ethylene plant which produces 600,000 tons of this highly explosive substance each year.

After twenty years as a major nuclear port for both the British and American submarine forces, Rosyth now has a devil's choice – compete for a contract for the refitting, refuelling and decommissioning of nuclear submarines or accept the nuclear waste from other installations which have won those contracts, as well as from Germany and Japan. Britain's Polaris fleet is now both outmoded by the advent of Trident and plagued with operational defects. Maintaining the Polaris in operational condition is particularly difficult given the confined spaces in which the work must be done close to and including radiation sources.[17]

It is to be hoped that the safety record in Naval Dockyards is better than that in Britain's Atomic Weapons Establishments. Greenpeace called for an independent investigation of an alleged appalling safety record of unreported deaths and fires, radioactive leaks and contamination fifteen years after the last official inquiry.[18] The report of a review by the Health and Safety Executive on the management of health and safety at atomic weapons establishment premises was released in October 1994. The HSE Director, John Rimington (former husband of the Director of M15) was reported as saying that safety standards are so poor that the Atomic

Weapons Establishment (AWE) would be refused a licence if it were a civil nuclear power station.[19]

The report noted among many other criticisms that:

> *When compared with other work places, the pattern of reporting [of abnormal events that might be hazardous] at AWE suggested that there was probably under-reporting of non-injury events. Trade union representatives told the review team that under-reporting might occur because staff were reluctant to report minor incidents which they perceived might work to their disadvantage, for example by leading to removal from work in designated areas where special bonuses were paid. There was no structured approach to the consideration of ill-health, and the possible uses of ill-health statistics seemed to be poorly understood. Although the AWE occupational health service contributed to epidemiological work by others, it did not itself undertake such work.[20]*

In 1993 it was reported[21] that millions of tons of silt and sediment contaminated with radioactive waste dredged up from the Rosyth Naval Base were thought to be the source of increased levels of Cobalt 60 along the Fife coast – from Dalgety Bay to Anstruther. 'Officials came to the opinion that the dumping of radiation-contaminated silt was illegal as no official authorisation was given by the Industrial Pollution Inspectorate. This has been rejected by the Scottish Office who say the authorisation for Rosyth Dockyard to discharge low level radioactive waste into the Forth also covers the dredging operations.' The Cobalt 60 is coming from the refitting and decommissioning work carried out on at the dockyard. And in November 1994 it was reported that the decontamination from Radium 226 at Dalgety Bay was on the increase again. A spokesman for the Scottish office was quoted as saying[22] 'We are not yet certain how this issue will be dealt with but a risk assessment study in the future is a high probability'.

So the Scottish studies have ranged from Thurso and Dounreay in the northeast to Sullum Voe in the Shetlands to Glenrothes in the south east. They have been conducted on a variety of hypotheses which we have examined closely in connection to the human reality of life in those parts of Scotland. We have discovered, even if the researchers have not noticed, that workers in the nuclear industry and the petrochemical industry often work in close proximity and that both communities have a high degree of childhood leukaemia in their under-fours. We have established that both industries use radioactive sources routinely in their operations. We find it more difficult to believe the hypothesis of viral infection in population mixes than in preconceptual paternal exposure to ionizing radiation. It may be that the simultaneous closing of Dounreay and the opening of the Britannia oil field installation at St Fergus, south-east of Thurso, will provide an opportunity to re-examine the question. A plan is before the Fife Regional Council to develop a fourth module at the Mossmorran Shell complex to increase the maximum intake of natural gas liquids from 4.9 million tons to 6.5 million tons a year in order to accommodate the fuel that will come ashore at St Fergus and travel to Mossmorran by Grangemouth via a 138-mile underground pipeline. Perhaps the workers on the new wave energy project off Orkney can be used as a control. But let us, for the sake of our children, apply some commonsense to the research designs.

Commonsense – is that all we can pit against the huge resources of scientific enterprise that have gone into the study of the biomedical hazards of ionizing radiation over the past fifty years? Living as I do on the coast of Fife, along the sea roads into Rosyth and Grangemouth, by Anstruther, with a child conceived a few months after Chernobyl whom I no longer allow to paddle off the piers built by Robert Louis Stevenson's father in the time before we strained the capacity of our planet to tolerate man-made radionuclides, it is all I have to pit against the didactic deadpan[23] reassurances of the biomedical researchers who tell me to lie back, shut my eyes against the evidence, and practise a stochastic stoicism. Ultimately, the political is personal. And as I complete this personal inquiry into the biomedical consequences of Hiroshima and Nagasaki, my heart goes out to the family of the seventeen-year-old girl from our village high school who died last week from leukaemia. Fortunately my daughter's seven-year-old classmate in the local primary school is in remission.

Notes

1. Leo Kinlen, 'Evidence for an infective cause of childhood leukaemia: comparison of a Scottish new Town with nuclear reprocessing sites in Britain,' *The Lancet*, 10 December 1988:1321–26.

2. Keith Ferguson, *A History of Glenrothes* (Glenrothes Development Corporation, 1982) p.124.

3. Glenrothes Development Corporation, *Factfile*, 1994.

4. Fife Regional Council, *The Fife Structure Plan* circa 1990:17.

5. Eric Baijal, 'A case-control study to investigate apparent leukaemia clusters in Fife', July 1988, report lodged with Fife Health Board Library, Cupar.

6. James D. Urquhart *et al.*, 'Case-control study of leukaemia and non-Hodgkin's lymphoma in children in Caithness near the Dounreay nuclear installation', *British Medical Journal*, 23 March 1991:302:688–92.

7. Roger J. Black *et al.*, 'Incidence of leukaemia and other cancers in birth and schools cohort in the Dounreay area', *British Medical Journal*, 30 May 1992:304:1401–5.

8. L. J. Kinlen *et al.*, 'Rural population mixing and childhood leukaemia: effects of the North Sea oil industry in Scotland, including the area near Dounreay nuclear site', *British Medical Journal*, 20 March 1993:306:743–8.

9. Tom Wilkie, 'Worker killed by record dose of radiation', *The Independent*, 9 May 1994:1.

10. Tom Wilkie, 'I don't want my husband's death to be for nothing', *The Independent*, 9 May 1994:3.

11. D. C. T. Eves, letter to the editor, *The Independent*, 1994:19.

12. Health and Safety Executive, *The Radiation Protection Adviser*, June 1994:5:2.

13. Tim Kelsey, 'Oil worker's widow blames rig radiation', *Independent on Sunday*, 11 December 1994:9.

14. Tom Wilkie, 'Dream of unlimited power fades to black', *The Independent*, 28 March 1994:3.

15. Nic Outterside, 'Dounreay faces inquiry into waste', *The Scotsman*, 18 November 1994.

16. R. J. Black *et al.* 'Cancer incidence in a population potentially exposed to radium-226 at Dalgety Bay, Scotland', *British Journal of Cancer*, 1994:69:140–3.

17. Tom Wilkie, 'Cracks found in pipework generator', *The Independent*, 11 May 1991:2. The safety record of Britain's nuclear fleet is discussed in Joshua Handler and William M. Arkin, *Nuclear Warships and Naval Nuclear Weapons: a complete inventory*, Neptune Papers No. 2, Greenpeace and Institute for Policy Studies, Washington, May 1988; Joshua Handler, Amy Wickenheiser and William M. Arkin, *Naval Safety 1989: the year of the accident*, Neptune Papers No. 4, Greenpeace and Institute for Policy Studies, Washington, April 1990.

18. 'MoD defends safety record', *The Courier and Advertiser*, 25 January, 1993:9.

19. Tom Wilkie and Susan Watts, 'Safety "lapses" at nuclear weapons plants attacked', *The Independent*, 18 October 1994:6.

20. Health and Safety Executive, *The Management of Health and Safety at Atomic Weapons Establishment Premises: a review by The Health and Safety Executive; part 1 an overview*, 1994:19.

21. 'Row over radioactive dumping', *The Courier and Advertiser*, 25 May 1993:4.

22. 'Beach radiation problem growing again', *The Courier and Advertiser*, 23 November, 1994.

23. J. W. N. Watkins, 'Confession is good for ideas', *Experiment*, BBC, 1964:64–70.

Index